To
EVERY MAN
a PENNY

Also by Bruce Marshall

Vespers in Vienna
George Brown's Schooldays
The World, the Flesh and Father Smith
Father Malachy's Miracle

To EVERY MAN *a* PENNY

a novel by Bruce Marshall

"When therefore they were come that came about the eleventh hour they received every man a penny."

—*Matthew 20:9*

TO EVERY MAN A PENNY
By Bruce Marshall

Copyright © 1949 by the Estate of Bruce Marshall. First edition. All rights reserved.

Copyright © 2025 Human Adventure Books. Second edition. Reprinted with permission. All rights reserved.

17105 Longacres Ln
Odessa, FL 33556

www.humanadventurebooks.com

All rights reserved

ISBN: 978-1-941457-31-3

In Memory of

ELIZABETH MYERS

A fine writer

and a brave woman

Foreword

In the period covered by my story, four different Cardinal Archbishops administered the archdiocese of Paris. My Cardinal Archbishop of Paris is my own creation and is intended to be the portraits of none of them. The three English Cardinals who gently enter the narrative are all real and I hope that the living one, for whom I have great admiration, will forgive the liberty I have taken with his virtues. All the other characters in the story, as the parish of Saint Clovis itself, are imaginary.

—Bruce Marshall

I

THE Cardinal always found it difficult to feel holy in hot weather, and even in the early morning of the twenty-ninth of June, 1914 it looked as though the feast of Saints Peter and Paul were going to be very warm indeed. With a regret that the discomfort of the body should so unfailingly affect the spirit, he alighted quickly from the taxi as it drew up in front of the church of St. Sulpice and hoped that there would not be too many people about to notice his buckled shoes and the scarlet stockings peeping from under his ordinary priest's cassock. Relieved to find that the Place was, at that early hour, almost deserted, the Cardinal walked along to the nearest newspaper kiosk.

"Good morning, Monsieur l'abbé," the newsvendor said, not recognizing his archbishop in such humble attire and indicating with a flourish his many wares. "What can I do for you? As you see, I cater for all tastes."

The Cardinal saw indeed: next to the conservative *Figaro* and the *Matin* lay the socialist *Humanité* and Jaurès' *Bonnet Rouge*; and, clipped side by side with the *Illustration* displaying on its front page a photograph of Pope Pius the Tenth, hung the *Vie Parisienne* depicting a naked young woman crouching her haunches and pouting a pair of inflated red lips towards a monster cherry which dangled just above them.

"Beautiful picture of the Pope," the newsvendor said, following the Cardinal's gaze.

"As far as I can see His Holiness seems to be keeping rather bad company," the Cardinal said with what he hoped was not too tolerant a smile.

He bought the *Figaro* and rapidly read the headlines. There was as yet no hint of the trouble which the informed were beginning to fear. Then he walked back towards the church, preparing his mind for the important business which lay ahead of him.

The Cardinal was about to elevate to the priesthood twenty-four deacons for service in the archdiocese of Paris. There was also a considerable number of deacons and subdeacons to be ordained, so that he had a long morning in front of him, distributing the Holy Spirit. The Cardinal never performed this rite without a deep sense of responsibility. He knew that what he was about to do could not be undone, since when God empowered souls His mark remained upon them forever. It was in order that he might pray privately upon this matter that he had left his residence early and without his chaplain. For he knew that as soon as he had begun to recite the words commanded by the doctors of the Church, he would have little time for reflection, but would have to do a great many holy things publicly and speedily.

Although his vocation was to promote sanctity, the Cardinal knew that he himself was no saint. Kneeling at the back of the church, he examined his conscience. The grosser sins were not there, of course, the angers and the greed and the jubilant fornications of the people, but the Cardinal did not fail to distinguish a number of the lesser. On Thursday he had talked at length about his recent visit to Rome, not so much as to communicate His Holiness' views on the politics of Kaiser Wilhelm as to impress a protonotary apostolic from Bayonne; on Friday he had allowed the thought of his forthcoming holiday in Brittany to disturb his mid-day recitation of the Angelus; and on Saturday he had laughed aloud when the Minister of Bridges and Roads had attended a public function with one of his fly-buttons undone. For these sins he asked forgiveness. He consoled his sense of unworthiness by recalling the words of Fenélon: "As the light grows, we see ourselves to be worse than we thought. We are amazed at our former blindness as we see issuing from our heart a whole swarm of shameful feelings, like filthy reptiles crawling from a hidden cave. But we must be neither amazed nor disturbed. We are not worse than we were; on the contrary we are better." Then he asked God to bless those whom he was about to ordain, that they might promote holiness among the people.

In the sacristy the Cardinal sat down on the chair which had been specially prepared for him and allowed his chaplain to change his shoes for the crimson satin slippers worn by bishops on the feasts of martyrs and the Holy Ghost. The Cardinal did not like his chaplain much, suspecting him of loving the liturgy rather than the truths which it mirrored. He reminded himself that he must love his Chaplain in Christ even if he could not like him for his own sake. Sometimes the Cardinal got rather tired of loving people in Christ: there was such a terrible lot of it to do.

They led him out into the sanctuary and sat him upon his throne where they carried his vestments to him, because such was his privilege as a bishop. The Cardinal kissed the long red stole because His yoke was sweet and His burden was light. They laid the holy vestments upon him, and the tunicle and dalmatic as well as the chasuble they put upon him, because he was a bishop and possessed the fullness of order. The Cardinal began the mass at the foot of the altar steps, but the prayers he read from his throne, because such was his privilege as a bishop. Then he knelt in front of the altar, and the young men who were to be ordained lay stretched out flat in their white albs, and they prayed that the Lord might have mercy and that Christ might have mercy and that the Lord might have mercy.

In 1914 as 1466, in Greek and in Latin, the litanies of supplication were roared, that the Lord might have mercy and Christ hearken, and that all the holy apostles and evangelists and all the holy disciples of the Lord might pray for them; that Saints Fabian and Sebastian might pray for them; that Saint Gregory and Saint Ambrose might pray for them; that Saint Augustine might pray for them; that all holy priests and levites, monks and hermits might pray for them; that the Lord would spare them and pardon them and rule and preserve His holy Church; that it might please the Lord to grant peace and concord to Christian rulers and to lift up their minds to heavenly desires; that it might please the Lord to bless, hallow and consecrate these chosen ones; that Christ might hearken and that the Lord might have mercy. Lying upon their faces, they prayed that the Lord might accomplish all these things.

The Cardinal was only forty-five, but the weight of his vestments and the heat oppressed him, so that he was already tired when he began to ordain the deacons and the subdeacons, that they might sing holy words and do holy things. Upon each of them he laid his hands separately, pressing the power upon them, as it had once been pressed upon him, by another bishop. Then he laid his hands upon all those that were to become priests and prayed that, as God had poured the superabundant graces into Eleazar and Ithamar and confirmed the apostles, so He might strengthen the greater frailty of His servants and renew holiness within them. And he crossed the stole on their breasts and gave them the yoke of the Lord and vested them with the holy vestments, and he prayed that by their gravity they might keep their ministry undefiled. And he anointed their hands with the oil of catechumens and closed their hands and bound them with a white cloth. And when the holy thing was done he laid his hands upon them again and kissed them and blessed them in the priestly order and charged them to lead a godly life and to pray for him to Almighty God.

II

THE church of Saint Clovis lay in a square in the center of Paris. The square had on occasion been called the Place de l'Empire, the Place Louis Philippe, the Place Napoléon Trois and the Place Thiers; by reason of a recent indignation it was, for the present, called the Place du Général Marchand. In spite of the fact that France was now a godless country ten masses were said there every Sunday. All these masses were well attended. The graph of piety, however, descended abruptly at noon, when the last mass was celebrated by the abbé Gaston for the lazy and the fashionable, who were frightened of going to hell for six reasons when they need be sent there for only five.

This afternoon the abbé Gaston had been invited by the rector to join himself and his assistant clergy for their after luncheon walk on the square, in order that he might meet the new curate who had recently been ordained by the Cardinal. The abbé Gaston was a small thick-set man of about thirty-five, unremarkable in appearance except for his black beard, which he wore because he had once been a missionary in North Africa, where beards were reputed to impress the heathen. He had retired early from this work because the colonial climate had not suited his health and he now lived comfortably enough in a nearby garrett on the small annual income of three thousand francs a year left him by his parents. He supplemented this income and exercised his ministry by acting as an extra and unofficial curate at the church of Saint Clovis.

It was the habit of the clergy to walk up and down the broad pavement on the south side of the church. Today the Chanoine Litry walked with his curates on either side of him, and, as he walked, the rector spoke of the reasons for the present distress of religion in France. These, he maintained, were twofold. Firstly, he said, the apathy of contemporary French Christians could be traced to the banishment of the religious orders and the introduction of lay education into the schools and the universities. Secondly, there was the regrettable reputation that France and, in particular, Paris held for the commission of, and connivance at, the sins of the flesh. It was not for nothing, the rector said, that the chief industries of the metropolis were the designing of women's satin dresses and silken shifts, the concoction of foolish hats for their heads and shoes to make them walk immodestly, and the mixing of perfumes, pigments, lotions, ointments and powders to conceal the ordinarily disagreeable colors, contours and odors of their bodies. The abbé Gaston smiled as he listened to the rector saying these things: he had heard it all before.

The other curates, however, did not smile, although they, too, had heard it all before. The senior curate, the abbé Vernet, gravely nodded his small grey head and the abbé Graber, the second curate, pursed his lips thoughtfully. Even the abbé Robert, the tubby little third curate, who ordinarily walked about the parish with a big smile on his round face, was solemn and the abbé Paquin, the fifth curate and recently ordained by the Cardinal, was obviously impressed. Alone the abbé Ronsard, the day-dreaming fourth curate, appeared to be paying no attention. The abbé Gaston hoped, for the abbé Ronsard's sake, that the Chanoine Litry would not notice this lack of attention: the rector disapproved of the noise the abbé Ronsard made when he ate apples and he liked his curates to listen with their eyes as well as with their ears when he talked.

Beside them on the pavement walked men and women who moved more hurriedly than the priests and did not return upon their steps; the purpose of their perambulations was neither to digest nor to discuss but to get somewhere else as quickly as possible. To them, however, were presently joined more leisurely persons who emerged from the neighboring restaurants to take the air before returning to work in their shops and offices. Among these was a group of pretty girls who came out from their frugal lunch in a dressmaker's establishment on the other side of the street. The girls began to walk slowly up and down the pavement, chattering and laughing in their colored frocks. The Chanoine Litry's demeanor stiffened immediately.

"Funny things, women's fashions," the abbé Gaston said. For more than a year now he had been trying to soften the rector's disapproval of the young women, and always without success. "Last year it was narrow skirts; this year it is wide skirts and boots."

"It is only the accent that changes," the Chanoine Litry said. "The doctrine always remains the same."

Up and down the priests marched, discussing now the merits of Saint Thérèse of Lisieux. Up and down the girls strolled, pretty beneath their wide hats. The breeze which blew in the priests' cassocks blew also in the girls' dresses, puffing them out into bright balloons of red and green and yellow. Above the grey roofs of Paris the sky was blue and the sun was gold. From the slates of the church came a flutter of pigeons, which alighted on the pavement and walked gravely, as though they, too, were thinking about the saints.

"I am beginning to think that these young women come here on purpose," the rector said.

"It's much more likely that they're beginning to think that we do," the abbé Gaston said.

"Monsieur l'abbé Gaston and I have divergent views about the merits of the modern young woman," the Chanoine Litry explained to the new curate.

"I like to think that Monsieur le Curé judges too much by externals," the abbé Gaston said.

"St. Cyprian went a little more deeply into it than that," the Chanoine Litry said and quoted: " 'For the rest, if you dress your hair sumptuously and walk so as to draw attention in public and attract the eyes of youth upon you and draw the sighs of young men after you, to nourish the lust of concupiscence and inflame the fuel of sighs so that although you yourself perish not, yet you cause others to perish: you cannot be excused on the pretense that you are chaste and modest of mind.' And now, Monsieur l'abbé Gaston, I think that it is time for you to be taking your catechism class."

Outside the church three or four workmen inside their rectangle of rope were resting from doing something incomprehensible to the gas mains. The abbé Gaston rather liked the workmen and he smiled at them. Although he knew that none of them had been to the sacraments for years he also knew that they were honest and hardworking and brave and that they would never do a mean thing, which was more than the abbé could say about quite a few of the Christians. The abbé waved to the workmen and one of them waved back with a half empty bottle of red wine.

"A man's thirsty in weather like this," the workman shouted.

"You're right," the abbé shouted back. "It's very hot."

Inside, however, the church was cool and dark. A scrabble of children was already sitting in front of the high altar, the boys on the gospel side and the girls on the epistle side. The abbé Gaston knelt for a few moments. He formulated no petition but gazed in silence past the ruby glow of the sanctuary lamp at the silk curtains on the door of the tabernacle. It was because of the peace which he experienced at such moments that the abbé Gaston had become a priest.

The children didn't appear to be very interested when the abbé Gaston began to tell them that God had created them to know Him, to love Him, to serve Him in this world and to be happy with Him forever in the next. The little boys fidgeted and the little girls looked out at the priest from round, perplexed eyes. But the abbé Gaston did not believe in keeping the children serious for too long and he soon had them roaring with laughter at his story of the negro in North Africa, who, on the fourteenth Sunday after Pentecost, 1908, had come to church wearing the abbé's green chasuble which he had stolen for fun. The abbé had to hurry over his funny story because the sacristan was hanging the big black frontal on the high altar, in preparation for a funeral. When he had finished his funny story, abbé dismissed the children with his blessing and told them to be sure and come again next week.

The children scampered out of the church, but one little girl of seven came up to the abbé and curtsied and shook hands with him. The little girl had blue eyes and soft gold hair and she wore a white dress with big blue spots on it. Her name was Armelle and the abbé liked her better than all the other little girls, not only because he knew her mother well, but also because she was a good little girl. The abbé walked gravely with her to the door of the church and stood waving to her until she was out of sight.

III

IT was perhaps natural that the clergy of the Church of Saint Clovis should hear of the war for the first time from the poetess. The poetess, it was said, had known about Agadir before the German Admiralty. The poetess was a red-faced, overdressed and loud-voiced woman in her middle forties, who had invented a new technique of versification which she claimed to have based on the principles of Euclid applied to the subconscious. She had recently acquired international renown for a stanza beginning:

> *The Pipes of Pan*
> *Play out for Emile Zola*
> *Whom Charon ferries across the styx*
> *With benign oars*
> *For a fee of nix.*

The abbé Ronsard had doubted whether the lines could be described as Christian; the Chanoine Litry had doubted whether they could be described as poetry.

"Viviani himself told me," the poetess said as she stood in the middle of the presbytery parlor and made dramatic gestures. "The mobilization order has already been signed. And priests are going to have to fight, too."

"It will leave us terribly short-handed," the Chanoine Litry said.

"It will mean a new lease of life for the Church in France," the abbé Gaston said. "When men see their priests fighting by their sides they will be forced to respect us."

"It is as well our cause is just otherwise the participation of priests in the combat would pose rather a difficult problem in theology," the abbé Vernet said.

"The cause of France is always just," the abbé Gaston said.

"All the same it seems a little difficult to visualize the geographical division of rectitude," the abbé Ronsard said.

"The Germans are a brutal and domineering race," the rector said.

"Perhaps they won't expect priests to fight," the abbé Graber said. "Perhaps they'll just make stretcher bearers of us."

"That would be the worst thing that could happen," the abbé Gaston said. "Men would never respect us if we did not share their dangers."

"It may indeed be a great opportunity for the Church," the Chanoine Litry said.

"The whole green loveliness of France will be Christian again," the abbé Gaston said.

> *"The soldiers march*
> *Across mountains of fire*
> *Into the rhomboid*
> *Of Valhalla,"*

the poetess said.

In the silence that followed the abbé Gaston remembered words which he had often heard the deacon sing out at mass: "*Sic et Pater meus coelestis faciet vobis, si non remiseritis unusquisque fratri suo ab cordibus vestris.*" Did not nations, as individuals, run the same risk of Divine punishment if they forgave not every one his brother from their hearts? Before the abbé could answer his own question there was shouting in the street outside as the poetess hadn't been as much in advance with her news as usual. And as soon as they all began to sing the *Marseillaise* the abbé Gaston forgot that he had even asked himself the question.

With joy in his heart the abbé Gaston walked back along the clamorous streets to his garret. There was, however, a fear in his heart as well that he might be too old to be mobilized right away and that they would call the younger and the stronger men first. But as soon as he reached the church his fear was dispelled: the billposter was sticking up a proclamation which said that the soldier of the second class Jean Marie Benoit Gaston had, along with a few others, been summoned to the aid of France in her hour of need.

The abbé had not much to pack: he had only one cassock and two pairs of boots and two changes of underwear and his breviary and he knew that they would issue him with his uniform at the depot. The caretaker, Madame Boulon, said that she would look after St. Blasius of Cappadocia. St. Blasius of Cappadocia was the abbé's tom cat whose habits didn't always rhyme with his name, although the abbé had succeeded in training him not to jump at the pigeons when they flew over from the church to walk on the window ledge. Madame Boulon said that she would have to ask the abbé to pay a little towards the cat's keep because prices were bound to go up with a bang now that the Kaiser had done all those terrible things. Anyway it wouldn't be long, that was one consolation, Madame Boulon said, because they'd be in Berlin within a month, so the gentleman on the third floor had told her.

The Chanoine Litry had not time to come to the station to see the abbé Gaston off to the war, so the abbé walked to the Gare de l'Est alone in the baggy pale blue uniform with which they had issued him at the depot. Because they had been short of kitbags, he carried his spare underclothes in an old newspaper tied up with string. He walked because all the buses and the tramcars were full and he expected that the underground railway would be crowded, too. The hot summer sun shone down on the abbé's face and made it shine with sweat as he walked along the rue du Quatre Septembre, but the abbé Gaston was too happy to care how much he sweated, because he was going to fight in a holy war for France. In the rue Réaumur the sky was clamped tight down above the roofs of the houses and on the Boulevard Sébastopol it was the same. The pavements were crowded with other soldiers with packs on their backs or paper parcels beneath their arms, and the other soldiers smiled at the abbé Gaston and the abbé Gaston smiled back at the other soldiers, because he was going to fight in a holy war for France. Sometimes some of the pretty girls that were with the other soldiers smiled at the abbé Gaston, too, and waved their hands, and although he was a priest forever and had the mark on his soul the abbé Gaston smiled back at the pretty girls and waved his hand as well, because he was going to fight in a holy war for France.

The abbé thought that he might have felt even happier if he, too, had had someone to come to the station to see him off. He wished for a few moments that his mother had still been alive and then decided that this desire was selfish as it would have hurt his mother to have known that her only son was going to fight in a war. Human relationships were one of the things that priests gave up and they had other joys instead. The fragrance of the psalms was one of these joys, and as he walked along the streets the abbé threw a little of their loveliness up at the sky. "*Quam dilecta tabernacula tua, Domine virtutum,*" the abbé murmured, and then he saw that somebody had come to see him off after all. At the entrance to the station Armelle was standing holding her mother's hand. The sun was shining on the little girl's soft hair and making it glow and she was wearing a print frock which made her look like a daisy. She ran towards the abbé as soon as she saw him and the abbé caught her up in his arms and held her high above his head. Then he pulled her down against his breast and kissed her and forgot all about how hard his beard must feel on her face.

IV

THE Cardinal had been called up also, by the Sacred College in Rome, to elect a new Pope.

On his way through Switzerland the Cardinal had had a dream. Lying in the sleeping car, he had dreamed that he had been elected Pope, because the Holy Ghost had inspired his brother Cardinals to decide that only a young man could rule a torn apart world. When he had been led by the Dean of the Sacred College to try on the three white cassocks already laid out, only the longest had fitted, because he was so tall. He had elected to reign under the title of Leo the Fourteenth and he had woken up just as he was about to give his blessing to the city and to the world. The Cardinal had been in a bad temper at breakfast that morning, partly because he was still only a cardinal, partly because there wasn't enough marmalade.

Walking along the corridors of the Vatican, he met the Cardinal Archbishop of Munich advancing towards him. The Cardinal knew his brother prelate quite intimately, though not as intimately as he knew Francis, with whom he had once shared a lemon sole in Ventimiglia. Ought he to obey his Lord and forgive his enemies? Or ought he to respect the wrongs suffered by the sons of France? Ought he to speak, smile, bow coldly or pass on without giving any sign of recognition? In scarlet silk and white lace His Eminence of Munich rustled towards him, with no indication on his face as to the operation of the Holy Ghost within him. The Cardinal passed his brother of Munich without a word, smile or bow.

For three hours that night the Cardinal knelt in prayer and asked the Lord to forgive him, but he ignored his brother of Munich again the next day when they met on their way to the Sistine Chapel.

V

IN the front line the abbé Gaston did not often receive letters. The Chanoine Litry wrote occasionally to give him news of the parish and to say that the girls on the Place due Général Marchand were behaving themselves immodestly with British officers on leave. An old missionary friend wrote once from North Africa to say that the vicar apostolic had visited them recently to conduct a confirmation. A firm of ecclesiastical furnishers had sent him a catalogue enumerating the advantages to be derived from the use of the special war time chasuble, gold on one side and black on the other. And once the publishers of *La Vie Parisienne* had sent him a complimentary copy by mistake. Two days ago, however, he had received a real letter which he had read over so often that he knew it by heart already:

"Dear Monsieur l'abbé Gaston,

I hope that you are well. I am very well. Mother sends her kind regards. I remember you every day in my prayers.

Big kisses from

Armelle."

The abbé folded the letter for the seventeenth time and put it back in his breviary, not many pages away from the holy picture which his mother had given him when he had been ordained. Then he closed his eyes and began to pray for all those who had been killed in battle, that the Lord might appoint for them a place of solace and of light and of peace. He prayed for those who had died in the sign of faith, and for those who hadn't he prayed also, for Marc Pradier who had stolen the farmer's chickens and for Guy Morin who had seduced the farmer's daughter, that Christ might cool them and comfort them. The abbé used the words of the missal as he prayed, because he thought that the words in the holy book were the best words.

Both because of his age and because of his calling, the abbé Gaston had not been allowed so far to take any part in the fighting. Instead he had been entrusted with ambulance duties. He had to expose himself to shelling, of course, but he had rarely to experience the bullets, mortars, mud and rain which were the daily lot of his comrades. He was waiting now in the field dressing station. An attack was imminent and casualties were expected.

The abbé wondered if it was because of his comparative comfort that piety had not spread through the battalion as rapidly as, at the beginning of the war, he had expected. Most of his companions respected his calling and few insulted it, although fewer still sought his spiritual counsel except when they knew that they were going to die. In the trenches they faced bravely death, pain and discomfort and out of the trenches they boozed, gambled and whored. Although such recreations were unlikely to be recommended by the moral theologians, they shocked the abbé less than he would have previously imagined. The sins of soldiers were the broad generous sins of the unreflecting, committed under extreme provocation; they were never the calculated meannesses of the respectable. The abbé thought that he understood better now why the Lord had so signally commended the centurion. He looked up from this meditation to see his friend the soldier of the first class Louis Philippe Bessier smiling down at him.

"Things going all right, Jean?" Bessier asked.

"So, so, Philippe," the abbé answered.

"Not come round to my way of thinking yet, eh?" Bessier asked.

"Not come round to your way of *not* thinking, you mean," the abbé answered.

They both laughed. Sometimes the abbé thought that the reason why they both got on so well together was that they were both interested enough in the same thing to disagree about it. In a wilderness of metaphysical apathy this divergence was enough to draw them together. Bessier was the first to stop laughing. His face was angry and serious as he began to argue.

"I am beginning to think more than ever that it is not against Germany that we should be fighting," he said. "I am beginning to think that the whole working classes of the world ought to be fighting the wealthy and the indolent."

"But that is not patriotism," the abbé said.

"It is socialism, Jean, and Christianity ought to be socialism if you really believe what you teach," Bessier said.

"Christianity is something more than a remedy for social evils," the priest said gently.

"Do you know how much a textile worker in Roubaix earns?" Bessier asked. "Or a miner in Lens? You do not know because in France the Church is the Church of the rich. For you sin is no longer cruelty but only young men getting into bed with pretty girls to whom they are not married. And the prettier the girl the bigger the sin!" Bessier laughed bitterly. "When I was home on leave in Paris I travelled on the underground. There was no room in second class so I went first. The women drew away from me so that the mud on my uniform should not dirty their dresses."

"They do not understand, that's all," the abbé Gaston said.

"They will never understand until they have been made to understand," Bessier said. They will never understand until the silk has been ripped from their backs. It is wrong that a few should be so rich and that most should be so poor." Bessier was no longer angry when he said this, but sad rather, and the abbé Gaston was sad with him, that so many things should be wrong in the world. "And that is why I say that it is not against the Germans in the trench opposite us that we should be fighting. It is against the rich men in Paris and in London and in Berlin and Moscow that we should be fighting. If I were a really brave man I should refuse to go on killing those who have done me no harm. But as I am only a relatively brave man I suppose that I shall choose the lesser courage and go back to the butchery."

The abbé Gaston was unhappy when Bessier went away again. He was unhappy because he knew that although Bessier had said true things there were even truer things to be said and he himself had not been clever enough to say them. The abbé was unhappy, too, because he was afraid that Bessier might be killed in the coming attack and then he himself would be very alone indeed, because Bessier would no longer be there and he would not have said the truer things to Bessier. Splinters of daylight began to appear round the edge of the entrance to the dugout. The abbé pulled aside the curtain of sacking and held up his face for a few seconds to the cool beginnings of the new day. There were still stars in the sky, but their sparkle was growing fainter. The blue of the horizon was turning gradually to green. Soon the attack would begin in the brittle beauty of the dawn.

The chaplain strode in with his big square boots sticking out from under his short cassock. The chaplain sometimes spoke kindly to the abbé Gaston and sometimes he walked past him with his nose stuck in the air. This morning the chaplain was in a communicative enough mood to ask the abbé's advice. The chaplain said that he had long been perturbed by the paucity of the spiritual consolation which he was able to give the dying and that therefore it was his intention to fetch a few Hosts from the neighboring church, in order that he might be able to give viaticum to those who desired it. He wanted to know if the abbé Gaston thought that there was any likelihood of the Blessed Sacrament being exposed to irreverence on the part of unbelievers and the lapsed. The abbé Gaston gave a ready response. The Lord, he said, hadn't trodden a special earth and it wasn't stained glass sinners and that He had gone among, but the real sweaty smelly kind. The abbé Gaston said that this was the meaning of the world: that the Lord had come to sinners and that He still went on doing so. The chaplain thanked the abbé Gaston for his answer and strode away to the church.

Outside the noise of the barrage grew great. The noise was as though boulders were being flung down mountain sides. The noise was so great that it sent an exhilaration through the abbé and made him feel brave rather than frightened. The abbé Gaston wasn't quite sure whether it was the French of the German guns that were firing for, in spite of the fact that he had been a soldier for nearly three years now, the abbé had not mastered the technique of hate. From time to time great flashes of light lit up the dugout, paling the candle flames. The earth rocked and roared and rumbled with many reverberations and still the abbé wasn't frightened, although he knew that he would have been frightened if he had had to go in to attack with his comrades. It was the bullets and the bayonets that were terrible, the men said. It was the places a man could get wounded in, the men said, and the gouged out eyes and the gaping bellies, the men said, and the long cold wet time for which those terrible things went on. The abbé wondered if the permanent pain of hell could really, as the theologians maintained, be more acute than the temporary anguish of modern conflict. Could God really consign a soul to an eternal Battle of the Somme for an unrepented fornication? Miserably the abbé ransacked his mind for a mitigation of doctrine. It was possible that hell was a state of deprivation rather than a place. In the end the abbé Gaston used theology to beat theology. God was Merciful with a mercy surpassing the kindness of men and in the knowledge of this clemency the abbé went on listening to the barrage with fresh courage.

The world was suddenly quiet again with a silence which could almost be heard. The abbé knew that this meant that the attack would be going in almost immediately. He did not quite understand why, but he knew that this was so: the abbé remained as ignorant as he could be about the details of carnage, because he was more easily able to believe in the holiness of the struggle that way. He began to pray silently for those who would so soon have the flying iron hurled at them, that their hurt might be lessened and that they might be given last minute graces. Then he took Armelle's letter out of his breviary and read it through again. He was glad to be able to think that there was one person alive who would miss him if he died.

The wounded began to arrive on their stretchers, and the chaplain came back from the church carrying the Body of God in his inverted steel helmet. The abbé Gaston was happy when he saw the chaplain in his short white stole, for he knew that this was the meaning of the world, even though dying men might come hardly to it. At first the wounded were quiet, but soon they were moaning as they lay waiting on their stretchers. In his smock the surgeon stood at the table and probed and cut and tied. The wounded men shrieked beneath the surgeon's touch and their shrieks mingled with the moans of those who were still waiting to have their wounds dressed. The chaplain went about hearing confessions and giving holy communion and always there was shrieking and always there was moaning, because when men were wrenched, blasted and cloven the agony was for each man alone. They brought in a man who had just had his jaw shot away and the chaplain couldn't get the Blessed Sacrament into his mouth and he had to call for the abbé Gaston to help him. Sometimes the abbé Gaston heard confessions, too, when men were dying quickly under their blankets, but mostly he gave injections of morphia and helped the surgeon to dress wounds. Outside there was the blast of shells exploding and the stutter of machine gun fire. Outside, for the generals and those who still fought in it, the battle went on.

Moving with his syringe along the line of stretchers, the abbé Gaston came upon the soldier of the first class Bessier, lying with a pallid face under a blanket.

"Philippe," the abbé murmured as he knelt by his friend's side.

"Stomach and legs," Bessier said from a twisted mouth. "Quick with your syringe."

"My poor Philippe," the abbé Gaston said, as he pressed the syringe into Bessier's arm.

"It's stupid to die in this war when I might have lived to fight in the real war," Bessier said.

"Please, Philippe, listen to me," the abbé Gaston said.

"Civil war's the thing," Bessier said. "Killing people, you know."

"It is foolish to be proud," the abbé Gaston said. He spoke unconvincingly for a few moments in the technology of piety. "Please, Philippe," he said.

"I'm sorry, Jean, but that would be cheating," Bessier said and closed his eyes.

The abbé laid his ear against Bessier's heart. Bessier's heart was still beating. The abbé looked up to see the Colonel standing beside him. The Colonel was lithe, clean, and unhurt and there was a great shine on his leather leggings.

"Wounded comfortable?" the Colonel asked.

"As far as can be expected, sir," the abbé Gaston said.

"Good." The Colonel's face was lean and hard, but his eyes were kind, and the abbé was sure that the Colonel tried to feel the men's hurt as his own. "Things are not going at all well up there," the Colonel said. "We may have to put you fellows in next time."

"It's all I ask for, sir," the abbé Gaston said, looking down at Bessier's silent, pale face.

The Colonel went away again. The sun shone in through the curtain of sacking and made big golden pools on the floor of the dugout. Outside the battle went on.

VI

THE English Cardinal had been visiting the British soldiers. On the way back he stopped to dine with his brother in Paris. The French Cardinal saw to it that Francis had the bigger helping of everything, because Francis had given him the larger portion of lemon sole in Ventimiglia.

They talked the holy shop of prelates, but chiefly they talked about the war, about which they did not think that the Lord could be very pleased. Alphonse said that if he were Benedict he would ex-communicate the German clergy and laity for crimes against humanity in which they had participated, but Francis said that theology was not quite as simple as all that. Francis said that, although the cause of France and of Britain was manifestly more just than that of Germany, it would require many centuries of qualified reflection to assess the subsidiary errors and rectitudes of the contestants. Any premature and official condemnation of Germany's actions might result in the creation of a new schism, and Alphonse must remember that the Church of God was a ladder let down to all men, Francis said. But Alphonse still maintained that Benedict ought to ex-communicate all Germans and especially the Cardinal Archbishop of Cologne, who, at the last Conclave, had deliberately kept him out of the bathroom for half an hour.

They decided in the end to pray for victory. This time, however, they would pray privately as last time, when they had prayed publicly, things had gone wrong. Side by side in the private chapel they knelt and prayed that God would grant supremacy to their arms and that He would mend the rent in Christ's garment, which was the Church.

VII

IN the Spring of 1918 the abbé Gaston had two people to write to him at the front. Bessier hadn't died of his wounds after all, and now he wrote as well as Armelle. He said that they had managed to patch up his stomach wonderfully. The surgeons had hoped to save his leg at first, but in the end they had to amputate just below the knee. Bessier did not think that this would prevent him earning his living as everybody said that they did wonderful things with artificial legs these days. Before the war he had been a clerk in a factory and he supposed that he could still go on doing this sort of work. And his fiancée didn't seem to mind marrying a man with only one leg. Bessier's letters were simple and uncomplaining. The abbé wondered if suffering had taught Bessier patience.

The abbé re-read some of Bessier's letters now and then put them back in his breviary along with Armelle's. In a few minutes he would be going over the top of the trenches with his battalion to attack the enemy for the first time. He was surprised that he did not feel more frightened. There was the fear of the judgement and there was the fear of pain. Until ten minutes ago, when they had given him his glass of rum, both these fears had been with the abbé. Now they were with him no longer. The abbé was even eager to attack and to avenge the pain which had been inflicted upon his comrades. "You will never be a good soldier until you have learned to be bloodthirsty," the abbé's corporal had told him. Listening to the barrage as it fell on the enemy's lines, the abbé Gaston felt quite bloodthirsty. Crouched beneath the parapet, the abbé forgot that it was his duty as a priest to be merciful and to forgive. Above his head the stars went slowly out and the sky turned from indigo to pale blue. On either side of him, anonymous, virtuous, courageous, with eternity upon them on a swoop, his comrades waited in their clumsy boots. Their steel helmets made them look like heads stamped on coins. Watching them, the abbé loved them and swore that he, too, would be brave.

The barrage ceased. The whistle blew. The abbé Gaston sprang with the rest, astonished that it should all be so easy. Above the stars were extinct. The sky was a blue sail, stretching, and somewhere birds were beginning to sing. On the right the smoke screen which was to prevent them being enfiladed from the hill skiffed along the ground like an indiscreet cloud. No sound came from the German lines. Running forward with his rifle at the trail, the abbé began to feel that he would like to go over the top every day.

Then the enemy's artillery crashed out. Rifles cracked and machine guns spattered. On both sides of the abbé men began to fall. On his right a man slithered to the ground where he lay trying to cram the coils of his entrails back into his stomach. On his left a boy of nineteen with blood pouring from where his eyes had been began to cry out for his mother. The abbé fell to the ground, too. He fell to the ground not because he was hurt, but because he was afraid and his legs would not carry him any further. The bullets that whistled past him made a noise like tissue paper being torn.

On the crest of a hillock in front of him the abbé could see a group of German soldiers firing a machine gun. As they fired the German soldiers swayed the barrel of the machine gun from right to left and from left to right. The sun was beginning to shine on their helmets as the German soldiers fired. The sun made the German soldiers' helmets glow so much that it was hard for the abbé to see their faces. The abbé Gaston remembered that it was a German machine gun which had wounded Bessier. The abbé realized that he would be shot for cowardice if he lay there much longer. He knew that he wasn't lying there because he didn't want to kill Germans, but because he didn't want Germans to kill him. The abbé got up again and began to run towards the machine gun. He had been told that attacking a machine gun single-handed was one of the bravest actions that a soldier could perform. The abbé Gaston wanted very much to be brave.

The abbé had been lying on the ground for three seconds. It took him fifteen seconds to reach the machine gun, but when he reached it the machine gun wasn't firing anymore. Another French soldier had crawled round behind the emplacement and thrown a hand grenade at it. The sun still shone on the German soldiers' steel helmets but the soldiers themselves were dead.

The abbé ran on. The smoke screen had spread out into a thick mist and he could no longer see any distance in front of him. As the abbé ran he could hear his heart beating and his water bottle banging against his equipment. He could see nobody on his right and nobody on his left but still he ran on through the smoke. Then suddenly the ground sloped away in front of his feet and he stumbled forwards into a shell hole. He did not fall on his face, however, but managed to regain his balance in time. In front of him stood a young German soldier. The German soldier lunged at the abbé with his bayonet, but he lunged inexpertly and the rifle slipped from his hand and fell to the ground.

Even before the shell came screeching through the air the abbé Gaston knew that he was not going to kill the German boy. He was not going to kill the German boy because he had once knelt in front of a bishop and the bishop had laid his hands upon him and made the mark upon his soul. The shell came screeching as soon as the abbé had finished thinking these things and the sky was heavy above the abbé's head. The abbé and the German soldier both flung themselves on the ground. There was an explosion near them. A fountain of stones and earth rose blackly into the air. The explosion went on for a long time in the abbé's ears after it had happened. The stones and the earth fell down again much more slowly than they had risen. The abbé waited until the stones and the earth had finished falling before he got up again. The German soldier did not move. The abbé saw that blood was oozing through his breeches.

"You are hurt?" the abbé Gaston asked in his stilted German.

The boy did not answer at once. His lips moved, but no sound came from them. It was some time before he could speak.

"It was like a house falling on me," he managed to say at length. "But it did not hurt with a sharp pain. When I try to move my legs feel as though they were nailed to the ground." The boy began to laugh. Then he turned and bit the earth of the shell hole. "The war is over for me now. They will have to send me home now." He laughed again for a little and then he began to weep. "But perhaps I shall die. You are a kind French soldier. Please tell me that I shall not die."

"Of course, you will not die," the abbé said, but he did not know that the boy would not die. He did not know that the boy would not die because in the seminary they had not taught him about bodies, but only about souls, which were immortal.

"If I die you will write to my parents?" the boy asked. His face was white and startled and young and lonely beneath the morning sun. "Promise me that if I die you will write to my parents."

"If you die I shall write to your parents," the abbé Gaston promised, but already the boy was unconscious. The abbé bent his head to the boy's breast: the boy was still breathing. In the pocket of the boy's tunic were the pitiful treasures that soldiers carried into conflict so that they might seem less alone. There were snapshots of a middle-aged woman and a man and of a girl with big eyes and soft hair. "To darling Otto from his loving Mado," the writing on the girl's photograph ran, and the girl with the big eyes and the soft hair looked very much like any other girl with big eyes and soft hair, although the abbé knew that to the boy she must have been very special because she had written these kind things to him. The abbé rummaged through all the boy's papers hoping to find a letter with an address on it, but there was none. There was only the boy's paybook with his name, which was Otto Braunschwig.

The boy was still breathing when the abbé left him and ran on with his name in his mind. The abbé hoped that the boy would not die and that the stretcher bearers would find him in time. He wondered if the boy was a Catholic. Perhaps he ought to have told him that he was a priest and to have heard his confession. He calmed his conscience by telling himself that there must be a special clemency for soldiers who were killed on battlefields. It was the politicians and the bankers and the business men who ought to have been making their confessions. Bless them, father, for they had sinned. They had plotted and they had planned and they had betrayed. They had charmed and they had cheated and they had been incompetent. They had boasted and they had bullied. They had guzzled and they had grabbed and they had grudged. Bless them, father, for they had sinned. Bless them, father, for they intended to sin again.

The abbé Gaston ran on blindly through the smoke and the din, following the direction which he imagined his battalion had taken. Soon there was another explosion and another fountain of earth and stones rose blackly into the air. This time it was the abbé who felt fall on his leg the weight which did not hurt with a sharp pain. The German stretcher bearers picked the abbé up after it was dark, for the French attack had been repulsed. They carried him through a deserted village and across a canal on which shells were bursting in spurts of orange fire. In the German casualty station the abbé saw them bringing in the boy whom he had befriended in the shell hole. The boy smiled and waved his hand when he recognized the abbé, so the abbé knew that it didn't matter that he had not been able to ascertain the boy's address.

VIII

IN the hospital ward the soldier of the first class Bessier was showing the soldier of the second class Gaston how well he could walk on his new artificial leg. Up and down between the two rows of beds Bessier went and all the other soldiers watched as well. The soldiers said that it was wonderful what they did nowadays and that really you couldn't tell that Bessier had had his leg cut off at all.

Bessier explained that that was because he had had his leg taken off below the knee. Bessier said that it made all the difference when you had your leg taken off below the knee. Having your leg off above the knee was quite another matter, he said. Then you had to have a pelvic band and a shoulder strap and all sorts of gadgets to help you along. You had to learn to control the automatic bending of the knee, otherwise you risked pitching forward on your face. And if you had no stump at all to put in the bucket you had to have a tilting table. There were some chaps with double amputations who had two tilting tables. Bessier didn't understand how they were going to manage because as soon as they got out on the pavement the civilian swine would knock them over, now that the war was over.

The abbé Gaston watched Bessier with even more sympathy than the other soldiers. Bessier was his special friend and he himself had come very near to losing his left leg. In the German hospital the abbé had lain with his leg in a high splint with a weight on the end. He had shrieked when the surgeon had come to dress his wound and even now he still yelled a little when they removed the plug of gauze with which his wound was filled. But now it was certain that no amputation would be required, although they had told him he would have to walk with a special boot, because his left leg would be shorter than his right. He would still be able to say mass, although it might be a bit hard for him on Christmas and All Souls' days, when priests had to say three masses running.

"And when are you going to get married?" the abbé asked Bessier when the demonstration was over and Bessier was again seated by his bed.

"In June, but it won't be in church," Bessier said.

"I didn't think that it would be," the abbé said gently.

"And our children won't be baptized either," Bessier said.

"There's no need to rub it in," the abbé Gaston said.

"It's only by rubbing some things in that one will rub other things out," Bessier said. "That's what they've done in Russia."

"I don't think that I very much approve of what they have done in Russia," the abbé Gaston said.

"It doesn't matter whether you approve or not," Bessier said. "The main thing is that they have done something in Russia. In Russia the poor no longer fight battles for the rich. Three hundred francs a month, that's what they're going to pay me when I get back to the office. My boss spends as much on an evening out with one of his women. Ever heard of Henri de la Porte du Bibier? In case you haven't, he's the managing director and chief shareholder of the Fonderies et Laminoirs de Bobigny where I work as a cost clerk."

The abbé Gaston was glad when Bessier left: he didn't like arguing with Bessier and he felt stupid not to be able to comfort him. The proper answers to Bessier's assertions always occurred to the abbé when Bessier was no longer there. The abbé lay in grateful silence, glad that he was so soon going to return to the safety of the recurring ceremonies of the Church. The abbé felt, however, that new words were required to express the old piety in order that men and women should be compelled to listen. In the German hospital the abbé had seen dreadful things. He had seen wounds which had made him realize that it wasn't only upon the French that the misery of war had fallen. Priests had a duty to prevent these terrible things from happening again, the abbé Gaston decided. He looked up from his meditation to find Armelle and her mother standing at the foot of his bed. Armelle was wearing a pretty new green dress.

"Good afternoon, Monsieur l'abbé," Armelle said and ran to kiss him.

The abbé caught the little girl to him and stroked her hair.

"It is good to see you again, child," he said.

Armelle sat at the top of the bed, holding the priest's hand, and her mother sat at the foot of the bed. Madame Dillier, the abbé knew, had had a hard time of it, bringing the child up. Madame Dillier's husband had died when his daughter was only three years old and Madame Dillier had been obliged to work in an office. The abbé liked it when Madame Dillier and Armelle came to see him. He knew them well enough not to have to do much talking. Today it was Armelle who did all the talking. Armelle said that Monsieur l'abbé Gaston must have been very brave to get such a sore wound from the Germans. She said that Monsieur l'abbé Gaston must get well in time to be able to say the mass for her first communion, which was to take place in May. She said that they had two new priests for catechism now. One was called Monsieur l'abbé Paquin and the other was called Monsieur l'abbé Moune. She liked Monsieur l'abbé Paquin much better than Monsieur l'abbé Moune although even Monsieur l'abbé Paquin she did not like nearly as much as she liked Monsieur l'abbé Gaston. The child's voice rose gaily above her new green dress. The abbé Gaston liked listening to it.

"Visitors, I see?" The Chanoine Litry did not look pleased as he came and stood by Madame Dillier, in the dark anonymity of his cassock. The rector was a good man and he loved the Lord, but he loved Him without laughing. The rector was grim as he began to catalogue the crimes recently committed by the clergy of the neighboring church of Saint Rémy. The clergy of the church of Saint Rémy had had a soft time of it during the war, the Chanoine Litry said. Only one of them had been called up and the remainder had la-di-da-ed around ministering to a lot of toothy old trout who were bound to save their souls anyway. They had had special preachers during Advent and Lent and opera singers in the choir and an organist who was an original enough agnostic to believe that man had evolved from the codfish but who wasn't quite so ignorant about music. The result was that they had stolen a good quarter of the congregation of Saint Clovis and a large proportion of the society weddings as well. The rector was still talking about the clergy of Saint Rémy when Armelle and her mother left.

"Well, how are we getting on?" the rector asked, drawing his chair in closer to the bed.

"Not so dusty, Monsieur le Curé," the abbé Gaston said.

"Military language, eh?" the rector said. "Well, I suppose soldiers will be soldiers."

"There was a charity about the men at the front," the abbé Gaston said. He wanted to make the rector understand about the war and about how the language of soldiers was not necessarily crude language. He wanted to tell the rector about the time that it rained for four days on end and of how Germans and Frenchmen had found themselves dying in the same mud together. He wanted to tell the rector about the day when the man standing next to him in the trenches had had his head blown off his shoulders. He wanted to tell him about how men who didn't believe in life after death were often kindly in adversity. But with the rector's face so close and cold and disapproving the proper words wouldn't come. The rector had heard it all before of course. The rector had heard it so often that he hadn't heard it at all. All the abbé Gaston could say was: "What I feel is that the soldiers weren't hostile to us. And I do not think that they are hostile to us now. All that we have got to do is to make them understand."

"Isn't that what the Church has been trying to do for nearly two thousand years?" the Chanoine Litry asked.

"This time it is more important than ever that we shall succeed," the abbé Gaston said. "The world has just been through a very terrible experience."

"The world does not seem to have learned a great deal from that experience," the rector interrupted.

"It is for us to make the world learn," the abbé Gaston said. "It is for us to do what the politicians will certainly fail to do. I feel that everywhere men are waiting for a message. If we do not give them the right message somebody else is going to give them the wrong message. Our opportunity is here and now. All that we have to do is to restate the old truths in a new language."

"That sounds to me surprisingly like modernism," the rector said.

"It is rather a reform of our rhetoric that I recommend," the abbé Gaston said. "Tirell and Loisy wanted to change the doctrines. I don't want to do that. All I want to change is the words. All I want is for us to use simple words instead of long ear-deadening phrases. I feel certain that we should be more successful if we did. And what's more I'm sure that the men who've just come back from the front would listen to us."

The Chanoine Litry shook his head sadly.

"Monsieur l'abbé Paquin who has also been to the front has been saying much the same thing to me," he said. "I wish that I could believe that you were both right. I am afraid, however, that you are both wrong. It is not because of the words we use that people won't listen to us. It is because the practice of our teaching would interfere with their pleasures. You are lying in a hospital bed, Monsieur l'abbé Gaston, and you do not know what is happening in the world. When you return to the parish your optimism will be tempered. Immorality has never been as widespread as it is at the present moment. The girls on the square have become quite shameless." The rector spoke for a long time about the girls on the square.

The abbé Paquin was the abbé Gaston's next visitor. He arrived shortly after the rector had left. The abbé Paquin was despondent. He said that he had returned from the war filled with a desire to convert the whole world and that the rector had accused him of heresy, schism and spiritual pride. He said that there was no hope for the Church when narrow-minded men like the Chanoine Litry ministered at her altars.

The abbé Gaston listened patiently. There was always hope for the Church, the abbé Gaston said, and there was certainty as well. The Church has a long patience, the abbé Gaston said.

IX

IN 1919 the Place du Général Marchand had become the Place du Maréchal Haig and the dresses worn by the dressmaker's girls when they walked on the square came down to their ankles. The Chanoine Litry said, however, that he would have preferred crinolines, although he supposed that their bulk would have prevented penitents from kneeling properly in the confessional. The rector was more than ordinarily concerned by the girls' misdemeanors. A new hairdresser's establishment had been opened on the other side of the square and thither the girls went at all hours of the day to have their hair tweezed, tugged, cut and twisted in a manner the rector considered calculated to encourage lewdness. What chiefly concerned the rector, however, was that the girls had discovered that it was quicker to walk through the church when they went to the hairdresser's than to walk round the church and cross the square in front of it or behind it. The girls entered the church by the northern door and left it by the southern and on their way through, he said, they never paused to pray. The Chanoine Litry hesitated to close the side doors of the church for fear of discouraging those who genuinely sought the peace of the Lord's House. Instead he instructed his curates that they were rigorously to reprimand any young women they saw crossing the church without making exterior signs of devotion.

The abbé Paquin did not like taking the catechism class. He felt that he did not teach it as well as the abbé Gaston, perhaps because he was not yet old enough to persuade the very young. The little boys and girls were restless when he spoke to them. When he asked them to say that God had made the world they said back that God had made the world. When he asked them to say that God could neither err nor be deceived they said back that God could neither err nor be deceived. But if he asked one of them, unprompted, to tell him who had made the world, he was quite likely to be told that it had been the Blessed Virgin Mary. He was glad when the time came for him to dismiss them with his blessing. He knelt to pray for the children when they had gone. It was Septuagesima and the curtains on the tabernacle were violet. The Church was rolling round her wise old year again. The abbé Paquin prayed that the children might be wise with her. *"Multi enim sunt vocati, pauci vero electi."* Perhaps the words which he himself had chanted on Sunday as deacon at the high mass held the answer. Perhaps many were called and few indeed were chosen. The Lord had said so. Had he been guilty of spiritual pride in supposing otherwise? Had the rector been right and he himself wrong? Were perhaps the old words the best after all? At any rate it was manifestly his duty to obey his superior. The Church was strong because it was founded on obedience.

A young girl entered the church by the northern door. She was pretty and she had shining black hair and she was fashionably dressed. Remembering the rector's instructions, the abbé Paquin watched her discreetly. She took no holy water from the holy water stoup. She passed in front of the high altar without genuflecting. She made no sign of the cross and she paused nowhere to pray. She made directly for the southern door. The abbé Paquin rose from his knees and overtook her in the passage just as she was about to go down the stairs.

The girl seemed surprised to see the young priest standing in front of her. Her eyelashes stood up in rows of little black spikes. Her lips shone damply like newly painted railings. Her dress was short and her heels were high and her stockings silk. From the bodice of her low cut blouse came a perfume penetrating enough to convince the abbé Paquin that it was sinful. "I have been watching you, Mademoiselle," the abbé Paquin said. "You have profaned God's House. You have passed through it without either asking God's blessing upon yourself or acknowledging His Presence. And it was not in order that young women might dress immodestly and plaster themselves with paint that our soldiers fought and died. You ought to be ashamed of yourself, Mademoiselle."

The abbé Paquin left the girl and went back into the church before she had time to reply. He had not liked the task which the rector had imposed upon him and he did not feel that his words had been very wisely chosen. He knelt and prayed that the Lord might give them effect. Then he went back to the presbytery, proud to be able to tell the rector that he had obeyed his instructions.

The new priest, the abbé Moune, was the only priest in the common room. He was a red-haired priest with small unspiritual eyes who had spent the war as an orderly in a naval supply depot at Brest. Lying back in the only comfortable chair, he was reading an illustrated sporting weekly.

"I've just been pitching in to one of those hoydens that the rector's been telling us about," the abbé Paquin said, unable to keep his recent adventure to himself.

"Monsieur le Curé will certainly be pleased," the abbé Moune said, without lowering his paper.

It was impossible to tell from the abbé Moune's expression whether he really thought that the rector would be pleased. It was equally impossible to tell whether the abbé Moune himself was pleased. The abbé Paquin never knew what the abbé Moune was thinking, not even when the abbé Moune was agreeing vociferously with the rector. The abbé Paquin did not think that he liked the abbé Moune. He was glad when the door of the common room opened and the rector himself entered.

"Monsieur le Curé, I have just been rebuking one of those girls," the abbé Paquin said eagerly.

"So I gather, but my instructions did not authorize you to insult the niece of Cardinal Archbishop of Paris," the Chanoine Litry said grimly. "Perhaps you will be able to explain this matter in the proper quarter. His Eminence has telephoned to say that he wishes to see you immediately."

X

THE Cardinal stood by his window and looked down on the glossy panorama of the city. The street lamps were already lighted, for night was beginning to fall.

In the high buildings, too, lights began to appear. The lights threw gold upon the river where it turned into two rivers to flow past the cathedral. Where Thomas of Aquin had carried his books bank messengers scurried with bills of exchange. Where Heloise's dress had blown in the wind young men walked in waterproofs. The Angelus rang out from the towers of the cathedral, casting a prayer upon the water. Looking down upon the sad streets, the Cardinal prayed for his careless parish.

"You seem very young to be a priest," the Cardinal said when the young man knelt to kiss his ring.

"Your Eminence ordained me in 1914," the young man said.

"I'm glad of that," the Cardinal said and looked earnestly into the face to whose soul his hands had given power and the mark. He did not remember ever having seen the face before. The Cardinal was sad sometimes when he thought of all the priests he had ordained and whose faces he could not remember. He thought of the first time when he himself had been reprimanded by authority. He had been a deacon at the time, with the yoke of Christ only half upon his shoulders, and the Bishop had learned that he had played the violin at a private dance given during the holidays by one of his sisters. "If you go on like this, young man, you'll never get anywhere in the Church," the Bishop had said. The Cardinal smiled at the recollection.

"I do not think that what you have said to my niece will do her any harm," the Cardinal said. "We must remember, however, that she has not been called as we have been called. Sometimes I think that it is difficult for priests to understand that it is harder for lay people to be holy than it is for us. They do not receive the same graces and the same privileges. We must remember, too, that we are links in mercy rather than in wrath. But in the main you were right. My niece is a very worldly young woman. Her name does not help her, either. It is Solange Buonacompagnia. Corsican, of course. And now shall we go into the chapel?"

In the chapel they were having Benediction of the Blessed Sacrament. The candle flames on the altar were blurred by clouds of incense. In an old gold cope the chaplain was swinging the thurible and the tiny congregation was singing the Tantum Ergo. The Cardinal and the young priest knelt side by side in a small gallery facing sideways on to the altar. Wrapped in the humeral veil, the chaplain raised the loneliness of God above the loneliness of men. Then he put the Host back into the tabernacle again. In a sweet blue mist they sang their praise to the Lord, because His mercy was confirmed upon them.

"I think that it will be inadvisable for you to continue as a curate at the church of Saint Clovis," the Cardinal said to the young priest when they had returned to his study. "I think that you will be much more suitably employed as my assistant chaplain."

There was a lot of work waiting for the Cardinal on his desk when the young priest had gone. There was his Lenten pastoral letter to sign and the list of his visitations to draw up. There were more churches in Paris than there were Sundays in the year and to some he would have to send an auxiliary bishop. The principal churches like Sainte Marie Madeleine, Saint Augustin and Saint Philippe du Roule he would, of course, have to visit personally. There were quite a lot of unholy things to be done in order that people might fail to be holy, the Cardinal thought.

XI

TEARS of excitement, pride and gratitude were drying in the abbé Paquin's eyes when he left the Cardinal's study. In the antechamber two pretty girls were sitting dangling their legs from a table. Their silk dresses were spread out like fans over the holy books. One of them rose as the young priest approached and ran to meet him. The abbé Paquin again found himself looking into the face of the Cardinal's niece.

"Monsieur l'abbé, please allow me to apologize," the girl said. "It was mean of me to report you to my uncle. Please tell me. My uncle hasn't punished you, has he?"

"Only by making me his assistant chaplain," the abbé Paquin said.

"Oh I'm so glad!" the girl exclaimed. "You'll probably end up a cardinal yourself yet. Like that you'll find it easier to forgive me." She called back to her friend. "Giséle, come and meet the new Pope. Giséle is even worldlier than I am," she explained. "She eats Neapolitan ices during Lent."

Giséle was fair and Solange was dark. Both girls were very young and both girls were very pretty. The abbé Paquin was surprised to find that he liked looking at their smiling eyes beneath their wide hats. The abbé Paquin thought that it was perhaps as well that the Lord had made the majority of women plain.

XII

THE abbé Gaston usually got up in the mornings as soon as he heard Madame Boulon bringing in the garbage buckets. Today, however, he could lie on in luxury because he wasn't saying mass until eleven o'clock, when Armelle was going to make her first communion. It was a month now since he had been discharged from the hospital. Although he limped a lot when he moved about the sanctuary he was still able to say mass all right and even to be subdeacon at the high mass on Sundays if the celebrant remembered not to take too long steps.

The abbé lay for a little thinking about Armelle's first communion and watching the pigeon as it strutted up and down the window ledge. St. Blasius of Cappadocia also watched the pigeon as it strutted up and down the window ledge, but he made no attempt to jump at the pigeon. The tom cat knew that, although his master took, for a theologian, an elastic view of his romances, he was opposed to certain forms of gluttony. From the street outside came the harsh cry of the rag merchant.

The abbé rose soon because he had his shopping to do before he said mass, and this took much longer than it had done before the war, as he limped so badly carrying his bag. He knelt and said his prayers before he began to dress. He prayed for all those that were dying that day, that God might grant them rest. He prayed for the living, that God might prosper them. He prayed for Armelle, that she might make a good first communion and serve the Lord all the days of her life. He prayed for those who were lying wounded on battlefields and for those who were sick in hospitals and for those in prisons. Finally, he prayed for himself, that God might make him a good priest.

The abbé found it difficult going downstairs with his shopping bag in one hand and his stick in the other, but he supposed that Bessier must find it even more difficult, with his artificial leg. Bessier had told him that the great secret as far as stairs were concerned was always to remember to put the bad leg down first and to pull it up last. This tip the abbé kept in mind now, as he had kept it in mind on the altar steps. Years ago an old priest had told the abbé that, although there were no rubrics about it, it was only polite to God to leave the chalice and the paten standing on the altar until one had recited the prayers after mass. Taking the chalice and paten down with one immediately after the last gospel suggested an indecent haste to leave the sanctuary, the old priest had said. Compliance with the old priest's counsel had been made easier by Bessier's tip.

Outside the square was full of little girls in their first communion dresses. Even in the greengrocer's shop when the abbé went in to buy his potatoes and his runner beans there were two little girls in white dresses. Everybody said that they thought that the girls looked very pretty in their white dresses and the abbé was glad that the little girls looked so pretty in their white dresses, because of the wonderful thing that the Lord was going to do to their souls. The abbé told the little girls that it was he who was going to say the communion mass, and the people in the shop all said that the abbé must be feeling very proud that he was about to celebrate so important a ceremony. The people in the shop all said that they were glad to see the abbé back among them again and that it had been very brave of the abbé indeed to have been so badly wounded in the war. The lady who kept the greengrocer's shop was especially effusive and she let the abbé have his runner beans for a few centimes cheaper than the price marked up.

The lady of easy virtue who lived in the centrally heated flat on the fifth floor was kind to the abbé, too, when he came back laden with his purchases and she met him at the entrance to the lift. The abbé Gaston was not supposed to use the lift as he lived only in a servant's room on the sixth floor and did not pay enough rent, but the centrally heated lady of easy virtue said that she was sure that the landlord would not mind his using the lift with her, as the abbé had been so badly wounded in the war. So up together in the lift they shot and the abbé hoped that the centrally heated lady of easy virtue's soul would soar as rapidly after death. The centrally heated lady of easy virtue said that the abbé must really meet her gentleman friend someday because funnily enough her gentleman friend had a beard, too, and she was sure that they had a lot of other tastes in common.

The poetess, too, was kind to the abbé when she overtook him crossing to the church. Youth was beautiful, the poetess said, and because she knew that the abbé Gaston understood Spanish she would recite to him her new poem about bull fighting:

"Corrida de toros,
Matadores, picadores,
Blood and sand
To beat the band
Se queda prohibido
Escupir
En el suelo..."

The poetess was still reciting her poem when they arrived at the door of the church.

The abbé didn't listen much to the poetess' poem. He was looking for Armelle, and he left the poetess and went towards her as soon as he saw the little girl coming up the steps with her mother. The sun was gold in the blue sky and Armelle's white muslin dress was like a soft wavy cloud against the blue sky and her eyes were grave above her smile. The abbé Gaston wanted to say quite a lot of things to the little girl. He wanted to tell her that what she was going to do was a happy thing and a glad thing because it was the meaning of the world and the light let into the world. He wanted to tell her that the state of grace was more beautiful than the summer sky above her head. Instead he kissed her on both cheeks and laughed when she said that his beard tickled. Then he gave her a holy picture for her prayer book and went into the sacristy to vest. The white satin vestments were already laid out. The abbé Gaston was about to pick up the amice when the abbé Moune entered in a hurry.

"I see that I have arrived just in time," the abbé Moune said, pointing further down the dresser to where the black vestments were also laid out.

"Requiem at twelve in the lady chapel. The notice came in late last night. Monsieur le Curé said that he thought it much more suitable that I should say the communion mass and that you should say the requiem. The rector said that in view of your limp it was preferable that you celebrate as few masses at the high altar as possible."

"But a little girl who is my special friend is making her first communion today," the abbé Gaston said. "I promised to say this mass for her."

"Monsieur l'abbé Gaston, I am repeating the rector's instructions," the abbé Moune said.

The abbé Gaston wanted to say many things. He wanted to say that it was not his fault that he had been wounded at the front while the abbé Moune had been skulking at Brest trying to convert tins of sardines. But these things he knew he could not say, because he was a priest. A priest could not accuse another priest of cowardice. A priest had no right to human affections. A priest had been nailed to Christ's passion the day of his ordination. And a priest's hands were safe hands and all priests' hands were safe hands, and it did not matter by which priest's hands the holy things were done. The abbé Gaston went out of the sacristy and knelt in a dark corner at the back of the church and prayed for the children who were about to make their first communion, that a grace might touch them.

Out in the sunlight the pigeons came tumbling down from the roof of the church. The little girls walked about the cobble stones in their white muslin dresses. The abbé Gaston told Armelle the reason why he had not been able to say her first communion mass for her and how sorry he was. The abbé said that the Church on earth was like that, with people at different stages on their journey all the time. When Talleyrand had been dying a young girl on her way to her first communion had been brought in to see him, and her visit had comforted Talleyrand, who hadn't always had holy thoughts. The abbé said that perhaps Armelle's first communion would bless and make beautiful the funeral of the dead man he was shortly going to bury. He said that he wouldn't be able to come to her party as it would be too late when he got back from the cemetery. He said that of course she could sing Au Clair de la Lune and Sur le Pont d'Avignon with her little friends.

XIII

IN February 1922 the Cardinal had had the dream about the three white cassocks again, because Benedict the Fifteenth had died, and it was once more necessary to elect a new pontiff, to guard the flame. This time, however, the Cardinal thought that Francis stood a much better chance than he did, but Francis himself said not. They were walking together in the garden of the Vatican when Francis said this. Towards them came their Eminences of Munich and Cologne, rustling in their sacred purple.

"My dear Alphonse, I'm so glad that the war is over because I've been waiting all this time to explain about keeping you out of the bathroom," the Cardinal of Cologne said, advancing towards his brother with both arms outstretched. "I didn't do it on purpose, you know. The bolt wasn't working properly, that's all."

The four Cardinals walked together, deliberating gravely. They agreed that the war had been a mistake. They thought, however, that one good thing had come out of it, and that was that the lesson had been so severe that a similar catastrophe was unlikely to recur. Their Eminences thought that a great opportunity for sanctification awaited the world. Their Eminences could distinguish signs of religious revival in many lands. They rejoiced that the rent had been mended in Christ's garment, which was the Church.

"New boy, eh?" Francis asked, indicating a dumpy little Italian Cardinal walking alone.

"Achille Ratti of Milan," the Cardinal of Munich said. "Created only a month or two ago. Hasn't an earthly of course."

The four Cardinals walked together, deliberating gravely. They rejoiced that the rent had been mended in Christ's garment, which was the Church.

XIV

IN 1922 nobody was grateful anymore to the abbé Gaston for having been so badly wounded in the war. The centrally heated lady of easy virtue no longer invited him to share the lift with her when he came in with his shopping bag full. Today his bag was more heavily laden than usual, because Bessier was coming for lunch and the abbé had bought two pork chops and a bottle of wine for their meal. Although the abbé had still to wear a special boot with a thick sole and a high heel, his wounded leg was much stronger now. The abbé managed the six flights of stairs easily enough by hanging onto the banister with his left hand and by carrying his walking stick in his mouth.

St. Blasius of Cappadocia was so interested in the smell of the pork chops that the abbé had to give him a raw runner bean or two to keep him quiet while he himself got on with the cooking. The abbé put the vegetables on to boil but decided that he wouldn't start frying the chops until Bessier came, as they would taste better that way. He removed his books from the table, cleaned the oilcloth with a damp rag, laid out the cutlery and glasses, sliced the tomatoes and uncorked the wine. Then, as Bessier was not due to arrive for some time yet, the abbé indulged in a little worldliness by clapping on the earphones of the crystal receiving set which the poetess had given him for understanding her poems about Spain so well. Miraculously, cracklingly, there came the sound of an invisible lady singing that she was forever blowing bubbles, pretty bubbles in the air. The abbé Gaston didn't think that the new invention was as wicked as the Chanoine Litry had made out.

Bessier was in a bad temper when he arrived. The rubber on the end of his stick had slipped on the oil on the platform of the underground and he had had a nasty fall. And Madame Boulon had shouted at him for trying to get into the lift. Artificial leg or no artificial leg, Bessier would have to walk upstairs as only the visitors of tenants who paid decent rents were allowed to use the lift, Madame Boulon had said. Bessier said that it showed how right Karl Marx had been when he had said that the struggle was between the proletariat and the rich. As Bessier said this he handed an illustrated magazine to the abbé and told him to look at page six.

The magazine was full of the photographs of fashionable young women, apparently doing the minimum of thinking about their salvation. Leaning against the doors of limousines, lounging on the decks of transatlantic liners, standing beneath monster umbrellas at lace meetings, drinking tea on the Riviera, showing their legs on golf courses, they smiled with white teeth at the world, as though they would never die. "Personalities at St. Moritz" was the heading on page six and beneath it was a photograph of a young woman and a young man seated on a high stool at a bar. "Mademoiselle Solange Buonacompagnia and Monsieur Henri de la Porte du Bibier, Whose Engagement Has Just Been Announced," the writing underneath the photograph ran.

"Good advertisement for Holy Mother Church, eh?" Bessier sneered. "A Cardinal's niece tippling in a bar while old people and children die of starvation."

"You mustn't get things out of proportion, you know," the abbé Gaston said gently.

"Listen," Bessier said. "Only last week that swine refused me a rise of thirty francs a month. He seems to be able to afford to pay for Mademoiselle Buonacompagnia's cocktails all right, doesn't he? If not being able to pay me a rise and going to St. Moritz for winter sports is not out of proportion, I should very much like to know what is. There is a misery in the world, Monsieur l'abbé Gaston, and as usual the Church seems to be doing nothing about it."

"The Church's ministers are always there for those who require consolation," the abbé Gaston said, beginning to smear butter on the bottom of the frying pan.

"It's not consolation that the workers want; it's justice," Bessier said. "A man called André Desmoutiers was condemned to death for murder last week. In case you don't know why he committed murder I'll tell you. André Desmoutiers fought as an infantryman during the whole of the war. He was at Vimy and he was at Verdun and he was wounded four times. In civilian life he was a roadmender, but when he was demobilized his municipality would no longer employ him as they said he wasn't fit to work anymore. Nobody else would employ him either. He couldn't live on his disability pension, of course, and he was forced to go round selling pencils and stationery from office to office and people like Monsieur Henri de la Porte du Bibier banged their doors in his face and told him that they no longer had any time for war heroes. In the end he murdered an old woman on the Boulevard Barbés for fifty francs."

"Murder's a cowardly crime all the same," the abbé Gaston said.

"Not so cowardly as the crime of doing your murdering at a remove," Bessier said. "Desmoutiers at least had the courage to do his killing with his own hands. And he killed for an elemental reason: because he was hungry. The rich are afraid to do their own killing; they delegate their killing to hunger and cold and they don't call their executioners in for elemental reasons: they call them in because they want to go on whoring in Biarritz and drinking cocktails in St. Moritz. And that's why you and I got wounded in the last war: so that the French and the British and the American rich men could go on smoking the big cigars and having the best women instead of the German rich men."

The abbé Gaston was sorry for Bessier sitting there being angry in his cheap cotton suit and horizontally striped shirt. He knew that much of what Bessier said was true.

"All the same you must not let yourself get bitter," the abbé said.

"How can I help being bitter?" Bessier asked. "I've got a wife and child now and although I work like a nigger I don't make enough to keep them. My job's not easy either: stock records and oncost and heaven knows what. And I've got to go out and write up grocers' accounts in the evenings in order to make both ends meet. And all so that Monsieur Henri de la Porte du Bibier can marry a Cardinal's niece."

"Let's leave the Church out of it, please," the abbé Gaston said.

"How can we leave the Church out of it when she's in it up to her neck?" Bessier answered. "Do you know what a rich woman coming out of St. Pierre de Chaillot said to a beggar the other day? The beggar asked her how she thought he was going to live without money or without food. 'In that case,' she said, 'you'd better go and croak.'"

When they had finished arguing the pork chops were burned and St. Blasius of Cappadocia had stolen half the runner beans. It was not a very successful luncheon party.

XV

IN the chapel of the monastery the Cardinal was making his confession to a Benedictine monk. His red stockings peeped out from beneath the curtain, but before the grille his face was redder still, for the Cardinal had sinned grievously. Bless him, father, for he had been guilty of spiritual pride, his thoughts had often wandered during his prayers and he had cleaned his spectacles on his alb while celebrating pontifical high mass.

The Cardinal said that it was lack of concentration in prayer which bothered him the most. When his thoughts wandered in the course of private prayer the remedy was simple, because all he had to do was to begin the petition over again. Such a procedure, however, was scarcely possible when his reflections strayed during his public supplications, otherwise the liberation of the congregation might be considerably delayed. Prayers that had to be sung gave him special concern. The Cardinal found that it was almost impossible for him simultaneously to get his notes right and to keep his mind on the matter of his orison. There was, too, the distraction of his mitre. In the course of his fifteen years as a bishop no assistant minister at mass had ever succeeded, at the first attempt, in placing his mitre comfortably on his head and invariably he himself had subsequently to adjust its position. Often he found himself worrying about this trifling annoyance a collect or two ahead, so that sometimes he did not know whether he was praying about the finding in the temple or the temptation in the desert. Finally, the Cardinal said, there was the business of his prayers for those who had preceded him in the sign of faith. Did his ghostly father think that it was wrong of him to pray for repose of the souls of the faithful departed while he was shaving in the morning? Ought this charitable act to be postponed until his hands as well as his mind were unoccupied? The monk did not think that his ghostly son had sinned too seriously. Spiritual pride and distraction in prayer were, of course, devices contrived by the devil to confound those who had succeeded in resisting the gaudier temptations by which less eclectic souls were ensnared. In these matters, as in others, it was the intention which mattered. As regards the wandering of his penitent's thoughts during the performance of public ceremonies, the monk thought that Meister Eckhart had said the really important thing. Meister Eckhart had said: "A celebrant of the mass who is over-intent on recollection is apt to make mistakes. The best way is to try to concentrate the mind before and afterwards, but, when saying it, to do so quite straightforwardly." Much more important was the content with which his penitent filled his periods of relaxation. The monk had read the other day of an American Cardinal who had publicly stated that he devoted the greater part of his leisure to perfecting his practice of a game called Mah Jong. While the monk did not think that such a diversion was even venially sinful, he considered it an unsuitable pastime for a prelate. A priest's holiday, and much more a Cardinal's, should always be a busman's holiday, and in this connection he would again quote Meister Eckhart: "Whoever has God in mind, simply and solely God, in all things, such a man carries God with him into all his works and into all places, and God alone does all his works. He sees nothing but God, nothing seems good to him but God. He becomes one with God in every thought. Just as no multiplicity can dissipate God, so nothing can dissipate this man or make him multiple."

His penitent must chiefly aim at not being made multiple. The monk ended by recommending the Cardinal to recite his prayers for the souls of the faithful departed while lathering rather than while shaving his face, if his penitent wished to avoid the risk of hurting his chin more than he advanced the liberation of sinners. For his penance the Cardinal would say one Hail Mary.

It was Passion week and the crucifix and the statues were covered with purple veils, because of the sad thing that had been done long ago. The little chapel was full of people waiting to hear vespers. The Cardinal went and knelt next an old woman who had just been absolved for losing her temper at Lisieux when, after queueing for more than an hour in the basilica, she had discovered that she had extended for benediction by the priest a packet of sausages instead of a statue of the Little Flower. The Cardinal hoped that his pectoral cross and sash and stockings wouldn't be noticed too much by the other clergymen who had come to learn how to behave in church. The Cardinal bent his head to say his penance. The

Cardinal was still trying to say it an hour later when the gold and the white and the purple and the flame had gone from the altar and only the smell of wax and incense remained. The Cardinal feared that he was becoming a very multiple man.

XVI

IN 1924 the dresses worn by the girls in the Place du Maréchal Haig showed more of their legs than would have been approved by the Council of Trent. The Chanoine Litry often commented on the display and said that if skirts got any shorter the result would be either the end of civilization or the union of the schismatic Churches. Today the girls had walked across the square to stand on the steps of the church to see Mademoiselle Buonacompagnia and Monsieur Henri de la Porte du Bibier walk out of the porch together when the Cardinal had finished marrying them. The abbé Gaston had to make his way through throngs of young women before he could find a place in the corner of the railings against which to lean and say his office.

The abbé Gaston did not like fashionable weddings and still less did he like paid singers in church. The abbé thought that a croak which came from the heart was more pleasing to the Lord than basses and tenors and sopranos at one franc fifty the tra-la-la. In spite of his double distaste the abbé had done his best to stay in church during the whole of the ceremony but the restlessness of the congregation and the operatic insincerity of the choir had been too much for him and he had come outside. He was just beginning to open his breviary when he saw Armelle working her way through the crowd towards him. She was wearing a pink dress in which the abbé did not remember having seen her before. Armelle was sixteen now and the abbé thought that she was beginning to look very pretty.

"What luck meeting you, my child," the abbé said, closing his breviary and stretching out both his hands to her. "And where's your mother?"

"Mother's ill, Monsieur l'abbé," the girl replied. "She says it's nothing much but she thinks she'd better stay in bed."

"And what about school?" the abbé asked.

"I stayed at home to do the cooking and look after mother, but mother said I could come to see the wedding," Armelle said.

The abbé nodded sympathetically. He knew that Madame Dillier's circumstances were those of thousands of other Parisian widows. Underpaid for keeping the customers' accounts in a department store, she had to do her housework and prepare her own and her daughter's breakfast before leaving for the office. At noon she had to rush home in the underground and prepare another meal. In the evening, after office hours, she often had shopping and mending to do as well as more cooking and washing up. The abbé found himself beginning to hate the fashionable people inside the church. They were insensitive not only to the sufferings which they did not see, but also to those which they saw. The abbé supposed that they were cruel because they were afraid to know that they themselves could suffer as the poor.

"Sometimes I am frightened when mother is ill," Armelle said. "She coughs a lot and sometimes it seems that she is never going to stop."

"I expect that she is tired and has caught a summer cold," the abbé said. "People do, you know."

"She coughs in winter as well," Armelle said.

"Then she must catch winter colds, too," the priest said. Armelle thrust her arm through the priest's and they stood for a little like that, with the wind blowing Armelle's hair about her head and her pink frock like a flag about her legs. The girls from the dressmakers' establishment stood all around them.

"I want to be a mannequin, too, when I grow up," Armelle said. "Mother says no and that I'd much better work in an office. But I don't want to work in an office. I want to be pretty and I want to wear pretty clothes. Please say that you'll help me, Monsieur l'abbé. Please say that you'll tell mother that you think it's all right for me to be a mannequin."

The abbé Gaston hesitated. He had heard many things about mannequins.

"What's the matter?" Armelle asked. "Isn't a mannequin a good thing to want to be?"

"A mannequin's like everybody else in the world," the abbé said. "She either serves God or she doesn't."

"Of course, I'd be a mannequin that served God," Armelle said.

"In that case I've no objection to you becoming a mannequin and I'll say so to your mother," the abbé Gaston said.

Armelle hugged the abbé's arm.

"I knew I could count on you," she said. "Tell me: is the bride very beautiful?"

"Very," the abbé said.

"Is it sinful to be beautiful?" Armelle asked.

"Of course not," the abbé said. "Who on earth put that idea into your head?"

"The rector said in the pulpit that beauty was a snare of the devil," Armelle said.

"Anyway the beauty of brides isn't sinful," the abbé said.

"And are brides always beautiful?" Armelle asked.

"They always think they are," the abbé said.

Policemen came up the steps of the church and began to clear a passage through the middle of the crowd for the bridal procession. One of the policemen sneered as he asked the abbé Gaston to move back. The abbé thought he knew why the policeman sneered. The policeman sneered because he considered the abbé a fool because he was a priest or a priest because he was a fool. The policeman sneered either because he thought that the abbé had given up delight for superstition or because he thought that the abbé was too stupid to earn his living any other way. The abbé scowled back at the policeman to show the policeman that he could be angry when he wanted. to be angry. Then he remembered the thing that had been done to him on the day of his ordination and he bit back his resentment and let the sun shine into his beard and tried to feel happy.

"Here they come," Armelle said.

The bride and the bridegroom came out of the church. The bride blinked a little in the sunlight and her white dress spread out on either side of her and her veil was a mist about her head. The bridegroom walked proudly beside her. Behind them followed a procession of gentlemen in black clothes and ladies in colored silks. Simultaneously, however, there came from the street a procession of shabbily dressed men and women waving their arms and shouting angrily as they advanced up the steps of the church. "We want a living wage," they cried as they followed their leader, who limped badly. Almost as quickly as the abbé recognized

Bessier, the policeman who had sneered hit out at the limping man with his baton.

XVII

THE abbé Paquin had never been in a worldly drawing room before. The drawing room was crowded with pretty young women all talking at once. The noise their voices made was like birds twittering in the trees, only it was much louder. Conscious of the cracks in his dusty boots, the abbé Paquin stood miserably with a frail cup of tea in his hand. The abbé Paquin had never drunk tea in his life before and he would very much have preferred coffee.

"Monsieur l'abbé, these are simply delicious; you must try one," Gisèle said. Gisèle was wearing a pink green silk frock which flowed about her limbs like water as she walked. The abbé Paquin wondered if her worldliness were still confined to the consumption of Neapolitan ices during Lent.

The plate which Gisèle offered the abbé Paquin contained cream buns. The young priest took one, although he really wanted a sandwich, of which he saw there were plenty on other plates. He had to take the cream bun in the same hand as held his cup of tea, as his left hand was already holding his breviary.

"I'll take your book for you," Gisèle said. "Careful. These buns are loaded, you know."

Carrying his cream bun in his left hand and his cup and saucer in his right, the abbé Paquin followed Gisèle across the drawing-room. He could not follow her straight across the drawing-room, however. He had to wind back when she wound back, and forward again when she wound forward again, through aisles lined by other young women with cups of tea and cream buns or sandwiches in their hands. The young women were clever enough to be able to talk to one another as they stood with their cups of tea and cream buns in their hands. The young women were also clever enough to listen to one another as they talked to one another. High society life seemed complicated, the abbé Paquin thought.

"We'll sit here," Gisèle announced, sitting down on a sofa and smoothing out her frock.

The abbé Paquin sat down, but he sat down too hard. The tea from his cup splashed over into his saucer and some of it splashed on to his cassock as well.

"If I were you I'd pour the tea from my saucer back into my cup before I started drying myself with my handkerchief," Gisèle said. "I'll hold your bun for you."

Relieved that nobody else had noticed his embarrassment, the abbé Paquin mopped vigorously at his cassock. Indeed he mopped so vigorously that he nearly spilled his tea again and managed to correct the balance of his cup only just in time.

"Tell me, Monsieur l'abbé," Gisèle said, handing the young priest back his bun and his breviary. "Why is the Church so narrow-minded about divorce?"

With his cream bun in one hand and his cup and saucer in the other and his breviary in his tap, the abbé Paquin found it difficult to reply.

"It is a matter of theology," he said gravely.

"All the same infidelity must be rather amusing, don't you think?" Gisèle said, looking at the young priest out of earnest eyes.

The abbé Paquin was bending forward to bite the cream bun when Gisèle said this. The startling nature of her statement made him bite too hard. The cream came spurting out of the bun and fell in a blob on his cassock.

"It looks as though you'll have to use your handkerchief again," Gisèle said. "Here, give me back that bun."

The young priest rubbed desperately at his cassock. The cream vanished but a white stain remained.

"I'm afraid there's nothing for it but to spit, although I expect you'll have to suck first," Gisèle said. "It's alright. It's quite simple really. It's not a matter of theology."

"I am afraid, Mademoiselle, that I do not understand," the abbé Paquin said.

"Listen, Monsieur l'abbé," Gisèle said. "If you spit on your handkerchief without removing the cream that's on it already you'll only succeed in rubbing more cream onto your cassock. Therefore, the first thing to do is to suck off the cream that is already on your handkerchief. You can pretend you're blowing your nose."

The abbé Paquin sucked.

"Now prepare to spit," Gisèle said. "I'll tell you when nobody's looking. All right. You can go ahead now. Spit."

The abbé Paquin spat.

"Now rub," Gisèle said.

The abbé Paquin rubbed. The stain disappeared.

"And now, Monsieur l'abbé, I am going to teach you how to eat a cream bun without making a mess of your cassock," Gisèle said. "The first essential is not to press too hard with the fingers."

The abbé Paquin did not press too hard with the fingers.

"And the second essential is not to bite too hard with the teeth," Gisèle said.

The abbé Paquin did not bite too hard with the teeth.

"And the third essential is to wriggle one's tongue about inside the cream, delicately, as though one were sipping Beethoven," Gisèle said.

The abbé Paquin wriggled his tongue about inside the cream, delicately, as though he were sipping Beethoven.

"There you are," Gisèle said. "And now perhaps you'll repay me by telling me a little about theology."

The abbé Paquin was nervous again. He thought that Gisèle was too young and pretty for him to be able to talk to her with ease. Underneath her silk stocking she was wearing a thin silver chain round her ankle and the abbé Paquin supposed that this was very worldly of her. He looked away from her ankle and saw that her eyes were smiling and friendly, and this gave him courage.

"There is one thing about the modern world that strikes me rather forcibly," the abbé Paquin said solemnly. "In the past the wicked admitted that they were doing wrong; today the wicked are at pains to prove that they are doing right. In other words, modern sinners are bad metaphysicians as well as bad Christians: they imagine that their practice not only modifies objective truth but deprives them of the right to believe in it."

"That is very clever, Monsieur l'abbé, but now I am afraid that we must listen to the poetess," Gisèle said.

"She's going to recite a poem about a man called Mussolini."

The abbé Paquin did not know whether he had bored Gisèle or not. He was afraid that he had been beginning to bore himself. The poetess, large in a striped skirt, advanced, towards the piano and declaimed:

> *"Blessed in name and in function,*
> *Benito Mussolini,*
> *Duce e luce,*
> *Leader and light,*
> *Thou hast put to flight*
> *The hordes of barbary,*
> *And we are grateful."*

Everybody applauded. The poetess thanked them and said that, while she was grateful for their praise, what really mattered was that they should all realize that in fascism alone lay the ultimate salvation of Europe. Everybody applauded again. The abbé Paquin looked round to see that Gisèle had gone and that Monsieur Henri de la Porte du Bibier was sitting beside him instead. Monsieur Henri de la Porte du Bibier looked about thirty-five years of age and had the accentuated Anglo-Saxon appearance of the successful French businessman.

"I understand from my wife, Monsieur l'abbé, that you have a request to make of me," Monsieur Henri de la Porte du Bibier said.

The abbé Paquin told Monsieur Henri de la Porte du Bibier that Bessier, who was in prison awaiting trial, was a friend of the abbé Gaston and that the abbé Gaston had asked him to use his influence to obtain his release. Monsieur Henri de la Porte du Bibier listened attentively.

"I am sorry," Monsieur Henri de la Porte du Bibier said when the abbé Paquin had finished. "I should like to be clement, but I am afraid that clemency is a gesture which the modern employee always interprets as weakness. The director of a great industrial undertaking cannot afford to be weak. He must crush rebellion wherever it manifests itself."

"But surely the request to be paid a living wage cannot be regarded as rebellion," the abbé Paquin said.

"It is for the owners of businesses to decide what wages they can afford to pay," Monsieur Henri de la Porte du Bibier said. "It is not for the workers to dictate to them. Oh, I think I know what you are thinking. You are thinking that if I chose to live a little less comfortably myself I might have more money to spare for my workers. But even Cardinals live more ornately than simple priests, Monsieur l'abbé. Privileges entail responsibilities and the power to assume them is learned not in years but in centuries. The new masters whom the workers are attempting to create will have no sense of responsibility because they will be unaccustomed to the exercise of power; the new masters will seek only to enjoy and the last state of the worker will be worse than the first. And that is why I am obliged to refuse your request."

In the drawing-room Monsieur Henri de la Porte's argument sounded convincing enough, but outside in the street it seemed less so. The limousines laden with the rich roared past glistening in the evening rain. The rich men who sat with their harlots on the terraces of the cafés did not seem to be thinking about their responsibilities. A sorry little procession of disabled men passed up the avenue on their way to rekindle the flame on the tomb of the unknown warrior, but nobody paid any attention to them. The Angelus rang out from the church of St. Pierre de Chaillot, but nobody paid any attention to it either. The abbé Paquin walked sadly homewards.

XVIII

IT was the spring of 1926. In the drawing-room of the Cardinal's residence the six Chinese bishops were telling the Cardinal about China. The Cardinal, they said, must not take too seriously the stories about the communists. The Christian religion was making great headway in China, they said. Thanks to the intercession of our Lady of Ping-liang-fu, Cathay would soon be sending missionaries to Europe.

The Bishop of Wu-Pao said that his whole diocese was under the protection of our Lady of Ping-liang-fu, who worked great miracles when the young men praised her on the pitch pipes. The Bishop Ping Fan said that, in his opinion, our Lady of Tung-ting-shui worked even greater miracles. But the Bishop of Kwang-yang-hu said that it was impolite to speak all the time of the shrines of China, when France, too, had her holy places. The Bishop of Kwang-yang-hu understood that these were three in number and that they were called the Casino de Paris, the Bal Tabarin and the Folies Bergère and that they were very great shrines indeed, as they were much spoken of by many men. The Bishop of Kwang-yang-hu said that he and his fellow bishops would like very much to visit the shrines.

The Cardinal said that he was afraid that the Bishop of Kwang-yang-hu had been misinformed. He was sorry to have to tell the Bishop of Kwang-yang-hu that the places which his lordship had mentioned were shrines of the flesh rather than of the spirit and were temples where men and women assembled to forget God rather than to remember Him. Happily, however, France had real shrines which outshone both in fame and sanctity the places which the Bishop of Kwang-hang-hu had mentioned. These shrines were called the basilica of the Sacred Heart in Paris, the cathedral of Notre Dame at Chartres and the grotto at Lourdes. The Cardinal said that he was surprised that their Lordships had not heard of these places and that he would be pleased to arrange that they should visit them.

After consultation among themselves the Chinese Bishops said that they still thought that it would be more suitable for them to visit the Casino de Paris, the Bal Tabarin and the Folies Bergère. The Chinese Bishops said that their Blessed Lord, while on earth, had always consorted with sinners rather than with those who professed virtue and that they saw no reason why they should be presumptuous enough to depart from His practice. They said that it was evident, from what the Cardinal had just said, that the people who frequented these places were heathen and required to have the gospel preached to them. While they were aware that the clergy of Paris must have already made plans for the evangelization of such pagans, they would urge, without vanity, that they themselves were more experienced in controverting with the ignorant and might more speedily persuade them to abandon their errors. The Bishop of Wu-Pao had once preached to three hundred girls in a house of pleasure at Yu-lin and had converted two hundred and fifty-two of them. The Bishop of Ping Fan had once preached most successfully on the market place at Tu Shan Hu, explaining to the assembled merchants that Adam and not P'an Ku had been the first man in the world.

The Cardinal said that, not only could he not recommend this mission, but that he would have to forbid it. The Cardinal said that the difference between France and China was, as far as he could see, that in China it was the pagans who indulged in worldly amusements while in France it was the Christians. He said that more harm than good would result from the attempt publicly to remind French Christians of their obligations of their religion. Their lordships must realize that it was much more difficult to convert the Christian than to convert the heathen. The Chinese Bishops said that this was indeed a great mystery and that they would pray to our Lady of Ping-liang-fu to help them to understand it.

XIX

PUNCTUALLY at twenty-five minutes to eleven every Sunday morning in 1926 a young negro entered the church of Saint Clovis by the southern door and deposited his pale grey felt hat, yellow chamois leather gloves and silver topped walking stick on the altar dedicated to St. Peter of Alcantara where, in full view of the preacher, he stood in prayer. In spite of the fact that he had often felt it his duty to reprimand the negro for his neglect of the word of God, for his insufficient attendance at mass and for his disrespect of St. Peter of Alcantara, the Chanoine Litry had been grateful to the young man for the regularity with which he committed these faults. The rector, who didn't like listening to sermons other than his own, had given orders that the negro's arrival was to be interpreted by the preacher as a sign that it was time for him to cease his exhortations.

Today, however, the rector hoped that his warning would be disregarded, because it was the abbé Moune who was preaching the sermon, and the abbé Moune preached very well indeed. His current series of sermons on the Sins of Modern Paris had emptied the neighboring church of Saint Rémy and the bars of the Chatham and the Ritz as well. On the third Sunday after Pentecost there had been no room for the negro's hat, gloves and walking stick on the altar of St. Peter of Alcantara and the young man had had to lay them on the altar of St. Gregory Thaumaturgus instead. The rector was beginning to congratulate himself on having secured the services of so admirable a priest. He settled himself in his stall and prepared to listen with pleasure.

Seated beside the celebrant on the sedilia, the abbé Gaston did his best to feel charitable. He tried to forget the indecent haste with which the abbé Moune ordinarily celebrated mass and the elementary mistakes in ritual which he made. He tried to forget the way the abbé Moune banged the tabernacle door when he had finished giving communion. He tried to forget the way the abbé Moune rushed out of church without making his thanksgiving in order to get the lion's share of breakfast at the presbytery. He tried to tell himself that his dislike of the abbé Moune's sermons was prompted by jealousy rather than by criticism of their content.

"Send us priests, send us holy priests." The abbé Moune gabbled through the bidding prayer and it was impossible for the abbé Gaston not to notice that the abbé Moune was rolling his eyes all over the church to see how big the congregation was. It was also impossible for the abbé Gaston not to notice that the abbé Moune rattled through the gospel in French and gave out his own text with emphasis and deliberation. It was equally impossible for the abbé Gaston to avoid the deduction that the abbé Moune attached more importance to his own words than to those of the Lord.

"Pity the poor preacher and pray for him, because he is trying to say big things with small lips," the abbé Gaston's spiritual director had said to him when he was a student at the seminary. It was in vain that the abbé Gaston tried to conform with this counsel and to tell himself that the abbé Moune might really, deep down inside him, be trying to speak the message. As soon as the abbé Moune spoke out with a ring and a clap the first words of his sermon the sneer appeared on the abbé Gaston's face and it stayed there until the abbé Moune had finished.

The abbé Moune was preaching on the sinfulness of contemporary fashions in women's dress and the congregation fairly lapped it up. Women with frocks even shorter than those which the abbé Moune was condemning sat with their eyes glued on the preacher, and the men listened, too. The abbé Moune preached with art. At times he shouted and at times his voice fell almost to a whisper. At times he threw back his head and rolled his eyes, at times he waved his hands, at times he leaned over the edge of the pulpit and pointed with his finger. The abbé Gaston had to admit that it was an effective performance.

The abbé Gaston himself had preached at the eight o'clock mass that morning. His subject had been the unsensational one of the duty of Christians to forgive offense. The abbé Gaston had said this compulsion of clemency was perhaps the hardest which the Lord had laid upon them. He had said that the best way of complying with it was to think of how often the Lord had had to be merciful to them when they disobeyed His commands from motives of malice, selfishness and human respect. The abbé Gaston had felt very deeply what he was saying, but he did not think that he had said it very ably. The congregation had coughed and wriggled all the time he was preaching and they had all turned 'round to stare when the beadle had been forced to expel a dog which had intruded into the center aisle. The abbé Gaston did not suppose that when they had left the church six people out of the whole congregation could have said what he had been preaching about. Listening to the abbé Moune, the abbé Gaston was conscious of his own shortcomings as an orator.

Ordinarily the abbé Gaston did not, like the rector and the other curates, go out on to the steps of the church after high mass on Sundays to talk to the congregation when they came out. He found it hard to be polite to the women in fur coats who put five centimes in the collection plate, and he knew that their congress was the confluence of a caste rather than the fellowship of those who had renounced the world. Today, however, he came out to talk to Armelle. He had noticed that she had not been accompanied by her mother at mass and he wanted to find out if Madame Dillier were ill.

Armelle was eighteen now, and she was looking very pretty in a short taffeta frock. The abbé noticed with distress the crimson lines on her lips. He thought that they detracted from her beauty and told a lie beneath her eyes.

"I don't want to sound oppressive, but why the paint?" the abbé asked.

"But, Monsieur l'abbé, everybody does it and I feel so much better with it," Armelle said. "You've no idea really."

The abbé supposed that he had no idea really. Often he had felt inclined to pass over at the altar rails women who knelt to receive God's Body with a scarlet smear on their lips. He had refrained from doing so because he had been afraid to deprive their souls of grace.

"I suppose it's alright if you say so," he said. He patted her cheek. The pat was meant to express the hope for which he could not find words, that she would continue to stand upon the right meaning of the world.

"Besides it'll be necessary in my new profession," Armelle said. "I'm starting as a mannequin on Monday at Bisberot's." She pointed gaily across to the shuttered dressmaker's on the other side of the square. "I want to thank you for telling mother that you approved. I don't think that she would have agreed otherwise."

The abbé Gaston was no longer sure that he approved. Perhaps, after all, there was something in what the rector and the abbé Moune said. Perhaps the classic toboggan slide was still as slippery as ever. Just then the abbé Moune turned from the group he was blandishing and raised his eyebrows in obvious disapproval of Armelle's appearance. The abbé Gaston observed his glance and knew that he was meant to do so. He reacted immediately.

"I'm glad to have helped you," he said. "One can serve God as a mannequin just as one can serve Him as a priest." He preached on at her for a few minutes without observing that he was wearying her into inattention. "And how's your mother?" he asked when he had finished.

"She's started her coughing fits again, but I don't suppose that it's anything serious really." Armelle said.

As usual the abbé stood and waved to Armelle until she had disappeared 'round the corner of the street. Then he turned to walk up the steps into the church where he had still to say the twelve o'clock mass. The horde of late worshippers pushed their way past him without paying any attention to his limp. Up the steps and into the temple they crammed, the bloated businessmen, the crapulous cads, the beautiful women with the unpitying faces, the Argentinians who loved the Lord in between selling frozen meat, the harlots who leased their bodies for a lifetime instead of for an hour, to honor God with a sketchy genuflection and a halfpenny in the collection plate.

"Your little protégée is growing up into a very beautiful young woman, Monsieur l'abbé Gaston," the abbé Moune said as he overtook the abbé Gaston at the top of the steps. "I'm not surprised that you are so fond of her."

"I'm fond of her mother, too, Monsieur l'abbé Moune," the abbé Gaston said.

"Of course," the abbé Moune said. "We've all of us always known that. Otherwise the friendship might have been misunderstood, mightn't it?"

"The friendship could not possibly be misunderstood except by the malignant," the abbé Gaston said, beginning to be angered by the other's tone.

"That is true," the abbé Moune said. "But a priest has a duty not to give scandal. Therefore he is bound to avoid even the appearance of evil."

"A priest is also bound to avoid even the appearance of unkindness," the abbé Gaston said. "Both Madame Dillier and her daughter come frequently to me for advice and I give it."

"I'm sure that you give them very good advice," the abbé Moune said.

"I hope so," the abbé Gaston said and continued deliberately. "I have just advised Madame Dillier that I see no reason why Armelle should not become a mannequin."

As the abbé Gaston had expected, the abbé Moune was horrified and said so.

"Monsieur l'abbé Gaston, did you not listen to my sermon this morning?" the abbé Moune asked.

"I did, Monsieur l'abbé Moune, and I am persuaded that you gravely misdirected the faithful," the abbé Gaston said. "You were both theologically and technically wrong. It's not the parts of their bodies that women show that rock chastity; it's the parts they conceal." As the abbé Gaston spoke the poetess came out of the church, wearing a short tight striped skirt. Plastered with paint, with ruts under her eyes and breasts like clockweights, she waddled down the steps, her loins revolving like turbines. "Do you really think, Monsieur l'abbé Moune, that the sight of that woman in her bath would tempt you to forget your priestly vows?"

"Really, Monsieur l'abbé Gaston," the abbé Moune said. "The rector's quite right: the army does not seem to have done you any good."

"I mean what I say," the abbé Gaston said.

"And I mean what I say," the abbé Moune said. "And I say that you are suffering from spiritual pride. I think that you are wrong about modern dress just as you have been wrong about everything else. You imagined that a great religious revival was going to take place during the war; you were wrong. You imagined that the soldiers returning from the front would sooner or later flock back to the churches; you were wrong. And in your theories about women's dress you are wrong just as you are wrong in exposing that young girl to the temptations she will undoubtedly encounter displaying her body in a dressmaker's shop. In fact, Monsieur l'abbé Gaston, you have been wrong so often that I am surprised that the rector doesn't ask you to transfer your services to another parish."

That Sunday the twelve o'clock mass didn't start until five minutes past twelve.

XX

IT was a long time since the Cardinal had seen Francis and as soon as he boarded the special scarlet train carrying prelates to the 1926 Eucharistic congress in Chicago he started to look for him. But Francis was nowhere to be found, not even in the bar, where archbishops sat perched on high stools discussing the possibility of the canonization of Bernadette Soubirous. "Didn't know they had Cardinals. Englishmen all Protestants. All go to hell," the apostolic exarch for the Podocarpathian Ruthenians of the Byzantine rite grunted when the French Cardinal asked him if he had seen the Archbishop of Westminster. The monkey-faced little Cardinal Archbishop of Sevilla with a head like a cannon ball with spikes stuck in it was scarcely more helpful. "I do not know where Frankie is, but I want very much to see Carlos Chapleen in *The Gorld Roosh*," he said. The French Cardinal thanked the Spaniard and returned to his sleeping compartment where he passed an uneasy night because his neighbor, the Cardinal Archbishop of Warsaw, snored. The Cardinal wanted to talk to Francis about the spiritual state of the world. The Cardinal thought that the world was sliding rapidly away from God. The Cardinal's assistant chaplain had said that there were two reasons for this. The first reason was that a mechanistic conception of the universe was working greater harm among the uninstructed who no longer felt themselves compelled to the practice of virtue by any supernatural imperative. The second reason was that the modern novelists had subverted morality by presenting pleasure as the only object worthy of pursuit. The Cardinal wanted to know what Francis thought about these two theories.

It was not until they were all assembled in the cathedral of the Holy Name that the Cardinal caught his first glimpse of Francis, sitting on the other side of the sanctuary behind a Portuguese prelate who was scratching his ear. The Cardinal blinked a wink, but Francis was too intent on his devotions to notice. And in the sacristy afterwards there was such a mob of Cardinals and Archbishops that the Cardinal found it impossible to reach Francis, who was disrobing at the other end.

"Let's beat it, bud," the young American Bishop of Saracen said. "Seeing all these clergymen together puts me off saying my prayers."

The Cardinal usually spoke French with Francis, who had studied at St. Sulpice, but he knew a little English, in which language he had once explained to an Irish Dominican the shortest route to the Gare St. Lazare.

"But I have an important matter to discuss with the Cardinal Archbishop of Westminster," the French Cardinal said.

"It'll keep till the swimming pool, won't it?" the Bishop of Saracen asked.

"But how do I know that I shall see Francis at the swimming pool," the French Cardinal asked.

"All the boys are going to the swimming pool," the Bishop of Saracen said. "He's English, ain't he? And the English are fond of baths. Sure he'll be at the swimming pool. Shorty and I will drive you along."

Shorty was the Bishop of Saracen's chaplain, and the abbé Paquin sat in front with Shorty, who did the driving, and the Cardinal and the Bishop of Saracen sat behind. The Cardinal told the Bishop of Saracen how greatly he had been impressed by the piety of the American laity and the Bishop of Saracen told the Cardinal how greatly he had been impressed by the learning of the French clergy. Holy Mother Church, they both agreed, was truly universal, one part completing the other and Rheims supplying what lacked in Poughkeepsie. It was a pity, they said, that the laity did not more warmly appreciate her wide embrace. It was a pity, too, they said, that the politicians, searching for a belt with which to bind the nations together, should overlook the cincture which God had already supplied.

There seemed to be more clergymen in the swimming pool than there had been in the cathedral, and as none of the prelates wore their pectoral crosses it was even more difficult to spot Francis than it had been before.

Once indeed the Cardinal thought that he recognized his English brother, but it turned out to be the Archbishop of Salamanca, doing a belly flop.

Standing on the diving board, the Bishop of Saracen said that he liked swimming because the constant contact with cold water enabled him to think more clearly about theology. There was, for example, the problem of the geographical location of heaven and hell, not to mention the pin-pointing of purgatory, concerning which the scriptures had been so reticent. It was quite evident, the Bishop of Saracen said, that the discoveries of Copernicus had disproved the notion, formerly widely held, that the sky was the converse side of a floor on which the saints walked and that the earth was a roof above the yells of the damned. The mathematics of Einstein, which represented space itself as curved, made the problem even more difficult. If heaven and hell were neither above the sky nor below the earth nor in space, then where were they? Ordinarily the question puzzled him, when he tried to solve it in pulpit or in study. As soon, however, as he dived into a swimming pool the answer became clear: heaven, hell and purgatory were not places at all, but states of presence or absence of God. So saying, the Bishop of Saracen dived into the water, swam neatly through the legs of the Cardinal Archbishop of Vienna and came to the surface on the far side of the Cardinal Patriarch of Lisbon.

The French Cardinal did not know how to dive. On his annual holiday in Brittany, accompanied by his vicar general, he waded out into the sea, held his nose between his fingers, bobbed beneath the water and felt brave because the vicar general wasn't as good at bobbing as he was. He realized, however, that such a procedure was unlikely to impress the Bishop of Saracen, who was now swimming with a leisurely and powerful sidestroke back to the diving board. Worse still, it might even force the American Bishop to conclude that the French hierarchy were inadequate theologians. When it was a matter of maintaining the reputation of the eldest daughter of the Church deceit might be called diplomacy. Walking quickly along to the shallow end of the pool, the Cardinal slid over the side, ducked and swam, with a clumsy breast-stroke, back towards the diving board, hoping that his subterfuge had not been noticed.

"*Vive l'amour*," the Bishop of Saracen shouted, waving an encouraging hand. Once again he dived into the water, his body curved in a perfect crescent, and came up close to the plodding French Cardinal. "That's French, isn't it?" he asked.

The Cardinal managed to splutter out that it would be more appropriate for the Bishop of Saracen to say "*Vive l'amour divin*" as the unqualified noun was apt to be misinterpreted in contemporary France. After that his wind gave out completely and he swallowed a lot of water and he was sure that he was going to sink. But the Bishop of Saracen came to his rescue and, locking his feet under the Cardinal's chin, towed him back to the diving board. "Swing me just a little bit higher, Obadiah, do," the Bishop of Saracen sang, running nimbly up the steps to the really high diving platform. "Come on, your Eminence," he said. "You've no idea how good this is for your theology."

Not daring to admit that he couldn't dive even from a low height, the Cardinal followed the Bishop of Saracen up the rungs of the ladder leading to the high diving platform. Years ago, in the company of Francis, he had ascended the campanile at Westminster Cathedral, from the summit of which he had gazed down on heretical London spread out in squares below. The Cardinal had felt giddy then, but he felt giddier now, standing behind his new friend and looking down on the water of the swimming pool, with archbishops floating all over it like lifebuoys. There was no retreat because already there were four impatient Canadian prelates lined up behind him. The Bishop of Saracen dived, going straight into the water like an arrow. Invoking assistance from the saints, the Cardinal followed, winding himself terribly as his stomach hit the water.

"Now do you understand better about the Trinity?" the Bishop of Saracen asked when at last they sat side by side on the edge of the pool, allowing the water to drip off them.

Still gasping, the Cardinal admitted that he had never understood about the Trinity and that he was prepared to leave the Trinity as it had always been, a very holy mystery. And he said that he contested his American brother's contention that diving and swimming sharpened the speculative faculties. As far as he was concerned they blunted his own and he doubted very much whether they sharpened his brother's. Heaven at least must be more than a state, the French Cardinal said, or the Lord's Risen Body could not have ascended into it. He would remind his brother of the words which he recited in the Nicene Creed: "*Et ascendit in coelum: sedet ad dexteram Patris.*" Our Lady, too, had been corporeally assumed into heaven and, on the last day, the just would walk there also, in their glorified bodies, as the Lord had promised. It was precisely because of this doctrine of the resurrection of the dead and its physical demands upon space that the German philosophers, in particular, had rejected Christianity. Incidentally, the Cardinal said, he would like very much to know what, in his brother's opinion, was the best means of counteracting the manifestly nefarious influence on contemporary thought of Hegel, Kant, Leibnitz and Schopenhauer.

"What those bums want is a kick in the ass," the Bishop of Saracen said and dived back into the water, coming up on the far side of the Bishop of Wu-Pao, who was practicing the breast-stroke on water wings.

They agreed, as they buttoned themselves back into clergymen, that it was as well that God had not made all things plain but had hung a curtain in front of His glory, through which He allowed chinks of light to peep out. They ought to be grateful to God for allowing them these glimpses of his grandeur. Such indeed was the theme of the Bishop of Wu-Pao, who preached the next sermon. Blessed, the Lord had said, were the poor in spirit, the meek, those that mourned, the merciful, the clean of heart and the peacemakers. They were blessed because they were candles dropped into the world to show unhappy men and women what the saints were like beyond the grave. The Cardinal saw Francis smile as the Chinese Bishop said these words, and the Cardinal smiled back at Francis, glad of the many happy things that God had let through into the world.

XXI

ON the first of May 1927 the abbé Gaston had no longer any need to put on earphones in order to hear the songs they were singing in London. He had only to press a switch on the outside of a little box for the music to come out loud and clear. Indeed he rarely required to do even this, because through his open window he could hear all the music he wanted from his neighbors' wooden boxes, which were generally switched on from seven o'clock in the morning till after midnight. Often, too, the noises coming from these boxes didn't sound like music at all and the words only occasionally made sense. "Making love to Joanna in a big armchair is like walking through Alaska in your underwear" might mean something in New York but it seemed to mean nothing in Paris.

What was worse, this perpetual trickle of din interfered with the abbé Gaston's devotions. In 1917 his daily prayer for the repose of the souls of the faithful departed whom he had known personally in life had taken him seven minutes; in 1927 the same prayer occupied eleven minutes. There were also the living and those who died in the battles that were still taking place all over the world to be prayed for. All these petitions took time, and, with his office and funeral and wedding masses to say, the hospital to visit and his own shopping, cooking and laundering to do, the abbé Gaston did not have much time. They also, because the abbé was not a saint and could not pray well when someone was shouting in his ear about not being able to dance the Charleston, required silence. If he got up early and tried to say his prayers before mass at least three wireless sets would be blaring away on the other side of the street. If he waited till noon the noise was worse. And if he waited till after midnight the centrally heated lady of easy virtue on the fifth floor was sure to be entertaining her gentleman friend and through the thin flooring would come the sound of what passed for jubilation on the other side of the

Atlantic. In the summer in Paris the abbé Gaston understood very well what the psalmist had meant when he had written: "Be still and know that I am God."

Today, however, the abbé was feeling cheerful. He had managed to say at least half his prayers while waiting to be served in the greengrocer's and only two wirelesses on the other side of the street and not fourteen were oozing tinned beatitude. Bessier was coming for lunch and St. Blasius of Cappadocia didn't look as though he were going to die after all. St. Blasius was fourteen years old now and of late the cat's lack of health had been worrying the abbé. Lying on his small square of blanket, the old cat purred when the abbé stroked him and looked with a golden, greedy eye at the gas ring where the pork chops were sizzling.

Bessier could walk without a stick now. He came into the abbé's small room so squarely and so steadily that it was hard to believe that he had an artificial leg. Bessier still said that this was because he had been lucky enough to have his leg amputated below the knee. He said that if he had had his leg taken off above the knee he would still have been using a stick and rocking from side to side like so many other poor devils.

"Well, Jean, you'll be glad to hear that I've landed a job," Bessier said, as soon as he had exchanged greetings with the abbé.

The abbé Gaston was glad to hear such news and said so. After his demonstration at the wedding of the Cardinal's niece and Monsieur Henri de la Porte du Bibier, Bessier had been in prison for almost a year. Since his release he had been able to find only temporary and ill-remunerated posts because other employers had distrusted his reputation as an agitator. This had made things difficult for Bessier who now had a son of four as well as a wife for whom to provide.

"You'll disapprove, I'm sure," Bessier went on. "It's the headquarters of the communist party that are going to employ me."

The abbé Gaston did not know much about communists except the little that he had read in the newspapers. That little was not good. It might be, however, that the French communists did not approve of the excesses committed by their Russian associates. As they sat down to eat their hors d'oeuvre the abbé asked Bessier to enlighten him upon this point.

"Communism is based on the Marxist dialectic," Bessier explained learnedly. "All through history there have been temporary syntheses of opposing theses until the new and subordinate thesis has had time to conquer the older and prevalent thesis. At present we are living in the synthesis of capital and labor. Capital is the older and prevalent thesis; Labor is the new and subordinate thesis and labor will eventually conquer."

The abbé Gaston said that he did not understand how so apparently academic a theory could justify the atrocities commonly reported to have been committed by the Bolsheviks.

"But it's not an academic theory," Bessier protested, brandishing a half-consumed radish. "Communism is a system of realist politics whose aim is the elimination of the privileged or wealthy classes. The chief enemy of communism is the rich man. To uproot him it considers all methods lawful and recognizes no morality except that of expediency. In order to achieve this object it will even permit the creation of a new privileged class and maintain it in power until such time as it is possible to establish true socialism."

"That sounds just like what Mussolini is attempting to do in Italy," the abbé Gaston said.

"Please never say such a thing again," Bessier said earnestly. "The fascists are even greater enemies of communism than are the rich. They are the enemies of communism because they argue that the end justifies the means."

"But on your own admission that is precisely the philosophy of communism," the abbé Gaston said. "Really, I fail to see any difference between fascism and communism."

"They're different and that's all there is to it," Bessier said. "Mussolini wants war, for one thing. Already he has forbidden Italians to emigrate from a country which cannot support her present population. Already Frenchmen are insulted when they visit Italy."

"I have heard that Russians cannot emigrate either," the abbé Gaston said: "I have heard, too, that foreigners are not welcomed in Moscow."

"Fascists are reactionaries," Bessier said.

"All progress is not necessarily forwards," the abbé Gaston said.

After that the pork chops didn't taste as good as the abbé had hoped, and St. Blasius of Cappadocia came in for more than his share. The abbé and his friend still weren't talking much to each other when they went out to walk on the square.

"Do you know what day this is?" Bessier asked suddenly.

Of course," the abbé Gaston said. "It's the feast of St. Philip and St. James."

Bessier stopped in his steps and burst out laughing.

"My poor imbecile, it's Labor Day," he said, clapping the abbé affectionately on the shoulder. "That means a special parade of the Red Army in front of the Kremlin in Moscow. That means workers' meetings in Berlin, Paris, London, Buenos Aires and New York. That means the celebration of the dawn of workers' solidarity the world over. It's that that matters and not your silly St. Philip and St. James who are both dead anyway."

"Their bodies may be dead, but their souls are with the Lord in heaven," the abbé Gaston said. "The Church says so."

"And all that they stood for is dead, too," Bessier said.

"That is a lie," the abbé Gaston said angrily. "That's the great mistake both sinners and freethinkers make. All over the world there are practicing Christians. Most of them are poor, shabby and unknown, and because they don't get their names into the papers you think that they don't exist."

"Their existence would appear to have little effect on the conduct of the world," Bessier said. "Look at those young women up there," he went on, pointing up at the first floor window of Bisberot's, where the girls had gathered to admire the fairness of the day.

"Do you think they care at all about your silly St. Philip and St. James?"

"Do you think they care about your silly Karl Marx either?" the abbé Gaston asked.

"Perhaps not now," Bessier said. "But one day they will care. As soon as they are told they will care. That's the great difference between your creed and mine. You can preach yours until you are blue in the face and nobody will pay the slightest attention. Whereas the workers of the world have only to hear our teaching once and they understand immediately."

"Perhaps that is because it is always easier to follow a lower philosophy than a higher one," the abbé Gaston said.

They continued their walk in silence. At the entrance to the underground the hawkers were selling the traditional bunches of lily of the valley. When he was a little boy the abbé Gaston's mother had always put lily of the valley in his bedroom on the first of May. Even when he was in the seminary she had sent him a small bunch by post, and the abbé had placed it in his tooth glass at the foot of his small statue of the Blessed Virgin, because May was the Month of Mary. Tonight there would be a special recitation of the rosary in church, with the Blessed Sacrament exposed and the rector and his curates all kneeling in a row in front of the high altar, praying that God might make them better priests.

At first the abbé Gaston noticed only the beauty of the day. The sky was blue and the sun was gold and the air was like water held in a glass. The pigeons fluttered down from the roof of the church and walked beneath the leaves of the trees. The abbé Gaston remembered the May mornings that had crept through his mother's curtains long ago. Then he began to remark the expressions on the faces of those who passed on the pavements about their business. Depressed, angry, arrogant, scowling, wretched, they came up from nothingness before him and vanished into annihilation behind him. Mean men wearing brown boots beneath striped trousers, scurrying girls with parcels under their arms, surly bank messengers carrying the symbols of other men's wealth, they passed with a vast disinterest in their regard, and with a suffering sometimes too, as though afraid of what the world might do to their anonymity. Out on the causeway the proud men rolled on their wheels. Behind the glass of the windscreens their faces did not look as though they were caring much about St. Philip and St. James, by whose merits they had gained. Nor did their faces look as though they understood that their privilege was due to the patience of the poor. Nor did each face behind its rectangle of glass seem to care about the comfort of the other faces behind their rectangles of glass. Honking their horns, overtaking on the right when they should have overtaken on the left, driving fast when they should have driven slowly, they screeched past with their 1927 women to their 1927 joys.

"All the same there's injustice in the world," the abbé Gaston said.

"I'm glad that you admit it," Bessier said.

In spite of the fact that Bessier had an artificial leg and the abbé had only a wounded one, Bessier walked more quickly than the priest. The abbé was glad when Bessier halted at the entrance to the underground.

"Let's take some lily of the valley over to your friend Armelle," Bessier suggested. "It might make her stick to St. Philip and St. James for a little longer."

The abbé Gaston hesitated. He knew that the rector would not approve. He also knew that it was unlikely that the rector would ever find out. The rector and his curates were not due to appear for their daily walk for at least half an hour yet and by that time Bessier and he would have been in the shop and out of it again. For the last three Sundays he had not seen Armelle at mass. It was his duty to encourage her to persevere and if he could do so by taking her a bunch of lily of the valley he did not think that the Lord would be displeased.

"All right; I'm game," he said.

Bessier and the abbé did not buy big bunches of lily of the valley because neither of them was rich. They bought two small bunches at two francs a bunch. Each with a bunch in his hand, they walked across to Bisberot's.

Inside the shop was dark after the brightness of the street. The shop seemed to be full of young women standing about in silk frocks and tweed costumes. Most of the young women held one hand on their hips and the other in the air, with the fingers curved. None of the young women either moved or spoke but they all wore expressions of concentrated aristocracy. The abbé Gaston coughed discreetly to attract their attention but the young women still went on standing as they had stood before. It was not until a little dumpy woman walked forward from the back of the shop that the abbé realized that he had been looking at wax mannequins.

"We wish to speak with Mademoiselle Armelle," the abbé Gaston said. "We are old friends of hers and we have brought her some lily of the valley."

The dumpy little woman smiled and clapped her hands and shouted up the staircase to Armelle that there were visitors for her with lily of the valley. But it wasn't only Armelle who came down to greet them. At least twenty other girls came, too, tumbling down the stairs in their colored frocks. Shouting and laughing, they surrounded the abbé Gaston and Bessier and said that to have lily of the valley brought them on the first of May meant that they would have good luck the whole year round. Bessier's and the abbé's bunches were split up into sprigs, because each girl wanted to have at least a bloom for herself. The girls were still arguing among themselves when Madame Bisberot opened the champagne.

"We've got to drink to this," she said as she went round filling the glasses. As soon as he had taken two or three sips of his champagne the abbé Gaston began to feel that Bessier had been right in a great deal of what he had said. But Bessier, he felt also, had been only half right, because there was another side to the question. If clergymen didn't always know what went on inside ordinary people, ordinary people often didn't know what went on inside clergymen. Both sides had gaps to fill. The abbé felt that he must say this quickly to somebody before he forgot it himself. So, when Madame Bisberot had replenished his glass, he turned to the young woman standing next to him.

"Mademoiselle, it is well that priests and laity should meet on such secular occasions," the abbé said. "Our consequently increased knowledge of one another can contribute only to the welfare of the whole Church Militant. If there are times, Mademoiselle, when clergymen appear to you to be distant and austere you must remember that theirs is a high calling, since they are the ministers of great mysteries. I think that this is a fact which is not always sufficiently appreciated."

The young woman appeared to think so, too, for she looked very grave and said nothing.

"And the clergy, Mademoiselle, should remember that as the laity do not share these responsibilities it is natural that they should be more light-hearted," the abbé continued but broke off as he saw Armelle approaching, so that he could include her in the conversation, too.

"Perhaps, Monsieur l'abbé, you'd better talk to me instead," Armelle said laughingly. "Clothilde's not an awfully good listener, I'm afraid. You see, she's got rather a lot of wax in her ears."

The abbé looked more closely at the face which he had just been addressing. Straight ahead the painted eyes stared, lifelike because they were so lifeless. Like spikes on the edge of a miniature fan, the eyelashes stuck up in solemn crescents of imbecility. From a window of spun gold the moon of pink and white face peeped out, claiming originality and expression by its lack of both. The abbé understood why he had made the same mistake twice. It was not because the dummies looked like young women; it was because the young women looked like dummies. He laughed at his mistake, and began to talk to Armelle as he had talked to the wax mannequin, about the gravity and the cheer that there should be always in all men's hearts. But almost immediately he realized that she wasn't listening.

"Armelle, what's the matter?" he asked. "You're not paying any attention."

"I'm sorry, Monsieur l'abbé," Armelle said, laying her hand contritely on the abbé's arm.

"Your thoughts have no business to be wandering when I'm talking on such a subject," the abbé Gaston said. "Armelle, why haven't you been at mass for the last three Sundays?"

"Mother's been ill again," Armelle said.

"You know as well as I do that that is no excuse," the abbé said.

Armelle's face hardened.

"Listen, Monsieur l'abbé," she said. "It's no good expecting me to behave like a saint."

"But that's precisely what I do expect you to do," the abbé said. "It's the reason why you were sent into the world." Overcome by emotion, the abbé took the oval of her small lineless face into his hands, trying to press some of his own thoughts into hers. "You think you know so much, don't you?" he said. "You think you're so very old. And you're so very young and you know so very little. Do you know, sometimes I think that God ought to have made people grow downwards instead of upwards. Like that beauty and wisdom might have been able to concur."

"All I know is I don't want to spend my life praying in stuffy churches," Armelle said sulkily.

With his glass of unfinished champagne in his hand, the abbé told Armelle that sanctity was not invariably accomplished by prayer. The abbé said that that was one of the great mercies which God had allowed to the world. One could become a cyclist or a footballer only by riding a bicycle or kicking a football, but one could become a saint by doing all sorts of unsaintly things in a saintly manner, the abbé Gaston said. One could offer to God's greater glory all sorts of things besides prayers. One could offer the depth one dug a ditch or the height one jumped or the way one wore a pretty dress, for if to pray was to work, to work was also to pray. The greatest crime which secularism had committed against humanity was to rob it of a worthy motive for its labor, the abbé Gaston said.

"Please, Monsieur l'abbé," Armelle pleaded. "We can talk of that later, can't we? It was sweet of you to bring me the lily of the valley. And now I think Madame Bisberot is expecting you to join us for our walk."

The abbé Gaston did not wish to join them for their walk because he was afraid of meeting the rector and his curates. But he knew that if he refused Armelle would never again allow him to talk to her about sanctity. He knew, too, that the Lord would have joined them for their walk. Wordlessly, he followed them to the door and soon was walking across the square with three pretty girls on either side of him. Towards him, grim in the black anonymity of their cassocks, came the Chanoine Litry and his curates. It was not until the rector had ignored his bow that the abbé Gaston realized that he was still carrying his champagne glass in his hand.

XXII

IN 1927 there were still many unholy things to be done in order to make men holy and, as the Cardinal's chief secretary, the abbé Paquin had to do a great many of them. The former chief secretary had died the previous year, on the feast of Saints Soter and Caius, popes and Martyrs. The former chief secretary's body lay in the Puy-de-Dome; the Cardinal hoped that his soul was in heaven.

One of the unholy things that had to be done was the opening of the Cardinal's correspondence. This task the abbé Paquin generally performed in the Cardinal's presence, passing to the prelate the letters which he thought His Eminence ought to see personally. These communications were many and varied. There were letters from foreign Cardinals and country priests. There were letters from mothers superior of convents asking for permission to expose the Blessed Sacrament on the feasts of their founders. There were letters from missionaries asking for funds. There were letters from monks requesting the Cardinal to bless choir stalls. There were letters from sports outfitters asking him to bless tennis rackets. Today there was also a letter from the Bishop of Saracen, who wrote:

"Your Eminence,

"There has been a great outbreak of holiness in the diocese. During the past year 22,342 converts have been received into the Church, and of these only 6,802 abjured heresy through marrying persons already professing the Faith. 322 new churches and chapels have been opened in the diocese and there is a waiting list of candidates seeking admission to the new Trappist monastery at Palm Shore Bend, formerly more famed for its bathing girls than for its anchorites. Palm Shore Bend has now bells as well as belles. It is strange that the new world should be accepting so readily what the old world is slowly rejecting. I like to believe that this is due to purity of heart rather than to simple-mindedness.

"At any rate, in a land inclined to extravagance, the Church has a double mission to perform: not only has it to evangelize the people, but it has to civilize them, teaching them to honor God in their pastimes as well as in their prayers. Recently, a Catholic young man and woman were publicly honored by their pastor for having danced together for twenty-four hours on end, whereas a Congregationalist couple had danced for only twenty-three hours and eleven minutes. I find it in my heart to wish that the heretics had danced the longer. Last week, too, a Catholic young woman of prominent social position in the diocese abjured her faith by being married in a diving suit by a Protestant minister at the bottom of a ten foot deep swimming pool. I am almost as disturbed by the diving suit as I am by the apostasy. The holy noises of the liturgy ought to make it impossible for Christians to be fools outside Christ.

"If, however, we require the discretion of the old rites to temper our exuberance, perhaps we can consecrate a portion of our effervescence to the preaching of the gospel. I hope that you will not be offended when I say that I think that our missioners are much more persuasive than are yours, speaking out the truth with force and conviction, hurling the rules at the people. I think that this is important. Elegance, while fitting in our converse with God, is often out of place when talking to ordinary persons, who understand fine things more easily when they are rudely expressed.

"An elderly woman in the diocese has recently had the stigmata implanted upon her. These manifestations occur every Friday about three o'clock in the afternoon. Wounds appear in her hands, in her feet and in her left side and blood pours from them. The woman, who is a farmer's wife, complains of no pain but says that she feels very weak when the manifestations have been taken away from her and has to drink large quantities of water. We are not making public these happenings and would ask you to treat this information as confidential. The necessity for such diplomacy is a sad commentary upon the spirit of our times.

"We have recently been visited by a slippery joker from the Vatican, who is concerned that illustrations in ecclesiastical publications should not incite to concupiscence. I gather that he will shortly be coming your way. So please, your Eminence, keep those parish magazines clean.

"Yours Cordially in Our Lord,

"✢ Cuthbert Aloysius O'Hara,
"Bishop of Saracen.

P.S. Shorty sends his love. C.A.O'H."

It was, however, the communication from the Holy See which demanded the Cardinal's immediate attention. Lately the Sacred Congregation of Rites had condemned the practice of placing electric candles on altars, pointing out that such did not express the Mind of the Church. The Cardinal had taken what steps he could to suppress this disobedience, but much as the clergy of the archdiocese loved God they appeared to love their electric candles more. There was also the matter of polyphonic music, concerning which the Sacred Congregation of Rites had been equally explicit but in this matter, too, the clergy had been recalcitrant, filling their churches with fiddlers and sopranos, who twanged and screeched God's glory in unbecoming strains. As soon as he saw the seal on the envelope, therefore, the Cardinal became uneasy.

"It's all right, Your Eminence," the abbé Paquin said when he had unfolded the thick parchment. "It's only the South American clergy."

"Thank heaven for that," the Cardinal exclaimed. "What have they been doing this time?"

This time the South American clergy had been doing all sorts of things and the Holy See was disturbed. Their chief misdemeanor was the speed and the carelessness with which they had administered the sacraments. True reverence, the letter pointed out, was the mean between speed and delay. In Patagonia, at Pinchinahuida, a parish priest had, on the feast of St. Casimir, celebrated mass in thirteen minutes and fifteen seconds. In Uruguay at Maysambu, a priest was in the habit of omitting the prayers after mass in order to consume sooner the poached egg which he had had his housekeeper prepare for him in the sacristy. Sometimes indeed this priest's gluttony was such that he ate the poached egg without first removing his vestments. In Venezuela, Colombia, Ecuador, Bolivia, Chile and Brazil similar irregularities had happened.

It was not, unfortunately, at the altar alone that these laxities had occurred. At Maguapalzinho in Brazil a priest, while walking in procession behind a bier, had been observed showing an acolyte how to ignite a firework. In many small villages throughout the peninsula it was customary for priests to smoke pipes or cigars while they sat in the confessional absolving penitents. While it was not contended that these breaches of decorum were as grave as those committed in the sanctuary, it was nevertheless evident that neither mourners nor sinners could be consoled or edified by such practices.

Although the sacraments, the letter went on to say, were as valid when they were inattentively administered as when they were applied with piety, it was also true that a rite rattled through did not appear to contain power, and there was no doubt that many unreflective and undiscerning persons had been discouraged from the practice of their religion by the slackness of their priests. It had, therefore, been decided to appoint a commission of inquiry. This commission of inquiry would be drawn from non-Spanish nations and would consist of unpromoted priests, each of whom would travel alone and report directly to Rome upon liturgical conditions in the section of the peninsula which he visited. Metropolitans and ordinaries would therefore select from their clergy such Spanish-speaking priests whose services they could spare and submit their names to the Sacred College in Rome, whose members would decide the final composition of the commission and the rules for its procedure.

"Circularize all parish priests," the Cardinal decided.

XXIII

"EVER since your return from the war your conduct has caused me concern," the rector told the abbé Gaston when he summoned him to the presbytery. "First of all there has been your constant antipathy to the abbé Moune and the really scandalous words with which you controverted his able sermon on women's dress. Then there has been your notorious preference for this young girl and your advising her mother to allow her to become a mannequin. And last of all there has been this disgraceful demonstration when you yourself appeared on the square in the company of a band of immodestly dressed young women, brandishing in your hand an empty champagne glass."

"I beg your pardon, Monsieur le Curé," the abbé Gaston said gently. "The champagne glass was not empty; it was half full."

"Monsieur l'abbé Gaston, I would remind you that I am not the most patient of men," the Chanoine Litry said.

"And the champagne glass was there by mistake," the abbé Gaston said. "Really, Monsieur le Curé, I'm most frightfully sorry about it all."

"Being sorry won't undo the scandal which your conduct has caused in the parish," the rector said.

"All I can do is to ask you to believe that I acted with the intention of serving our Lord," the abbé Gaston said. "If I have ever opposed you it was because I felt that it was my duty to oppose you."

"I think that I am willing to believe that," the rector said.

"I know that walking about the Place du Maréchal Haig with a half-filled glass of champagne in my hand may seem a strange way of teaching all nations," the abbé Gaston said. "Yet it was to promote the gospel that I took the lily of the valley to Armelle Dillier. The champagne happened afterwards."

"Your friendship with that young girl is most unsuitable," the rector said.

The abbé Gaston was silent for a little. He did not know how to tell the rector about his feelings for Armelle. He could scarcely say that he loved Armelle as his daughter because he was supposed to love all women as his daughters. He supposed that he loved her specially because he had known her ever since she was a child, and he did not feel that there was anything wrong about this tenderness. But the proper words wouldn't come when he tried to explain this to the rector.

"The conversion of the world's a big job, Monsieur le Curé," the abbé Gaston said at length. "One's got to use all sorts of methods and one's got to try and try again."

"You simply cannot make two thousand million saints," the rector said, but he spoke gently and it was gently, too, that he continued. "You have been wrong so very often, too," he said. "You were wrong about the ex-soldiers. I cannot but believe that you are wrong again about this girl."

"There's a lot of virtue in unexpected places," the abbé Gaston said. "And perhaps good actions redeem bad environments more than bad actions damage good environments."

"I can see that we are unlikely to agree," the rector said patiently. "So perhaps it would be as well if we were to separate for a little. The Cardinal has asked for the names of Spanish-speaking priests whose services can be spared, and I have forwarded yours." The rector told the abbé Gaston about the special mission which the Holy See was sending to South America.

The abbé Gaston was silent. He wanted to say that he limped too badly to be sent on a special mission to South America. He wanted to say that he didn't want to leave Armelle and St. Blasius of Cappadocia and his happy ordinary duties about the parish. He wanted to say all these things but he said none of them. Outside on the pavement a crocodile of small girls unwound in front of the window with a dumpy old nun tied on to the end of the procession. The old nun had a smile on her lumpy wrinkled face as she walked in her big blue skirts through the loveless mob in the streets. Anonymously serving God she passed, unconscious of her own beauty. The abbé Gaston knew that when she was dead she would lie in a nameless grave, with her good deeds for a tombstone. The abbé knew, too, that those good deeds would soon be forgotten, because there would be other nuns peeling potatoes, scrubbing floors, teaching children, going to China. The Church of God was an obedience, after all. The nun and her children vanished round the back of the church, with the pigeons flying above their heads.

"Of course, I'll go if you want me to, Monsieur le Curé," the abbé Gaston said. "And I'm sorry if I have been a nuisance to you."

"We all of us make mistakes sometimes," the Chanoine Litry said. "And so that you needn't worry too much about Mademoiselle Dillier I'll ask the abbé Moune to keep a special eye on her."

Once again the abbé Gaston didn't say what he wanted to say, in case he had been wrong about the abbé Moune as well. When he arrived back in his small room he found St. Blasius of Cappadocia stretched dead beneath the window sill. He knelt and stroked the tired striped fur. Then he knelt and said a little prayer, just in case there might be a corner of purgatory roped off for repentant tom cats.

XXIV

THE Bishop of Saracen had been right. As soon as he had finished expurgating parochial magazines in America, the slippery joker from the Vatican sailed for France.

The slippery joker said that he did not think that he needed to tell the Cardinal that any short stories published in religious magazines ought to be edifying. For that reason, works by Emile Zola, Anatole France, Voltaire, H. G. Wells, E. M. Hull and Dean Farrar were to be eschewed. Special attention should be paid to the romantic aspect of such narratives as were published. Embraces between lovers must be restrained. Of even greater importance was the matter of illustrations. Saints, martyrs and confessors should be chastely and decently clothed. Canonized virgins should wear their haloes demurely and not at a tilt. St. Lawrence should always be kilted with a loincloth when he lay on the gridiron. Especial care should be taken with the portrayal of angels, the slippery joker said.

The abbé Paquin said that he hoped that their illustrious visitor was not echoing an *ex cathedra* utterance of the Pope's, because he very much doubted the wisdom of what had just been said. Our Lord, the abbé Paquin said, had not walked an aseptic earth. Our Lord had lived in a world of blasphemers, hypocrites, idolaters, thieves, murderers, adulterers and fornicators. He had smelt the stench of drains and the perfume of harlots. The men who had nailed Him to the Cross had been rude men and the language of those who had mocked Him had been rude also. Christ's agony had been no more genteel on Calvary than it would have been on the Boulevard Barbès. The whole glory of the atonement was that it had been carried out in creation gone wrong. This also was the glory of the saints, that they had been good in a bad world. The abbé Paquin saw every reason why parochial magazines should not print stories about businessmen who asked their typists to change into sackcloth and ashes before they came in to take down dictation. The abbé Paquin said that the unreality of such narratives forced readers to conclude that the ideals which inspired them were unreal, too.

The slippery joker from the Vatican did not agree. The slippery joker laid on the table two illustrated magazines whose covers depicted naked young women without even a halo or a gridiron to give them a semblance of chastity. The slippery joker said that it was useless for the Cardinal or for his chaplain to contend that neither of these journals was published under ecclesiastical authority. What mattered, the slippery joker said, was that such periodicals were accessible to the faithful, who were unlikely to be stimulated to virtue by their perusal. And it was also useless for the Cardinal to state that the faithful were unlikely to purchase such journals. For one thing, it was always difficult to estimate just how faithful the faithful would be, and, for another, it wasn't even necessary for the faithful to spend money in order to read this literature. The periodicals of which he complained were, the slippery joker had discovered, offered free of charge by all barbers in the metropolis to their customers. In spite of his patent ecclesiastical status the slippery joker himself had been handed these journals that very morning when he had gone to have his hair cut. It was crime enough that the laity should be subjected to the influence of such literature, but it was intolerable that the clergy should be exposed to it, too, and urgent steps must be taken to avoid the continuance of this scandal. An ordinance must be published at once forbidding all clerks in holy orders to frequent any establishment where hair was publicly clipped or beards were shaven. Instead hairdressers should be invited to visit monasteries, friaries and presbyteries on set days, where communities could be barbered collectively. Such hairdressers would be ordered to bring with them only their shears and not their literature. And in the meantime, parochial magazines must be kept very, very edifying, the slippery joker said.

XXV

WITH his arms outstretched, the abbé Gaston stood at the altar and prayed the most merciful Father to bestow upon His Church His peace, to keep her, to gather her together and to guide her. It was the feast of St. Anacletus, Pope and Martyr, 1929. Vested in a skimpy scarlet Spanish chasuble, the abbé Gaston was saying the eight o'clock mass in the parish church of Pueblo de Biedo. Holding the Host like a little moon above the ciborium, the abbé murmured the ritual greeting and went down to give God's Body to His assorted saints. Lined along the linen cloth they knelt, a young woman in a mantilla, a middle-aged man in dungarees, an old lady in a shawl, a cavalry officer, a boy of twelve and a commercial traveler from the Argentine. The abbé gave communion to them and prayed that God might keep their souls unto everlasting life.

In the presbytery the Reverendo Don Miguel Ortiz, parish priest of Pueblo de Biedo, was breakfasting on a tin of sardines and a cup of black coffee. With the finger and thumb of one hand he fished the sardines out of the tin and popped them into his mouth, and with the finger and thumb of the other he held open in front of him the Diario de Fuerto Pobre in which he was reading the bullfighting news. There was a dark smear on his unshaven chin and, as he sat down opposite his host, the abbé Gaston wondered how the priest managed that the bristle should always appear the same length. Elated by his vision of the Universal Church, the abbé Gaston attempted to communicate some of his enthusiasm to the Reverendo Don Miguel.

"I was very edified this morning," the abbé said. "There was an officer at communion."

The Reverendo Don Miguel gulped down his coffee and blew a strong breath of acetylene across the patterned oilcloth.

"The general is in town," he said. "He has come to inspect the garrison."

"Perhaps he'll come to mass tomorrow," the abbé Gaston said. "It's Sunday, you know."

"This time it is His Excellency's turn to visit the brothel in the morning, the Reverendo Don Miguel said, tipping the sardine tin into his mouth so that he could drink out the oil. "Last time His Excellency came to Pueblo de Biedo he came to mass in the morning and went to the bullfight in the afternoon and to the fireworks and the brothel in the evening. This time it is His Excellency's turn to go to the brothel in the morning and to the bullfight in the afternoon and to the fireworks and the brothel in the evening."

"But that is a mortal sin," the abbé Gaston said.

"His Excellency Don Estebán de los Puentesamarillos is also a very mortal general," the Reverendo Don Miguel said with a tolerant smile lighting the depths of his dark eyes. "Generals are like that, you know."

"Our generals aren't," the abbé Gaston said. "Most of them are very religious men."

"His Excellency Don Estebán de les Puentesamarillos is a very religious man, too," the Reverendo Don Miguel said. "It's just that he's not very good at being religious."

"All the same even generals have got to make an effort to correspond with sanctifying grace," the abbé Gaston said, beginning to sound to himself quite like the Chanoine Litry. "During the war our Marshal Foch set a very high example in that respect."

"What war was that?" the Reverendo Don Miguel asked. "The one against England?"

"The war in which France and England and the United States of America fought against Germany," the abbé Gaston said, striving to conceal his irritation.

"Of course," the Reverendo Don Miguel said. "Stupid of me to forget. And Germany won, didn't she?"

"Germany did not win," the abbé Gaston almost shouted. "Germany lost. And it was fitting that she should lose. In 1914 Germany was a tyrannical, unjust and domineering nation."

"Worse than Peru?" the Reverendo Don Miguel asked.

"And France and England and the United States of America stood for righteousness," the abbé Gaston said.

"You surprise me," the Reverendo Don Miguel said, "I always thought that it was the other way about."

"Perhaps we'd better get back to talking about His Excellency Don Estebán de los Puentesamarillos," the abbé Gaston said.

"There's really no need to talk about him," the Reverendo Don Miguel said, taking a stub of half-smoked cigarette from his pocket, lighting it and sticking it on the surface of his lower lip, so that it wagged up and down when he spoke. "His case is uninteresting. When he is too old to go to the brothel he will repent. He will die in a state of grace and his soul will look very beautiful. Our Lady will pray for him and our Lord will forgive him. He will go to heaven. Perhaps he will not be sitting very near the big saints, but he will have his place among the small ones."

Was this what the theologians called the grace of perseverance, the abbé Gaston wondered. The abbé did not know, anymore than he knew what the Reverendo Don Miguel was thinking inside his scrubby prickly head. Their doctrine was the same, but their interpretation of it was different. And who was to say that the Reverendo Don Miguel's was not more consonant with the teaching of the Lord, Who forgave the penitent thief on the cross and paid the last workers in the vineyard as the first? Might not His Excellency Don Estebán de los Puentesamarillos, for all his wantonings, be a better Christian than those who, in the arithmetic of disbelief, walked past Calvary with their hats on their heads? The abbé Gaston did not know. The abbé began to think that he had a very imperfect understanding of theology.

"*Mire Usted*," the Reverendo Don Miguel said, as though perceiving the abbé Gaston's perplexity, "the world is a very wicked place. If the world were not a wicked place there would have been no need for the Holy Jesus to come down from heaven and die on the cross. There would have been no need for the Catholic Church and the Sacraments. And it is not by being unhappy about the world's wickedness that we shall make the world an any better place; it is only by praying and by preaching and by administering the sacraments that we shall do that. *Mire Usted*, I know that I do not pray very well because most of the time the flies tickle the back of my neck and they interrupt me. I know also that I do not preach very well because when I try to tell the people about our Lord and our Lady and the saints they yawn and do not pay very much attention. But with the sacraments I know that I cannot fail, because they are the great fire which God has lighted in the world for men to warm their hands at.

'My kingdom is not of this world,' the Holy Jesus said but He instituted the Catholic Church all the same, because He still hoped that His Excellency Don Estebán de los Puentesamarillos would be able to jump on to the buffers of the last train. God's mercy is infinite; always remember that," the Reverendo Don Miguel said, licking round the inside of the sardine tin to make sure that there was no oil left.

God's mercy certainly required to be infinite, the abbé Gaston thought as ten minutes later he sat down in his bedroom and set about compiling the latest installment of his report, and perhaps Europe was more in need of God's mercy than South America, where people still believed brave things about the world. In Santa Maria del Fuego, the town which the abbé had visited previously, the parish priest had neither smoked in the confessional, lit fireworks at funerals or consumed poached eggs behind the high altar. He had, however, kept an uncooked chicken in the sacristy and allowed his canary to slake its thirst from the holy water stoup, and these facts the abbé noted unemotionally. Then he added another paragraph to his commentary.

"In South America, as in Spain," the abbé wrote, "one feels that the people believe that the Christian religion is objectively true and that behind electricity, telephones and tram cars throb the invisible dynamos of God. In this general acceptance of the supernatural lies, paradoxically, a danger for the clergy, who tend to be less alert than in modern countries, where heresy has to be refuted. There is consequently the risk that an unpersuasive priesthood may one day produce an unpersuaded people. This possibility is likeliest in industrial towns, where the selfish lives led by wealthy Christians may dispose the working classes to accept the doctrines of the atheistic revolutionaries. This is already happening in Spain, in particular in the towns of Barcelona and Oviedo. Only the simultaneous practice of both the great commandments can prevent similar occurrences in South America and indeed in every country in the world."

When he had read through what he had written the abbé Gaston leaned out of the window to look for the postman. The Reverendo Don Miguel had told the abbé that the postman who delivered letters at the presbytery was always very punctual, being due at half-past ten in the morning and never arriving later than three o'clock in the afternoon. The abbé hoped that this exemplary postman would be even more punctual than usual today because he had written to the United Bank of the

Pope and the Railway in Santiago to ask them to forward his correspondence to Pueblo de Biedo, and he was expecting a letter from Armelle. The abbé had not heard from Armelle ever since he had been in South America, although he had written to her six or seven times. Today, however, he hoped to hear from her as in his last letter he had made it very plain how much her silence was alarming him.

But the postman seemed unwilling to accelerate his punctuality. At twelve o'clock the pavement was still empty except for an old woman who was trying to trim a goat's beard with a razor blade. "A watched postman never boils," the abbé murmured, smiling to himself as he parodied the proverb. To help the postman to boil, he walked away from the window and started to compile a statistical summary to attach to his report. But he was too anxious to be able to work well, and soon he was adding the nun who had played a mouth organ in a refectory to clergymen who smoked in confessionals and confusing acolytes who ignited thuribles with cigarette lighters with bishops who went to sleep during sermons.

The postman arrived, punctually late, at three o'clock and he brought quite a few letters for the abbé Gaston. There was a letter from Bessier, a postcard from the Chanoine Litry, a receipt from his landlord for the payment of rent and an advertisement from a firm of clerical outfitters for a waterproof cassock. There was no letter from Armelle.

The abbé was still worrying about not having heard from Armelle when he went down into the church to help out the Reverendo Don Miguel with the Saturday evening confessions. Before he went into the box the abbé knelt and prayed, as he always did, that the Lord would lend him wisdom to counsel souls in their difficulties. As it was also his habit to pray that God would send him a really big sinner to reconcile to Him, he asked that God would direct to him His Excellency Don Estebán de los Puentesamarillos. Glancing down the church, the abbé noted that no smoke was coming from the Reverendo Don Miguel's confessional.

As usual, the really big sinners seemed to be in no hurry to present themselves. There was the banal hugger-mugger of penitents who had been inattentive during their prayers, missed mass on Sundays, lost their tempers with their husbands or snarled at their wives, forgotten to abstain from meat on ember days and been generally uncharitable, vain, ambitious, greedy, drunken, licentious in hearts and motor buses, worldly and puffed up. Once indeed the perfume of a fashionable young woman came through the grille to the abbé, concentrated upon him as on Anthony in the desert, but all the fashionable young woman had done was to have used by mistake a rosary blessed for her aunt. It was only when he had been sitting in the confessional for three hours that the abbé pushed back the slide to see a gold braided uniform kneeling in an attitude of contrition. On the breast of the uniform rows of gold and silver medals dangled from other rows of multi-colored ribbons and above the uniform curved the steep switchbacks of a monster military moustache. Tracing the sign of the cross over the bowed head, the abbé murmured a brief prayer of gratitude and prepared not to be too shocked.

His penitent, however, was not Don Esteban de los Puentesamarillos, but the captain of the local fire brigade. The captain of the local fire brigade had sinned grievously, although he hadn't sinned quite as grievously as Don Esteban de los Puentesamarillos. The captain of the local fire brigade had, in a fit of temper, thrown his wife against the fire engine. He claimed, however, that, although blameworthy, this action represented a certain spiritual progress, because previously he had been in the habit of throwing the fire engine against his wife. He would point out, however, that the fire engine in question was a very small fire engine. Indeed, the proportions of the fire engine were so minute as to constitute for him a further occasion of sin, because he was in the habit of claiming at the counters of cafés, and with a lack of Christian reticence, that it was a disgrace that Pueblo de Biedo should have such a tiny fire engine when the neighboring town of Palamanca had one twice as big.

In lulls between penitents it was the abbé Gaston's habit to stretch his legs, walking up and down the aisle and reciting his office. This evening, however, there was no such lull for more than four hours and it was only when he had finished absolving the fishmonger who had stolen a bicycle and restored it as soon as he had discovered that the back tire was punctured that the abbé was able temporarily to leave his box. There was still no smoke issuing from the Reverendo Don Miguel's confessional and there were no penitents outside the box. There was also no Reverendo Don Miguel inside the box. Two hours later, when the Reverendo Don Miguel returned from watching the six bulls driven through the street for the next day's fight, the abbé Gaston was still wondering whether or not to open in his report two columns or one for priests who neglected their spiritual duties for secular diversions and parked chewing gum on the walls of their confessionals.

XXVI

STANDING with a Dresden china teacup in his hand in his niece's drawing-room, the Cardinal wondered whom to avoid speaking to next. The poetess solved his dilemma for him.

"You really must meet the statesman, Your Eminence," the poetess said.

The statesman was one of the first politicians whom the Cardinal had met when he had been a newly consecrated young bishop. The Cardinal had been astounded to discover that a man who conducted the affairs of a country could be so stupid. Suspecting, however, that the poetess was even more stupid, the Cardinal allowed himself to be reintroduced to the statesman.

"We've met before, Your Eminence," the statesman said. "I was in Roads and Bridges then, if I remember rightly."

"And aren't you still?" the Cardinal asked.

"Dear me, no," the statesman said. "Since then I've been in Posts, Telephones and Telegraphs, Merchant Marine, War, Navy, Education and Foreign Affairs."

"It must require a great deal of effort to keep so many subjects in your head," the Cardinal said.

"I don't," the statesman said. "That's the great virtue of popular democracy. One doesn't need to remember anything at all."

"I seem to remember that you are a socialist," the Cardinal said.

"Far from it," the statesman said. "I started out that way, of course. We all do. But I soon learned that socialism was a pseudo-idealistic aberration based on a false understanding of economics. Now I veer towards the center."

"That means you are a Republican?" the Cardinal asked.

"Of course not," the statesman answered. Republicans are latent Monarchists. I am a Republican Socialist. Which means that I am neither a Republican nor a Socialist. It's very simple really,"

The Cardinal wondered what he was going to say to the statesman next. There were so many subjects that were dynamite. He couldn't talk to the statesman about ecumenical councils, plainchant, lay education and birth control and the statesman couldn't talk to him about freemasonry, divorce, lay education and birth control. It was the statesman who found a topic.

"Personally I prefer beer," the statesman said.

"I rather like tea," the Cardinal said.

"Every cup of tea you drink means another penny in the coffers of the Anglo-Saxons," the statesman said. "I don't like the Anglo-Saxons. Just look at the way the English and American tourists behaved when the franc was at the bottom of the well in 1926. Fortunately we had Poincaré to pull us out of the mess, although I don't mind admitting that I was able to give him a few tips. Now it's the turn of the Anglo-Saxons to be in the mud. The effects of the Wall Street crash won't be confined to America. Sooner or later they'll be felt in England, too."

"Perhaps they may be felt in France as well," the Cardinal said.

"Nonsense," the statesman said. "France is sitting pretty. We've a balanced budget. We've a bigger gold reserve than any other country in the world. It won't be long before both England and America have to come begging to us on their knees and I for one shan't be sorry."

The Cardinal did not like the statesman's uncharitable tone.

"Clemenceau," the Cardinal said. "What a pity he's dead."

"France will find other Clemenceaus," the statesman said.

There did not seem to be much more that they could say about Clemenceau because he had already been dead for nearly a year now and so it was hard to distinguish his ghost from Napoleon's. The Cardinal was glad when his nephew-in-law came to rescue him.

"If I were you I shouldn't waste my time talking to a silly snot like that," Henri de la Porte du Bibier said. "He's a reactionary rat. France will get nowhere as long as she is governed by the present gang of baggy-trousered blunderers," he went on. "We want to do as they have done in Italy and make a thorough clean up. Parliamentarism and universal suffrage have been proved a flop and democracy a delusion. It is incomprehensible that we should ever have made the experiment when one remembers that the foolish persons in the world far outnumber the reasonable. Politicians elected by a majority are politicians elected by numbskulls and if they are not numbskulls themselves they are mountebanks and blackguards."

"It is God's way to use frail men for mighty purposes," the Cardinal said gently, but the Cardinal was thinking of the Church as he spoke and not of the Third French Republic.

It was his niece who accompanied the Cardinal to the door.

"Happy, Solange?" the Cardinal asked, patting her cheek.

"I'm beginning to think that the most that one can ask from life is the absence of misery," Madame Henri de la Porte du Bibier replied.

"That sounds rather cynical for a young woman of your age, but perhaps it is not such bad theology," the Cardinal said. He gazed with affection into the eyes which he had known since childhood and was sad to see that they no longer looked so young.

The statesman overtook the Cardinal on the pavement.

"You keep bad company, your Eminence," the statesman said. "Between you and me that man's a fearful reactionary."

XXVII

JOSTLED in the underground, the abbé Gaston often found it hard to love his neighbor as himself. Today the operation was even more difficult than usual. The abbé had just returned from South America and there had been nobody at the station to meet him. Having given away his last ten francs note to a needy nun on the boat, he had been unable to indulge in the unapostolic luxury of a taxi, as it was unlikely that the driver would be willing to debit the fare to the Sacred Congregation of Rites. Wedged in between a young man carrying a trombone and a young woman carrying a pair of skis and with his thin straw travelling bag at his feet, the abbé Gaston was borne rapidly along the subterranean railway.

DUBO, DUBON, DUBONNET, the black and yellow slogan on the walls of the tunnel ran, meaning that Dubonnet was both beautiful and good, but the information did not soothe the abbé's discomfort or make it easier for him to love the young man with the trombone. Because he had been disabled in the war, the abbé had the privilege of traveling first class in the underground for a price slightly below that of a second class ticket, but the concession didn't make the points of the young woman's skis stick into his left ear any the less sharply. Looking round the crowded carriage, the abbé found it almost impossible to believe that his fellow passengers had been created in God's image, and he wondered how the Lord was going to love such ugly faces if they ever succeeded in getting into heaven. But perhaps, the abbé thought, an alchemy would be worked upon them at the judgment and those dreadful, arrogant, disbelieving noses would rise beautiful, humble, trusting noses at the sound of the last trump. It was only by reminding himself that his own soul, seen supernaturally, might be even more hideous than the countenances bobbing about like balloons all around him that the abbé was able, finally, to calm his distemper.

There were seats labelled as specially reserved for the disabled, but the fat business men sat on unperturbed, reading their neighbor's newspapers. Watching the stony stare in their unlighted eyes, the abbé Gaston wanted to go round and hit them over the head with his stick, not because he himself had to stand up while they were sitting down, but because their indifference to his own discomfort slighted also other men who had been wounded in the service of France.

When the abbé got out at his destination an employee was watering the platform with disinfectant. The abbé wanted to hit the employee across the head, too, because the disinfectant turned the platform into a sheet of grease on which the rubber on the end of his stick was liable to slip. Carrying his bag in one hand and his stick horizontally in the other, the abbé hobbled slowly towards the steps.

The Place du Maréchal Haig did not seem to have changed much since the abbé had last seen it. The pigeons still came swirling down from the roof of the church and the trees were bare with recurring November. Madame Boulon didn't seem to have changed much either. Clad in her dressing-gown and picking her teeth with a hairpin, she was sitting in an armchair listening desultorily to the drool of concupiscent cannibals emitted by her wireless set.

"So you're back from South Africa?" Madame Boulon asked as she handed him the key of his room.

"South America, you mean," the abbé Gaston corrected.

"All those countries," Madame Boulon said. "And what language do they speak in South America?"

"Spanish and Portuguese," the abbé Gaston said.

"All those languages," Madame Boulon said. "Why can't everybody speak French and be done with it?"

The abbé left Madame Boulon to her daily dose of noise and went upstairs to his room. On the staircase he met the centrally heated lady of easy virtue, coming down to do her shopping. The abbé tried not to dislike the centrally heated lady of easy virtue for passing him without recognition.

The pair of grey socks which the abbé had left out of his luggage at the last moment still lay on the bed to remind him of his loneliness and of God's patient conservation of geography. The small square of mat on which St. Blasius of Cappadocia had used to sleep still lay on top of St. Augustine's *De Civitate Dei*. The chair and the table and the wireless set and the washingstand were covered with dust.

It did not take the abbé long to unpack his best cassock, his two shirts, his two sets of underclothes, his four pairs of socks and his one and a half pairs of pyjamas. Although it was nearly lunch time he did not immediately set about cleaning his room but went straight downstairs again and across the square to the dressmaker's. The abbé knew that Armelle might not like him calling publicly upon her in the middle of the morning and he was afraid that she might receive him coldly. But it was more than two years since he had last had news of her and he wanted to find out at once if she was well and why she had not written to him all the time he had been in South America.

The wax mannequins in the window were no longer wearing the same sort of dresses or the same sort of faces. Their dresses were no longer short above the knee but short below the knee with a slit at the side. Their faces were no longer jubilantly witless with short hair but reflectively witless with longer hair. The abbé wondered if the Chanoine Litry found the new fashions more godly than the old. He also wondered if Madame Bisberot had had to buy whole new mannequins or only new wax heads. It seemed to the abbé uneconomical to replace the whole mannequin when the same effect could be achieved by merely removing the old head and sticking on a new one. After all, even Parisian dressmakers couldn't change the fashion in female bodies. Only God could do that and Darwin himself had admitted that He didn't do it either quickly or often. But perhaps they didn't make wax mannequins with detachable heads. Perhaps wax mannequins with detachable heads hadn't been invented yet. He must speak to Madame Bisberot about it. There might be money in the idea. They might be able to go into partnership together. He would give his share of the profits to the North African missions or to the Society of St. Vincent de Paul. The project was not inconceivable. After all, there were presumably holy priests who had dabbled in cough mixtures.

But as soon as the abbé saw Madame Bisberot he knew that he was not going to be able to talk to her about wax mannequins with detachable heads. Instead of a smile of welcome there was a frown of impatience on her face as she came waddling towards him in her short black dress. The abbé saw at once that she did not remember him.

"Yes, what is it?" she asked abruptly.

"It's about Armelle," the abbé said nervously. "If you please, I should very much like to speak to her."

"Armelle?" Madame pressed her forefinger against her cheek and threw back her head as though to allow an invisible wheel to rotate inside it. "Sorry. Never heard of her," she said when the wheel seemed to have come to a stop.

"But she works here," the abbé said.

"She may have worked here but she no longer works here now," Madame Bisberot said. "Of that I am quite certain."

"Her name is Armelle Dillier," the abbé persisted. "Surely you must remember her? A friend of mine and I brought her lily of the valley nearly two years ago and you were kind enough to treat us to champagne."

"Of course!" The wrinkles on Madame Bisberot's face smoothed out instantly and the pouches changed into dimples of laughter. "Those were the good old days, weren't they?" She called up the staircase as soon as she had finished laughing. "Yvonne, what happened to the little Dillier?"

There came back a rapid rigmarole whose sense the abbé Gaston could not distinguish.

"Yes, I remember now," Madame Bisberot said. "'She was amongst those I had to get rid of. The stock exchange crash in New York hit us badly, you know. Many of our best customers were Americans. I had to reduce staff. Mademoiselle Dillier was one of the first to go."

The abbé became frightened.

"Was that because her services were unsatisfactory?" he asked.

"I am afraid so," Madame Bisberot said.

"What sort of unsatisfactoriness?" the abbé asked.

"Flighty," Madame Bisberot said.

"There's flightiness and flightiness," the abbé Gaston said.

"I'm afraid, Monsieur l'abbé, that it was flightiness," Madame Bisberot said. "In a flighty profession there's no room for flightiness. I hope that you understand what I mean."

The abbé understood so well that, instead of calling at the presbytery to report his return, he went back down into the underground again. The disinfectant which had been spilled earlier in the day was now a treacherous greasy paste and once again the abbé could not lean any weight on his stick. The platform was crowded with people who looked as though they had been born there. Bored, malevolent, cretinous, sad or lascivious, they stood waiting for the train to shoot in. Even although the abbé knew that the underground was a sort of miracle of the loaves and fishes in reverse, the abbé wondered how they were all going to get into the train. The sight of a priest with a white beard among them soothed the abbé's despondency with the realization that the Church was still going about her business.

But when the train came in it was the priest with the white beard who barged the most efficiently. Whirling his arms and shoving with his shoulders, the holy clerk banged bellies and trod on toes with far greater skill than the heathen, who were parted before his onslaught. Elbowing past his competitors, the priest beat a young mother and a girl of four in a race for the last vacant seat on which he sat down with a contented grunt and gazed at the unsuccessful with a glassy eye. None of the other passengers rebuked the priest, stared at him or seemed to disapprove his conduct. Jammed together in their lighted cube, they were drawn out of advertisements about brassiéres, macaroni and starch towards advertisements about fur capes, furniture and boot polish.

The abbé Gaston had been able to get into the carriage only because a man carrying a flower pot had pushed him from behind. Crammed against the doorway, the abbé glared at the priest, but the priest sat on unseeingly, alert only when he was trying to read the advertisements on the back of his neighbor's unfolded newspaper. Once indeed the priest seemed to catch the abbé's glare, but he looked away again quickly, unimpressed by the similarity of their calling and imperceptive of the other's wrath. The abbé Gaston gave it up as a bad job.

The caretaker of the block in which the Dilliers had their flat looked very like Madame Boulon. Clad in a dirty apron and with her tousled hair sticking up from her head like a black bath sponge, she was standing at her stove frying a horsemeat sausage. The smell was terrific, but the noise coming from the wireless set was even more terrific. The noise was about stars above and love and dove and skies are blue and true and you. The smell was only about garlic. The caretaker scowled at the abbé when he opened the door.

"What is it?" she rasped.

"I'm afraid I've forgotten whether the Dilliers live on the fifth floor or the sixth floor," the abbé Gaston said.

"The Dilliers used to live on the sixth floor right but they don't live here any longer because they've cleared out," the caretaker said, giving a prod with a fork at the horsemeat sausage.

"But where have they gone to?" the abbé asked in fear and astonishment.

"Mother Dillier's gone to the cemetery and the daughter's gone I don't know where," the caretaker said.

"Do you mean to tell me that Madame Dillier has died?" the abbé asked.

"I said so, didn't I?" the caretaker said.

"But this is terrible," the abbé said. "And where has Mademoiselle Dillier gone? Didn't she leave any address?"

"The landlord turned her out because she couldn't pay her rent and where she's gone I neither know nor care," the caretaker said.

There were times when the abbé Gaston regretted the Christian compulsion to meekness and this was one of them. The abbé would have liked to empty the contents of the frying pan into the caretaker's hair and smash the wireless set across her head. Instead he remembered the law of mystical substitution and offered his suffering to God.

The abbé Gaston was still offering up his suffering when he returned to the Place du Maréchal Haig and found the Chanoine Litry and his curates already walking there. The rector had more grey hair on his temples than when the abbé had last seen him. The curates seemed older, too. They all welcomed the abbé Gaston with discreet affability but showed little interest in the details of his mission. Outside the church a hearse was waiting for a coffin and the undertaker's assistants stood lounging about with their hands in their pockets. Looking at his companions, the abbé Gaston saw that the abbé Ronsard was missing and concluded that he must be officiating at the funeral. Neither the rector nor his curates seemed interested or sorry that another of their parishioners had died. Instead they listened attentively while the abbé Moune went on talking at the top of his voice about the Uniate Eastern Churches. The abbé Gaston didn't listen, however. The abbé Gaston thought about the dead person over whom the abbé Ronsard was praying and about the nature of eternity into which it seemed unfair that some should arrive earlier than others. The abbé Gaston wondered if the explanation could be that eternity was circular, like part of the underground railway in London.

The abbé Gaston was still thinking about eternity when the girls from Madame Bisberot's came out on the square. There were not so many girls as usual, but they were all pretty and wore the same sort of slit skirts as the abbé Gaston had seen in the window that morning. The expressions on the priests' faces became grim.

"That reminds me, Monsieur l'abbé Gaston," the rector said. "The mother of your young friend is dead."

"I have heard that, Monsieur le Curé," the abbé Gaston said, trying to speak without emotion. "I have also heard that her daughter has been turned out of her flat for not being able to pay her rent."

"You seem to have lost no time in inquiring after your friends' welfare," the abbé Moune said.

"It seems that I had reason to do so," the abbé Gaston said.

"Monsieur l'abbé Moune did all that could be expected of him," the rector said. "Madame Dillier died in February. Monsieur l'abbé Moune himself buried her. And when the girl was dismissed by her employer he offered to help her and was insulted by her for his pains."

The abbé Gaston said nothing. He was thinking that if the abbé Moune had really looked after Armelle properly the girl need never have gone away. Even if she had insulted him it had been more than ever the abbé Moune's duty to have watched over her. Bessier was right, the abbé thought bitterly: clerical charity was almost always inadequate.

"You must not take this too much to heart, Monsieur l 'abbé Gaston," the rector said gently. "You did your best for the girl and God can ask no more of you as far as she is concerned. And now I have more pleasant news for you. The Daughters of Charity have opened a new orphanage at Auteuil and because of the shortage of priests it has been agreed that the most important of the city parishes should take turns in providing them with a chaplain. I want you to look after them on Thursdays."

But the abbé Gaston was still feeling too sad to be able to listen very much.

XXVIII

THE Cardinal was happy because he had found a new technique for saying his prayers with sincerity, and thus was able to avoid multiplicity. This technique consisted in saying alternate prayers at different speeds, first a prayer quickly, then another prayer slowly, then another prayer quickly again. In this way he was able to avoid distraction in his quick prayers and to mean what he was saying in his slow prayers and, he hoped, to honor the Lord in both.

This morning, therefore, when the Angelus bells rang out over the city, decanting their blessing on the heedless, the Cardinal faced his duty with confidence. Standing at the window and looking out at the sky, he murmured the text and plunged into the first *ave* at a rate. Rapidly as he prayed, however, he did not pray more speedily than his chaplain walked. And before he had come to the end of his petition the abbé Paquin was standing beside him, holding out a letter.

"Personal," the chaplain said. "From the Bishop of Saracen, I think."

Controlling his irritation, the Cardinal took the letter from the chaplain and turned back to the window to go on with his praying. But by this time he was out of tune with the bells and, as he could never pray properly a clang or two behind, he decided to wait until the bells had stopped ringing before beginning again. To mortify himself the Cardinal decided that he would not open the Bishop of Saracen's letter but would just wonder what the Bishop of Saracen had written to him about instead.

Watching from his window, the Cardinal saw that nobody in the street below paused to pray beneath the benediction of the bells. It had not been so in Dublin, where the Cardinal had recently been attending another eucharistic congress. This was perhaps the greatest calamity that had fallen upon France: that men no longer dared to wear their religion out of doors. It was also probably the greatest calamity that had fallen upon the world, because Paris wasn't the only city where men were born and lived and died among plate glass and advertisements instead of shrines. The Cardinal sometimes thought that the backward peoples were those who had been sensible enough to stop at their destination when they had reached it and the progressive peoples those who had been blind enough to go charging past it. When the bells stopped ringing the Cardinal was surprised to find that he hadn't been thinking at all about what was inside the Bishop of Saracen's unopened letter.

The Cardinal began the Angelus for the second time. The first prayer went with a swing and the second with a suck and the third with a swing again, because that was the correct variation. The Cardinal was just about to ask the Lord to pour grace into his heart when the abbé Paquin came in again.

"Well, what is it this time?" the Cardinal asked, unable any longer to conceal his irritation.

"If you please, Your Eminence, it's a Hindu bishop," the chaplain said.

"Don't talk nonsense," the Cardinal said. "Hindus don't have bishops."

"This one's been converted," the chaplain said.

"How very inconsiderate of him," the Cardinal said. "All right. Show him in."

It was three o'clock in the afternoon before the Cardinal was able to recite the twelve o'clock Angelus, and then the new technique didn't work properly. It was twenty minutes past three when he slit open the letter from his brother in God, the Bishop of Saracen.

XXIX

THE abbé Gaston liked preaching to the nuns, because they listened so attentively. He liked talking to their calm faces, so earnest beneath their white coifs.

This afternoon the abbé took his text from the gospel for the sixteenth Sunday after Pentecost: *"Amice, ascende superius,"* "Friend, go up higher." The abbé said that this was a very wonderful parable of the Lord's, and a very subtle one, too, because it showed that false humility could be almost as great a sin as pride. In no life, the abbé said, was spiritual equilibrium more necessary than in a nun's or a monk's or a priest's, because not only had nuns and monks and priests to obey their superiors but often they had also to command in God's Name. All Christians began their career in the Church as babies at the baptismal font. If God called some of those babies to become nuns or monks or priests those babies had no right to refuse the promotion. If God called some of those nuns or monks or priests to become sisters superior or abbots or bishops those nuns or monks or priests had no right to refuse the promotion. It was possible, if there was a great dearth of wisdom and sanctity among ecclesiastics, that he himself might one day be elected Pope. If so it would be his duty to accept the triple tiara humbly, although he didn't think that he would be able to resist sending the nuns his photograph. The nuns giggled at the holy joke.

When he had finished his sermon the abbé gave Benediction of the Blessed Sacrament. The nuns sang the litany of the Blessed Virgin Mary and the abbé was happy as he knelt before the Host. He liked the sound of the nuns' voices singing *"Sedes Sapientiae."* Above all he liked the stillness before him and behind him. Heaven, the abbé felt, could scarcely be more beautiful. As he climbed the altar steps to take the monstrance into his hands the abbé thanked God for this pocket of beatitude in which He allowed them to rest. The abbé held the Host very high as he blessed the nuns because he wanted to bless the rest of the world as well.

The nuns always fussed over the abbé in the parlor afterwards. Today they brought him coffee and cake and they all stood round in a circle to watch him eat. The nuns couldn't stand very close to one another in case the wings of their coiffs became entangled, so they all had to lean slightly sideways, like ships on a rough sea.

"We've a new orphan since we saw you last, Monsieur l'abbé," Sister Anastasie said.

"He walked in all by himself," Sister Marie Thérèse said.

"He's never been baptized," Sister Scholastica said.

The abbé almost sighed aloud as he realized how tired he was. He had been up all the previous night at two death beds. He had said mass at six o'clock, assisted at a wedding, given the last sacraments to a patient in the hospital, taught a catechism class, officiated at a funeral and accompanied the corpse to the cemetery. Before preaching to the nuns he had also heard their confessions. He had no desire to add a baptism to his labors. But the abbé knew where his duty lay. The child might die that night and it would be the abbé's fault if his soul went to limbo forever. The abbé rose with resignation.

"In that case we'd better lose no time," he said.

"He's a kitten, Monsieur l'abbé," Sister Scholastica shrieked, unable to keep the secret any longer.

They all laughed loudly at the joke and Sister Marie Thérèse went to fetch the kitten. The kitten was very young and had blue eyes and walked on the table with his tail stuck up in the air. The kitten purred when the abbé stroked him and meowed for more when the abbé gave him a morsel of cake. The nuns had heard all about St. Blasius of Cappadocia and they said that the abbé could take the kitten with him if he wanted. The abbé mustn't think that he was depriving them. As soon as the kitten had appeared in the refectory Sister Anastasie had said that they must give him as a present to the abbé Gaston.

"You're quite sure he's a boy?" the abbé Gaston asked shyly.

The nuns were quite sure that the kitten was a boy, because Sister Marie Joseph had examined him most closely and she ought to know, because she had studied botany.

"In that case we'll call him St. Francis Xavier in honor of today's saint," the abbé Gaston decided.

St. Francis of Xavier didn't like being shut up in a basket and he meowed all the way to the underground. It was difficult for the abbé to walk down the long flight of steps with his stick and his ticket in one hand and the basket in the other. It was still more difficult for the abbé when he had to give his ticket to be punched. The scruffy slut who was waiting to punch it didn't make any attempt to help him but sat shouting to the scruffy slut who was punching tickets on the other side of the rails about how many Strasbourg sausages she had eaten for lunch. Benediction of the Blessed Sacrament seemed a long way off.

In the train itself things weren't much better. The abbé sat with the basket on his knee. Next him sat a young woman with protruding cold boiled eyes. Her body was encased in a tight fitting sheath through which it looked as though it might burst at any minute. Opposite the abbé sat a middle-aged man and woman so disinterested in each other as to appear to be married. None of them smiled when the kitten meowed in its basket and the people standing up in the corridor didn't smile either. Anxious to be able to believe in the humanity of his fellows, the abbé smiled at them, trying to intrigue them into temporary love through the kitten in the basket, but none of them smiled back. Even when the abbé took the kitten out of the basket to give it air and the kitten gave a pink meow instead of an invisible one none of them smiled back. Congealing in liberty, equality and fraternity, they were rushed from Calvary through Trocadéro, Iéna and Alma Marceau. Even if God liked such people the abbé Gaston knew that he didn't.

The restaurants round the Place du Maréchal Haig were brightly lighted. Inside amber icebergs glossy men sat with glossy women, stoking their bodies in order that their souls could go on disobeying God. On the pavements a forest of synthetic concubines walked, on the prowl for an early penny. In the darkness their faces looked like moons hung by invisible threads, but when the abbé got close up to them he could see that they had hands and legs as well, The abbé said a silent prayer for them, but he did not pray too hard because he did not think that they were as wicked as a lot of women who came to church. The abbé Gaston hoped that the Lord would be very kind to tarts.

It was not often that such women spoke to the abbé, and when they did he always answered courteously, remembering how the Lord had spoken to Mary Magdelene. He was courteous, therefore, when a young woman with a lighted cigarette in her mouth bumped into him and excused herself. He excused himself, too, and bowed gravely back. Then he recognized her.

"Armelle!" he exclaimed. "What on earth are you doing here?"

The girl was obviously startled and displeased by her encounter.

"Please, Monsieur l'abbé, there's nothing to get excited about," she said.

"But there's everything to get excited about," the abbé said. "Why, it's more than two years since I last saw you." Examining her, the abbé was surprised to find that she was not expensively dressed. She wore a cheap blue costume and an artificial silk pink blouse pinned at the neck with a glass brooch. "Armelle, my dear, need it have come to this?" he asked.

"Please don't preach to me, Monsieur l'abbé," Armelle said. She tried to smile as she spoke, but her pale face was sad beneath her smile, and her lips were sad, too, beneath the dab of the lie upon them. "You're a good man and you've always been kind to me and I like you a lot, but I don't think you understand about what I've been through."

"Tell me about it," the abbé said gently.

"There's not much to tell," Armelle said. "Mother died. She left very little money. There were the funeral and the doctor to pay for. Then I got the sack from Bisberot's."

"I think I understand," the abbé said. "But the rector and the abbé Moune? Didn't they offer to help you?"

"Priests often offer but they rarely help," Armelle said.

"But surely you told them that you were in trouble?" the abbé Gaston said.

"I told Monsieur l'abbé Moune," Armelle said. "He offered me ten francs and said that he would pray for me."

"I never heard of such a disgraceful thing in all my life," the abbé Gaston said. "Ten francs indeed! But why didn't you write and tell me?" he asked. "I haven't much money, I know, but I could have helped you. Why didn't you answer my letters? You must have known that I was worried about you."

"I'm sorry, Monsieur l'abbé, truly I am," Armelle said. "But South America is a long way off and in the meantime I had to live. And then when you wrote I was ashamed. Please try to understand."

The abbé understood only too well. "*Considerate lilia agri quomodo crescunt: non laborant neque nent,*" the Lord had said. But even the lilies of the field couldn't grow in Paris, without toiling and without spinning. St. John the Baptist would have had a hard time of it living on locusts and wild honey on the Boulevard de Clichy. Heroisms possible in a desert of sands were impracticable in a desert of streets.

"Well, I am going to do more than pray for you," the abbé said. "And I'm going to give you more than ten francs," he said, taking Armelle's hand in his and noticing with a pang the blisters of peeling pink varnish on her nails. "And the first thing I'm going to do is to take you home and cook you a good meal. After that we can make plans. But one thing is certain and that is that you're finished with this sort of life forever." He let go her hand, hung his stick over his arm and laid the basket with the kitten in it on the ground. Then he took her face between his hands as he had used to do when she was a child and looked tenderly into her tired eyes. "Armelle, what you've been doing is very wrong," he said.

"Please, Monsieur l'abbé, I know all that," Armelle said. There was a weariness on her face as she spoke, but the abbé thought there was a gentleness also.

"And it's not only you I've got to cook dinner for," the abbé said, trying to make her smile. "I've got to cook dinner for St. Francis Xavier as well. St. Francis Xavier's my new kitten," he explained, indicating the basket on the pavement, from which meowing was beginning to come again.

The smile which the abbé had hoped for spread over Armelle's face. It made her look very young.

"I adore kittens," she said. "Please let me carry him for you. It's cruel to keep him shut up in that basket."

"You'll have to hold him tightly in case he runs away," the abbé said, bending down to open the basket. The kitten wriggled as he lifted it out, but by that time Armelle had taken to her heels and was gone.

XXX

SISTER Marie Joseph had not been so soundly grounded in botany after all, for St. Francis Xavier had turned out to be a girl and the abbé Gaston had been obliged to call him St. Elizabeth of Hungary, hoping for the best. The good, however, had speedily degenerated into the worst. A pious belief about over-consumption of fish had given place to a certainty about kittens. In the end there had been three of them: a grey one, a black one and a striped one. They played now with the abbé's rosary as he sat trying to meditate upon the five sorrowful mysteries.

The abbé knew that he ought to have drowned the kittens as soon as they were born, when they were too young to suffer much. But their tiny mews when he had taken them out of their basket and St. Elizabeth's reproachful regard had made the deed impossible. Bessier, to whom the abbé had explained his predicament, had told him that his clemency had been a cowardice. When working class mothers hadn't enough food to give their children it was intolerable that kittens should live like capitalists, Bessier had said. If these kittens were allowed to go on living they would turn into cats. The cats would beget other kittens. The process, unchecked, would ultimately result in the overpopulation of the world by cats. The cats would sack Paris and London and New York. They would swarm over the Himalayas. They would invade Russia and India and China. They would upset the prophecies of both Karl Marx and St. John the Divine. If the abbé Gaston had any loyalty to his religion it was his duty to drown those kittens, Bessier had said.

Today, therefore, the fourteenth of October 1930, as soon as he had finished saying his rosary, the abbé Gaston had made up his mind to drown the kittens. The water was already in the slop pail. The small sack, weighted with stones in the bottom, was laid out on the bed.

The abbé had always found it difficult simultaneously to recite the prayers of the rosary and to meditate upon the mysteries assigned to each decade. He supposed that this was because he was not saintly enough to do two holy things at once. Today he found the spiritual gymnastic more than ever beyond him as he had not only to refrain from thinking about drowning the kittens but also to keep disentangling the kittens from his rosary. In the end, however, the last bead was said. The abbé made the sign of the cross, picked up the striped kitten and advanced towards the bag.

At first the striped kitten seemed to like being shoved in the bag, for as soon as the abbé had got its hind legs to follow its front legs the kitten popped its head out again and tapped the abbé's hand with its paw. Then the abbé tried inserting the kitten's hind legs first, and the kitten meowed a lot and pulled himself out of the bag quickly. Then the abbé tried holding the mouth of the-bag wide open and dropping the kitten in sideways and closing the top of the bag quickly again. The kitten liked this even less and meowed so much the abbé let him out at once. The kitten forgot his misery immediately and ran back to the other kittens on scurrying, noiseless feet. The abbé decided that the only thing to do was to drop the three kittens together into the bag sideways.

St. Elizabeth of Hungary didn't seem to realize what was happening. She lay watching the abbé with big benign eyes as he hobbled about the room after the kittens. It took the abbé some time to capture the kittens because they were all rushing round the room after one another. And even when he had caught them he did not succeed in getting them into the bag sideways. The striped kitten flopped in head first, the grey kitten fell in tail first and the abbé had to push the black kitten in on top of the others and hold his head down while he closed the top of the bag and fastened it with string. The abbé poised the wriggling bag above the pail of water and the wriggling bag meowed in a tremendous treble. The abbé untied the string round the top of the bag and let the kittens out again. Even if their descendants were to overthrow the Third French Republic, the abbé Gaston could not drown the kittens, not even in holy water.

The liberated kittens ran about the floor, crouching, arching their backs and springing at one another. The abbé Gaston sat down and wondered why God had made cats multiply so quickly. But he knew that it wasn't because of God's hidden purpose that he hadn't been able to drown the kittens; it was because the kittens were small, warm, furry and graceful. In the summer he could swat flies with the best of them. And perhaps flies were very beautiful indeed when scientists looked at them through the microscope. Perhaps flies suffered just as much as kittens when they were destroyed. And flies were intricate creations of God, fashioned with patience. And lizards, which God had also created, preyed on flies and kittens preyed on lizards. The abbé Gaston gave it up. Animals, like men, must have fallen from grace.

There was no other way out of it, the abbé decided. He must make another attempt to give the kittens away. The Jesuits, the Dominicans, the Oratorians, the Benedictines and the Little Sisters of the Poor had already refused to take them. There seemed, however, to be no reason why he should not try some of the local shopkeepers. Perhaps it was foolish of him not to have thought of them before. After all, the shopkeepers were under a certain obligation to him for purchasing his foodstuffs from them. Freshly hopeful, the abbé bundled the striped kitten into the shopping bag and made his way down the six long flights of stairs.

It was eleven o'clock in the morning and the Place du Maréchal Haig was filled with traffic. A column of motor cars and buses and taxi-cabs roared and screeched round the church. When the policeman held up his white bâton to allow the pedestrians to cross, the drivers at the back of the column honked their horns in protest. As soon as the policeman lowered his bâton the motor cars and the buses and the taxi-cabs surged forward again, crushing their wheels against one another, swerving past one another, cheating one another. The abbé had some difficulty in crossing the road. because the policeman waved the traffic on again before the abbé had reached the other side.

The grocer was sorry that he couldn't take Monsieur l'abbé Gaston's kitten because he already had a white cat with a black blob over its right eye. The greengrocer was sorry but he couldn't take Monsieur l'abbé Gaston's kitten because he already had a tortoiseshell cat. The baker was sorry but he couldn't take Monsieur l'abbé Gaston's kitten because he already had a grey cat. The fishmonger was sorry but he couldn't take Monsieur l'abbé Gaston's kitten because he never had any cats at all.

But when he came to the hairdresser's shop the abbé Gaston was unexpectedly lucky. The hairdresser said that he had been looking for a kitten for a long time and that he would be only too pleased to give

Monsieur l'abbé Gaston's kitten a home. And as Monsieur l'abbé Gaston was going to give him a present, the hairdresser insisted on giving Monsieur l'abbé Gaston a present. The hairdresser was sure that Monsieur l'abbé Gaston would like his hair cut and his beard trimmed and his nails manicured.

The leather chair by the window was higher than an archbishop's throne and much more comfortable, and when the hairdresser tilted it back the abbé felt as though he was lying in bed. The hairdresser said that he would begin with Monsieur l'abbé's hair first and that if Monsieur l'abbé would dangle his right hand Mademoiselle Fifi would start on his nails. Mademoiselle Fifi was a pretty girl with hair like syrup and big blue eyes. Mademoiselle Fifi said that it was getting quite dark early at night now but that soon it would begin getting lighter again. After that Mademoiselle Fifi did not have much to say so the hairdresser gave the abbé Gaston a paper to read. The paper was full of drawings of girls who looked like Mademoiselle Fifi.

Watching the foolish looking abbé Gaston's face reflected in the mirror, the abbé Gaston noticed that the foolish looking abbé Gaston's beard was getting quite grey. Indeed it was getting so grey that it could no longer be described with accuracy as pepper and salt but rather as salt and pepper. Soon it would be all salt and then he would have to think very seriously about making his soul as holy as his beard. But his own beard was not the only thing that the abbé noticed in the mirror. He noticed also that the chair on his left was no longer vacant but was occupied by a white sheet surmounted by an inverted tin can. Between the top of the white sheet and the bottom of the tin can ran an isthmus of rugged face which the abbé recognized as belonging to the poetess.

It was difficult for the abbé to talk to the poetess because the hairdresser was now beginning to trim his beard and Mademoiselle Fifi came and sat between them in order to manicure the abbé's left hand. But the tin can on top of her head did not prevent the poetess from talking. The poetess said that she was glad to see a priest taking an interest in his personal appearance. She herself was a great believer in beauty culture which, she claimed, did for the body what the sacrament of penance did for the soul. If one was as young as one felt it was also one's duty to look as young as one felt. Recently she had been an auburn poetess. In future she was going to be a blonde poetess. The poetess said that she would have hair like silken sheaves of corn, in honor of the goddess Ceres. The poetess said that the goddess Ceres was a very poetical goddess.

The poetess was still talking when the abbé heard tapping on the window pane. He turned to see the angry face of the abbé Moune pressed almost flat against the glass. As soon as he perceived that the abbé Gaston had seen him, the abbé Moune began to gesticulate wildly, but his semaphores were too rapid for the abbé Gaston to be able to interpret them. Then the abbé Moune started to jerk his thumb towards himself, opening and shutting his mouth to utter slow soundless words, and scowling as he did so. The abbé Gaston began to understand that the abbé Moune was angry about something and wished to speak to him immediately.

But the abbé Gaston had no intention of foregoing the dry shampoo which the hairdresser had offered him, as this was a luxury which he was seldom able to afford. He calmed his conscience by telling himself that if the abbé Moune was as angry as all that he could easily come into the hairdresser's shop and tell him what he was being angry about. So as not to be obliged to look at the abbé Moune still signaling frantically outside the window, the abbé Gaston pretended to be listening to the poetess. He also exchanged a few words with Mademoiselle Fifi who was just finishing manicuring his left hand. He also flicked over the pages of the magazine which the hairdresser had given him, but he could distinguish clearly neither the text nor the drawings because he wasn't wearing his glasses.

The abbé Moune was waiting on the pavement when the abbé Gaston came out of the barber's shop. The abbé Moune was so angry that he could scarcely speak.

"Don't you know the rules?" the abbé Moune spluttered. "Don't you know that priests are now forbidden to patronize barbers' shops?"

"You forget that I've been in South America," the abbé Gaston said patiently.

"I forget nothing," the abbé Moune shouted. "I don't forget that you've always been a scandal to this parish. I don't forget that you've always gone your own way and disobeyed your superiors."

All the anger that the abbé Gaston had been trying for weeks to suppress was suddenly released. He forgot that he was a Christian priest and that the abbé Moune was another Christian priest. He remembered only the abbé Moune's inadequate charity to Armelle when she had been in distress.

"And I don't forget that you were asked to look after Armelle when I was away," the abbé Gaston shouted. "I don't forget that when she was jobless and penniless you offered her ten francs. Ten francs, Monsieur l'abbé Moune! You didn't think I knew that, did you? And do you know what your ten francs did to her? Well, I'll tell you. They made her end up on the street."

"I always knew that she would end up on the streets," the abbé Moune said. "But it wasn't my ten francs that did it. It was your allowing her to become a mannequin."

"Ten francs!" the abbé Gaston went on shouting. "Ten francs for a girl who hadn't a centime in the world."

In the end a crowd gathered round them.

XXXI

IT was the Cardinal's day for chiding recalcitrant clergymen.

His last interview had wearied him. It had been with a Dominican friar who had insulted the women in a fashionable congregation by what he had said in a sermon on the subject of cosmetics. The Dominican had said that in his opinion the majority of women were so ugly already that he couldn't understand why they bothered to make themselves look any uglier. The Dominican had said that he wished that women would get it into their heads that they had to be both young and pretty if their faces were to withstand the scars and rusts that it was now fashionable to paint upon them. The Dominican had said that women didn't make themselves look either less old or less ugly by smudging blue bruises under their eyes or coloring their lips until they looked like coils of wet indiarubber. The Dominican had said that his advice was an earthly tip rather than a supernatural counsel, as personally he was in favor of the practice, because it reduced immorality. The ladies of the congregation had lodged a complaint. But the Dominican had defended himself ably. He had pointed out to the Cardinal that the women would not have complained if he had told them that their souls were stinking and twisted and parched, as was the common practice of preachers. He claimed that he had as much right to insult the part of women that was mortal as others to insult the part that was immortal. The Cardinal did not feel that he had been very successful with the Dominican.

The Cardinal liked the look of the little priest with the grey beard as soon as he saw him come limping into the room.

"I do not think that you are to blame in the matter of the hairdresser's shop," the Cardinal said, glancing at the papers in front of him. "It was the duty of your rector to advise you of the regulation on your return from South America, but apparently he omitted to do so. Personally, I find the prohibition both irksome and stupid, but as a man under authority I am bound to enforce it. Brawling in the public street, however, is quite a different matter."

"I think that I understand that, Your Eminence," the little priest with the grey beard said.

"But do you understand it enough?" the Cardinal asked. "That is the point. There is a tendency in some quarters to believe that the world will be more speedily converted if clergymen cease to be circumspect. That is not the case. As far as human agencies are concerned men and women will be converted only by priests humbly and dully performing their duty. And they will be converted neither in great numbers nor with great speed, because Christianity is a difficult religion, as our Blessed Lord Himself has said."

"Please believe that I understand that most thoroughly," the little priest with the grey beard said.

"You, Monsieur l'abbé, have not been circumspect," the Cardinal went on. "Although I am willing to believe that your disregard of convention was prompted by the highest motives, I cannot think that it has been a very successful disregard of convention. Take the case of this young woman about whom most of this trouble has arisen. The abbé Moune appears to have pointed out to you the dangers to which she would be exposed if she were employed as a mannequin. You maintained that such dangers were negligible. The abbé Moune was right and you were wrong."

"The abbé Moune had no right to offer the girl the paltry sum of ten francs when she was homeless and unemployed," the little priest with the grey beard said vehemently. "Charity as inadequate as that is tantamount to forcing the girl on to the streets."

"It is neither for you nor for me to assess what the abbé Moune could or could not afford," the Cardinal said gently. "The abbé Moune may have needed the rest of his money. So far as I know, he is not wealthy."

"I am sorry, Your Eminence," the little priest with the grey beard said. "I shall admit that I had not looked at the matter in that light before."

"I have always thought that it is sad that the ungodly thoughts which go on inside other people should be as real as the ungodly thoughts which go on inside me," the Cardinal said. "You and I can both console ourselves by thinking that the virtues which go on inside other people are also as real as any which may go on inside ourselves."

"That I promise Your Eminence I shall in future try to think," the little priest with the grey beard said.

"And try to think also that the Church is very old and very wise," the Cardinal said. "Often, I know, she seems worn and battered, and often there seem to be rents in her armor, and sometimes she creaks a little as she shifts from one century to another. But the wear and the tear and the holes and the rust are of men and not of God," the Cardinal said.

"I shall try to think all these things, Your Eminence," the priest with the little grey beard said.

"Often, too, priests appear tired and careless," the Cardinal went on. "Sometimes they are ugly and sometimes they are stupid, but always there is the mark upon them."

"I shall try to remember that also, Your Eminence," the little priest with the grey beard said.

"And remember that the real reason why men and women don't come to the wedding feast is because they don't want to come to the wedding feast," the Cardinal said.

"That, too, I shall try to remember," the little priest with the grey beard said.

"As you are not one of my own archdiocesan priests I ought either to withdraw your faculties or ask you to transfer your services to another parish," the Cardinal went on. "I am going to do neither of these things. Instead, I am going to ask for your promise that you will be more circumspect in future and avoid sensational attempts to set the world right. I am also going to ask you to apologize to the abbé Moune."

"These things I promise Your Eminence that I shall do," the little priest with the grey beard said.

The Cardinal thought that the little priest with the grey beard had tears in his eyes as he rose from receiving his blessing and turned to go. The Cardinal prayed for a little that he might have been more successful with the little priest with the grey beard than he had been with the Dominican friar. Then he asked the abbé Paquin to show in the suburban curate who had knocked down a nun with his bicycle and had failed to dismount.

XXXII

SOMETIMES the abbé Gaston took heart from the number of confessions he heard at Christmas and Easter, but as it was always the same sort of confessions he heard at those seasons he was forced to conclude that the majority of his penitents slipped speedily back into disobedience. Today, Christmas Eve, 1930, kneeling in the church, the abbé prayed that his ministering would be potent and his counsel persuasive.

The falling darkness was already beginning to filter through the stained glass and to spread out in a haze in front of the high altar, shrouding it in mystery. The lighted confessionals lining the side aisles glowed like cottage windows along a road. In them the rector and his curates were already at work, polishing souls. Long rows of penitents were also waiting outside the abbé Gaston's confessional, but the abbé knelt on for a little, saying his prayers.

"*Jesus, Jesus, esto mihi Jesus,*" the abbé prayed. He prayed that this Christmas might not be as other Christmases, whose charity had evaporated into litter on damp pavements. He prayed for Bessier that God might enlighten his indignation. He prayed for Otto Braunschwig, that he might be made happy. He prayed for the abbé Moune, that his hurt might be healed. He prayed for Armelle, that God might stretch out His hand to her. He prayed for those who were dying in forgotten beds and far away wars. He prayed for himself, that he might be made holy. "Oh, my God I'm a stinker," he prayed and went into his box and switched on the light.

Bless them, father, for they had sinned. They confessed to Almighty God, to Blessed Mary ever a Virgin, to Blessed Michael the Archangel, to Blessed John the Baptist, to the Holy Apostles Peter and Paul, to all the Saints and to him, their ghostly father, that they had sinned exceedingly by thought, by word, and by deed: they had sworn at their grandmothers, they had thought about their bank balances while they were saying their prayers, they had pilfered lawnmowers, typewriters and hair nets, they had eaten meat on Fridays, they had lain with whores, they had travelled first class with second class tickets, they had stuck tin tacks in their enemies' back tires, they had winked at lewd women and stroked girls' knees, they had wanted to become President of the Republic, they had attended spiritualist meetings, they had bragged that they could play the pianoforte better than Paderewski. Wherefore they begged Blessed Mary ever a Virgin, Blessed Michael the Archangel, Blessed John the Baptist, the Holy Apostles Peter and Paul, all the Saints and their ghostly father to pray for them.

It was quite dark in the church when the abbé at last switched off the light and left the confessional. There were still penitents waiting in lines in the darkness, but the abbé told them that they would have to go to one of the other priests, as he himself had to go and hear confessions at the hospital. The abbé knelt for a little in the darkness and thought of all the other Christmases which the church had seen. Year by year through all those centuries men and women had knelt to worship God in a lighted hollow in the middle of the night. Perhaps time was a little like that, the abbé thought, a constantly recurring strip of patterned space unrolled from eternity and rolled back into it again.

Outside the stars hung high in a cold sky. The shop windows were sheets of silver and gold and the buses sailed round the square like lighted galleons. Although the abbé didn't like the secular Christmas, he felt that there was a new charity abroad in the street and he liked to think that some of it had seeped out from the church. Men and women didn't seem to have the same tight look about their lips as they hurried home with their parcels beneath the leafless trees. The newsvendor, who ordinarily ignored the abbé, shouted a "Good-evening, Monsieur l'abbé" from behind her pile of papers, and the abbé returned her greeting. Even the clot of bus drivers and conductors standing at the terminus seemed less surly than usual. Round the square came the procession of schoolgirls with the same old fat nun tied on to the end. The abbé took off his hat to the nun, and the nun bowed to the abbé, saluting the similarity of their servitude. Perhaps, the abbé thought, Christmas wasn't going to fail again this time after all.

This hope helped the abbé to set out for the hospital with greater confidence. The abbé never liked going to the hospital. He didn't like the doctors and surgeons who often treated him with contempt. He didn't like having to wrestle for the souls of stubborn moribunds. He knew, however, that he was never nearer the Lord than when he was doing these uncomfortable things, because the Lord had not preached goodness in centrally heated churches.

The abbé began his rounds in the men's wards, because these were the most difficult and he wanted to get the unpleasant part of his duties over quickly. He had to find out how many wanted to go to holy communion the next day so that he could bring the necessary number of Hosts from the church. He had also to hear the confessions of those who wanted to make them. The procedure was delicate because it had to be carried out without offending the prejudices of freethinkers and apostates. An Irish priest, who had once said mass in the church of Saint Clovis on his way to the Grand Prix, had laughed when the abbé Gaston had explained his difficulties to him. "Sure, and you're making a mountain out of a molehill," the Irish priest had said. "Sure, and all I've got to do when I enter a ward in Inchigeelach is to shout out 'Hands up, all those who are in a state of mortal sin' and then I hear their confessions." The abbé had often wished that things were as simple in Paris as in Inchigeelach.

But today things were easier than usual. It was a man with both his legs off and with his trunk held perpendicular by staves of wood who set the fashion in repentance. His example was followed by others, including three men who hadn't been to the sacraments for upwards of thirty years. The socialist patients, however, remained aloof, as also did a man who said he was an atheist because his grandfather had once lent his best silk handkerchief to a priest and the priest hadn't returned it. In spite of these failures, the abbé was well pleased when he entered the maternity ward.

In the third bed on the left from the doorway a young woman lay with her fair hair spread out in damp strands on her pillow. Her face was pale and drawn. Her eyes were unnaturally bright. The abbé Gaston recognized Armelle.

The abbé Gaston sat down beside Armelle's bed. He took the girl's hand in his and stroked it. Once or twice Armelle tried to withdraw her hand but the abbé went on holding it. A nurse passed up the center of the ward, carrying a large can of water. The nurse glanced disapprovingly at the abbé as she passed and vanished behind screens at the other end of the ward.

"Please be angry with me quickly, Monsieur l'abbé," Armelle said.

How would St. John Vianney have gone about it, the abbé Gaston wondered. For forty years the Curé of Ars had sat in the confessional of his parish church, sometimes for as long as seventeen hours a day. To him had come thieves and blasphemers and lechers and women of the town and by him they had been converted and consoled. The Curé of Ars hadn't sought high words about God still being true in spite of geology and Kant. The Curé of Ars had used simple words and had made strong men weep.

"I'm going to have a baby, Monsieur l'abbé," Armelle said. "I'm going to have a baby and I don't even know who the father is." Her eyes were big and round as she spoke and there were tears in them, too. But the tears didn't run down her cheeks. The tears toppled over and dried beneath her eyelids.

The abbé Gaston sought desperately for inspiration.

"Listen," he said. "It's Christmas."

"The Little Jesus," Armelle said. "That's pretty."

The abbé Gaston knew that the Little Jesus was lots of other things besides pretty. The abbé Gaston knew that the Little Jesus was also the splendor of the Father, the king of glory, the sun of justice, the author of life, the king of patriarchs and the light of confessors. The abbé Gaston knew that the Little Jesus was also might and right and recompense and retribution. The abbé Gaston knew that the Little Jesus was immanent and transcendent and that He was wrathful and merciful and that He was the ultimate mystery at the bottom of test tubes. But the abbé Gaston said none of those things to Armelle.

"At Christmas we've got to be pretty, too," the abbé Gaston said.

The abbé knew that what he had said was not profound, but he knew also that he did not require to be profound. The truths that God wanted men and women to understand were not profound, otherwise He could never have expected men and women to understand them. The truths which God wanted men and women to understand were the simple laws of rectitude in defiance of which they could expect to be happy neither in this world nor the next. In an age distinguished for its brilliant exposition of falsehood, this ordinary, willful, worldly, unhappy young woman had had the wit to realize that the Little Jesus was indeed pretty. The abbé Gaston slipped on his thin silk stole and listened.

The nurse passed down the ward again, carrying her can. The nurse scowled at the abbé as she saw him sitting there with his stole over his shoulders, but the abbé was too busy listening to Armelle to notice. Once again, the abbé was wishing that he possessed the wisdom of the Curé of Ars.

"You've just got to be truly sorry and our Blessed Lord will forgive you," the abbé said when Armelle had finished her story. "And try always to remember that the world is twice a cheat: it cheats you out of God and in the end it cheats you out of itself as well." The abbé felt that there were lots of other things that he ought to say. There was the great truth about the meaning of the world, and about holy things going on silently and invisibly. There was the great truth about religion being a mathematic and not just a guess at cosmology. There was the great truth about mockers being cowards in their hearts and really desiring the consolations at which they scoffed. But the proper words wouldn't come to the abbé to help him to say any of these things, perhaps because he was tired, he thought, or perhaps because he wasn't wise enough or holy enough to say them. "And now your soul's in a state of grace again and that's the most beautiful thing in the whole wide world," he said when he had finished absolving her. "And tomorrow I'll bring you holy communion," he said. "And you must not worry about the baby," he said. "We'll look after the baby when it comes," he said. "And we'll look after you, too," he said.

The nurse was waiting for the abbé Gaston when he came away from the bed. "That girl's very ill and she oughtn't to be disturbed" the nurse said. "She's going to have her baby soon and she's very run down."

"I've been hearing her confession," the abbé Gaston said.

"It's taken a long time," the nurse said.

"Perhaps yours would take even longer," the abbé Gaston said as he continued happily on his round.

In 1914 the abbé Gaston's private income of three thousand francs a year had gone quite a long way; in 1930 it went about a sixth of the distance and the abbé had to rely a great deal on his mass fees and the small sums of money which the Chanoine Litry gave him. Although he knew that it was fitting that those who served the altar should live by the altar, the abbé didn't like the idea that he was praying pork chops into his frying pan and so he did without pork chops as often as possible.

Necessity as well as scruple forced him to be frugal, because he had the rent of his garret as well as his food to pay for.

Three thousand francs a year meant that the abbé could spend two hundred and fifty francs a month. On the fifteenth of January he had to pay three hundred francs a month for rent, but to meet this liability he had already set aside one hundred and fifty francs. The abbé thought that he could afford to spend a hundred francs on Armelle provided that he lived for the next five weeks like St. John the Baptist, St. Anthony of Padua, St. Francis of Assisi and the Seven Holy Founders of the Servite Order all rolled into one. He decided that he would buy Armelle a bottle of champagne and some grapes.

Although it was late when the abbé got back from the hospital the shops round the square were still open, because it was Christmas Eve. The abbé felt awkward when he went into the wine merchant's as he hadn't been inside the shop since the price of ordinary wine had gone up to one franc seventy-five centimes a bottle. But the wine merchant greeted the abbé affably and said that he had good champagne at fifty francs a bottle. He had, however, even better champagne at seventy francs a bottle. Invalids, the wine merchant said, always preferred the champagne at seventy francs a bottle to the champagne at fifty francs a bottle. The champagne at seventy francs a bottle made invalids feel that they were having a holiday on top of a mountain in Switzerland whereas the champagne at fifty francs a bottle made them feel only as though they were lying out in a garden in the suburbs. The abbé Gaston took the champagne at seventy francs a bottle.

The grapes were dear, too, because they were out of season and the fruiterer said that he had to import them from North Africa. The fruiterer also said that if there was one thing that invalids liked better than grapes it was pears. Grapes made invalids' complexions shine but pears made their souls expand, the fruiterer said. When the abbé came out of the fruiterer's shop he had only enough francs left to purchase an indiarubber cat for the baby from a huckster on the square. The huckster said that indiarubber cats that squeaked amused new born babies very much indeed.

The abbé arrived back at the entrance to his house at the same time as the centrally heated lady of easy virtue, who also had been buying champagne. The centrally heated lady of easy virtue said that her gentleman liked champagne very much indeed, and, perhaps because it was Christmas Eve, she invited the abbé to share the lift with her. As they were dragged creakingly upwards the centrally heated lady of easy virtue told the abbé that what she liked best about Christmas was that it made her feel like a little girl. Observing the wrinkles about her eyes, the abbé wondered if St. John Vianney would have told the centrally heated lady of easy virtue that Christmas didn't make her look like a little girl. Soon even the tweezings and pluckings and pinchings and paintings of the beauty specialists would be in vain. Soon there would be no more gentlemen friends and bottles of champagne. He had been quite right in what he had said to Armelle: the world cheated sinners twice. The abbé decided that he must preach about that to nuns sometime and then they would know for certain that they had missed nothing.

The abbé Gaston never said mass at midnight on Christmas without a deep feeling of thankfulness for the glow which God had let into the world. It was, therefore, with a grave demeanor that he crossed the darkened square at a quarter to twelve to say his three low masses at the altar of St. Peter of Alcantara. The Chanoine Litry, of course, was saying his three masses at the high altar, and the abbé Moune was celebrating at the Lady Altar, because of the number of communicants that were expected.

Although it was almost midnight the restaurants and cafés round the square were blazing with light, crowded with those who thanked God for the glow by guzzling turkeys, getting drunk, wearing paper hats, blowing whistles and fornicating upon one another in the dance. The abbé had a theory that one day France was going to pay dearly for the vulgarity of its hedonists who had travestied an agape. He was glad, therefore, when the beadle let him into the church at the side entrance and closed the door on progress making Babylon out of Bethlehem.

The abbé was happy again when he began the mass, asking God to deliver him from the unjust and deceitful man. With love in his heart he recited the canticle of joy: *"Tecum principium in die virtutis tuae in splendoribus sanctorum: ex utero ante luciferum genui te."* The Lord was clothed with strength and had girded Himself with power. The abbé forgot the heathen in the streets. The abbé didn't notice that the big negro had hung his walking stick round St. Joan of Arc's neck and stuck his gloves on the stone spike on top of her helmet, out of reverence for what was happening at the altar. The abbé read the three glorious gospels with glee. From left to right and from right to left he moved, tracing the mercies anew. Not once but thrice he bent over bread and wine and consecrated them.

Not once but thrice he went down to the communion rail, to load men and women with the Holy Thing.

When it was all over the abbé knelt for a long time in the empty church to make his thanksgiving. Then he went home and slept with St. Elizabeth of Hungary curled up at the foot of his bed.

The abbé Ronsard was saying the mass of the aurora at the high altar when the abbé Gaston went across to the church to get the Hosts out of the tabernacle to take to the hospital. Although it was only six o'clock in the morning the church was crowded. The abbé Gaston wondered where all the Christians got to on ordinary week-days.

Walking along the pavement to the hospital holding the Holy Thing in the pyx, the abbé Gaston apologized to the Lord for carrying Him through the streets so shabbily. The Lord ought to have gone to the hospital in procession, with chants and with music and with incense and with banners, and people ought to have knelt down as the Lord passed and to have praised Him. In the ages that had been called dark, perhaps because men had been able to see into eternity instead of just past the next bus stop, priests had carried God to the sick openly, for all men to see. In the ages that were called dark it was the sinners who had lived in the darkness and even they had known the meaning of the world. Progress, the abbé thought, was a bigger mystery than religion, especially when it progressed backwards. Beneath his cloak the abbé Gaston wore a white stole because white was the color of the Blessed Sacrament, and he held the Holy Thing a little underneath his stole, so that God might be sheltered from the meanness of the world.

The doctors and the nurses didn't bow to the abbé as he entered the hospital. Most of them knew his errand, but only a few of the nurses made a sketchy sign of the cross. The doctors looked straight in front of them because they didn't believe in the Lord God any longer but only in the Third Republic and potassium permanganate. Once again the abbé Gaston knew that his loneliness was near the Lord's, but he didn't like it at all and he didn't think that the Lord had liked it either.

The abbé began by giving holy communion to the man with both his legs off and his trunk held perpendicular by staves of wood. Then he gave holy communion to the three men who hadn't been to the sacraments for more than twenty years and prayed that they might persevere. He proceeded rapidly round the wards, entering the maternity ward last of all. He gave communion to three women who were just about to have babies and to another woman who had just had one. With only one Host left in his pyx he advanced towards Armelle's bed. Screens were drawn round it. The nurse to whom he had spoken the previous evening came out from behind the screens. Once again she was carrying a can of water but this time she did not scowl when she saw the abbé.

"Please try to believe that I am as sorry as you are, Monsieur l'abbé," she said.

The nurse had told the abbé that a woman with a tumor on her neck as big as a lemon was going to die, too, and wanted to repent, so the abbé Gaston went and heard her confession and gave her the Host which he had brought for Armelle. When he came back again the nurse had finished washing Armelle's body and had brushed her hair. Armelle's hair was soft and golden in the sunlight and fluffy a little at the ends. The abbé knelt down and prayed for a few minutes. Then he rose and sat down by the side of the bed. From the street came the sound of homeward bound revelers blowing paper trumpets. With her eyes closed, Armelle froze slowly into sanctity.

"It was a hemorrhage," the nurse explained. "She wasn't very strong, you know. Fortunately, the baby's all right."

The abbé had forgotten about the baby. While he was still thinking about the baby the doctor joined them. The doctor told the abbé more about the baby.

"A girl," the doctor said. "Five and a half pounds. That's slightly underweight, of course. But with proper feeding she'll probably do all right. The mother had relations, I suppose?"

"Not a soul in the world as far as I could make out," the nurse said.

"Wife to all men and sister and daughter to none, eh?" the doctor said, but he did not say it unkindly.

"Please," the abbé said gently. "I used to know her mother. And I prepared her for her first communion."

"Religion doesn't seem to help people much, does it, Monsieur l'abbé?" the doctor said, but the doctor did not say this unkindly either.

"Perhaps it would be truer to say that people don't help religion much," the abbé Gaston said.

"Religion won't fill your belly when you're hungry," the doctor said. "If that girl had had enough to eat and hadn't been obliged to walk the streets when she was pregnant her child wouldn't be motherless now. Money could have prevented that. Money can do anything, Monsieur l'abbé."

"Money is the measure of man's refusal to obey our Lord's command to love his neighbor as himself," the abbé Gaston said.

The doctor shrugged his shoulders.

"Have it your own way," the doctor said. "The girl will have to be buried in a pauper's grave, whatever you say."

"That she will not," the abbé Gaston said. "I shall look after the funeral."

"She asked for you before she died," the nurse said. "She said that she wanted you to have these."

The abbé recognized the glass brooch and the glass necklace which the nurse handed him. The sun shone on them when he took them in his hand. He put them sadly away in the pocket of his cassock.

"And the baby?" the doctor asked, a little impatiently, the abbé thought. "Public Assistance, I suppose?"

"Of course not," the abbé Gaston said' "I shall look after the baby, too."

"That's rather unusual, isn't it?" the doctor asked.

"Christianity is unusual," the abbé Gaston said. "That's chiefly what's the matter with it," the abbé Gaston said.

The abbé Vernet had finished singing the high mass when the abbé Gaston entered the church to pray, but there were still low masses going on, because every priest had to say three masses that day, in thanksgiving for the chink of light that had been let into the world. The abbé Gaston had a lot to pray about. He asked God to grant to Armelle a place of refreshment and of peace, and to help him to find money to pay for her funeral. He asked God to help him to find a home for the baby. He asked God to forgive him if he had loved Armelle too much out of God and not enough in God. He asked God to help him to love all Christians and all those who weren't Christians. The abbé was still praying when the last mass ended and the candles on the altar were extinguished. The sacristan changed the tabernacle curtains from white to red, because tomorrow was the feast of St. Stephen, the First Martyr. God's clock clicked on.

XXXIII

THE statesman was inaugurating his forty-seventh war memorial. It was raining and the sub-prefect had to hold an umbrella over the statesman's head while he read his speech. The statesman said some highly original things. The statesman said that those who had died for their country had inscribed their names forever on the golden scrolls of history. He said that those who had shed their blood together were bound by ties of unbreakable brotherhood. He said that he was deeply moved to inaugurate this shrine to their everlasting memory. He said that democracy was now freed from the shackles of dogma. He said that the nations of the earth desired a just and a lasting peace. The statesman said that those who had died for their country had inscribed their names forever on the golden scrolls of history.

XXXIV

WHEN Armelle was buried her coffin had to be brought in at the side door of the church because a first class funeral had just finished at the high altar and the coffin of a rich man was being carried out through the front door. But the policeman on point duty wouldn't allow the ninth class horse-drawn hearse to pull up outside the side door, because he said it interfered with the traffic, and so the hearse had to pull up on the other side of the square outside the de luxe plumber's, in whose windows there was a display of pink and pale green wash-hand basins and baths. The undertaker's assistants howked the coffin out of the hearse with energetic apathy.

The traffic roared on through the square as it had always roared: Citroens, Peugeots, Renaults, dripping from Agincourt, via Napoleon. The policeman didn't hold the traffic up specially for the coffin and the undertaker's assistants had to trot across in a gap between buses. As he followed them the abbé could hear Armelle's body rattling about in the coffin and he was frightened that one of her arms might have come unjoined where the medical students had dissected it and sewn it roughly on again. Two pretty girls with long silk legs passed along the pavement in fur coats. They did not look at the coffin. Biting out at the world with young white teeth, they passed on to talk nonsense for another fifty years.

The abbé Gaston said Armelle's requiem in the chapel dedicated to St. Peter of Alcantara. Three harlots from the Place du Maréchal Haig were the only mourners. The abbé recognized them because he had seen them hanging about under the trees at night. He was touched to observe that they were dressed soberly and that they had not painted their faces.

The abbé said Armelle's requiem rapidly because he was afraid of sobbing out aloud if he tarried over the words. "*Fratres, nolumus vos ignorare de dormientibus, ut non contristemini sicut et ceteri, qui spem non habent,*" he read to the three harlots in the epistle, and the three harlots seemed to understand that they must not be ignorant about them that were asleep, or sorrowful as others that had no hope. "*Absolve, Domine, animas omnium fidelium defunctorum ab omni vinculo delictorum,*" he prayed in a gulp of hope. "*Dixit ei Jesus: Ego sum resurrectio, et vita,*" he read in the gospel, and the three harlots seemed to understand that, too, about Jesus being the resurrection and the life.

The abbé Gaston kissed the altar and uplifted his hands as he began the great prayer in which he consecrated bread and wine to the Body and Blood of Christ. In nearly thirty years of priesthood the abbé had never doubted that God sent Himself to men this way. It was to do this that the abbé had become a priest. It was because of this that he was happy when he walked along ugly streets. It was because of this that he pitied men as they rode past in their Rolls-Royces. "*Te igitur, clementissime Peter,*" he prayed, astounded as ever by the beauty of the words and astounded that other men should not find them lovely, too. "*Quam oblationem tu Deus in omnibus, quaesumus, benedictam, adscriptam, ratam, rationabilem, acceptabilemque facere digneris: ut nobis Corpus et Sanguis fiat dilectissimi Filii tui Domini Nostri Jesu Christi,*" he whispered. If God did not infallibly answer that prayer there was no light coming from under the door, and the world was a mechanism and the spirit an illusion. The abbé bent and the bell tinkled thinly as he pronounced the holy words. The three harlots bowed their heads. When the solemn thing was done the abbé prayed that the Lord might be mindful of Armelle, who had gone before Him, and that the three harlots might one day have lot and fellowship with the apostles and martyrs, with John, Stephen, Mathias, Barnabas and Ignatius. The lucid names passed like lanterns through the darkness of the world. When the mass was over the abbé prayed that the Lord would keep Armelle from the tainted horde, and he sprinkled the bier with holy water and censed it and prayed that Armelle's soul might be snatched from the gate of hell.

The three harlots were waiting on the pavement when the abbé came out of the church and they asked the abbé if they might drive with him to the cemetery and they all got into the carriage together. Two of the harlots sat opposite the abbé and one of them sat next him. Outside the window of the carriage the grey streets of Paris uncoiled from an invisible bobbin and the shops of the Galeries Lafayette and the One Hundred Thousand Shirts were plastered glossily against the glass. Once a man took off his hat across the parapet of a urinal as the hearse passed but for the most part the living were unresponsive to the spectacle of death as it passed them.

In the cemetery the narrow slot of Armelle's grave looked very deep and the coffin made a crunching sound as it was lowered into it. The wind blew the abbé's surplice and the harlots' skirts into pillows of billowing pattern. The abbé prayed briefly that God might shine eternal light upon Armelle and that her soul might rest in peace. Then they all got into the carriage again. On the way back one of the harlots told the abbé that Armelle had always made them laugh a lot because she had been able to touch her nose with the tip of her tongue and to wiggle her ears without moving her scalp. The abbé said good-bye to the three harlots outside the church and the three harlots walked away in their squeaky shoes.

XXXV

THE Cardinals and the Archbishops and the Bishops of France met in council. They sang the mass of the Holy Ghost and they asked God to guide them in the difficult task of persuading to probity and purity the members of a Latin race.

Their Eminences, Their Graces and Their Lordships gently chided the faithful. They cautioned them against the tendency to avoid moral responsibility by calling God nature. Nature was God's creation and was subordinate to Him and the fact that rivers flowed down mountains did not mean that it was impossible for mountains to flow down rivers, if God so willed, Their Eminences, Their Graces and Their Lordships said. The prelates also counselled the faithful against the false wisdom of unbelief. They said that it was foolish of lawgivers who mocked at sanctity to expect those whom they administered to behave like saints. The heart also had, as Pascal had pointed it out, its reasons for believing, Their Eminences, Their Graces and Their Lordships said.

Shouting his mouth off in the Maritime Alps, the statesman said that France was becoming a modern country. The statesman also said that the modern world was becoming a modern world. He said that science was going to make all men happy. He said that improved methods of agriculture would soon make undernourishment a thing of the past. He said that the recent number of successful transatlantic flights was making the world small and that a small world would be more comfortable to live in than a big world. He said that it would soon be possible to lunch in Paris and dine in New York on the same day. He said that soon it wouldn't be only airplanes that were flying the Atlantic, but great big hotels as well, with a bathroom attached to every bedroom. The recent developments in aerial transport alone gave him great confidence in the future, the statesman said. The statesman said nothing about the Holy Ghost. The statesman did not believe in the Holy Ghost.

XXXVI

THE abbé Gaston found carrying baby a through the streets even more difficult than carrying a kitten, because he couldn't put the baby in a basket. The abbé had to walk because there was no underground station near the hospital and because he wasn't able to afford a taxi after having paid out one thousand, six hundred and fifty-two francs, thirty-five centimes for Armelle's funeral. In any case he had to call back for the indiarubber kitten which he had foolishly left behind in his room. The abbé carried the baby in both arms, the way the hospital nurse had shown him. It was impossible for him to use his stick, which he had hung across his elbow.

The centrally heated lady of easy virtue was just coming out of the house when the abbé came in with the baby. The centrally heated lady of easy virtue looked ten years younger as soon as she saw the baby and she insisted on coming back in again right away, so that the abbé might take the baby upstairs in the lift. The centrally heated lady of easy virtue told the abbé that she had once been a baby herself. She said that she had always been very fond of babies and that her gentleman friend was also very fond of babies. The centrally heated lady of easy virtue said that her gentleman friend had once been a baby, too, and that he often used to talk about the experience, when she was entertaining him. The centrally heated lady of easy virtue said that she had always thought that it was against the Pope for clergymen to carry babies in their arms through the streets. She said that she was glad to see that she had been mistaken because if there was one thing she believed in it was kindness to babies. She asked if the baby was going to stay long with the abbé and seemed disappointed when the abbé told her that the baby was an orphan whom he was taking to be brought up by nuns that very afternoon.

The centrally heated lady of easy virtue waved to the baby as she sailed away downstairs in the lift again.

To the abbé's disappointment the baby didn't seem very interested in the indiarubber cat, although the real cat was very interested in the baby. With her tail erect and her body arched, St. Elizabeth of Hungary walked three times round the baby and then curled up beside it on the bed. When the abbé lifted the baby up again the bed was wet. For all his inexperience the abbé knew at once that it was the baby and not St. Elizabeth of Hungary that was to blame, because saints didn't do that sort of thing and babies did.

The baby was a baby without any spare parts. To substitute for a dry napkin the abbé had to use the big white handkerchief which a protonotary apostolic from Basutoland had once given him for a birthday present. The removal of the damp napkin was easy enough, but the application of the handkerchief was more difficult, as the abbé was neat neither at making triangles nor at inserting safety pins. In the end, however, he managed to arrange the handkerchief strategically and he didn't think that he had stuck the safety pin in the baby because the baby hadn't yelled.

In the underground the abbé managed to get a seat fairly easily, because it wasn't the rush hour with men charging one another like bulls to get into the carriage first, but only the quiet period with women jabbing one another with umbrellas to get into the carriage first. As the train rolled away into the tunnel the abbé began to jog the baby up and down on his knee, because he thought that babies liked travelling that way best. He told the baby that the little round red lights which went flashing past the window like rubies had been little round white lights like pearls until the wheels of the first carriage of the train had touched an electric wire which turned them to red. The abbé told the baby that the lights changed like this in order that another train shouldn't run into them from behind. The baby seemed very interested. The majority of the passengers smiled at the baby, and the abbé Gaston thought that their smiles lent beauty to eyes, noses, and ears that seemed to have slipped away slightly from God's image. The abbé Gaston smiled joyfully back at the passengers.

It was the abbé's day for visiting the convent and the nuns were already assembled in the chapel when he arrived. The abbé left the baby with a lay sister in the parlor and went into the chapel to preach to the nuns. Standing at the altar rail the abbé told the nuns that what the world needed most was more laughter and smiles. The abbé said that he knew that he had no need to tell them that, because they were nuns, and nobody on the whole earth smiled and laughed more than monks and nuns. From Alaska to Amiens monasteries and convents rocked with laughter, only it was with holy laughter. Monks and nuns smiled and laughed because God was High and His mercy sure. That was one of the great lessons which monks and nuns had to teach ordinary men and women, who often smiled and laughed only because both they and their fellows were low. Christianity was a companionship as well as an asceticism, the abbé Gaston said. People ought to laugh and joke and nudge one another in the ribs when they came out of church on Sundays instead of passing one another like strangers emerging from a department store, the abbé Gaston said. The abbé rather rushed through benediction that afternoon because he was in a hurry to get back to the baby.

The abbé found the nuns all gathered round the baby when he came into the parlor. The nuns were so interested in the baby that they forgot to offer the abbé his usual coffee and cake.

"See, it's smiling," Sister Marie Thérèse said.

"Nonsense, it's wind," said Sister Marie Joseph, who had studied botany.

"I don't believe you; it's the Holy Ghost," Sister Anastasie said.

"It can't be the Holy Ghost because it hasn't been baptized yet," the abbé Gaston said.

"We'll keep it of course," Sister Marie Thérèse said.

"If we're going to keep it for a long time it ought really to be a girl," Sister Scholastica said.

"It is a girl," the abbé Gaston said.

"You're quite sure of that?" Sister Marie Joseph asked.

"I know I haven't studied botany but I'm pretty certain," the abbé Gaston said, blushing beneath his beard.

XXXVII

THE Cardinal had been dreaming again, and in the little Benedictine Chapel he was confessing his dream to the monk. The Cardinal had dreamed that the Pope had died and that a great American friend of his had been elected Sovereign Pontiff in his stead. The new Holy Father had chosen to reign under the somewhat unusual title of Buster the First and his first proclamation had been startling. From the chair of Peter, to the city and to the world, the new Pope had declared that all his predecessors had been wrong on an important doctrine of theology: free love was not a mortal sin but an immortal virtue. As a result of this declaration Christendom had been instantly united. Heretics and schismatics had abjured their errors. The Turkish nation had been converted in a body and Scotland had not been far behind. Russia had forsaken communism. Argentina, always devout, had sent three cruisers and a battleship to fire a salute of honor at the mouth of the Tiber. There had been a special display of fireworks at Port Said. The Cardinal felt that it was wrong of him to have dreamed this dream.

The monk said that the Cardinal must not too greatly distress himself. Although dreams were a weapon of the devil, one was not responsible for one's dreams unless one had been reading evil literature which prompted them. And the matter of his penitent's dream was so fantastically heretical as to be almost innocuous. The doctrine of the Church had always been safeguarded by the Holy Ghost and would continue to be so safeguarded, even during the Pontificate of an American. Truths already defined could be amplified; they could never be minimized or contradicted. Conduct which had been declared sinful yesterday could not be declared virtuous tomorrow. Nor would the promulgation of the particular falsehood in question have the consequences suggested in his penitent's dream. The sins of the spirit as well as the sins of the flesh kept men from knowing the truth and following God, and the sins of the spirit were manifold and subtle. Purity was not so difficult, as his penitent could discover for himself by walking along the beach in the summer at any popular seaside resort; humility, meekness, benevolence and patience were much more hard to achieve and it was the lack of these virtues which chiefly prevented men from recognizing God when He shone. While it was imprudent to underrate the intelligence of Satan, the monk didn't think that the dream which the devil had suggested to his penitent had been very clever. Of course, it mightn't have been the devil after all; it might have been lobster mayonnaise.

XXXVIII

"BIRTH control, Monsieur l'abbé," the veterinary surgeon said, lifting St. Elizabeth of Hungary in his arms and listening to the beat of her heart. "Really, I'm surprised at you."

"I'm rather surprised at myself," the abbé Gaston said. "But it's better than murder. By now I must have given away kittens to every religious community in France. I'd have to start on China next and by the time the kittens arrived there they'd be cats and having kittens themselves."

"Perhaps it's all right in cat theology," the veterinary surgeon said, laying St. Elizabeth of Hungary down on the operating table again. "I don't like doing it, though. Kittens turn out so much better than human beings as a general rule. Children aren't nearly as attractive as kittens and they rarely grow up into anything as pleasant as cats. Between you and me, I'd much rather sterilize stockbrokers."

"Personally, I'd be all for it," the abbé Gaston said.

St. Elizabeth of Hungary was a striped St. Elizabeth of Hungary. She was also a curious and an intrepid St. Elizabeth of Hungary. She jumped from the operating table on to the ledge of the cabinet and began to look through the glass door at the rows of shining steel instruments behind. Then, with her tail in the air, she jumped back on to the operating table again and arched her back and began to purr when the veterinary surgeon stroked her head.

"See what I mean?" the veterinary surgeon said. "A duchess wouldn't do that."

"I see perfectly," the abbé Gaston said.

"What's the matter with the world is that there are far too many people in it," the veterinary surgeon said. "Two thousand million of them and most of them ugly, selfish, arrogant, mean, scheming mediocrities who imagine that their shattering resemblance to one another is a proof of their genius and originality."

"I have rarely heard my fellowmen so accurately described," the abbé Gaston said.

"Sterilize the lot and in a hundred years the world would be safe for cats," the veterinary surgeon said.

"Once again I'd be all for it," the abbé Gaston said.

"You seem to be much more broadminded than the majority of your colleagues," the veterinary surgeon said.

"Oh, I'm very narrow-minded really," the abbé Gaston said. "Like you I am distressed by the conduct of my fellow human beings. I think that they are ugly and I see them performing mean and despicable acts. Personally, I'd like to drown the whole caboodle at once and make an end to the sorry spectacle. But I know that's not the way that God looks at it."

"Of course, if you're going to bring theology into it," the veterinary surgeon said.

"Here's the fifty francs you asked for and please try to bring veterinary science into it," the abbé Gaston said.

XXXIX

MONEY was as money did, the statesman said. The position of the Bank of France was very sound, the statesman said. The coffers of the Bank of France would soon be full of gold, the statesman said. Hitler would never come to anything, the statesman said. Hitler could never stand up to the sort of politicians France possessed, the statesman said. The note issue of the Bank of France was backed by gold, the statesman said. Money was as money did, the statesman said.

XL

THE abbé Gaston often envied people when he saw them walking easily about the streets, running for trains, riding bicycles and jumping on buses when they were moving. The abbé Gaston would have liked to have been able to do these things, too.

But the abbé Gaston never envied hale people or pitied himself when he marched with the disabled ex-service men's association to rekindle the flame on the tomb of the unknown warrior under the Arc de Triomphe. Then he rather pitied hale people and was ashamed of himself for not having been more seriously wounded. The legless trunks in wheel chairs, the seared and scarred and sewn up faces, the shot away noses, the shining, scorched empty sockets in which eyes had lain, the bumps and the lumps and humps that had been whole flesh, the limps that were so much worse than Bessier's or his own made him also a little proud of his own tiny participation in their mutilation.

The abbé knew that all of them had not fought for God as he had fought for God. He knew, too, that some of them had not fought very much for France, but only because they had been caught up in the struggle and in order to save their lives. But he knew that their suffering had made them no longer safe, mean, calculating men. He knew that most of them were in a real sense martyrs, witnesses to a compulsion nobler than egotism. The abbé always marched gladly with them.

On the eleventh of November 1931, as on previous armistice anniversaries, the abbé Gaston and Bessier marched side by side up the Avenue des Champs Elysées in the ragged procession of the halt, the maimed and the blind. Bessier could now walk without a stick, because he had a new light aluminum leg. Indeed the leg was so light, Bessier said, that you had to be careful when there was a high wind blowing, in case the leg flapped about like a flag. Bessier also said that he could keep in step with the Garde Républicaine if the Garde Républicaine would keep in step with him.

This evening, however, there was no question of Bessier's keeping in step with anybody, because everybody marched at his own gait, clippety-clop, anyhow. There were men with a leg off above the knee who marched with a sideways lurch to the left. There were men with a leg off above the knee who marched with a sideways lurch to the right. There were men with a leg off above the knee who marched on long crutches. There were men with a leg off above the knee who marched on short crutches. There were men with both legs off above the knee who were pushed in wheel chairs by men with only one leg off below the knee. There were blind men who tapped in front of them with white sticks on the causeway. There were blind men who marched arm-in-arm together. There were men with smashed pulped faces who marched normally. There were men with an arm off who marched normally. There were men with an arm off who did not march normally because they had lost a leg or two legs as well.

They wore no uniform in this draggle of the blistered, blasted and bludgeoned soldiers of France. They wore no uniform except the poverty of their civilian attire. And even their threadbare clothes differed from other threadbare clothes as the lacerations upon the bodies of those who wore them. There were shiny brown jackets on top of shiny blue trousers and there were shiny blue jackets on top of shiny brown trousers. There were striped trousers on top of yellow boots and green jackets on top of striped trousers. There were darns on elbows and shirt tails showing through pants. There were bowler hats and straw hats and caps and no hats at all. There were homburg hats with regimental numbers stuck on them. There were overcoats with medal ribbons wound round the buttonhole of the lapel. There were mackintoshes, jerseys and shirts that were striped sideways. There was the disgusting, holy stench of poverty.

They were growing older, the men who had once fought for France, and the lines on their faces weren't all wounds. The young men with the whole bodies and the lineless faces watched them with disinterest from the pavement. With their new breasts high in their blouses the silken young women walked over the fallen leaves on their long enticing legs. With their glass faces behind glass screens the rich tore past in their limousines. It was so long since France had been saved that it seemed she had never been saved at all.

The lamps round the Place de L'Etoile glistened in the mist. The buses came charging round from the avenues with the lighted up passengers screwed into their seats. The disabled men limped across with their flags and stood within the railings of the arch. Upon the arch were inscribed the names of other victories and the men who had died and been wounded to win them had been forgotten, too. The flags were lowered, and the new flame leapt against the sky. The statesman made a speech.

The statesman said that those who had died for France had not died in vain. The statesman said that they had inscribed their names forever on the golden scrolls of history. The statesman said that the defeat which France had suffered in 1871 had now been finally avenged. The statesman said that the grateful sons of France venerated also the marks which war had left on the bodies of those who still lived. The statesman said that the wounded, too, had inscribed their names forever on the golden scrolls of history.

The statesman finished his speech. The flags were drooped again and the bugles sounded the last post. The disabled Frenchmen stood as nearly to attention as disabled Frenchmen could. But the buses charged past with the lighted up people all hating one another inside. The young women walked on the pavements in their colored waterproofs. But the abbé Gaston did not notice the buses or the people on the pavements. The abbé Gaston stood with the army of France. The abbé Gaston stood with the men who had done brave things.

XLI

THE cat woke up to her simple day, blinking at the sun with her early morning pin-point eyes. Watching her, the abbé Gaston wondered briefly if it were not better to be a cat after all, to have a happy life here below and to go pop out when you were dead. But all cats did not have a happy life here below. There were cats which never had enough to eat; there were homeless cats which wandered the streets; there were pole cats; there were cats which were ill-treated by small boys. How were those cats to be compensated for their miseries on earth by a dreamless sleep when cats which had no miseries got a dreamless sleep also? The abbé gave it up. Probably the Lord would make it clear about cats, too, on the last day.

Almost as soon as the abbé knelt to say his prayers the wirelesses started. The wireless on the sixth floor on the other side of the street began first, blazing shrieks that sounded like hyenas being disemboweled but which the abbé knew by faith to be emitted by American young women singing about love. Then the centrally heated lady of easy virtue's wireless started throwing up its quota of racket from the floor below, sending out the groans and moans which, so the abbé had been informed, were the noises contemporary Cubans made when they thought about señoritas and stars and moons. Finally the wireless on the third floor on the other side of the street began to ooze out a noise like the sound of the taste of Turkish delight, and this the abbé understood to be secular organ music.

In 1927 it had taken the abbé eleven minutes to pray for the souls of the faithful departed; in 1932 it took him seventeen minutes and today it looked as though it would take him even longer, because of the wirelesses. The abbé began to be glad that he was not saying mass till eleven o'clock, when he had to officiate at a funeral.

The bell rang before he had got very far with his prayers. It was Madame Boulon, with a letter, Madame Boulon looked at the abbé's pyjamas with disapproval. It was evident that Madame Boulon expected priests to be like cake, the same inside as outside, cassock all the way through.

The letter was from the abbé's bank manager and was very short and ran:

> "Dear Sir,
> "Unless immediate steps are taken to reduce your bank overdraft, now standing at Frs. 1413,50, we shall be obliged to sell at best some of your securities deposited as collateral.
> "Yours faithfully,
> R. Merville,
> Manager."

The abbé knew enough about finance to understand that a loss of capital meant a loss of revenue. He knew also that a loss of revenue would mean that he would have to eat even less than he ate now. He knew also that to eat less than he was eating now might endanger his health and make it impossible for him to go on carrying out his duties at Saint Clovis.

Although the abbé Gaston had never thought it of much use to pray for material favors, his predicament was such that he decided that he had better seek guidance. So he knelt by his bedside and told the Lord what the Lord already knew. He told the Lord that he had incurred the overdraft in order to pay for Armelle's funeral and to prevent her being buried in a pauper's grave. He told the Lord that in nearly two years he had been able to reimburse the bank only slightly more than two hundred francs. He told the Lord that he had tried to eat as little as possible in order to pay the bank back but that there had been extra expenses for the child's keep, as the nuns weren't very well off and he had felt bound to help them with small contributions from time to time. When he had finished telling the Lord these things the abbé knelt on for a few minutes in silence. But the Lord gave him no help at all. This did not surprise the abbé. He knew that the Lord was much more interested in the souls of His children than in what sort of shoes they wore. The abbé rose to his feet and began to dress.

There was nothing else for it, the abbé decided. Either he would have to sell some of his furniture or to economize still further on his food. As he had sold his wireless set to help the nuns out there was only the bed, two chairs, the table and the washhand stand to sell and none of these he could do without. It would have to be the food. Ordinarily he spent about three hundred francs a month on food. If he were to reduce this to a hundred and fifty francs a month he could repay the overdraft in ten months. He would have to cut out quite a lot of things, of course. But he would have to cut them out for only ten months whereas if he started to allow the bank to sell his bonds he would have to lower his standard of living permanently.

On his way downstairs the abbé made up his mind that he would start straight away. If he were to save a hundred and fifty francs a month that meant that he must buy five francs' less worth of food each day. The laws of arithmetic were as inexorable as those of theology. Today he had been going to have a small steak for lunch and a boiled egg for supper. A steak cost three francs and an egg cost seventy centimes. He would do without both the steak and the egg. He would also do without fruit. Like that he would easily save five francs. This very afternoon he would call on the bank manager and hand him five francs. Every day for ten months he would call on the bank manager and hand him five francs. On Mondays he would hand him ten francs because of course he wouldn't be able to see the bank manager on Sundays. The bank manager would be very pleased with him if he did this. The bank manager wouldn't be angry with him anymore.

The centrally heated lady of easy virtue came in at the front door just as the abbé was going out. It wasn't one of the centrally heated lady of easy virtue's days for smiling at the abbé because she passed him with her nose in the air. But her shopping bag smiled at the abbé. Her shopping bag smiled so broadly at the abbé that it showed all its teeth, and its teeth were bottles of wine and carrots and French beans and potatoes and packages in white paper which the abbé was sure must contain cold ham and meat. It was evident that the centrally heated lady of easy virtue didn't have a bank overdraft.

"Good morning, Monsieur l'abbé," the butcher shouted from his doorway. "Beautiful steak today." The butcher was a big red faced man who hadn't been to mass since the Third Sunday in Lent 1901, but he always had lovely steaks and the abbé hoped that they would be accounted unto the butcher for righteousness. "Sorry, but it's not my day," the abbé answered, trying not to look as he passed at the raw chunks of meat laid out in the window. Ordinarily the carcasses hanging on the hooks disgusted the abbé, but today they tempted him like the inside of a cathedral.

"Good morning, Monsieur l'abbé," the baker shouted from his doorway. "Fine chocolate éclairs today." The baker was a small man and much more devout than the butcher, as it was only twelve years since he had stopped coming to mass. If there was one thing that the abbé liked better than reading the lives of the saints it was eating a chocolate éclair and he often hoped that the Lord would forgive him this lewdness especially as he could rarely afford to buy the fresh chocolate éclairs but only the stale ones. "Sorry, never eat chocolate éclairs on ember days," the abbé replied, trying not to see the pyramid of éclairs in the baker's window and hoping that the baker wouldn't realize that it wasn't an ember day at all but the feast of St. Raymond Nonnatus instead.

"Good morning, Monsieur l'abbé," the wine merchant shouted from his doorway. "An excellent little lot in today. A bit dearer than usual perhaps, but well worth the money. Twenty-four francs the dozen and two francs twenty-five by the bottle." It cost the abbé quite an effort to say no, not only because he liked wine even more than he liked steak and chocolate éclairs, but also because the wine merchant was a really religious man, attending mass regularly every Easter.

It was in the greengrocer's that the abbé finally made his purchases. He paid two francs for carrots, leeks and French beans, a franc for potatoes, a franc for cheese, fifty centimes for milk and twenty-five centimes for tomatoes. When he had finished making his purchases his shopping bag was not very heavy.

In the dressmaker's window the wax mannequins stood about with their eyelashes sticking up like black pins. With their arms on their hips, they stared authoritatively out at the rim of the world as though about disdainfully to board airplanes, launch battleships, explain Einstein or reject the turbulent advances of maharajahs. The abbé noticed, however, that both their hair style and their expressions had changed again. Their hair was now swept over their brow in ordered disorder and their expressions were no longer reflectively witless but arrogantly imbecilic. Suddenly the abbé knew that the Lord didn't confine His supernatural interventions to allowing St. Benedict to see St. Scholastica's soul rising as a white dove to heaven or to sending a troop of angels to transport the body of St. Catharine from Alexandria to Mount Sinai. Suddenly the abbé knew that the Lord was interested in bank overdrafts as well. Suddenly the abbé knew that the Lord had answered his prayer.

Although this time Madame Bisberot recognized the abbé Gaston as soon as she entered the shop, she didn't smile as she came to greet him, and the abbé thought that he knew why she didn't smile. In his mind the abbé had always blamed Madame Bisberot for Armelle's death and once or twice, when he had met her in the street, he had bowed to her rather coldly. But today the abbé was prepared to be agreeable to Madame Bisberot, because he knew that the Lord had sent him to her.

"Yes? What is it?" Madame Bisberot asked in her old abrupt manner.

"Please, it's about an invention," the abbé Gaston said.

"This is not the Pasteur Institute or the Ministry of War, Monsieur l'abbé," Madame Bisberot said. "This is a dressmaker's shop: it's dresses we're interested in, not submarines."

"I know, Madame, but it's about the dummies in the window that I wish to speak to you," the abbé Gaston said.

"Well, what about them?" Madame Bisberot asked.

"I see that you've had to change them again," the abbé Gaston said. "Their hair and their expressions aren't the same as the last time I looked at them."

"And I'm going to have to change them still again in the next few weeks," Madame Bisberot said, switching her hostility from the abbé to the wax mannequins. "The windswept fashion in hairdressing is going out almost as soon as it came in. Next spring hair is going to be brushed further back from the ears and expressions are to be slightly more genial. Changes in fashion are supposed to make dressmakers' fortunes, I know, but they don't in a time of slump because nobody can afford the changes in fashion. And yet we've still got to go on changing our dummies or nobody would buy anything at all. And a fine lot of money it costs me, I can tell you."

"That's what my invention's about," the abbé Gaston said.

"Don't talk nonsense," Madame Bisberot said. "How can submarines have anything to do with wax mannequins?"

"But it's not submarines that I have invented," the abbé Gaston said. "It's submannequins."

"What next?" Madame Bisberot said.

"It's quite simple really," the abbé Gaston said. "It has struck me that while fashions in women's hair and faces change their bodies remain unaltered."

"That is not quite true," Madame Bisberot said. "The fashion in women's bodies *has* changed. Before the war it was fashionable for a woman to have a figure like an hourglass. Now it is fashionable for her to have a figure like a guardsman."

"But however much women may desire to change the shape of their bodies it is still not possible for them to do so," the abbé Gaston said. "They may tinker with their faces and their hair; they cannot tinker with their trunks."

"That's all you know," Madame Bisberot said.

"All the same the main details must remain unaltered," the abbé Gaston persisted.

"I thought that it was souls you were supposed to be interested in, Monsieur l'abbé," Madame Bisberot said.

"My contention is quite theological really," the abbé Gaston said. "Every time the fashion changes you are obliged to buy a whole new wax mannequin although it is only the hair style and the facial expression which are different. Any change in the appearance of women's bodies is really a change in the appearance of their clothes." The abbé Gaston felt a little guilty as he said these worldly things, especially when he remembered what the Cardinal had said to him, but the Lord had guided him, he knew, and the Lord was higher than the Cardinal, he also knew.

"That is substantially true," Madame Bisberot agreed.

"Now if you were to have such a thing as a wax mannequin with a detachable head you would save yourself a lot of money because you wouldn't need to buy a whole new wax mannequin every time the fashion changed," the abbé Gaston said, a little nervous now that he had come to the important part of his proposition. "On one wax mannequin the saving would be considerable; on twenty to thirty it would be enormous."

Madame Bisberot's expression grew thoughtful. She held her head on one side and then on the other. She placed a finger on the point of her chin and rolled her eyes up to the roof. Then she lowered her eyes again and tapped several times on the point of her chin with her finger.

"Yes, there's something in it," Madame Bisberot said at length. "Perhaps not for this time, but for next time. No, it's not a bad idea really."

The abbé Gaston smiled. He could feel his smile cutting right across his face.

"I'm glad that you like my little invention of the submannequin," he said.

Madame Bisberot's expression clouded.

"Invention, did you say?" she asked. "Have you taken out a patent?"

"Patent?" It was the abbé Gaston's turn to look perturbed. "Is that necessary? You see, I wanted to know your opinion first. And if it was favorable I thought that you might be willing to put me in touch with other dressmakers."

Madame Bisberot reflected for a moment. Then she spoke earnestly to the abbé. She said that the submannequin was a very useful invention really but that it required careful handling. With all due respect to Monsieur l'abbé, she did not think that the clergy had the necessary experience to handle a complicated matter like the marketing of a new invention. Nor were the other dressmakers in Paris competent to deal with the question, because the other dressmakers in Paris were thieves, liars, rascals, blackguards, mountebanks, varlets, doublecrossers, twicers, ruffians, rogues, swindlers, subborners and poltroons. Only an honorable and intelligent dressmaker like herself could handle so revolutionary an invention. Of course there was money in the idea, but there was a lot of boring details to be attended to first. Madame Bisberot said that she would feel honored if Monsieur l'abbé would allow her to attend to those boring details on his behalf. In the meantime she would keep in touch with Monsieur l'abbé and as soon as the boring details were arranged she would let him know. There would be royalties, of course, but all in good time.

The abbé Gaston knew enough about business to know that in good time generally meant in bad time. His smile vanished.

"You see, the point is I've got a bank overdraft," he said.

"In that case you can certainly afford to wait," Madame Bisberot said and went on to explain to the abbé about bank overdrafts. Madame Bisberot said that only rich people had bank overdrafts and that the bigger a person's bank overdraft was the richer he was. While a man who owed a hundred thousand francs to his bank was well off, a man who owed a million francs to his bank was wealthy. Madame Bisberot said that she herself had a bank overdraft, only hers wasn't a rich bank overdraft, but a poor bank overdraft. Listening to Madame Bisberot, the abbé Gaston realized that commerce, like religion, had its mysteries.

"I am afraid that my bank overdraft is a poor bank overdraft, too," the abbé Gaston said. "Indeed it is because it is so poor that I am attempting to sell my invention. You see, I incurred my overdraft in order to prevent Armelle Dillier from being buried in a pauper's grave. She once worked in this shop, you may remember."

Madame Bisberot remembered so well that she wept. Her indiarubber face screwed up just as though it were laughing, but her celluloid eyes squeezed water tears all down her indiarubber cheeks. So that was why Monsieur l'abbé had bowed so severely to her in the street? Monsieur l'abbé must believe her when she told him that this was the first news she had had of that poor girl's death. If she had known that Mademoiselle Dillier was going to die she would never have dismissed her. And when the abbé told her that Armelle had left behind a baby girl Madame Bisberot wept so much that she had to jam both her fists into her eyes, and in the end her grief became so great that she had to run into the back shop and weep over the cash register. Even from the front shop the abbé Gaston could hear her gulps of sorrow. Her tears seemed to make a clinking sound as they fell on the floor, but soon the abbé realized that it was only the cash register weeping as well. When Madame Bisberot came out into the front shop again the cash register had wept two thousand franc notes into her hand.

Monsieur l'abbé must honor her by taking the money, Madame Bisberot said. Monsieur l'abbé must take the money to show her that he understood how sorry she was about Mademoiselle Dillier dying and leaving behind that poor little baby girl. It didn't matter at all if the money came to a little more than the amount of Monsieur l'abbé's poor bank overdraft. Monsieur l'abbé must not think that the money she was giving him represented charity. The money that she was giving Monsieur l'abbé represented an advance on account of the royalties that would be earned by his very wonderful invention of the submannequin. Madame Bisberot said that there would be more royalties later, too, and that Monsieur l'abbé must not hesitate to ask her for them when he felt that he required them.

"Good morning once more, Monsieur l'abbé," the wine merchant shouted from his doorway. "My new wine's selling fast. You haven't had second thoughts, have you?" The abbé had had second thoughts; he bought three bottles.

"My chocolate éclairs are still here, Monsieur l'abbé," the baker cried from his doorway. "You haven't had second thoughts, have you?" The abbé had had second thoughts; he bought six chocolate éclairs.

"My steaks are still fresh and tomorrow's Friday," the butcher yelled through a pair of cupped hands. "You haven't had second thoughts, have you?" The abbé had had second thoughts; he bought two steaks, two juicy ones.

It wasn't until he was crossing to the church for the funeral that the abbé realized that he had forgotten to complete his private prayers for the repose of the souls of the faithful departed. It was too late to begin them over again because already the undertakers' assistants were carrying the unvarnished coffin up the steps of the church. A group of cheerful mourners followed, talking eagerly among themselves. The abbé was tempted to upbraid them for their demeanor and to chide them for not being able to follow even a corpse in silence, but he smoothed his ire by reminding himself that perhaps it wasn't necessary to feel sorry for the dead man. Perhaps the dead man was already with God, enjoying delights greater even than the simultaneous consumption of wine, steaks and chocolate éclairs. With these thoughts in his mind, the abbé went into the sacristy to put on his vestments.

XLII

IN 1933 the statesman had discovered a new phrase, and it was a very good phrase, because it didn't matter which way round he used it, upside down or upside up. The statesman said that the sinews of war was money. The statesman said that a country which lacked gold could not make war. The statesman said the sinews of war was money. The statesman said that money was the sinews of war.

XLIII

IN February 1934 the Cardinal had discovered a new way of saying the Angelus with concentration: this was to recite alternate prayers from opposite ends of the room, walking rapidly from one position to another: when his thoughts were wandering very badly he used three positions instead of two, praying in front of the fireplace as well as in front of the door and the window. The Cardinal thought that the necessity for rapid locomotion in between prayers banished the leisure for distraction.

Today, however, was one of his bad days. No matter how frequently he displaced himself, the Cardinal could not help interrupting his prayers with thoughts about the trouble which had fallen upon France. While he was still trying to pray the statesman was announced.

"It's about this Stavisky business," the statesman said. "You've heard about it, I suppose?"

For days the Cardinal had heard about nothing else. All through the feasts of St. Polycarp, St. John Chrysostom, St. Agnes, St. Francis of Sales, St. Martina, St. Peter Nolasco, St. Ignatius and the Purification of the Blessed Virgin Mary he had heard of the network of fraud which had spread out from the Credit Municipal de Bayonne. The financial details of the matter had largely escaped him because as a priest he was more used to thinking in terms of grace than in those of credit. He knew, however, that the son of a Russian immigrant called Stavisky had started the swindle. He knew that the Credit Municipal de Bayonne was a pawnshop which had inflated its assets by stating an excessive value on the counterfoils of receipts given for articles pledged with it in security for loans. He knew that on the strength of these counterfoils bonds had been issued and that the money obtained had been used to bolster up other doubtful enterprises. He knew that politicians had been involved and that there had been rioting in the streets.

"I should require to be a blind, deaf and dumb Trappist monk not to have heard of it," the Cardinal said.

"The people are foolish," the statesman said. "They do not understand. The government has promised that the whole truth shall be made known. The people must be patient."

"Patience is a fruit of the Holy Ghost and for years you have taught the people to disregard the fruits of the Holy Ghost," the Cardinal said.

"I didn't come here to argue with Your Eminence," the statesman said. "I came here to ask you a favor."

"It's yours if it's in my power to grant it," the Cardinal said.

"Your Eminence, the situation is serious," the statesman said. "Every day there are riots in the street. Prominent politicians are insulted by the crowd when they are recognized. The Croix de Feu plan to overthrow the government. Of course the communists want to overthrow the government, too, but it's the Croix de Feu who constitute the main danger. Your nephew-in-law, Henri de la Porte du Bibier holds an important position in the Croix de Feu. I want Your Eminence to use your influence with him. Tell him that what he and his friends contemplate is folly. Tell him that the government is sure of the loyalty of both the police and the military. Tell him that we shall not hesitate to deal energetically with rebels. Tell him to be patient."

"*Servi subditi estote in omni timore dominis non tantum bonis et modestis, sed etiam dyscolis*," the Cardinal remembered that St. Peter had written in his epistle. But if servants were to be subject to their masters with all fear, not only to the good and gentle, but also to the froward, what were the servants to do when one set of froward masters was froward enough to oust another set of froward masters? Where did the servants' loyalty begin and where did it end? Was this loyalty due only to the froward only while the froward were in office and was it automatically transferred from the outgoing froward to the incoming froward? And was it lawful to prevent excessively froward masters from being replaced by others who were perhaps less froward? The Cardinal could not help feeling that St. Peter had not been granted a vision of the Third French Republic.

Violence was always wrong, the Cardinal decided, and promised the statesman that he would do all he could to help to preserve peace in the public predicament.

XLIV

THE Cardinal had long been perturbed by the thought that it was difficult for secular priests to make others pious and remain pious themselves. The Cardinal knew that secular priests had to empty themselves out in order to fill others with grace and that their weariness was often all that they had left to offer to the Lord. Accordingly the Cardinal had, in the month of February 1934, entrusted his confessor with the task of conducting a retreat for one half of the archdiocesan clergy; the other half was to be preached to during the doldrums of the Sundays after Pentecost. Kneeling in tightly packed rows, the clergy of Paris prayed that they might be delivered from the snares of the devil, from everlasting death and from the neglect of God's inspiration. Holy, with their knobbly faces and in their shiny cassocks, they knelt and prayed that God might make them holier.

The monk did not spare them, although he understood their plight. The monks said that the great danger for them was that they were too familiar with the holy thing and that because of this familiarity they often failed to order divine worship in a seemly manner. He said that the way clergymen clicked, clucked, coughed, sneezed, fidgeted and scratched their ears in churches did great disservice to the cause of religion. He said that their patent disregard for one another's sermons led the laity into contempt for the Word of God. He said that for clergymen to maintain electric candles upon their altars was a greater sin than for clergymen to call publicly upon cinema actresses. From what the monk had read, there might be a temptation to commit a visit to Mae North; there could be none to commit an electric candle.

The monk said that they must always remember that they were priests, stamped with a special seal. The monk said that it was not only with their mouths that they preached the gospel but also with their arms and with their legs and with their eyes. For it was when they stood at the altar that they most expressed the Mind of the Church, and the Mind of the Church was not hurry and scurry and flurry, but dignity and simplicity and repose. The monk said that the reflection of this austerity should always be upon them, even when they walked among the worldly. The monk said that they should always remember the mark which had been placed upon them, at their ordination.

The priests knelt again and prayed that God might sanctify them. Bound in his linen and steady silk, the monk gave them benediction of the Blessed Sacrament. Holy, with their knobbly faces and in their shiny cassocks, the priests prayed that God might make them holier.

The abbé Gaston never liked walking for a long distance in the streets with the Chanoine Litry or the abbé Moune because usually they forgot about his limp and walked too fast for him. The abbé was glad, therefore, when, on leaving the chapel, they suggested that they should go on ahead and leave him to follow more slowly, and he tried not to suspect the motives for their haste. He also tried not to think about the big riot which had been forecast for this evening when the parliament met in the Chambre des Députés to debate on the Stavisky scandal and about the danger to which he himself was exposed. Instead he thought about the monk's sermon and concluded that the preacher had got the cinema actress' name wrong; the abbé was pretty certain that the monk should have said Mae South.

The night was dear and dark blue and shining, and the abbé could almost taste the sting of the stars on the tip of his tongue. The abbé was sometimes afraid when he looked up at the stars, because his contemplation of them made God seem both immense and far away, and yet the abbé knew that God was in the Holy Thing, too. Limping along the rows of street lamps, the abbé concluded that God must be both big and small, elastic according to the circumference of His confinement.

The district was inhabited by the wealthy. Huddled under a doorway, a beggar sat, with his crutches lying beside him and his cap inverted between his knees. Although it was already late, well dressed people were still passing in the street but none of them paid any attention to the beggar. From pink rectangles of window came the cushioned sounds of padded life. In their lighted limousines the lighted women rode past the beggar as they would have ridden past Calvary. The abbé gave ten francs to the beggar and decided to do without meat the next day and sausages the day after. Another priest was waiting at the bus stop when the abbé reached it. The abbé saw with pleasure that it was the Chanoine Paquin. It was the first time he had seen his young friend since the latter's recent promotion.

"Good evening, Monsieur le Chanoine," the abbé Gaston greeted.

"There's no need to be insulting just because I've sunk into hierarchy," the Chanoine Paquin laughed.

The Chanoine Paquin's reply made it easier for the abbé not to feel jealous. The abbé sometimes found it difficult to contemplate with equanimity the rapid rise of many of his juniors. Two of the abbé's contemporaries were now archbishops, in spite of the fact that they had been mediocre at theology and had muddled up the Manicheans and the Pelagian, and two friends of his, both ten years younger than he was, were now auxiliary bishops. The abbé sometimes thought that he wouldn't have made such a bad bishop himself.

The Chanoine Paquin told the abbé Gaston that he had been on a special mission for the Cardinal, trying to dissuade Monsieur Henri de la Porte du Bibier from attempting to overthrow the government by force. The Chanoine Paquin said that the Cardinal himself had already pleaded vainly with his nephewin-law and would have tried again had he not had to leave Paris for Lisieux. The Chanoine Paquin said that he did not think that he had been more successful than his master. Monsieur Henri de la Porte du Bibier had listened very inattentively, he said, and had left the house hurriedly to keep an engagement.

"It's for tonight, they say," the abbé Gaston said. "And yet things seem normal enough here. Beggars sitting on the pavement and the rich passing them by."

"This isn't the center of the town, remember," the Chanoine Paquin said. "And history never looks like history while its actually happening."

"I agree with you there," the abbé Gaston said. "Important events are held in a magic lantern slide only after they've happened."

"It is only when it has become the past that the present can ever be great," the Chanoine Paquin said. Their bus came rumbling up the Avenue. It was a very old bus, with rattling windows and steam issuing from its overheated engine. Perched high above the circular bonnet the driver sat at the monster wheel. The grubby conductor didn't seem to be worrying much about history as he tugged at the chain of his bell. The two priests sat down on one of the hard wooden seats. Opposite them sat two men, both looking miserable. Watching them, the abbé Gaston thought that he knew why the two men were both looking miserable. The abbé thought that the two men were looking miserable because at the end of a long stretch of rent bills, electric light bills and gas bills they saw only the undertaker's bill and no reward beyond for their frustration. For the two men Christianity had been exploded in the laboratory and romantic love in the chemist's shop. Debunking had debunked even debunking.

"You see there's nothing much happening here," the Chanoine Paquin said to the abbé.

"But it's happening all right, Monsieur l'abbé," one of the two men seated opposite said with a sudden gleam in his acid eye. "The Croix de Feu are cleaning up France tonight."

"I beg your pardon, Monsieur," the other man said, anger suddenly subduing the misery on his face. "It's the communists who are cleaning up France tonight."

"Daladier's a midden and Hitler's a sewer and Mussolini's a cesspool and Stalin ain't lavender," a woman sitting under a tilted pink hat on the other side of the bus said.

The two men glared at each other and then they both glared at the woman under the tilted pink hat. The bus rolled on with the map of its route hung across the center of the aisle like a temperature chart. At the stop outside Clemenceau's former house there was a crowd waiting, but the conductor jangled his chain and shouted that the bus was full. Five homeward bound bus conductors jumped on as the bus lumbered forward again and stood on the platform smoking amputated stubs of cigarettes in one another's faces. The officiating bus conductor shook all their left hands with his left hand and said good evening, how were they and that things were going to hum that night. The homeward bound bus conductors shook the officiating bus conductor's left hand back with their left hands and said good evening, how was he and that things were going to hum that night.

At the stop at the Place du Trocadero three passengers got off and six other homeward bound bus conductors got on. Although there were three vacant seats inside the bus all the bus conductors remained on the platform smoking in one another's faces and telling one another that Daladier was a midden and that things were going to hum that night. As the bus rolled along the Avenue Kléber towards the Place de l'Etoile the abbé Gaston wondered what bus conductors thought about, riding along the same streets day after day at the same time. In a sense their perpetually recurring motion was liturgical, but the abbé didn't suppose that the bus conductors looked at their vocation that way. But the abbé had not much time to think about this because before the bus had gone very far it was stopped by a mob of angry young men who surrounded it, shouting loudly.

The abbé Gaston knew that he was not a brave man. He had not liked being a soldier at the front and he preferred sleeping in a warm bed at night to having his entrails torn out for the Lord's sake. Since he had been wounded he had been even less brave, not wishing to be hurt again. His heart was thumping with fear when the hooligans made them all get out of the bus. He was still frightened when he stood on the pavement watching the hooligans board the bus with tins of petrol in their hands. The Chanoine Paquin, he noticed, didn't look too brave either, nor did any of the other passengers. Only the woman wearing the tilted pink hat was brave enough to argue with their aggressors.

"It's not French," the woman wearing the tilted pink hat said. "Mark my words. All this will end badly."

"The government's not French either, mother," one of the young men shouted back at her. "That's why we're going to burn this bus."

"It's against law and order," the woman wearing the tilted pink hat said.

"The government's against law and order, too," the young man said. "We're Croix de Feu. We're out for law and order. That's why we're going to set fire to this bus."

"And to think that we live in the twentieth century," the woman wearing the tilted pink hat said.

The abbé Gaston felt that the Chanoine Paquin and he should have argued with the young man, too, and have attempted to dissuade the hooligans from their purpose. St. Paul would have remonstrated resoundingly with the rioters, the abbé knew, reminding them about sounding brass and tinkling cymbals. But the time was no longer when one could risk rousing the populace to shout out for about the space of three hours. The Church of God was manicured these days. The abbé remembered with relief his promise to the Cardinal. But he still felt a coward as he watched the young men clamber on top of the bus and sprinkle it with petrol. It was impossible to tell what the Chanoine Paquin was thinking.

Even when the first flames burst from the bus and lit all their faces with pink it was impossible to tell what the Chanoine Paquin was thinking.

"Underground, I think," the Chanoine Paquin said. To the abbé Gaston it didn't sound at all like the sort of thing that St. Paul would have said to the Thessalonians.

The underground which ran from the Place d'Italie to the Place de l'Etoile was the one which the abbé Gaston detested most after that which ran from the Place de l'Etoile to the Place de la Nation. The trains consisted of old rickety carriages filled with unwashed, smelly people. Tonight, however, the train was almost empty when it came in and the two priests found seats easily enough.

"Do you really think it's a revolution?" the abbé Gaston asked.

"It certainly looks like one," the Chanoine Paquin said.

"Do you know, I think that we should have said or done something when those ruffians set fire to that bus," the abbé Gaston said.

"The Cardinal wouldn't have liked it," the Chanoine Paquin said. "The Cardinal thinks that we are living in difficult times. He thinks that we should keep quiet until things blow over."

"All the same there's such a thing as playing too much for safety," the abbé Gaston said.

The abbé Gaston and the Chanoine Paquin parted company at the Etoile. The abbé's next train came rounding into the station in a great golden rush. The first class carriage was crowded with hefty men who looked like baboons and the abbé had to stand. The hefty men were all jabbering excitedly among themselves. The hefty men said that Daladier was a midden and that the mounted police were middens, too, and that it was a pity if it was true that Henri de la Porte du Bibier had been killed in the rioting because Henri de la Porte du Bibier wasn't a midden at all. Wedged in among the angry louts, the abbé was again conscious of the inadequacy of his witness. Paul of Tarsus would have preached to those square jaws and those blunt noses and those cauliflower ears, and the square jaws and the cauliflower ears and the square jaws would have been converted, abandoning their violences for submission to the Lord. The abbé consoled himself with the thought that when St. Paul had pitched into the Galatians the words had been new.

The train drew into another station and the hefty men all got out. The train rattled on almost empty through the tunnel. The abbé found a seat and took out his breviary. The Latin words soothed the abbé and he bounced them joyfully on his lips.

The ticket inspector in his blue uniform came lurching along the passage between the seats. As the ticket inspector knew the abbé by sight he did not ask him to produce the pass which entitled him to travel first class for less than second class fare. Instead he told the abbé that the train would not be stopping at the Place du Maréchal Haig because of the rioting on the square, but only at the next station up the line. The ticket inspector said that politics disgusted him.

"Why don't you try religion instead?" the abbé Gaston asked, deciding that here at last was an unspectacular opportunity of exercising his apostolate. The ticket inspector told the abbé that he had, in fact, often thought of trying religion but had always been discouraged because religion appeared to be against so many things. The ticket inspector said that he had read in a book that religion was against pride, free love, bad temper and laziness and that he thought that was rather a lot of things for religion to be against if it wanted to appeal to Frenchmen. The abbé told the ticket inspector that he was really looking at the matter upside down. The abbé said that religion was against certain things only because it was for other things and that the things religion was for were humility, generosity, chastity, meekness, temperance, brotherly love and diligence. The ticket inspector said that the things religion was for sounded even more depressing than the things religion was against and that he thought that he had better stick to politics after all as politics were only against the people who disagreed with you.

The train rushed through the empty station of the Place du Maréchal Haig with a clang and a bang. It tore into the next tunnel, shooting past the strips of **DUBO DUBON DUBONNET** as though they were Swiss mountains. Although the abbé knew all the five bends in the tunnel by heart and was adept at keeping his balance when the train turned the corners quickly tonight he was thrown from one side of the carriage to the other when he rose to cross to the door in readiness to get out. "Rough sea tonight," the ticket inspector said, coming after the abbé to help him. The ticket inspector got out of the train, too, when it stopped because he had to wait for the next train, he said, to see if there were any blackguards travelling first class with second class tickets. "And remember to keep your head down if there's shooting," he shouted after the abbé as the priest made his way slowly along the slippery platform towards the exit.

The abbé hoped that there wouldn't be shooting, because with his limp he found it difficult enough to walk in ordinary non-rioting crowds. He took courage from the demeanor of two women climbing the long flight of steps in front of him and from the fragments of their conversation which floated back. "Three francs fifty the meter at the Printemps," one of them said. "It's only three francs twenty-five at the Belle Jardinière," the other woman said. "What I always say is that it pays in the long run to buy good stuff," the first woman said. "All the same I think you look best in your fluffy dress with the lace on the collar," the second woman said. From the banality of their remarks the abbé could imagine the platitude of their faces and he did not think that from the point of view of moral theology it mattered whether they wore fluffy dresses or sackcloth and ashes.

The exit from the underground was in a side street which was empty when the abbé reached it. He hurried gratefully along the pavement hoping that the ticket inspector had made a mistake and that the Place du Maréchal Haig would be empty, too. But as soon as he reached the boulevard the abbé realized that the ticket inspector had not made a mistake. Men came running along the pavement shrieking: "Down with Frot! Down with Cot! Hang that assassin Daladier !" Other men were tearing up the iron grilles from the foot of the trees and others were rushing wildly about brandishing empty bottles. In the doorways of cafés prostitutes stood on lighted legs, huddled in their tubular fur capes. From the Place du Maréchal Haig came the roar of angry voices.

Three times within three minutes the abbé was nearly knocked over. He edged in towards the cafés for safety and leaned against a hoarding, wondering whether he should try to slide his way through the crowd or go back and wait in the side street until the riot was over. He had still not decided what to do when he saw the lighted cone of a cigarette winking from a neighboring door. The glow that it made when it turned red illuminated the girl's face above it. The abbé recognized one of the harlots who had attended Armelle's funeral. The girl came over to speak to him.

"Good evening, Monsieur l'abbé," the girl said, holding out her hand. "Remember me? I'm Lucienne." She was wearing a thin pale green costume with a white blouse. Her lips were damp and glistening.

The abbé gravely shook hands with her.

"Of course, I remember you perfectly," he said.

"What a business, isn't it?" Lucienne said. "The mounted police have been firing, too, and quite a lot of people have been killed." The stiff spikes of her eyelashes made her eyes look as though they were embedded in shells. "The world's quite a sad place really. When you kick the bucket nobody cares."

The abbé wanted to say that the important thing was to know in what direction you kicked the bucket, but he felt that this was one of the occasions when one preached better by being silent. In a lull between rioters a titanic tart waddled past in a prairie of fur coat. The two harlots saluted each other like archbishops. "Not much doing tonight, dearie," the titanic tart shouted, churning away into the gloom.

There was another rush of men along the boulevard. They came from the Place du Maréchal Haig and they ran along both pavements and the middle of the road. They shouted as they came but there were so many of them shouting that it was impossible to hear what they were shouting. They came running all together at first and then they split up into small groups in which they came to a halt further along the boulevard. When they had stood in groups for a little they came surging back again, shrieking and yelling as they pushed their way towards the Place du Maréchal Haig.

"You're frightened, aren't you, Monsieur l'abbé?" Lucienne asked.

"Quite considerably, Mademoiselle," the abbé said.

"I'm frightened, too," Lucienne said. "I'm frightened when they shout but I feel quite brave when they're silent."

"I think that it's because of my wound that I'm frightened," the abbé Gaston said. "You see, I don't keep my balance very easily."

"I'll help you home if you don't mind being seen with me," Lucienne said.

The abbé wanted to go back and wait in the side street, but he felt that he could risk neither hurting Lucienne's feelings nor appearing less courageous than she. The girl took his hand and led him quite smartly up the street. As soon as they reached the back of the crowd the crowd began to move forward, too. Then another crowd joined them from behind and the abbé and Lucienne were carried forward in the rush. When the rush stopped the abbé saw with surprise that they were standing in the Place du Maréchal Haig. There were clouds over the sky now but when the abbé looked at the roof of the church it seemed as though it was the church that was sailing under the clouds. From the distance came a muffled noise of firing.

"The swine," Lucienne said. "Sideways, Monsieur l'abbé, sideways."

They slid sideways along the back of the crowd, which wasn't so difficult as they kept close to the shop windows. From time to time the crowd gave a roar of anger and then there was silence again and only the stars went on, with the clouds fluffing over them like transparent shawls. In the de luxe plumber's window the darkness had washed the color from the pink and pale green wash-hand basins and baths. Much sooner than he had expected the abbé found himself standing outside his own doorway.

"Really, Mademoiselle, I don't know how to thank you," the abbé said.

But Lucienne didn't wait to be thanked. In her thin little green costume she slid away along the square again. From time to time the abbé saw her white glove stuck up above the heads of the crowd and supposed that she must be waving to him. He waved back weakly, a little afraid of compromising himself. In front of him the crowd began to move forward again, pressing across the square in a compact mass. Standing in his doorway, the abbé watched the sea of heads move forward. At first the mob moved slowly but its momentum gradually increased. Soon the square was empty except for the titanic tart standing forlornly at the lamp-post on the corner. Above the church the clouds thinned out and the stars shone through brightly.

In the distance there were more sounds of firing but the shots sounded innocuous, benevolent almost, like champagne corks being extracted. Then the firing drew nearer and dribbles of people came running back into the square. Suddenly there was a crack of rifle fire quite close on the right. A man came walking quickly towards the abbé and his left leg made a jerking motion as he walked.

"Philippe!" the abbé exclaimed in surprise.

"Quick; they're after me," Bessier said.

The abbé pressed the automatic button and the door opened. He pushed Bessier in first, closing the door behind him. The glass shook in the heavy iron frame as the door clanged behind the abbé. "Gaston," the abbé called out, so that Madame Boulon might know who it was that had entered the house. There was the sound of feet running quickly past on the pavement outside.

"That's them," Bessier whispered. "They'll be back again in a minute. They'll search every house on the square. They'll know I can't have gone far with this gammy leg of mine. Don't put on that light, for heaven's sake."

The abbé drew back his hand just in time. He felt in the darkness for the door of the lift, deciding that neither he nor Bessier could climb all those stairs rapidly in the dark. He pressed the button. There was a click and the lift began to creak wheezily down the oiled center shaft. The lift was an old lift and it took a long time to come down. There was the sound of feet running rapidly past on the pavement again. The lift made a sucking noise as it slid to a standstill behind the iron gate.

"That damned thing'll wake the dead," Bessier whispered.

They both got into the lift. One of the inside doors kept swinging open again and the wood creaked and the door gave a crack when the abbé finally succeeded in holding it closed with his foot. The lift creaked and wheezed upwards as it had creaked and wheezed downwards but this time it made a rattling sound as well. Inside the lift there was a smell of turpentine, garlic and centrally heated lady of easy virtue. It seemed to take a long time before they reached the fifth floor. When they got out the abbé didn't send the lift down again because of the noise that it would make. The dry wood on the steps of the narrow staircase leading to the sixth floor squeaked and groaned beneath their feet. The silence as they stood on the narrow landing sounded even more menacing.

The abbé opened his door and switched on the light. St. Elizabeth of Hungary lay curled on the bed; asleep on a crumpled copy of *La Croix*. From the street below came fresh shoutings and roarings which merged into a snarl as the sharp rap of rifle fire was again heard. Before he closed the window the abbé looked down on to the square. Men were running in all directions and policemen in steel helmets were pursuing them. When the abbé closed the window the noise dulled a little but it still sounded very loud. Bessier stood with a nervous smile on his pale lips. The abbé saw that Bessier's forehead was cut and that his left eye was bruised.

"Thanks, old man; that was sporting of you," Bessier said. "Those swine of mobile guards. I'll do one of them in one of these days."

"Tonight the boot seems to have been on the other foot," the abbé said.

"As long as they don't start searching the houses on the square," Bessier said.

"From the noise down there I think they've got more important fish to fry," the abbé said, filling the kettle and putting it on the gas stove. "I'll heat some water for you to wash. Like that you'll at least be a Christian to look at."

They were both silent, listening to the shouting on the street below. Gradually the shouting grew fainter and fainter until they had difficulty in hearing it at all. The lid of the kettle began to clatter and the water sizzled out of the spout with a splash. The abbé put out the gas. There was a ring at the bell.

"I told you so," Bessier said.

"Quick; the window," the abbé Gaston said. He switched out the light and opened the window. "Put your feet on the window and hang on tight and don't look down. I'll try not to put the light on again." The abbé shut the window again when he had helped Bessier out on to the slates and went to open the door. But it was not the police; instead it was the centrally heated lady of easy virtue with her yellow hair all fuzzy about her head. The centrally heated lady of easy virtue said that she had been awakened by the sound of shouting and shooting on the street below and that she had been frightened, because she was all alone that night as her gentleman friend was away on business. She hoped that it wasn't civil war that had broken out. Indeed the noise had been so terrible that at one time she had almost thought that it was the end of the world which was taking place, although she supposed that this was foolish of her, because surely the Pope would have tipped them the wink about it in the newspapers so that she and her gentleman friend could have had time to repent properly. The abbé Gaston told the centrally heated lady of easy virtue that as far as he knew the noise which had awakened her had not come from civil war but only from a riot about Stavisky. And as for the end of the world, the abbé said, the centrally heated lady of easy virtue would know for certain when that was going to take place, because there would be signs in the sun and in the moon and in the stars as well as in the Place du Maréchal Haig, and upon the whole earth distress of nations, by reason of the confusion of the roaring of the sea and of the waves. The centrally heated lady of easy virtue thanked the abbé for his information and said that it was foolish of her not to have thought of

Stavisky before and that she was glad that she and her gentleman were going to be able to go on having fun together for a little longer.

"It was only the lady from downstairs," the abbé explained as Bessier climbed back into the room.

"The tart, you mean?" said Bessier, who had heard all about the abbé's neighbor.

"The tart I do not mean," the abbé Gaston said. "She's got an immortal soul. She may easily end up in the right place and I in the wrong."

"All the same it was decent of you," Bessier said. "It might have been the police. And if they had found me hiding on the roof you'd have got into trouble."

The abbé did not answer. He went over to the kettle and poured out some water for Bessier to wash in. "And now perhaps you wouldn't mind telling me what mischief you've been up to," the abbé said.

"I've been setting fire to a bus," Bessier said.

"But that's what the Croix de Feu are doing," the abbé Gaston said. "I've seen them at it."

"It's not the same thing at all," Bessier said. "Their setting fire to buses is reactionary; ours is progressive."

"Sounds Greek to me," the abbé said.

"It's quite simple really," Bessier said. "The fascists set fire to buses in order to perpetuate; the communists set fire to buses in order to create anew."

"The Athanasian creed seems simple in comparison," the abbé said. "And now to bed with you. I'm not letting you out of my sight again tonight."

While Bessier was undressing the abbé finished saying his office. Then he knelt down and said his prayers and when he had finished saying them Bessier was asleep. The abbé thought that Bessier looked very helpless and alone when he was asleep. Perhaps that was the cure for setting fire to buses: everybody in France seeing everybody else in France asleep. The abbé put out the light and lay down under the coverlet on the edge of the narrow bed, so as not to disturb Bessier.

XLV

IN London the Lord had called His Servant Francis to leave the Church Militant and in Westminster Cathedral the priests were praying that God, Who had made Francis a bishop, might bid him now to enter the company of the saints. In their scarlet and in their ermine and in their fine linen the Cardinals and the Archbishops and the Bishops prayed that Francis might enter into everlasting rest.

Lonely in the pile of prelates, the French Cardinal wondered what Francis would have thought about the Ursuline nun. The Ursuline nun had been worrying the Cardinal a lot of late. The nun claimed to have discovered a new method of protecting big cities from bombing in time of war. All you had to do, the nun said, was to cover towns with a moveable steel lid, which slid out from under the earth on one side of the city like the cover of a soup tureen, curved up into the air over the city and came down and touched the earth on the other side of the city, thus sheltering the whole town with an impenetrable dome until the air raid was over. And if the steel was strong enough, the nun said, the bombs would bounce back again and might even hit the hostile aircraft which had dropped them. The Cardinal wondered what Francis would have thought about this invention.

The French Cardinal was sad when they laid the black vestments upon him. With sorrow in his heart he prayed that God might not enter into judgment with His servant Francis but might succour him with His favor. With a mist before his eyes he prayed that the Lord might have mercy and that Christ might have mercy and that the Lord might have mercy. Then he sprinkled the catafalque with holy water and blessed it with incense and prayed that God might snatch from the gates of hell the soul of Francis who had been his bishop.

XLVI

THE statesman liked dining at the Elysee. He liked the look of the Garde Républicaine lining the stairway and he liked meeting other famous men and women. Above all he liked the feeling of directing the world effortlessly. When the Pouilly was properly iced it was really quite easy to direct the world effortlessly.

This evening in September 1935 the statesman sat between the wife of the Italian statesman and the wife of the Finnish statesman. The wife of the Italian statesman had a hooked nose and deep brown eyes and looked as though she might once have been passionate beneath palms. The wife of the Finnish statesman had pale blue eyes and looked as though she had never been passionate at all.

"The weather for the time of year is exceptional," the wife of the Finnish statesman said.

The banality of the remark did not surprise the statesman. When the statesman had been a young man he had supposed that the powerful talked intellectually, but now he knew better. He knew now that the powerful talked even more foolishly in private than in public. That was one of the two main reasons why it was so easy to direct the world; the other was that if you made a mess of it the mess was such a big mess that people rarely noticed it.

"Paris must certainly seem a bit of a change after your igloos," the statesman said.

"Your Excellency is mistaken; I am not an Eskimo," the wife of the Finnish statesman said.

The statesman employed the technique he always used when asked parliamentary questions to which he could not reply: he smiled and said nothing. He had used this technique with sensational success when, as Minister of the Fleet, he had been taken to task by the Deputy for Tarbes for having publicly confounded battleships with destroyers. He had smiled and said nothing for so long that he had finished by convincing the Deputy for Tarbes that battleships were indeed destroyers. It proved, however, more difficult than he had anticipated to convince the wife of the Finnish statesman that she was an Eskimo and in the end he was forced to turn in embarrassment to the wife of the Italian statesman. As far as he knew, there were no igloos in Abyssinia.

"The excellent food and drink provided by our illustrious host help one to forget the clouds on the political horizon," the statesman said.

"Between you and me they do things better at the Palazzo Venezia," the wife of the Italian statesman said. "And as far as Italy is concerned there are no clouds on the political horizon. Italy is no longer a nation of mendicants. Italy is a great nation. And Mussolini is a great man."

"Of course, of course," the statesman said soothingly. Sometimes the statesman regretted the disappearance of the old diplomacy which had made it possible for opponents momentarily to agree that each other's wrong was right however loudly they might shout that it was a dastardly crime afterwards. No matter how long he smiled at her the wife of the Italian statesman seemed unlikely to believe that Mussolini was a mendicant.

"The Abyssinians are savages," the wife of the Italian statesman went on. "It is once again the mission of Italy to civilize the world. Mussolini has said that the twentieth century will be the century of our power."

"A subtle way of speaking, certainly," the statesman said.

"And the British are hypocrites," the wife of the Italian statesman said. "They have colonies which they have conquered by the force of arms. Just look at India."

"Personally I have never quite approved of India," the statesman said.

"And if they send their navy to Gibraltar the valorous Italian airmen will blow it to smithereens," the wife of the Italian statesman said.

"After all it's only a fleet of rowing boats," the statesman said.

"And Germany is strong, too," the wife of the Italian statesman said. "Hitler is Mussolini's friend. It is to Hitler's advantage to be Mussolini's friend. Hitler may not be saying much just now, but you can take it from me that he is thinking a lot," the wife of the Italian statesman said.

"Deep thoughts, no doubt," the statesman said.

In the drawing-room afterwards the German statesman held his liqueur glass up to the light.

"The friendship of a country which can produce such brandy is worth cultivating, Your Excellency," the German statesman said.

"Your Excellency is pleased to flatter France," the statesman said.

"Your Excellency means that I am pleased to tell the truth about France," the German statesman said. "I am also telling the truth when I suggest to you that you should not pay too much attention to the assertions made by your talkative companion at the dinner table. If Hitler wants Germany to be strong it is because Hitler is a lover of peace."

"Si vis pacem, para bellum," the statesman said.

"I perceive that Your Excellency is a man of both culture and discernment," the German statesman said. "And Hitler is not so foolish as to risk the enmity of Napoleon brandy for the friendship of Chianti."

"Of course they can't fight for toffee," the statesman said.

"Not even for macaroni," the German statesman said.

"It is an impertinence for the Italians to compare their blackguardly threats to Abyssinia with the benign colonial policy of His Majesty's Government," the British statesman said.

"I have always had the greatest respect for the achievements of the British race," the statesman said.

"India is a model example," the British statesman said. "If we are despots at least we are benevolent despots."

"I have always admired the sagacity and the restraint of the British rule in India," the statesman said.

"And if the wops get too cheeky the Home Fleet will dot them one on the eye," the British statesman said.

"The French Navy has always had the highest esteem for the British Navy," the statesman said.

"You'll send destroyers, I presume?"

"Battleships, my boy," the British statesman said.

The statesman smiled and said nothing. He was always getting the damned things mixed up, like stalagmites and stalactites.

Afterwards there was music. The statesman supposed that it was Chopin but was willing to believe that it was Beethoven. He prepared not to listen in comfort. After all he had earned his leisure: he had spoken his mind frankly and courteously. But before his eyes closed they met the cold stare of the wife of the Finnish statesman. He smiled at her but she did not smile back, and the statesman concluded that he had not succeeded in persuading her that she was an Eskimo.

XLVII

THE abbé Gaston was preaching to the nuns about silence. The abbé said that the great mystery of silence was that silence was eloquent. That was one of the chief differences between paganism and Christianity, the abbé said: the false gods spoke in thunderstorms and rocks rolling down mountains; the true God spoke in silence. And that was why monks and nuns laid much stress on the value of silence, the abbé said.

The abbé Gaston said that the fact that silence was holy did not mean that all noises were unholy. There were certain noises that were very holy indeed. They were holy noises because they were beautiful noises. The sound that the sea when it broke on the shore made was a holy noise because it was a beautiful noise and it was a beautiful noise because it was a priestly noise, rhyming God's patience in the lap and suck of waves. The noise that oars made when they were dipped in water was also a holy noise and the noise that the birds made when they sang in the trees were holy noises, too. Especially, however, was the liturgy of the Church a holy noise because it was a lovely and a recurring noise, reflecting not only eternity but the kind of noises that would be heard in eternity. The abbé said that the repetition of beautiful noises always made them more holy, because the regular recurrence in time of lovely sounds was the nearest they could get to the static bliss of the next world. But the noises that were repeated had to be beautiful if they were to be holy. The sound coming from an organ whose keys were played on by a nun at the same time every day was a holy noise; the sound coming from an organ whose keys were sat on by a bishop at the same time every day was not a holy noise. The nuns always loved it when the abbé made a joke and Sister Anastasie had to clap her hand in front of her mouth so as not to laugh out aloud.

The abbé said that the modern world did not go in much for silence. What was more distressing still, the abbé said, was that, not content with the senseless noises they let out of their own silly mouths, people had had to go and invent machines to make even more senseless noises for them. The abbé said that in his opinion the ugly clang and clatter emitted by modern wireless sets were responsible for more heresies than the Arians, the Manichæans, the Macedonians, the Pelagians, the Nestorians, the Eutychians, the Albigenses and the Waldenses all put together. Modern wireless sets had persuaded the people that in order to be happy they had to listen to morons caterwauling about sinful itch from morning till night.

It was true, of course, that people could turn off a wireless set and that they couldn't turn off a Eutychian, but it was even more true that it was easier to turn on a wireless set than to turn on a Eutychian. In the abbé's opinion the invention of broadcasting was the worst evil that had befallen the world since the Great Schism. After all the Eastern Church had only muddled up the procession of the Holy Ghost; the broadcasters had made it impossible to think about the Holy Ghost at all.

Even from the devil's point of view, the abbé said, broadcasting appeared to be a work of supererogation, since modern people could get all the cacophony they wanted in the streets without having to listen to tin pails being kicked down stone stairs in their houses. One would have thought that the screechings, the roarings, the whizzings, the buzzings, the burrings, the honkings and the hootings emitted by contemporary traffic sounded out enough noisy purposelessness to satisfy even the most atheistic ear, but apparently that was not the case. Modern people had to listen to ugliness all the time. The dignity of even secular diversion had been destroyed. In the old days the frivolous had danced cotillons and waltzes; today they danced things called Charlestons and cancans. The abbé said that he didn't know what these new dances were like but his knowledge of the English language, supplemented by a conversation with an American Jesuit, had enabled him to hazard that the cancan was called the cancan because ladies when they danced it banged empty petrol cans together. The abbé thought that the nuns would agree that it was quite impossible for ladies to think about the Holy Ghost when they danced the cancan. When he had finished his sermon the abbé gave the nuns benediction of the Blessed Sacrament. The abbé tried to give it as the monk had given it in the little chapel, but he thought that he was a little more wobbly, because of his bad leg.

Afterwards the nuns took the abbé into the recreation room so that he could speak to Michelle. Michelle was nearly five years old now and she had her mother's golden hair and misty blue eyes. Indeed when he spoke to the little girl the abbé found it difficult to resist the illusion that he was talking to Armelle and he had to remind himself that it was more than twenty years since Armelle had first made mistakes in her catechism to him. The abbé watched Michelle and the other children play. The orphans were mostly little girls but there were some little boys as well. Sister Scholastica played *Dansons, les Capucines* on the piano and the children danced gravely in thin cheap check pinafores. Sister Marie Therese said that she hoped that the abbé Gaston thought that *Dansons, les Capucines* was a holy noise. The abbé Gaston said that he was sure that there was nothing of the cancan about *Dansons, les Capucines* and that it was quite possible for the children to think about the Holy Ghost while they danced it.

XLVIII

THE statesman said that gold was an outworn medium of exchange and that one country's currency could be valued in terms of another country's currency only if both countries' visible and invisible exports were simultaneously expressed in the coefficient of their reciprocity. The statesman said that it was all very simple really.

XLIX

SOMETIME when he saw the hard-faced rich people rushing about the square the abbé Gaston understood the impatience of Karl Marx. On the feast of Saints Protus and Hyacinthus, Martyrs, 1936, the abbé, preparing to join his colleagues for their after luncheon walk, felt that there was quite a lot to be said for Bessier's point of view. In spite of the stay-in strikes and the threat to their selfishness, the padded men and their sleek women still sat in the expensive restaurants, challenging the empty bellies of the poor.

In front of the church workmen were repairing the gas mains. Deep in their trenches the hairy men stood, howking out the brown earth. The workmen no longer smiled at the abbé as he passed. Instead they stared at him with a mocking look in their eyes. The abbé thought that he knew why the workmen looked at him like that. The workmen looked at him like that because they imagined that his religion was a lie against both science and charity and that the abbé knew this as well as they did. In 1914 workmen had been willing to believe that piety was felt by tender hearts; in 1936 workmen imagined that piety was simulated by brass necks. The abbé smiled at the workmen, trying to kindle kindliness in their eyes. The workmen scowled back, hating him from their hole.

A new young policeman stood on the square, controlling the traffic with sullen apathy. The limousines, the taxi-cabs, the lorries and the buses roared round the church, skittering away to Neuilly, Auteuil and Montparnasse. Although the policeman saw the abbé waiting to cross he looked away deliberately and waved the traffic on with his baton. The pavements began to be crowded with shabby workers swarming back to their drudgery. The rich didn't look at the poor and the poor didn't look at the rich and neither the rich nor the poor looked at one another as they passed down the drain of liberty, equality and fraternity. There were a lot of people waiting with the abbé Gaston to cross the square when the policeman at last lowered his baton.

The pretty girls from Madame Bisberot's weren't walking on the square today, because they were having a stay-in strike, too. With their colored frocks spread out like inverted flowers, they stood lined up along the first floor window, jamming their faces against the glass. The abbé tried not to look up at them as he passed. He also tried not to look at the wax mannequins in the lower window either, in case their expressions and their hair style should have changed again. The abbé always liked to believe the best about people and, although he was beginning to suspect that taking money for his invention was against Canon Law, he did not want to discover that Madame Bisberot owed him anymore royalties on the submannequin.

The other priests came out of the presbytery and joined the abbé beneath the trees. Although the Chanoine Litry was quite grey now his jaw was as determined as ever and the uncharitable said that he was disappointed that he had not been made a bishop. The abbé Moune was now senior curate as the abbé Vernet had been appointed rector of a church in Kremlin-Bicétre. Both the abbés Graber and Robert had also been transferred to suburban churches and they had been replaced by two very young curates, whose clean, northerly appearance pleased the abbé Gaston. The abbé Ronsard still blinked studiously behind his spectacles. Because they had come out of the presbytery first, the abbé Gaston was forced to walk with the rector and the abbé Moune.

"So our friends are on strike today, too," the rector said, glancing at Madame Bisberot's first floor window. "They look just like fish in bowls," the abbé Moune said.

"There's no reason for them to be on strike either," the rector said. "In these days the wages of sin is mink."

The abbé Moune laughed heartily, opening his mouth and showing his gold teeth like collar studs all in a row. But the abbé Gaston did not laugh. Instead he felt miserable and angry. The abbé Gaston knew that the wages of sin was not mink but poverty and disease and suppurating holes in faces and being buried in the common ditch. Remembering his promise to the Cardinal, however, he was silent.

"All the same these strikes are becoming too much of a good thing," the abbé Moune said. "The workers are beginning to lose all sense of proportion."

Once again the abbé Gaston restrained himself. He knew that if the employees were selfish now it was because the employers had been selfish first. To his surprise the rector expressed his thought for him.

"The employers haven't always been too good, you know," the Chanoine Litry said.

"Two blacks don't make a white," the abbé Moune said. "And it's not justice that the workers want; it's revenge. If you don't believe me just look at what is happening in Spain."

The abbé Gaston became miserable again. He had hoped that nobody was going to talk about Spain, because Spain these days was an even more inflammatory topic than France. Although the Spanish civil war had been going on for more than two months now the abbé had not yet been able to make up his mind what to think about it.

"There at least the issue is quite clear cut," the rector said. "There it's black hatred of religion that's at the bottom of all the trouble. The Spanish bishops have said so. They have said that the guns of Franco are the voice of the gospel."

"And the same thing will happen in France if we are not careful," the abbé Moune said. "The workers are the enemies of religion, I tell you."

"I don't think that the issue is clear cut either in Spain or in France," the abbé Gaston said, his voice trembling as he spoke. "And if the workers are the enemies of religion it is because the Christians have first been the enemies of the workers." The abbé also wanted to say that it was blasphemous to suggest that guns could ever be the voice of the gospel. He wanted to say that it was in hearts and not in shells that the Lord had put His high explosive. But the abbé was too angry and unhappy to say either of these things. He became angrier as he observed the rector and the abbé Moune exchanging amused, semi-tolerant glances.

"Perhaps you wouldn't mind telling us a little bit more fully what you mean, Monsieur l'abbé Gaston," the rector said.

But the abbé Gaston was still too hurt and angry to be able to speak coherently. He wanted to say that men couldn't shell and bomb and machine-gun other men into virtue. He wanted to say that the gospel of the Lord was a mercy and that it would be preached persuasively only by men who were merciful. "To the shame of religion it's often the unbelievers who have set the highest example in charity," was all that he managed to get out.

"So it's because of charity that they are murdering priests in Spain?" the abbé Moune asked. "And it's because of charity that they are digging up the bodies of dead nuns in Barcelona and exposing them to mockery in the streets?"

"You misunderstand me willfully, I think, Monsieur l'abbé Moune," the abbé Gaston said. "Men are rarely cruel without a reason." Once again the abbé tried to say calm and clever things and once again he failed. He tried to say that barbarity was often a barometer of the barbarity which provoked it. He tried to say that if Spanish Christians had loved their neighbors as themselves there would have been no civil war in Spain. But all he could say was that men did not readily hate the good.

"And Russia?" the abbé Moune asked ironically. "You seem to forget that Russia is backing the Spanish government. Is Stalin also unable readily to hate the good?"

"And Germany and Italy?" the abbé Gaston asked. "Is Mussolini a crusader? Is Hitler an evangelist?"

"You'll be talking about the Jews next," the abbé Moune sneered.

"Of course I'm going to talk about the Jews," the abbé Gaston said, but still the wretchedness was upon him and he could not talk. This time the abbé wanted to say that it was cruelty that was the crime, whether it was committed against Christian or infidel, because it was a wickedness done to men who were alone in their bodies. He wanted to say that God had made all ears and eyes and hair and laid His hand upon them and blessed them, and that all flesh was God's goodness at men's mercy. But as before the words would not come and all that he could do was to repeat what he had already said before. "Of course, I'm going to talk about the Jews," he said.

"It might be more prudent to change the subject altogether," the rector said. "They tell me that the Cardinal's off to Poland this week."

"He was in Holland last month," the abbé Moune said. "Getting a bit of a gadabout if you ask me."

"Oh, I expect he's quite religious really," the rector said.

Already in 1936 the abbé Gaston had begun to pray that God wouldn't require him to die by torture, because he didn't think that he would make a very good martyr. Only that morning he had read in the newspapers of a Jew who had been stripped naked by the Germans and beaten with barbed wire till he died. The abbé didn't think that he could recite the creed for very long if he were being beaten by barbed wire. He hoped that the Lord wouldn't ask too much of him in a world which was becoming daily more and more like a bad detective novel.

Tonight the abbé was going to dine with Bessier and his wife at the Buttes Chaumont and he was riding in the underground. On one side of the carriage there was a little yellow lamp which was extinct and on the other side there was a little blue lamp which was lighted. The white crescent of lettering on the lighted little blue lamp said Porte St. Gervais because the line branched off into two lines at the Louis Blanc station, one going to the Porte de la Villette and the other to the Porte St. Gervais. From previous observation the abbé knew that the driver usually switched off the little blue lamp as soon as the train left the Louis Blanc station, as after that there could be only one possible destination. But sometimes, the abbé also knew, the driver anticipated this operation by switching off the lamp at the Gare de l'Est station or at the Château Landon station. Sometimes, too, the driver postponed the operation until he had reached the Jaurès station or the Bolivar station. The abbé decided that if the driver switched the lamp off this evening accurately at the Louis Blanc station it would be a sign that the Lord would not require him to become a martyr.

At Chaussee d'Antin the usual crowd of workers invaded the carriage and still more got in at Le Peletier and Cadet. The abbé succeeded in conquering his resentment at their travelling first class with second class tickets but he found it difficult not to be annoyed by the way their heads obscured his view of the little blue lamp. When the train reached Poissonière he became very impatient because the next station was the Gare de l'Est and he wanted to know whether or not God was going to require him to be a martyr. But when the train ran into the Gare de l'Est most of the workers got out and the abbé once more had a clear view of the little blue lamp. The driver did not put it out.

The abbé began to look forward to dining with Bessier. Especially did he look forward to telling Bessier about his argument after lunch with the rector and the abbé Moune. He was sure that Bessier would approve of what he had tried to say. The abbé began to rehearse what he would say to Bessier and he was still formulating sentences when the train rattled into Jaurès. With a start the abbé looked up at the little blue lamp; it was out.

Had the driver put the little blue lamp out at Château-Landon or had he extinguished it correctly at Louis Blanc? Or had he waited until the train had reached Bolivar? The abbé did not know, and it was impossible for him to be certain whether the Lord intended him to become a martyr or not. The train rounded slowly into the Buttes Chaumont station in a long loop of lighted loveliness. The abbé Gaston got out.

The Buttes Chaumont station was sunk so deep beneath the ground that there was a lift to take passengers to the surface. As the first class carriage was placed in the middle of the train, the abbé always found it hard to walk along the platform quickly enough to get into the lift before the operator closed the door. This evening, to make things more difficult, the platform was greasy as they had been watering it with disinfectant and the abbé had to hobble along without using his stick in case the rubber cap on the end slipped. Although there were passengers who had got out of the second class carriages at the head of the train the abbé was the last to arrive at the lift. The liftman scowled at the abbé and clanged the door noisily.

The lift rose slowly up the shaft. The lift was crowded with working men and women who looked just as surly as the liftman. The abbé tried to smile at the working men and women but none of them smiled back. Even at one another the working men and women did not smile. Glowering at one another, the masters of tomorrow stood in their moving pen. Roped together by time and by trial, they looked away from one another and tried to be separate from one another.

The lift stopped. The liftman got out and talked revolution with the liftman of the lift that served the other line. "And you'll see in twenty-four hours it'll be all over," the liftman said to the other liftman, and together they stood with wooden faces and thought with mournful glee of the night of the long knives and of the glad morrow when it would be their turn to drive down to Deauville in Hispano-Suizas and fornicate with the best actresses. The other passengers walked dolefully up the short flight of steps into the evening sky. The abbé followed them.

It was at once evident that the abbé was in a communist district. Even the outside of the tin urinal was plastered with political inscriptions: TO THE STAKE WITH FRANCO; GUNS FOR THE SPANISH REPUBLICANS; MAKE THE RICH PAY; LONG LIVE THOREZ; and the abbé supposed that the inscriptions on the inside were even more illuminating. There was, however, an absence of zeal in the demeanor of the people who hurried by on the pavement, and to the abbé they seemed undistinguishable from those he had seen walking there in 1921 and 1926, when the new doctrines had been less popular. Even when he left the park and turned down the steep slope towards the district where the tough workers lived the people seemed little different. The same bored policemen stood at the entrance to the commissariat. There were the same blowsy women standing in their doorways and there was the same smell of garlic and rancid butter in the air. Even the Spanish barber who had cut the abbé's hair too short in 1924 hadn't changed. The abbé began to wonder whether communism mightn't be a holy feeling hidden in the heart or a lust that came out only after dark. In his shiny old black cassock the abbé walked slowly down the hot evening street with the children playing in the gutter and the wirelesses blaring full blast and nobody paying any attention to him.

Communism wasn't apparent in Bessier's reception of the abbé either. Bessier lived in a flat in a tumble down house with an advertisement for Byrrh painted on one end of it and an advertisement for Cinzano painted on the other. Bessier was very glad to see the abbé. Bessier hadn't forgotten how the abbé had saved him from getting into trouble with the police two years ago. Madame Bessier was glad to see the abbé, too. She came running across the kitchen drying both her hands on her apron and said that it was very kind of Monsieur l'abbé to have come such a long way to see them. The abbé said that he would willingly have come ten times the distance for the sort of dinner that he hoped Madame Bessier was going to give him. They all laughed loudly at the abbé's joke and Henri, Bessier's fifteen year old son, joined in.

Madame Bessier went back to her stove to finish her cooking and Bessier and the abbé sat down at the kitchen table to drink vermouth and talk about the war. Bessier asked if the abbé remembered the time when they had both been looking over the parapet at night and had imagined that the blades of grass blowing about in the wind were Germans crawling on their bellies towards them. The abbé asked if Bessier remembered the time when the corporal instructing them in arms drill had got the motions wrong himself. Bessier asked if the abbé remembered the time when they had marched for a day and a night in the rain to relieve a battalion in another part of the line and then had discovered that the order had been a mistake and had to march the whole way back again. Those had been the good old days, they said, and they had been very different from the bad new days, they also said. But the abbé knew that they said these things only because the passage of time had blunted the edge of bygone miseries. Most bad new days became good old days when they had retreated sufficiently into the past. Even the night of the long knives might become a good old night once progress got really going.

The dinner was plentiful and excellent. There was soup and there was an omelette. There was fish and there was liver and there was chicken. There was caramel pudding and there was fruit. There was white wine and there was red wine and there was champagne. The abbé knew that Bessier didn't earn much money from his employment with the communist party and that this dinner was Bessier's way of showing his gratitude for what he had done for him in 1934. It was not until the coffee and the liqueurs that the abbé had an opportunity of telling Bessier about his argument with his colleagues earlier in the day.

"You're coming along, aren't you, Jean?" Bessier said when the abbé had finished his tale. "But you've no need to worry. The Republicans will win. The forces of reaction are bound to yield to the forces of progress." Bessier spoke earnestly and in his preaching voice. "It's a law and you can't get away from it."

The abbé began to realize that Bessier had misunderstood him. He had not wished Bessier to imagine that he wished the Republicans to win. He had only wished Bessier to understand that there were priests in the world who would not condone injustices just because they were committed by Christians.

"It all depends on what you mean by progress," the abbé said gently.

"That's easy," Bessier said. "Progress consists in the abolition of superstition and privilege and prejudice and inequality."

"And that's why they dig up the bodies of dead nuns in Barcelona, I suppose?" the abbé asked, not so gently.

"Of course there are excesses," Bessier said.

"Excesses!" the abbé said. "Throughout the whole of Republican Spain the churches are closed. And that when Spain is a very special country, like Ireland and Poland: one of God's fleeces that are always dewy with grace."

"And it's to keep the dew on the fleece that the rebels committed mass murder at Badajoz?" Bessier said. "It's to keep the dew on the fleece that the Reverend Fathers Hitler and Mussolini send guns and airplanes and shock troops?"

"And it's to abolish privilege and prejudice and inequality that Stalin sends his Russians?" the abbé Gaston said.

"Of course, if you're going to believe everything you read in *Gringoire,*" Bessier said.

"Of course, if you're going to believe everything you read in *L' Humanité,*" the abbé Gaston said.

"It's much better to believe what you read in Châteaubriand," Bessier's son said unexpectedly. "Châteaubriand says that Spaniards are Christian Arabs."

They both laughed at that and were friends again.

St. Elizabeth of Hungary was one of the few cats the abbé knew which could meow and purr at the same time, and before he went to bed that night the abbé sat with her on his knee, stroking her and telling her about the international situation. The abbé said that what was wrong with the world was that people were being forced to choose between two fanaticisms, both of which were wrong. The abbé said that the only hope for the world was for people once again to be fanatical about the right things. St. Elizabeth of Hungary rolled over on her side and put her paws over her eyes and meowed and purred.

L

IN 1937 the cardinals and the archbishops and the bishops and the priests prayed for peace. They put on their jeweled vestments and they raised their hands to heaven and they prayed for peace. They asked the Lord to have mercy and Christ to have mercy and the Lord to have mercy. They asked all the holy angels and archangels to pray for them. They asked all the holy orders of blessed spirits to pray for them. They asked all the holy patriarchs and prophets to pray for them. They asked all the holy apostles and evangelists to pray for them. They asked all the holy disciples of the Lord to pray for them. They asked all the holy innocents to pray for them. They asked St. Cosmas and St. Damian to pray for them. They asked all the holy bishops and confessors to pray for them. They asked all the holy doctors to pray for them. They asked all the holy priests and levites to pray for them. They asked all the holy monks and hermits to pray for them. They asked St. Cecily to pray for them. They asked St. Anastasia to pray for them. They asked all the holy virgins and widows to pray for them. They asked all the holy men and women and saints of God to make intercession for them. They asked the Lord to deliver them from anger, hatred and ill-will, from plague, famine and war, by His baptism and holy fasting, by His cross and passion, by His holy resurrection and by His admirable ascension. They asked the Lord to have mercy and Christ to have mercy and the Lord to have mercy.

LI

THE abbé Gaston never found the nuns' confessions very exciting to listen to, because there was nothing of the man-who-broke-the-bank-at-Monte-Carlo about them. But in a sense they were more exciting than the remorse of wives who had been tempted to set fire to their husbands while they slept, because they were all about the slips and the slides and the slithers of holy women who were trying to be good. Exciting or dull, the nuns' confessions took a long time.

Today Sister Marie Thérèse confessed that she had sinned excessively in thought, word and deed. She had been erratic in her recitation of the *Salve Regina* at compline, and once she had even muddled it up with the *Memorare*, which had meant that she had had to start at the beginning again and had finished up much later than the other nuns. She had allowed herself to be irritated by the way Sister Scholastica kept on coughing during the litany of the Blessed Virgin at benediction. She had also taken pleasure in Sister Marie Joseph's discomfiture when Sister Marie had gone to sleep in the organ loft during mass and Sister Anastasie had sent Sister Jeanne Françoise to her to waken her up.

Sister Scholastica, too, had sinned excessively in thought, word and deed. She disliked meat and liked fish so much that she found that days of abstinence were to her occasions of pleasure rather than of mortification. Earnestly desiring to climb up into her salvation and not to toboggan down into it, she wondered whether she ought not to apply for a dispensation to eat fried liver and bacon on Fridays, ember days, vigils and Wednesdays in Lent, and bloaters on feast days. She had allowed herself to be irritated by the noisy way Sister Marie Therese blew her nose during the litany of the Blessed Virgin at benediction. She had not only failed to offer up for the sins of the world the cold draught blowing in under her bedroom door but had even grumbled about it and had been jealous of the other nuns for not having draughts blowing in under their bedroom doors.

Sister Marie Joseph, too, had sinned excessively in thought, word and deed. During mass she had fallen asleep over the organ and she had been so angry with Sister Jeanne Françoise when she had been sent to waken her up that she had sworn at her and said: "When you're my age, you'll fall asleep over organs, too, you worldly young flibbertigibbet." She had also removed the thick mat outside Sister Scholastica's bedroom door and replaced it by the thin mat outside her own. She did not know whether this was really a sin or not, as she was unable to decide whether she had removed the mat more to ensure her own freedom from draught or to provide Sister Scholastica with the additional means of mortification for which she was always clamoring.

It was late when the abbé Gaston left the confessional.

The lines were stretching across from Mademoiselle Buonacompagnia's face now, running out from her eyes, and there was a shine on her nose as well, only she was no longer called Mademoiselle Buonacompagnia or even Madame Henri de la Porte du Bibbier, but Sister Jeanne Françoise, because she had become a nun, praying to God. She stood waiting patiently while the abbé Gaston stood finishing talking to Michelle. Michelle was nearly eight now and she was telling the abbé that she, too, wanted to become a nun when she grew up, only she didn't want to become an ordinary nun, but a driving-underground-trains nun.

"Please, Monsieur l'abbé, there's a man dying in the house opposite and they want you to come at once," Sister Jeanne Françoise said. Although there were no other nuns standing near her, from habit she stood with her huge white bonnet at a tilt, as though it were a halo in which other haloes might become entangled, like shock absorbers on motor cars.

"People really ought to learn to stagger their deaths," the abbé said, rising wearily. He did not like the deathbed repentances of the rich whose last minute contrition was generally inspired only by prudence. But the Lord had made the rules and he as His priest must keep them. *"Volo autem et huic novissimo dare sicut et tibi,"* the Lord had said. If the Lord chose to give to the laborers enrolled at the eleventh hour as to those who had borne the burden of the day and the heats, that was the Lord's business.

The relatives of the dying man did not treat the abbé as though he had come about the Lord's business. The relatives of the dying man treated the abbé as though he were a plumber come to repair a leak in the cistern. They treated him with the contempt with which the stupid rich always treat the learned poor. But the abbé knew that it was for this that the Lord had put the mark upon him.

The dying man's confession was much more exciting than the nuns', although he, too, hadn't broken the bank at Monte Carlo, but only cheated honestly, in business. The dying man hadn't muddled up the *Salve Regina* with the *Memorare*, because he hadn't recited either of them for fifty years, although he had been provided by his parents with a solid religious foundation to blow up. The dying man hadn't made any tepid communions because he hadn't made any at all since his first communion, which he thought had been quite fervent. The dying man had been proud, covetous, lustful, angry, gluttonous, envious and slothful. Apart from that the dying man considered that he had been quite a good Christian because he thought that he hadn't done any harm to anybody except that lately he had been in the habit of leaving the hot water taps in the bathroom running on purpose, because he didn't like his landlord and the charge for hot water was included with the rent. The dying man hoped that he wasn't going to hell because he thought that it must be rather sultry there if all that the clergy said were true.

The abbé Gaston told the dying man gently that it was fortunate for him that the Lord had promised that the last workers in the vineyard should be recompensed as the first. The abbé Gaston told the dying man that this was a very holy mystery indeed and that he himself did not properly understand it. This much, however, he did understand and that was that the reward was the possession of God and that the punishment was the loss of God. The abbé said that it was not the high temperature of hell which hurt most, but the loss of God, which went on forever. Death, the abbé said, was an alchemy, which changed not only bodies into dust but worldly souls into spiritual souls so that they desired what they had formerly despised. Even murderers and crooners would be changed by death, the abbé said, but as long as they repented in time they wouldn't go to hell, but only to purgatory, which was the temporary deprivation of God's presence. The abbé agreed with the dying man's conjecture that purgatory would be probably even more unpleasant than travelling in winter from Marseilles to Paris in a third class carriage with wooden seats and the windows open, but said that the dying man would have the guarantee of seeing God face to face at the end of his sufferings, which was more than could be said for the Gare de Lyon.

It took the abbé a long time to hear the dying man's confession and then he had to go back to the nuns' chapel and bring him holy communion. It was very late indeed when he at last left the dying man's house.

In the underground train the abbé's ticket inspector friend came lurching along between the seats as the carriage swung in and out round the bends between La Muette and the Rue de la Pompe. The ticket inspector smiled as he recognized the abbé.

"Religion still against as many things as ever?" he asked.

The abbé Gaston said that, being himself a very worldly man, he was sorry to say that this was indeed so. "Pity," the ticket inspector said. "Now if religion were like politics. In politics the rules are always changing. Perhaps that's what makes them so exciting. Look at Monsieur Vincent Auriol for example. When he was Finance Minister in 1936 he said that the names of Frenchmen who didn't declare their foreign assets would be posted up on the walls of their houses. Of course most people didn't pay any attention. And now that the franc has been devalued Frenchmen are allowed to bring back their dollars and their pounds and exchange them into francs at a fine profit and nobody says anything to them for having disobeyed Monsieur Vincent Auriol. And the poor devils who were patriotic and obeyed Monsieur Vincent Auriol lose a hundred francs to the pound. Are you sure there isn't a catch in religion, too? The present Pope's against having a good time, I know, but are you sure that the next Pope won't say it's all hunky dory?"

The abbé said that he himself would like very much to have a good time, but that he was afraid that the next Pope would still say that it was a sin.

"Even in sport the rules change," the ticket inspector went on. "What's offside today is onside tomorrow. Referees are always changing the things they're blowing their whistles about. You're quite sure the Pope will be always blowing his whistle about having only one wife?"

"Quite," the abbé said. "When the Pope blows his whistle about marriage he blows it infallibly."

"It's too difficult," the ticket inspector said. "If I were Pope I'd make marriage like kicking the ball into touch. It's much more fun when the rules change. Even in international politics the rules change. Just look at Hitler, for example."

"Just look at him," the abbé Gaston said.

"He doesn't bother about rules or referees," the ticket inspector said. "He's his own referee and he blows the whistle when he wants."

"That's why you've got to have rules," the abbé Gaston said and tried not to speak unctuously.

"You really think he means business?" the ticket inspector said.

"Of course he means business," the abbé Gaston said. "This is only the beginning. It's Austria today. It will be somewhere else tomorrow. In the end it will be the whole world."

"Poor France," the ticket inspector said.

"Poor France has brought many of her troubles on herself, I'm afraid," the abbé Gaston said.

"France isn't harming anybody," the ticket inspector said. "France is only asking to be left in peace."

"Sometimes I think that France is even more stupid about material matters than she is about spiritual matters," the abbé Gaston said. "It's not enough not to harm anybody. If nations want to be left in peace they've got to earn their peace. It's no good having a forty hour week and talking about inaugurating a Ministry of Leisure when your potential enemies are working sixty hours a week making munitions."

Walking slowly up the steps at the Place du Maréchal Haig, the abbé wondered if he had said the right thing to the ticket inspector. Hadn't he seemed more eager to defend the lesser loyalty than the greater loyalty? And wasn't that precisely in what the error of mankind consisted: that men were Frenchmen and Englishmen and Germans and Italians first and Christians afterwards?

Out on the square Frenchmen didn't seem to be worrying much about being Frenchmen first and Christians afterwards. Out on the square Frenchmen didn't seem to be worrying much about being Frenchmen. The cafés and the restaurants were crowded and there was a queue outside the cinema. At the theatre on the other side of the street it was the interval and men and women were standing about the pavement owning the world in evening dress. On the terraces of the cafés Arabs were selling rugs and monkey nuts. The pretty prostitutes walked slowly beneath the trees, their frocks shining with night. Nobody seemed to be worrying about Hitler and Living-space and Guns for Butter and what ten thousand airplanes could do to Paris in an hour. When men failed to react to ever approaching earthly danger it was perhaps not astonishing that they should refuse to be stampeded by the threat of remote apocalyptic commotion.

The colored poster outside the cinema theatre displayed a naked young woman stretched like a peeled banana on a hearthrug in front of a fire. A man in a dinner jacket looked down at her with a lugubrious leer, but the leer hadn't quite come off, because the management of the cinema had foolishly stuck fiscal stamps for two francs forty on the south west corner of the leer. The poster said that the film being shown inside was called *Fifteen Minute Wife* and that it combined mirthprovoking comedy with excitement, voluptuousness and the stark tragedy of a beautiful woman's fate. The audience released from the cinema just as the abbé passed did not appear to have been experiencing mirthprovoking comedy or excitement or voluptuousness or the stark tragedy of any fate other than their own. Dismally they hurried out into the night and dismally the opaque men and women who had been waiting in the queue shuffled forward to the cash desk.

The crowd from the cinema marched in a mass along the boulevard until it reached the corner of the square, where it split up into groups of individuals, disappearing in different directions. But some of the crowd stopped outside the deluxe plumber's window; and the abbé concluded that they must be gazing at the pink and pale green wash-hand basins and baths which they could not afford, because these were the new respectability, as American female film stars were now reported to have bathrooms to match their under-clothes. Most of them, however, were moving on again when the abbé reached the window and saw that it wasn't the deluxe plumber's exhibits at which the crowd had been staring, but at a young girl lying on the pavement. The girl was dressed in a black costume with a red woollen jumper showing above the jacket. Her skirt was drawn up above her knees and her thighs were bare where the top of her silk stockings amputated her legs. The girl wore no hat and a strand of fair hair fell forward over her eyes. She made no movement and appeared to be asleep. The remnants of the crowd from the cinema hurried away from a spectacle which reflected what the world could do to them, too, if they had no money. The abbé Gaston was left alone beside the girl. He bent down and touched her shoulder.

"Mademoiselle," the abbé said softly.

The girl's body moved a little under his touch. Her eyes fluttered open and stared blankly up at the sky. Then they closed again. The abbé bent and touched her again. He felt people standing behind him but he did not look round at them. This time he touched the girl's cheek and he held his hand against her cheek until she opened her eyes again.

"*So müde bin ich,*" the girl said. She did not look at the abbé as she said this but still kept looking up at the sky until she closed her eyes again.

The abbé knew a little German, but he knew much more Spanish, and it was Spanish that came to his tongue.

"*Se ha hecho daño?*" he asked. "You've hurt yourself?" The girl spoke with her eyes still shut.

"*Auch bin ich hunrig,*" the girl said. "*Seit drei Tagen habe ich nicht gegessen.*"

The abbé knew enough German to know what that meant: the girl was hungry and had not eaten for three days. In spite of the fact that he was a priest the abbé experienced the classical resentment of those who have the misery of others thrust inescapably upon them. He was even angry with the girl for making him know her wretchedness and he had to struggle with himself not to accept the sooth with which the worldly hardened their hearts. Charity did not begin at home but where unhappiness first manifested itself, the abbé let himself know. Charity was not handing pain and loneliness over to the police. Charity was emery on one side and cotton wool on the other, and it was to hurt himself for the Lord's sake that he had become a priest.

"*Venga conmigo,*" he said, reaching down with his hands and taking hold of the girl's. "*Kommen Sie mit,*" he corrected into German. "Come with me." The abbé felt a little pleased with his trilinguality.

The girl allowed him to help her to her feet. Her dress fell down about her legs as she rose and she smoothed the rest of it down with her hands. She swayed a little as she stood upright and had to clutch on to the abbé's arm. There were more people standing round them now but the abbé tried not to look at them. With the girl's arm in his he walked with her a little into the square. He knew that people were still staring after them and he walked on with the girl until they stood together in the darkness under the trees. The girl let go his arm when they stopped walking. The abbé saw a glimmer of distrust in her eyes as she looked at his cassock. The girl swayed slightly on her feet and the abbé caught hold of her again.

"You do not seem to be very strong," he said in careful German. "You must be careful."

"I speak a little French," the girl said. "In fact I think that I speak French better than you speak German."

"That wouldn't be difficult," the abbé Gaston said. "I speak German like a Spanish cow." He laughed a little at his own joke but the girl did not laugh with him.

"I do not think that I like priests very much," the girl said.

"I am not asking you to like me," the abbé Gaston said. "I'm asking you to come and have something to eat."

There was not much light where they stood, but occasionally a shimmer of light fell on the girl's hair from the passing buses. The girl's hair shone when the buses passed and it was very soft and gold. But her face the abbé could not see very clearly although even when there were no buses passing the abbé knew that it was sad. The abbé saw only her hair when the buses passed and in the new deep blackness that the buses left behind them her body and her hair both vanished and her face was a wispy disc of moon hung between the trees.

"I do not think that you understand," the girl said. "I am a Jewess. I am an Austrian Jewess and often I think that I am a communist as well."

"You're cold and you're hungry and you're in distress," the abbé Gaston said. "All I want to do is to help you."

"Men always want things from girls they help," the girl said. "When they are ordinary men they want their bodies and when they are priests they want their souls." Her voice was cold and hard as she spoke her cynicism but her hair was warm and glowing again as the light from another bus fell on it. Then suddenly she began to weep and her voice was warm, too, as she told him what had happened to her. "They made me wash the pavements in the Kärtnerstrasse in Vienna," she gulped. "They poured acid over my hands. They took my body with my dress on. They tore my blouse and slobbered over my breasts." The tears streamed down her long cheeks.

She wept so much that her body became limp and she leaned heavily on the abbé as he helped her across the square. People stared at them as they passed, but the abbé was too busy thinking about the world being a bad detective novel to notice them staring. Up to now he had known about the cruelties inflicted on the Jews only from the newspapers, but now he knew it from the sobbing girl clinging on to his arm as well. It was like coming out of the seminary all over again. In the seminary he had learned about sin at a remove. He had learned about the permutations and combinations of perfidy as he had learned about the exports and imports of Australia. It had been a shock to discover that the misdemeanors so politely plotted by the professors in graphs smelled so badly when their gases came filtering in through the grille of his confessional. It was a new shock to find out that the cruel and the cold thing was very real, too.

There was no light coming from behind Madame Boulon's glass door when the abbé helped the girl into the house. The abbé hoped that this meant that Madame Boulon was asleep because he realized that he would have to make unauthorized use of the lift if he were to get the girl upstairs easily. "Gaston," he said not too quietly and not too loudly in the darkness, so that Madame Boulon would hear if she were awake and not waken if she were asleep. There was no answer and when he listened carefully the abbé thought that he could hear the sound of snoring.

Tonight the lift was on the ground floor. The doors made a noise as the abbé helped the girl to get in, but they did not make as much noise as on the night when he had hidden Bessier from the police. The lift made a moan, too, as it started out on its upward journey, but it did not make too loud a moan.

The girl shook her head and blinked when they stood at last in the strong white light of the abbé's little room. Her face was long and sad. The abbé could not make up his mind whether she was beautiful or not because her hair drooped over her eyes. Her hair was gold in the light but it did not seem so soft as when the glow from the buses had fallen upon it. The abbé helped her across to the bed on which St. Elizabeth of Hungary lay curled up asleep. The girl smiled a little as she sat down and began to stroke the cat.

"I like cats," she said in her precise French. "We used to have two cats at home. They were both very affectionate cats."

"St. Elizabeth of Hungary is a very affectionate cat," the abbé Gaston said. "Sometimes I like to think that she is an intelligent cat as well." He lighted the gas ring as he spoke and began to busy himself with the pots and pans.

"Our cats were both affectionate, too, but I do not think that they were very intelligent," the girl said. "One cat we had had since it was a kitten and the other cat was a lost cat which sought shelter with us. That's right; stare at me," she said in a sudden burst of temper. "I know that I have not a very beautiful face but my body is well made and it is for their bodies that men chiefly like girls." She pulled off her jacket as she spoke and threw back her shoulders so that the little balls of her breasts were rounded against her jumper. "Or did not they teach you such things in your seminary?"

"I apologize, Mademoiselle, if I have been looking at you in such a way as to make you feel uncomfortable," the abbé Gaston said.

"Oh, it is natural enough, I suppose," she said. "We talk about cats but while we are talking about them perhaps we are thinking silent and unkind things about each other." Her harshness vanished as suddenly as it had appeared and her face became long and gentle and sad again and she came and stood beside him as he cooked. "I beg your pardon for having spoken to you like that," she said. "I think that I am a little unhappy. You are kind to me and I am sorry." She smiled briefly up at him. Her smile trembled across the sadness of her face. Then she grew grave again and went back and sat down on the bed.

Simulating preoccupation with his task, the abbé watched the girl discreetly. A psychologist had once told the abbé that, viewed separately, the right and the left eyes gave two different aspects of the character of the person observed: the right eye showed the simulation held up to the world, and the left eye the loneliness before God the Father. It was the left eye which the girl exposed to the abbé as she sat on the bed, and in it the abbé thought that he could discern a frightened humility and tenderness sometimes absent from her speech. Her weeping had washed much of the lipstick from her mouth so that, in spite of the conventional provocation of her dress, her young person seemed at the mercy of men rather than imposing itself upon them. When he was young the abbé had sometimes felt drawn towards young women's bodies and he had had to pray a lot to cool himself. But now that he was getting old young bodies seemed to the abbé sad things rather than gay things, because experience had taught him that how surely they, too, would become old bodies, sinking into repose as God traced His summons upon them. Slowly the lust of the flesh became the want of the spirit. It wasn't only upon walls in Babylon that God's finger wrote. Watching the girl as she stroked the cat, the abbé thought that he could see the beginnings of that writing in the sadness of her face.

"Soup and liver and coffee," he said when he had finished.

The girl nodded. There was no smile on her face. It was almost as though she wasn't grateful. The abbé felt irritated as he watched her walk slowly over to the window and back again.

"I feel that it is my duty to be honest with you," the girl said. "I am not only a Jewess and do not believe in your things. I think that the things you believe in are false things and stupid things. I think that the world needs to believe in new things."

"Have it your own way," the abbé Gaston said patiently, carrying a plateful of soup across to the table. "In the meantime you'd better eat."

She sat down at the table. For a little she sat staring at her soup in silence and her hair fell over both her eyes, like a curtain. Then she pushed her hair back from her eyes and began to sup her soup slowly, but each time she bent her head down towards the plate her hair fell down over her face again. The abbé gave her bread and she began to eat ravenously. It was clear that she was very hungry. When he had handed her the liver the abbé sat down on the bed and began to read his office so that he should not appear to be watching her.

"God must be very greedy to require so much praise," the girl said as she began to drink her coffee.

"Perhaps it's rather that we require to praise God," the abbé Gaston said gently.

"It all seems so unnecessary," the girl said.

"Anyway it's the rule, although why it is the rule I do not know that I am clever enough to explain," the abbé Gaston said.

"Perhaps you'd better start to convert me," the girl said when she had finished drinking her coffee.

"Instead I'm going to leave you to sleep," the abbé said. "You'll find a clean pair of pyjamas in that drawer." He began to button himself into his overcoat cassock, with the miniature war ribbons sewn on to the lapel. "I apologize for not being able to provide you with clean sheets but my only other pair is at the laundry. And don't worry about breakfast. I'll be back in the morning in time to cook it for you."

The hard look vanished from the girl's face and the mocking look vanished, too. Instead a softness came upon her and she smiled again, and this time the smile remained a little longer than it had before.

"I think that you are very kind, but I cannot take your bed like this," she said. Her face was sad again as she spoke, but the gentleness was still there.

"The bed is narrow and I hate the thought of sleeping on a chair," the abbé said.

"But where will you sleep?" the girl asked.

"Don't you worry about me," the abbé said. "I'll be all right in the church. Besides, it won't be the first time that somebody's slept there," he added, trying to humor her out of her seriousness with a bad joke.

She did not laugh. She came and stood in front of him with her long sad face almost on a level with his. The abbé tried to see her left eye as unhappier than her right eye, but he could not see her right eye clearly, because of her droop of hair.

"I think that you are a good priest and I am sorry if I have said unkind things to you," she said. "My name is Rachel Wolf, but I should like it if you would call me Rachel."

"My name is Gaston," the abbé said. He pulled back her hair from her right eye so that he could see into it more clearly, but her right eye was round and unblinking and unhappy, too. "Please smile again," he said. "Things will be all right in the morning. You'll see."

The abbé let himself into the church with his private key. The church was in darkness except for the red lamp glowing in front of the tabernacle and for the watery light of the street lamps quivering in through the stained glass windows. The church was still with the silence of God's Hand held out. The sanctuary lay steeped in the shadows of old prayers. *"Sic non potuistis una hora vigilare mecum?"* the Lord had said to Peter. The abbé decided that he would watch with the Lord, not for an hour, but for the whole night, as men had done in the Middle Ages.

To the abbé the middle ages never seemed very far away when he thought about them in the presence of the Blessed Sacrament. The abbé liked thinking about the Middle Ages, because they couldn't hurt anymore. Time, the abbé thought, hurt less and less as it seeped into eternity. Perhaps eternity wasn't like the underground railway in London after all; perhaps eternity was rather like a bath sponge, sucking Napoleon in alongside of St. Thomas of Aquinas, although the abbé didn't suppose that they would have much to say to each other. The abbé watched for an hour and seven teen minutes with the Lord before he fell asleep. In the silence of the dark church the Lord watched on alone.

The abbé was ashamed of himself next morning when the early sunlight splashing into the church awoke him, but he hoped that the Lord would forgive him because of all the confessions he had had to hear the night before. In any case he hadn't time to be ashamed of himself for long, because he was down on the roster to say the first mass at six o'clock. He washed himself at the small tap in the sacristy and vested jubilantly, crossing the stole on his breast right side over left, because that was the way the bishop had crossed it, when he had changed him from a deacon into a priest. The abbé always liked saying mass in the early morning, when the world was new and shining and men hadn't had time to make it dirty again. He was already fully vested when the still sleepy server arrived to light the candles on the altar.

Although it was a week day the church was crowded because it was the first Friday of the month and the Lord had promised St. Margaret Mary Alacoque that anyone who went to communion nine first Fridays of the month running would be granted the grace of final perseverance. When the time came for the people's communion the abbé had to pass along the altar rails nineteen times. As he watched the sober demeanor of those who knelt there the abbé wondered if they were the same people who pushed and shoved and struggled in order to get on buses and underground trains. The future of civilization seemed to depend on the answer. His limp had seemed to be getting less lately and it no longer bothered the abbé at all to have to say the prayers after mass at the foot of the altar steps and to go up the steps again afterwards to fetch the chalice and paten afterwards, out of politeness to God.

The morning was still bright and new when the abbé Gaston came out of church, and the abbé held up the spade of his beard to it and was glad. As he walked along the pavement he met the Chanoine Litry coming towards him and prepared to pass him with a formal bow. To his surprise, however, the rector returned his greeting with a broad smile and indicated that he wished to speak to the abbé.

"A fortunate encounter, Monsieur l'abbé Gaston," the rector said. "I have been wanting to speak to you in private for some time now, but somehow the opportunity has never seemed to occur."

The abbé Gaston began to feel uneasy. Sometimes the rector was more dangerous when he smiled than when he frowned. The abbé began to examine his conscience. He did not think that he had been preaching from any of the rector's favorite texts or using the wrong matter at baptism. The latter was what the most recent row had been about, when an enquiry had been made as to why babies had been liking baptism so much and it had been discovered that the abbé Ronsard had been putting sugar instead of salt on their tongues.

"We have been drifting apart, you and I," the rector went on. "Perhaps originally it was a little your fault, but latterly I have felt that it has been more mine."

"That's all right, Monsieur le Curé," the abbé Gaston said. "I realize quite that I have a turbulent nature."

"That is just the point," the rector said. "Of late your nature has been far from turbulent. Of course we've had our little differences of opinion about the Spanish Civil War, but others would appear to uphold your point of view. And you've been polite and pleasant in your bearing towards Monsieur l'abbé Moune. In short, you've become quite a reformed character, Monsieur l'abbé Gaston."

"Perhaps I shouldn't go so far as to say that, Monsieur le Curé," the abbé Gaston said, thinking of Rachel sleeping in his bed in his pyjamas and wondering if the rector would speak to him quite so affably if he were aware of the fact.

"And I want to do more than say so," the rector said. "I want to reward you tangibly. In fact, I am considering the possibility of asking you to come and live with us in the presbytery. I should have to ask permission, of course, as you were not ordained for this archdiocese. Tell me, how does the proposal strike you?"

The abbé Gaston thought two different sets of things about the proposal: an unpleasant set and a pleasant set. In the unpleasant set were the realizations that he would have to listen every day to the rector's conversation at table, that he would be in constant association with the abbé Moune and that he would probably have to get rid of St. Elizabeth of Hungary as the rector did not like cats; in the pleasant set were the realizations that he would no longer require to spend his private income of three thousand francs a year on food and rent and that he would enjoy greater prestige in the parish. On the whole, the pleasant set of realizations seemed to outweigh the unpleasant set.

"You do me a great honor, Monsieur le Curé," the abbé Gaston said. "Of course I shall be very pleased to accept."

"Then it's settled," the rector said. "The formalities will take a little time, of course, but I have no doubt at all as to the outcome."

The abbé Gaston continued joyfully on his way across the square. With three thousand francs a year to spend on what he liked he would be rich. Such an income was just the right size: not too big to prevent him from getting into heaven and not too small to prevent him from buying a new cassock when he required one. He would be able to go away to the seaside for a holiday and say his office on the sands. He wouldn't of course be able to stay at the best hotels with the best faced people, but he would be able to afford a boarding house without bugs in the beds. He would be able to contribute towards Michelle's keep at the convent and to buy her a pretty dress for her first communion. The abbé was still busy with his calculations when the sight of Madame Boulon standing in her doorway reminded him again of Rachel. The possible misinterpretations of his sheltering the girl suddenly struck him. Madame Boulon had only to see Rachel leaving the house in his company to put her own construction upon the motives for his kindness and to tell every one in the district her own version of what she was bound to regard as a scandal. The story would reach the rector's ears and in the end it would reach the Cardinal's and then there would be no going to live in the presbytery. The possibility that Madame Boulon would not see them leaving the house together was not to be relied upon, as the caretaker rarely failed to look over her curtain when she heard footsteps in the passage outside. He could of course ask the girl to leave the house alone, but even then Madame Boulon would be almost certain to see her and ask her what flat she had been visiting. The only thing to do was to tell Madame Boulon the truth now and to hope that she would believe him.

"Good morning, Madame Boulon," the abbé greeted. "I've something to tell you. There's a young girl been sleeping in my room. I invited her to spend the night."

Madame Boulon's rheumy eyes glittered. "One lives and one learns," she said.

"That's just where you're wrong," the abbé said sharply. "Most people live and they don't learn. I found this girl fainting on the pavement. She's an Austrian Jewess and she's been driven out of Vienna by Hitler."

"The things that man gets up to," Madame Boulon said. It was impossible for the abbé to tell from her expression whether she believed him or not. "He'll be putting the gondoliers in a constipation camp next."

"Vienna, not Venice," the abbé Gaston corrected, without smiling. "I myself slept in the church. I'm telling you this because I don't want there to be any misunderstanding."

"All those miseries," Madame Boulon said. "Of course, Monsieur l'abbé, I understand perfectly."

The abbé hoped that Madame Boulon did understand perfectly. He wondered if she would understand more perfectly if he were to give her twenty francs. The centrally heated lady of easy virtue had given Madame Boulon fifty francs to understand perfectly when neighbors had complained to the police that the centrally heated lady of easy virtue had omitted to draw her curtains before giving a naked champagne party in honor of her gentleman friend's brother-inlaw.

"After all, sleeping in a church can't be anymore uncomfortable than sleeping in a train and churches don't move on wheels," Madame Boulon went on.

"The late Monsieur Boulon was great at sleeping in trains. I remember in 1904 he slept all the way from Paris to Bordeaux and in 1905 he kicked the bucket." The abbé Gaston had heard before about the late Monsieur Boulon who, to judge from the photograph standing beside the butter dish on Madame Boulon's mantelpiece, had been a cod-eyed man with a thick moustache curved like a scenic railway. According to Madame Boulon, the late Monsieur Boulon, although believing that the whale which had swallowed Jonah had really been a submarine invented by the admittedly precocious Egyptians, had kicked the bucket fortified by the rites of Holy Mother Church. Apparently, too, the late Monsieur Boulon had been great at other things besides sleeping in trains. The late Monsieur Boulon had been great at science, geography, military strategy and politics. Indeed so great at military strategy and politics had the late Monsieur Boulon been that, if he hadn't konked out so piously in 1905, there would have been no need for Foch and Poincare at all; instead there would have been Marshal Boulon and President Boulon, for the late Monsieur Boulon could easily have done both jobs at once. "But you're not going to sleep in the church every night, are you?" Madame Boulon asked. "This girl can't go on living in your room forever."

The abbé Gaston was surprised how readily he agreed with Madame Boulon.

"No, she'll have to find work of some sort," he said.

This thought was uppermost in the abbé's mind as he climbed the six long flights of stairs to his room. In spite of the compulsions of charity he couldn't risk compromising the easier future which had so unexpectedly been opened to him. He was thinking so hard about this that he forgot to knock at his door before he opened it with his key. But the girl was already dressed and was standing brushing her hair in front of the small rectangular mirror. And the bed had been made.

"I hope that you do not mind me using your brush," the girl said, without turning round and talking her stilted French to the abbé's reflection in the mirror. Her face bobbed up and down in the mirror as she moved her head against the movement of the brush. Academically, the abbé supposed that she was beautiful, but as on the previous evening he saw her beauty as pathetic. Watching her, the abbé wondered what St. Anthony had made all the fuss about and decided that the female body must be more attractive when served up hot in a desert.

The girl went on brushing her yellow hair until it became soft and shining and golden in the sun. When at last she turned from the mirror she was smiling and the length as well as the sadness seemed to have gone from her face. Even her left eye, over which her hair did not droop, was unperturbed and gay.

"Last night it was you who did the cooking; this morning it shall be I," she said. "Please to sit there on the bed. I am very clever at making coffee."

She moved quickly about the room, her slit black skirt opening and shutting over her glossy silk legs. The abbé wondered if her hair were dyed. Women's hair these days, he thought, was like an act of contrition: it was impossible to tell if it was sincere or not. The abbé, however, had his own method of testing the sincerity of a woman's hair: when a woman's hair looked as though it would make a tinny noise if it fell off her scalp on to the floor the abbé judged that it was insincere hair, and when it looked as though it would make no noise at all the abbé judged that it was sincere hair. Blondes, he knew, were especially to be suspected because, as he understood from his cosmopolitan penitents, both gentlemen and those who weren't gentlemen preferred them. Rachel's hair, he decided, looked sincere enough. He didn't think that it would make any noise even if it fell off into a marble holy water stoup.

"You have been very kind to me," she suddenly said. "Please to believe that I am very grateful. When I have eaten my breakfast I shall go away and I shall not trouble you again."

The abbé often wished that the Lord had made Christianity a little easier or at least allowed a handicap to bad players. The abbé felt that he would have made a fine Christian if he could have had one afternoon off a week on which to go round stuffing himself with chocolate eclairs and being rude to people he didn't like. In the parable of the good Samaritan the Lord had defined the indefinite neighbor whom men should love as themselves. *"Vade, et tu fac similiter,"* the Lord had said. The abbé felt that he ought to be let off a little of the parable of the good Samaritan, too.

"You must continue to stay here until you have found employment," he said, trying not to think of the promise which the rector had made him that morning.

"You cannot sleep in the church every night," she said. She put the coffee and the bread on the table and they sat down together. "And I do not think that it will be easy for me to find work in France. For one thing I understand that there are regulations against foreigners working in France. And for another thing French girls are rather good at my profession. Oh, my profession is not at all what I see that you are thinking," she said with a smile which stretched her lips but did not light her eyes. She rose from the table and swayed slowly across the room with one hand on her hip and the fingers of the other dangling in the air. "My profession is to persuade ugly women that they can look as attractive in pretty dresses as I do."

The abbé Gaston was startled. He looked at her in amazement.

"Don't tell me that you're a mannequin," he said.

"Do I not look like a mannequin?" she asked, coming close to him. She brought her face down to his and threw her hair back from her forehead and made her eyelashes stand up like two little rows of black pins. Then she fluttered her eyelashes at him. "Do I not make you feel irresolute when I do that?" Her body was hard and thin as she walked away from him again and seemed to the abbé, like modern railway engines and motor cars, to be shaped more for travelling through the air at a high speed than for responding to emotion. But before he had finished thinking about this she was sitting down at the table with him again, talking to him across her coffee cup. "I was not always a mannequin," she said. "Once I was a student. But one requires money to be a student. When my parents died I could not go on being a student. I became a mannequin. I think that I was a very successful mannequin. But when Hitler came to Vienna the Christian mannequins would not allow me to work anymore because I was a Jewess. And my Christian landlady turned me out of my lodgings because I was a Jewess. In Vienna nobody would shelter me and nobody would help me to leave. I had to spend all my money and cheat a little the railway company in order to come here. Perhaps now you will understand why I find myself unable to believe your things. Perhaps now you understand why I think that I am a little a communist. That is why I think that a new truth must come upon the world. Men will be kind to one another only when they are forced to be kind to one another."

At the seminary the abbé's professors had spent hours teaching him how to confound heretics. When a professor had pretended to believe that man could be saved by faith alone or that the good works of all unbelievers were sins, the abbé had known exactly how to refute his arguments. He had been able to defend the decisions of the Councils of Constantinople, Ephesus and Chalcedon and to prove by syllogism the truth of the Christian religion. But once he had left the seminary this ability had deserted him. Perhaps it was because the heretics always seemed so very much more fluent than he was, or perhaps it was because they no longer believed the right wrong things about religion. The abbé had been unable to convert either Bessier or the ticket inspector. There was a new hard cold thing about the world, compared with which the abbé thought that the errors of Calvin were a bull's eye in dogmatic theology. He began to dislike the girl in front of him for having said the new hard cold thing again because he didn't quite know how to prove that she was wrong. He began to dislike her for being a Jewess. Then he looked into her left eye again and saw it sad and knew at once what it was that the Lord would have him do.

"If you are a good mannequin, I think that perhaps I can help you," he said.

Remembering his promise to the Cardinal not to do anything theatrical and still wanting to go and live with the other priests in the presbytery, the abbé prayed that the Lord would keep the coast clear when he went downstairs with Rachel. But the Lord didn't keep the coast clear. The Lord crowded the coast with centrally heated lady of easy virtue coming out of her flat on the fifth floor with her shopping bag in her hand. And this morning the centrally heated lady of easy virtue was both observant and talkative.

"Good morning, Monsieur l'abbé," she greeted. "I did not know that you had such pretty parishioners."

"Mademoiselle is not one of my parishioners," the abbé answered coldly. "Mademoiselle is a Jewish refugee from Vienna. I am going to try to find her work."

The centrally heated lady of easy virtue's eyes gleamed as she shook her head lugubriously. The centrally heated lady of easy virtue said that she had heard some very terrible things about what Hitler had been doing lately. She said that she had heard that he had ordered his scientists to invent a bomb which as soon as it exploded would freeze thousands of Frenchmen to death in big blocks of ice which would never melt until another scientist came along and invented a bomb to heat them to death as well. She said that Monsieur l'abbé's kindness to a pretty girl in distress relieved her depression at Hitler's wickedness about the block of ice. Funnily enough her gentleman friend was always being kind to pretty girls in distress, too, and the prettier they were the kinder her gentleman friend was towards them. The centrally heated lady of easy virtue said that Monsieur l'abbé and her gentleman friend really must meet one of these days and have a nice long conversation about pretty girls in distress.

They met the centrally heated lady of easy virtue again at the bottom of the staircase, talking excitedly to Madame Boulon, who was talking excitedly back. Both the centrally heated lady of easy virtue and Madame Boulon stopped talking as the abbé and Rachel passed. The abbé could feel them staring at his back as he walked up the side of the square with the girl.

"I feel that I am causing you some embarrassment," Rachel said.

"That's all right," the abbé said, although he didn't feel that it was all right at all.

"You may call me 'Rachel', if you want to," the girl said. She did not turn to look at the abbé as she said this, but walked on with her long sad face held straight in front of her.

In Madame Bisberot's window the same wax mannequins stood, launching invisible battleships and chilling the lust of hidden potentates. But their hair was no longer swept in ordered disorder over their brows; instead it was long at the back and curled round up into the neck again. And the abbé saw that their expressions were no longer arrogantly imbecilic but menacingly idiotic. He had not time, however, to consider the implications of this change because Madame Bisberot came forward to greet them as soon as they entered the shop. The abbé was nervous about what he had to say to Madame Bisberot.

"Mademoiselle is a Jewish refugee from Vienna," he began. "She has been chased out of her country by Hitler."

Like the centrally heated lady of easy virtue Madame Bisberot shook her head lugubriously, but there was no gleam in her eye. Madame Bisberot said that she had heard that Hitler was so wicked that he had invented a bomb which would kill everybody in Paris twenty four hours after it had been dropped. She said that this bomb was so special that it would explode so silently that even the Secret Service wouldn't hear it. The dangerous part of the bomb was that it was filled with a chemical which would make people sneeze until they died. Madame Bisberot said that she had obtained this information from a doctor friend of hers.

"Perhaps things will not be as bad as we imagine," the abbé Gaston said. "In the meantime I am trying to find employment for this girl. You see, she is a mannequin."

Madame Bisberot regretted. She would have liked to have been able to oblige Monsieur l'abbé, but even to please him she could not increase her staff at the present time. Her bank overdraft was still a very poor bank overdraft, and it looked as though it would become an even poorer bank overdraft. Women weren't buying new dresses anymore, perhaps because they, too, had poor bank overdrafts, perhaps because they were afraid of the sneezing bomb, when it would do just as well to sneeze off an old dress as a new one. Madame Bisberot regretted. Madame Bisberot regretted infinitely.

The Lord, the abbé knew, spoke to people out of all sorts of queer places. The Lord had spoken to Moses out of a burning bush. The Lord spoke to the abbé now out of a frigid forest of wax mannequins.

"I see that fashions in hair and expression have changed again," the abbé said quietly. "I hope that my invention has come in useful. I hope that both you and other dressmakers have been able to make use of it." The abbé did not look at Madame Bisberot's face as he said this, because he did not wish to see her blush. "I'll tell you what," he went on, still not looking at Madame Bisberot's face. "I'll waive my right to the royalties on the submannequin if you'll give this girl employment. She'll make a very good mannequin, too," he added. "She's got a good figure. She goes in and out at the proper places." The abbé himself blushed a little when he realized what he had said.

But Madame Bisberot did not blush. Madame Bisberot laughed. As soon as she had finished one fit of laughter she started off on another.

It was some little time before she could speak. What Monsieur l'abbé had just said was French, she said. It was so French that it wasn't Italian or Spanish or German. Monsieur l'abbé could have no idea how much good it did her to laugh like that. When she laughed like that it took her mind off the sneezing bomb. When she had finished laughing Madame Bisberot was still laughing, but she managed to say that of course she would employ Mademoiselle as a mannequin. And what was more Mademoiselle could live with her in the flat above the shop if she wanted to, because what she really wanted was a mannequin who would help her with the housework. She thought that she would be able to arrange about the work permit all right and Mademoiselle could start in right away if she wanted to. Only Monsieur l'abbé must not think that it was because of the royalties that were due to him that she had engaged Mademoiselle; it was because he had made her laugh so much.

When the abbé walked out into the street again he looked to right and to left to assure himself that neither the rector nor the abbé Moune was in sight. If neither the centrally heated lady of easy virtue nor Madame Boulon talked too much perhaps the Lord was going to let him off easily with the parable of the good Samaritan after all.

LII

THE Cardinal did not know Arthur as well as he had known Francis, because he had never eaten fish with him in Ventimiglia, and so he did not know quite what to talk to him about as they drove together in a taxi from the Piazza dell' Esedra to the Vatican. The throne of Peter was again vacant and a successor to Pius the Eleventh had to be chosen.

Arthur said that they must remember that the Holy Ghost was upon them in a very special manner, helping them to direct the Church until the new Pope should have been elected. Arthur said that he had studied the prophecies of Malachy and that if they were true it didn't seem that there were many Popes left to rule before Christ should come again in glory. Alphonse said that it wasn't only Malachy's prophecies that were being fulfilled but God's. Nation was rising against nation and there were at least three possible antiChrists to choose from. Alphonse also wondered what airplanes would do on the last day when the Lord came in a cloud with great power and majesty, but Arthur said that he thought that the Lord would be able to look after the airplanes all right, because He was Almighty.

LIII

AS he walked along the street the abbé Gaston often felt that he was made of glass and that people could see his failure to be really holy showing through. He felt so more than ever today as he skirted round the back of the church to take the catechism class. Ordinarily the abbé would have walked round the front of the church, because that was the shorter way. But he was afraid of meeting the rector and his curates walking in the square in case he should also meet Rachel walking with the girls from Madame Bisberot's and be forced to recognize her in the presence of his colleagues. For more than a week now the abbé had avoided walking with the clergy on the square. The abbé was still hoping that nothing was going to happen to stop his going to live in the presbytery.

In front of the high altar the usual scrabble of children were fidgeting, whispering and yawning. The abbé knelt and prayed that what he was going to say to the children might remain in their hearts. The abbé had taught the catechism to so many children now and he did not think that very much of it had remained in their hearts. The abbé prayed very hard for the children.

The abbé tried to tell the children about sanctifying grace. Sanctifying grace was the most beautiful thing in the whole world, the abbé said. Sanctifying grace was more beautiful than the sun shining on the sea in summer or the patterns that the moon made at the foot of tall trees at night, the abbé said. It was a shimmering ladder let down from heaven to earth, the abbé said. When he had finished teaching the children the abbé went into his confessional, because the eve of the first Friday of the month had come round again.

In spite of more than thirty years' experience the abbé Gaston never quite knew how to treat the serious sinners who came to confess their faults. The abbé was always afraid that if he upbraided them too severely he might discourage them from perseverance, and he was also afraid that if he were too lenient with them he might appear to condone their trespasses. He preferred, however, to be mild rather than recriminatory, because he thought that this was the way the Lord liked best.

So this afternoon the abbé was kind to his penitents, exhorting them rather than reproving them. In any case there was not much need for him to be severe, because the slicers of throats and the tumblers of virgins rarely attempted to perform the nine first Fridays of the month. This charity persisted even when he slid back the grille to release a smell of alcohol, perfume, turpentine and fountain pen ink, which the abbé knew from previous experience to be the smell of the poetess. As he murmured the ritual blessing the abbé could see that he no longer had to deal with a blonde poetess, but with a russet poetess whose hair looked insincere enough to make a noise like a ship's anchor if it slid off her scalp into a marble holy water stoup. The poetess said that she had been making spiritual progress, because this time she had sinned in the bar of the Ritz Hotel instead of in the bar of the George V Hotel. The abbé was gentle with the poetess, too.

When he came out of the church the abbé was feeling pleased with himself and he hoped that the Lord was feeling pleased with him, too. But his sense of righteousness vanished when he saw Rachel coming slowly towards him along the pavement. The girl was carrying a long cardboard box under her arm. She had about her the look of loneliness and unprotectedness which the abbé had remarked before upon his familiars when he had observed them walking alone in crowded streets. Even the abbé Moune, the abbé thought, looked helpless before God when he walked unaccompanied upon the pavement. A smile lighted the girl's face as she caught sight of him and made him ashamed of having tried to avoid her.

"Rachel," he said as he advanced to greet her.

"Monsieur l'abbé," she said. "You see that I have learned the polite way to address you."

"Never mind about politeness," the abbé Gaston said. "How are you getting on? That's what I want to know."

"Madame Bisberot is very kind," the girl said. "I help her in the house. I walk in elegant dresses for ladies to look at me. I carry parcels for Madame Bisberot, too. She has given me a new dress and a new hat. Do you like them?"

The abbé did not think that he understood much about women's hats. As soon as he was beginning to get used to one shape of shapelessness the fashion changed and he had to begin getting used to a new shape of shapelessness. The abbé didn't think that he liked hats that looked as though they were meant to be eaten. He thought that he preferred hats that looked as though they were meant to be hats, and the women's hats that he liked best were broad hats like his mother had worn when he was a little boy. Rachel's hat was not a broad hat. It was neither a narrow hat nor a broad hat nor a high hat nor a low hat. Indeed to the abbé it did not look like a hat at all. Instead it looked more like a seagull's wing stuck in a dish of pêche melba and the abbé did not think that he liked it very much. But he was surprised to discover that he liked her dress. Her dress was of dark blue velvet and had a small lace collar.

"I like the dress," he said.

"I am glad that you like my dress," she said. "I think that it is very pretty, too."

Her simple copy book sentences began to disturb the abbé. He still could not see into her right eye because of her hair falling over it, but beneath the strange geometry of her hat her left eye was brooding and solemn.

"You are lonely," the abbé said. "You must not be lonely. You must try to make new friends. You must try to forget all the terrible things that have happened to you."

"You are kind," she said. "It is ungrateful of me to be sad when I talk to you; but soon perhaps I shall forget."

Every night before he went to bed the abbé prayed for the lonely, for the bereaved, for those who were in agony, for those who were being tortured and for those who were being killed by violence. But because he could not see the sufferers for whom he prayed he found it hard to feel their pain as his own as he was sure that God wished him to feel it. Even seeing Rachel's loneliness he could not swallow it down within himself and be miserable about it as though he were lonely, too. He was so close to her that he could see the little prickles of sweat where her nose had been badly powdered. He liked her all the more for this imperfection but he could not get the hurt from her heart into his heart where he knew it ought to be.

"Time heals everything," the abbé said. He knew that this was a stupid thing to say and a lie, too, because these days time brought new hurts rather than healed old hurts. The abbé knew that he ought to have said that it was God Who healed everything, but he didn't know the right old words with which to confound the wrong new words. He knew that modern men and women were destroying civilization by saying foolish things wisely, but he didn't know how to tell them that they were doing so, because he himself could say wise things only foolishly. He wanted to tell Rachel as she stood before him in her absurd hat and blue velvet dress that she, like everybody else, was unhappy because she had got the meaning of the world wrong. All over the world the holy lamps seemed to be going out, but the abbé knew that they wouldn't all go out, because the Lord had promised that they wouldn't. The abbé wanted to tell Rachel this, too, but once again he couldn't find the words. "That really is a very pretty dress," he said again.

Neither the abbé Moune's right eye nor his left eye was looking lonely as he came strutting up to them. Ordinarily sunk deep in their sockets, his little green eyes were incandescent with curiosity. His red hair was brash above his ears and he showed all his teeth in an arrogant grin.

"A new parishioner, I see?" the abbé Moune said, looking closely at the girl.

"Not exactly," the abbé Gaston said, knowing that it was wrong of him to be afraid of the abbé Moune just because the abbé Moune wanted religion to be like travelling in a first class railway carriage, and the Lord wanted it to be like riding a bicycle on a tight rope. "The difficult feat of equilibrium known as corresponding with sanctifying grace," he had recently preached in a sermon to the nuns. The abbé Gaston didn't think that the abbé Moune would understand that as well as the nuns had done, because for the abbé Moune correspondence with grace was a respectability, like not walking about the streets with your shirt tail sticking out of your trousers.

But the girl was more direct.

"No, I am not a new parishioner," she said coldly and turned to shake hands with the abbé Gaston. "It has been pleasant to have met you," she said. "I hope that we shall meet again soon. I thank you for all your kindness to me. I am glad that you like my new dress."

"What a quaint way of talking," the abbé Moune said, watching the girl as she walked slowly across the square.

"She is a foreigner," the abbé Gaston said.

"And another mannequin, too, eh?" the abbé Moune said as Rachel entered Madame Bisberot's shop. "I thought you'd given up that sort of thing."

"That girl's an Austrian refugee," the abbé Gaston said, trying to speak without emotion. "She's a Jewess and she had to leave Vienna because of the Nazis. She is a mannequin by profession. I found her when she was homeless and starving. I saw no harm in helping her to obtain work." The abbé Gaston was afraid that his fear of forfeiting the rector's invitation to live in the presbytery was making him justify himself too patently.

"More atrocities, eh?" the abbé Moune said. "Between you and me I shouldn't pay too much attention to all you hear. A lot of these reports are greatly exaggerated if you ask me."

"There is a misery abroad in the world and it is our duty to succour it," the abbé Gaston said, beginning to get angry.

"It is the duty of Christian priests to succour the very real distress of Christians rather than the hypothetical miseries of infidels," the abbé Moune said.

"Concentration camps aren't hypothetical," the abbé Gaston said.

"I'm getting a little tired of hearing about concentration camps," the abbé Moune said.

"Not as tired as the Jews of being in them," the abbé Gaston said.

"I'm also getting a little tired of hearing about the Jews," the abbé Moune said.

The abbé Gaston became so angry that he no longer cared whether the rector invited him to live in the presbytery or not. He forgot all about his promise to the Cardinal. He remembered only that there were two falsehoods in the world and that one of them was not less a falsehood because some Christians supported it.

"Monsieur l'abbé Moune, I sometimes wonder why you became a priest," the abbé Gaston said. He did not wait for an answer. He went straight down into the underground, as he had still to preach and give benediction at the convent, because the nuns had to go on being kept holy, too.

LIV

IN Lent the Cardinal did not wear his scarlet cassock, but only his old purple archbishop's one. He also wore a tippet and a cowl with white fur round the edge, which the liturgy allowed him to wear over his head when he was listening to other priests praying and which tickled his head much less than a mitre. In Lent 1939 the Cardinal listened as much as possible to other priests praying because he was getting too old to do all the public praying himself with his neck wobbling about all the time.

On Good Friday, therefore, a young bishop sang the pontifical mass of the pre-sanctified in black vestments and the Cardinal sat on his throne with the Chanoine Paquin beside him, to show him the place in the holy book. The young bishop prayed that the Lord might bestow His blessing upon the Church and gather her together and keep her in all the earth. The young bishop prayed for the Pope and for all bishops, priests, deacons, and subdeacons, acolytes, exorcists, lectors, doorkeepers, confessors, virgins and widows, that God might pour out His grace upon them. The young bishop prayed for catechumens, that they might be born again in the waters of baptism, and for prisoners, that God might break their chains, and for those at sea that God might grant them a secure harbor. And when the holy thing was done they extinguished the candles and stripped the linen cloth from the altar, and the cathedral was cold and empty, because of the sadness that there had been in the world.

LV

IN September 1939 the abbé Gaston's wound became suddenly fashionable again, because France had declared war on Germany once more. Whenever the centrally heated lady of easy virtue met the abbé going into the house she invited him to share the lift with her, because she said that he was a hero who had fought for France. And the day that he came home in his military chaplain's uniform even Madame Boulon said that the abbé could use the lift as much as he liked.

The abbé Gaston's uniform wasn't really a uniform at all. It consisted of field boots, a very short cassock, a forage cap and a cigar. The field boots and the forage cap the abbé had obtained from the military depot at St. Ouen; the short cassock he had manufactured himself by cutting a foot off the bottom of his second best one; and the cigar he had obtained from the general, who had said that this was the most important item in a military chaplain's outfit.

Indeed it was thanks to the general that the abbé had been called up for military service at all, because the abbé was over age and had been so badly wounded in the last war. But the general had said that in his opinion older priests and wounded priests made the best chaplains of all, especially when they smoked cigars. The general had said that there was something about a cigar in a chaplain's mouth that made soldiers respect religion even if it didn't always inspire them to obey it. To emphasize his contention the general had given the abbé a box of a hundred cigars. The abbé had already smoked five of them, partly because he knew it annoyed the rector to see one of his curates walking about the streets smoking a cigar, partly because he liked smoking cigars.

The abbé was smoking the butt end of a cigar as he did his packing. He had begun the cigar when he had gone to say good-bye to the shopkeepers, and he had puffed out great clouds of smoke in their faces to impress them with the potency of religion. The butcher had said that it was high time that France taught that fellow Hitler a lesson. The baker had said that the sooner one began a war the sooner it was over and that he was glad the abbé Gaston was beginning it now and not waiting until next spring. The wine merchant had said that he would stand the abbé Gaston a free bottle of champagne the day Hitler was marched through the Place du Maréchal Haig as a captive. Madame Bisberot had said that a friend had told her that the soldiers would be all back in their homes for Christmas, and that her friend should know as her husband was a colonel in the regular army.

St. Elizabeth of Hungary was impressed by the abbé's cigar, too, because the smoke got into her eyes and made her retreat to the other end of the room. But the abbé was too worried about his packing to notice the cat's discomfort. The abbé's only suitcase was the straw travelling bag which he had taken to South America and he was wondering if it was strong enough to withstand the rigors of war. Fortunately he had not much to pack because he didn't need to take his best cassock. There were in fact only his pyjamas and his socks and his underwear to pack. .As it was possible that the war might last longer than Madame Bisberot anticipated the abbé decided that he had better pack his summer as well as his winter underwear, so he put in the two pairs of woollen combinations with darns and no holes in them and the two pairs of woollen combinations with holes and no darns in them. When he had finished packing the abbé fastened a leather strap round each end of the travelling bag.

The abbé was leaving for a town in the Oise that afternoon and he was ashamed to think that his destination wasn't really dangerous, because everybody knew that the Germans would never get as far as that, with the Maginot Line to stop them. The centrally heated lady of easy virtue had offered to keep St. Elizabeth of Hungary while the abbé was away at the front but the abbé had felt that it was better to leave the cat with Madame Boulon who had looked after St. Blasius of Cappadocia during the last war and whom he could pay without embarrassment. Madame Boulon said that she would be very pleased to look after St. Elizabeth of Hungary because the late Monsieur Boulon had been very fond of cats, too.

While he stood not listening to Madame Boulon talking about how accurately the late Monsieur Boulon had foreseen both the present and the previous catastrophes, the abbé stroked St. Elizabeth of Hungary, who was standing with her back arched on the back of Madame Boulon's armchair. The cat meowed and purred simultaneously as he stroked it. The abbé wondered if he would have loved the rector better if he, too, had had striped fur and had meowed and purred when he was stroked.

The rector had invited the abbé Gaston to lunch and the abbé took his suitcase with him, because he was leaving for the station immediately afterwards. The abbé rather wished that he hadn't been carrying his suitcase because then he would have been able to march across the square with more of a swagger. As it was he walked with as little of a limp as possible and he blew out big clouds of cigar smoke, because he didn't want people to think that he was a weak broken down military chaplain but a strong fiery energetic one. He threw back his shoulders as he saw people turning to stare at his field boots and his forage cap and the medal ribbons set out in a row on the breast of his cassock. The policeman on point duty held up the traffic specially for him. This unexpected courtesy cheered the abbé into hoping that this new war was going to do what the old war had failed to do: unite all Frenchmen in brotherhood.

Something of this hope seemed to be shared by the clergy when the abbé met them in the dining-room of the presbytery. The Chanoine Litry had a grin on his face and he joked with the abbé Gaston about his military appearance. Even the abbé Moune was kindly and seemed to have forgotten their quarrel about Rachel, although the abbé Gaston knew that he must have spoken to the rector about it, because no more had been said about his coming to live in the presbytery. The abbé Gaston felt sorry for them all in their long plain everyday cassocks, because they weren't going away to fight in an exciting war like he was, but were staying at home to go on with the drudgery of failing to turn the laity into saints.

Outside on the square the old nun passed, tied on to the end of her platoon of schoolgirls. Although the schoolgirls must have changed they still looked the same, pegged at the same interval in God's patience. The nun still looked the same, too, but the abbé Gaston supposed that she must have moved up an interval or two since he had last seen her. The nun's knobbly face looked the same as other people's knobbly faces, but the abbé knew that it wasn't the same as other people's knobbly faces, because the chemistry of grace was invisible. Even the Church was invisible, because it was only churchmen that men saw, and churchmen soon passed and were succeeded by other churchmen. The abbé Gaston thought gratefully after the old nun as she disappeared into the distance.

"We are all very proud of you, Monsieur l'abbé Gaston," the rector said as they sat down to table. "We think that it is very brave of you to volunteer for the army at your age."

"Oh, I don't think that I'm very brave really," the abbé Gaston said, and he knew that this was true.

The abbé Gaston saw at once that the rector intended the meal to be a special occasion. The best silver was laid out on the best tablecloth, and instead of the usual red rot-gut there were two bottles of Pouilly and Saint Emilion. And when plates of radishes, sliced cucumber, tomatoes, sardines, potato salad, tunny, liver sausage and cold hardboiled eggs in mayonnaise appeared the abbé Gaston could scarcely restrain an ill-mannered and worldly expression of approval, for the abbé was very fond indeed of assorted hors d'œuvre. A rector who provided his curates with hardboiled eggs in mayonnaise was, the abbé thought, the next best thing to a striped furry rector who meowed and purred at the same time.

But the abbé Gaston was disappointed when the rector, instead of inviting his guest to help himself first, heaped great quantities of radishes, sliced cucumber, tomatoes, sardines, potato salad, liver sausage and hardboiled eggs in mayonnaise on to his own plate. There were only twelve slices of bisected egg on the dish and the abbé noticed with distress that the rector took four. The abbé's distress increased when the rector began circulating the dishes of hors d'œuvre the wrong way round the table, starting with the abbé Moune, who was seated on his left, instead of with himself, who was seated on his right. And the abbé Moune did not spoon out hors d'œuvre; he dug them out, and when he had finished digging, there were only five slices of egg in mayonnaise left. The abbé Gaston was apt enough at calculation to realize that if neither the abbé Ronsard nor one of the two younger curates forewent his share of hardboiled egg, there would be no hardboiled egg left for himself and perhaps no tunny either, to judge by the rapidity with which the contents of the other dishes also were disappearing. The abbé Gaston found himself almost glaring across the table at the abbé Ronsard as the meek little man switched his glinting spectacles on to the hardboiled eggs as though they were a problem in theology. The abbé Ronsard took two slices of hardboiled egg and a very untheological quantity of sardines.

"This time I think that there is cause for spiritual optimism," the rector said, filling his glass with Pouilly and passing the bottle to the abbé Moune, who filled his glass, drank the contents at a gulp and filled his glass again before he passed the bottle to the abbé Ronsard. "And I am not alone in this opinion," the rector went on. "I understand on the highest authority that the Holy Father is on the eve of making a most important pronouncement."

The abbé Gaston nodded unenthusiastically. He didn't care what sort of pronouncement the Holy Father made unless it were about clergymen eating too many hardboiled eggs in mayonnaise. The first young curate, expressing his admiration for the wisdom of the Supreme Pontiff, took two slices. The abbé Gaston stared hard at the second young curate and the remaining slice of egg. The stare was meant to intimate to the second young curate that as neither of the young curates had been called up for military service it was the second young curate's duty to leave the remaining slice of hardboiled egg for him. The second young curate was beginning to work round from the radishes to the remaining slice of hardboiled egg when the siren went.

Even when the abbé Gaston had heard the siren sound on Thursdays at noon as a practice for progress the sound had made him feel frightened. But today was the feast of St. John Mary Vianney and it wasn't a Thursday at all and France had declared war on Germany only the day before, so it looked as though progress itself was due to arrive at any moment. The abbé had read a great deal about progress, quite apart from what he had heard about it from Madame Bisberot and the centrally heated lady of easy virtue. The abbé had read that bombs dropped from ten thousand airplanes could reduce Paris to a heap of rubble within five minutes. The abbé had read that Hitler possessed a hundred thousand airplanes. Looking round the table, the abbé Gaston saw that his colleagues had read the same things, too. The abbé Moune had stopped shoveling himself full of hors d'œuvre and the second young curate had come to a full stop between the potato salad and the liver sausage.

The abbé Gaston knew what was going on in his colleagues' minds because the same thing was going on in his. In spite of their knowledge that, if they had practiced the virtues they had enjoined upon their parishioners, the biggest high explosive could only blow them into immediate contemplation of the Beatific Vision, they all seemed to want to postpone contemplation of the Beatific Vision for a little longer. They all seemed to want to go to the air raid shelter, but none of them wanted to be the first to suggest doing so. It was the abbé Moune who solved their dilemma for them.

"I don't know about you others, but I'm going to obey regulations," the abbé Moune said, rising from the table and pushing back his chair. "Remember what that man on the wireless said? There's nothing brave about making oneself a nuisance to other people."

The other clergymen remembered with alacrity what the man on the wireless had said. They agreed that it was only fair to the air raid warden that they should retreat at once to the shelter, where the air raid warden had a right to expect to find them, alive or dead. And the abbé Ronsard said with a faint smile that their going to the air raid shelter might even save the Lord trouble at the general resurrection. The abbé Moune was first through the door, although the rector wasn't long after him. The abbé Gaston was the last to leave the room and when he got out on the street the others were already hurrying across the square towards the air raid shelter, which was in the cellar of the house next the dressmaking establishment. The abbé Gaston had never seen the abbé Moune walk so quickly before, not even leaving the altar.

The abbé Gaston knew that he couldn't hurry across the square like the others had done, not only because of his limp, but also because of his field boots and his forage cap and the medal ribbons on his breast, which he must not disgrace. So, although he longed to be in the shelter with the others, he stood on the steps of the presbytery and lit one of the cigars which the general had given him, puffing out a cloud of smoke to make himself feel braver. The sight of the smoke reassured him and he soon felt very much the military chaplain again, rendering unto Clausewitz the things which were Clausewitz's.

Above his head the sky was blue and speckless, stretched like a taut sail. On the other side of the square the pink and pale green wash-hand basins and baths in the de luxe plumber's window shone in the afternoon sun. On the street the traffic had stopped and the policeman on point duty was shouting at a taxi driver not to honk his horn in case Hitler might hear. In front of the church a woman lay stretched out on the pavement with a newspaper spread out over her head. Apart from the bus conductors congregated round their vehicles at the terminus, there were very few people on the square, perhaps because it was the lunch hour, perhaps because the population of Paris had decided to obey the man on the wireless. In the de luxe plumber's window the pink and pale green wash-hand basins and baths went on being brave.

In spite of the fear on their faces the few people on the square smiled when they saw the abbé's field boots and his forage cap and his cigar, and the abbé tried not to think that men seemed to respect the religion of love only when it abased itself to share their hatreds. This time, more than ever, France's cause was just, the abbé knew, and he smiled gaily at the bus conductors when they smiled at him.

"Hitler hasn't dropped any of his chocolates yet, Monsieur l'abbé," one of the bus conductors called out.

"I shan't pick one up and eat it if he does," the abbé Gaston answered with a laugh.

The conductors all laughed at the simple joke and the abbé thought how surely a common danger welded men into fraternity. It had been so before and it was so again, only this time men must catch hold of their fraternity with both hands so that God's kingdom might come also. The abbé stuck his beard up into the sky and looked to see if he could see an airplane, but the sky was as empty of airplanes as of angels ascending and descending. The abbé was rather ashamed of walking across to the air raid shelter under the gaze of the bus conductors.

Down in the cellar the abbé Gaston found the rector and his curates lined up against one wall and Madame Bisberot and her girls lined up against the other. The abbé smiled at Rachel, who smiled back, and at Madame Bisberot, who waved her fingers at him. The rector and his curates went on staring in moody silence at the girls, who were obviously doing their best not to giggle. Conscious that his military aspect and his cigar made him a member of both worlds, the abbé Gaston tried to lessen the tension.

"This is a military occasion and I rather think that I'm the senior officer present," he said. "These mattresses are made to be sat on, you know."

The girls giggled openly. The young curates smiled. Madame Bisberot slapped her thigh.

"That's an idea," she said. "It's easily seen you've been in danger before."

The abbé Gaston tried not to throw out his chest with too much pride. He saw that the girls were looking at the medal ribbons on his breast. He flourished his cigar as though it were a sword.

"This is nothing," he said. "There's no use getting frightened until you hear a noise. And even then it's no use getting frightened because you never hear the noise that kills you."

The girls sat down, gathering the spill of their frocks about their long silk legs. In their green and in their purples and their reds, the abbé Gaston thought that they looked rather like flowers. The priests sat down, too, and the rector sat down last of all, still with a scowl on his face. In the distance a door banged.

"There goes one," Madame Bisberot said.

"Monsieur l'abbé says that the noise you hear never kills you," one of the girls said.

"In that case it is of silence that one should be frightened," Rachel said.

"It is the silence which you don't hear which kills you," the abbé Gaston said.

"That is very unsound doctrine, Monsieur l'abbé Gaston," the rector said acidly. "The silence one doesn't hear in this world one will hear immediately in the next."

The abbé Gaston knew that the rector was right: he had been talking nonsense theologically as well as militarily. *"In momenta, in ictu oculi,"* St. Paul had said "in a moment, in the twinkling of an eye." Unable to answer the rector's accusations, the abbé decided to ignore it.

"Down flat on your mattresses," he said, trying to bring the conversation back to military necessity. "There's less of you to be hit that way by stones falling perpendicularly."

"There's plenty of me to be hit all ways up," Madame Bisberot said. "And in any case I should have thought that the proper position for priests to be bombed in was on their knees."

"I began being frightened to the greater glory of God and I intend going on being frightened to the greater glory of God," the rector said with a wry smile.

The abbé Gaston caught at the rector's smile and tried to transfer it to the faces of the girls, and succeeded a little, although he knew that they hadn't really understood the point of the rector's remark. "Still no sign of trouble," he said and as he spoke on at them the girls smiled more broadly, and their smile wasn't a giggle at all, but gentle and friendly. He held his hand to his ear, rather grotesquely. "At least I don't hear anything," he said. The girls went on smiling.

"That's the great secret of the sneezing bomb," Madame Bisberot said. "It doesn't make any noise at all when it explodes. People don't know anything about it until they start sneezing."

This time the abbé Gaston smiled at the rector, hoping to light a smile on his face, too. The Chanoine Litry's face did not seem to change much, but his eyes twinkled a little as he spoke.

"That sounds like a form of chemical warfare," the rector said.

Madame Bisberot told the rector about the sneezing bomb. She said that it was chemical warfare because it had been invented in a chemist's shop one day when the man behind the counter had given Hitler a lozenge that had made him cough more instead of less and that had put the idea into Hitler's head of making people sneeze themselves to death. When Madame Bisberot had finished telling them about the sneezing bomb the curates and the girls were all laughing together and the rector was laughing louder than any of them. Madame Bisberot joined in the mirth, too, and laughed till the tears ran down her cheeks. Watching them laugh, the abbé Gaston thanked the Lord for making them all merry Christians together. He blew out a jubilant cloud of cigar smoke and prayed that, by the intercession of Blessed Michael the Archangel, who stood at the right hand of the altar of incense, the Lord might bless it and receive it for an odor of sweetness.

"All the same the real chemical warfare must be very dreadful," Rachel said gravely when they had finished laughing. "Perhaps it is not right for us to laugh when so many people are suffering such terrible things in Poland."

"I agree, Mademoiselle," the abbé Ronsard said, turning the solemn wheels of his spectacles on Rachel. "It is all very sad and terrible."

"It is difficult for me to understand how Christians can approve of modern war," Rachel said.

"The Church teaches that war is justifiable in self defense," the rector said.

The Church taught, but only God could explain, the abbé Gaston thought, unable to reconcile mercy with high explosive. For a few moments he was even ashamed of his field boots and his forage cap, because they were the emblems of force rather than of gentleness.

"We fight against evil things," the abbé Gaston said unhappily and listened on into the silence for the terror which might come upon them. Observing that the rector and Madame Bisberot were still smiling at each other, he was again encouraged to hope that good might come out of evil. After all both the centurion and St. Ignatius Loyola had been soldiers and the Lord had raised the words of the one and the person of the other to very high positions indeed. Thinking about the Lord's approval of soldiers, it was almost with cheerfulness that the abbé looked at his watch and saw that it was time for him to be leaving for the station.

"You can't go until the all clear's sounded," Madame Bisberot said.

"Orders are orders," the abbé Gaston said, glad to have something immediately military to do. "There are certain risks which a soldier has got to take," he said proudly and did not even try not to say it too proudly. He rolled his cigar into the corner of his mouth and swaggered down both sides of the cellar, saying goodbye to Madame Bisberot and the priests and the girls. Both the rector and the abbé Moune were so cordial when they shook hands with him that the abbé Gaston was not embarrassed when Rachel rose and accompanied him to the door of the cellar.

She was wearing the blue velvet dress in which he had last seen her. There were now blurs of smoothness on it in parts, rather like grass which had just been rolled, the abbé thought. She threw back her head and the droop of her hair was flung back, too. Both her eyes were sad when the abbé looked into them and her long face was sad, too.

"I want to thank you," she said. "You have been very kind to me."

"Nonsense," the abbé Gaston said.

"I wish that I could believe all the beautiful things that you do, but I cannot because the world is ugly," she said.

"Faith is a metaphysic; therefore it is neither beautiful nor ugly," the abbé said, but he saw at once that she did not understand, perhaps because the new words had not yet been said often enough for repetition to have dulled their meaning. "Try to be happy," he said, patting her face held up to him above the somber folds of her dark blue dress.

The abbé had to cross the square again to fetch his straw suitcase from the presbytery. The bus conductors were still gathered round their buses and they waved to the abbé as he passed and the abbé raised his cigar in the air as a sign that religion was really a manly affair and that everybody was going to believe in it again soon. The soldiers hurrying along the pavements reminded the abbé of those other soldiers whom he had seen hurrying there in 1914, but there was not the same gaiety in their demeanor. The abbé was still thinking about the demeanor of the soldiers when he polished off the slice of bisected hardboiled egg in mayonnaise still remaining in the hors d'œuvre dish.

LVI

THE statesman said that the French people must be united, because union was strength. The statesman said that Britain and France were stronger than ever because they were more united than ever. The statesman said that money was the sinews of war. With the money of Frenchmen France would make steel and with steel France would forge the victorious arms. The statesman said that Frenchmen who died in defense of their country would inscribe their names forever on the golden scrolls of history. The statesman said that the sinews of war was money.

LVII

THE abbé Gaston did not smoke his cigar in the pulpit when he came home from being brave at the town in the Oise and the rector asked him to preach at the high mass on the fourth Sunday in Lent, 1940. Instead he wore a pink stole and the ministers at the altar wore pink vestments, too, because the introit began "Rejoice, O Jerusalem" and it was not fitting for priests to wear purple vestments when such happy things were sung and said. It was the first time in more than twenty-five years that the abbé Gaston had been asked to preach at the Sunday high mass, because that was a privilege reserved for the rector and the abbé Moune, who shot out the heavenly sooth with logic and eloquence.

    The abbé's field boots showed grandly out from beneath his cassock as he marched down the aisle behind the beadle, and he climbed the steps of the pulpit as though it were an observation post. Before beginning the bidding prayer he scanned the congregation as though it were a battalion paraded for his inspection. And indeed there was a military atmosphere about the church. The flags of France and Great Britain were festooned above the high altar. There were British as well as French soldiers in the congregation and stuck up on the Chanoine Litry's confessional there was a notice to say that English was spoken, because the rector knew all about sin in five languages. But it wasn't only soldiers who were waiting to hear the abbé Gaston preach. The nuns from the convent sat together all in a row and Michelle was with them, dressed in a new pink Sunday dress. Even from the pulpit the abbé could see the excitement on Sister Scholastica's face. And Madame Bisberot and Rachel were there as well, sitting demurely in front of the font. And for once the negro was unpunctually early instead of punctually late and his pale grey hat, yellow chamois leather gloves and silver mounted walking stick were already devoutly laid out on the side altar dedicated to St. Peter of Alcantara, but the negro's hair was now white instead of black, because the negro was becoming an old negro. Even the centrally heated lady of easy virtue was there and she gazed up at the abbé with a damp devout look on her face. But it was Bessier's presence which chiefly astonished the abbé and made his voice tremble when he had to pray out aloud to God to send them priests, holy priests.

The abbé's voice was still trembling when he began his sermon because he knew that it was going to be very difficult for him to convert so many different kinds of people at once. He spoke gently through his beard, because he thought that was the way the Lord would have spoken and he smiled at the people with his eyes, because he knew that the Lord Jesus had always gone softly into men's hearts. But before he either spoke to the people or smiled at the people the abbé prayed that the Lord might lend wisdom to his words, because he knew that he was not sufficient to think anything of himself, because his sufficiency was from God.

The abbé said that he had been very disappointed when he had watched the congregation coming into the church that morning to remark that people were still saying short private prayers as usual. A sketchy sign of the cross, a bored stare at the altar, a mumble with their lips and the faithful's devotions were done and they were down on their hunkers again, if he might use a military phrase. The abbé said that it was very wrong of the faithful to be down so quickly on their hunkers again, in such troubled times.

The abbé said that he sometimes thought that it was because of George Bernard Shaw that men no longer prayed, and this was wrong of them, because their gallant allies the British were often better at running railway trains than at understanding theology. Even in the recent past France had been blessed with men and women who had known how to pray. It was because of men and women like Saint Jean Marie Vianney, Saint Thérèse of Lisieux, Saint Marie Bernarde and Saint Jeanne de Chantal that France was great and not because of men like Anatole France, Emile Zola and Guy de Maupassant, who had spread abroad the philosophy of disillusionment and cynicism, which was responsible for their present distress. Saint Jean Marie Vianney, Saint Thérèse of Lisieux, Saint Marie Bernarde and Saint Jeanne de Chantal had done a great service to France because they had shown other Frenchmen that it was possible for them to be holy, too. Anatole France, Emile Zola and Guy de Maupassant had done great harm not only to France but to the rest of the world as well, because their writings implied that men were never honest or good or humble from disinterested motives, and this was a false statistic, the abbé said. The power politics of Hitler and Mussolini were only an extension of the philosophy of Anatole France, Emile Zola and Guy de Maupassant, because they were a greater disobedience, the abbé said. It was because of her saints and not because of her writers that the Lord had allowed France once more to defend the right, and it was because of her saints that the Lord was going to grant France a very great favor indeed, the abbé said.

The abbé said that military secrets were generally very strictly kept and known only to officers of the rank of lieutenant-colonel and upwards. Although he himself was not an important enough soldier to be a lieutenant-colonel there was one military secret which he knew, and as all the other soldiers at the front knew it, too, the abbé said that he did not think that General Gamelin would be very angry if he told the congregation about it. This military secret was that France was going to win the war and quite soon. The abbé said that he didn't think that General Gamelin would like him to tell them the exact date because that would warn Hitler too much. But the congregation could take it from him that some time between Pentecost and the first Sunday in Advent the war against Germany would be won. It wasn't because of fear that the German soldiers hadn't attacked the French soldiers, but it wasn't because of fear that the French soldiers hadn't attacked the German soldiers, but on account of strategy or tactics or both. The abbé said this good news ought to persuade the faithful that sitting down on their hunkers too soon was not only heresy and schism but black ingratitude as well.

The abbé Gaston smiled again at all the people when he had finished preaching to them, but he didn't look down into their faces too closely, in case he should discover that he hadn't converted as many people as he hoped.

The abbé Gaston had converted the nuns all right, because they told him so after mass, on the top of the steps outside the church. Sister Scholastica said that she was going home to say her rosary right away and Sister Marie Joseph asked if the rumor were really true that in this war the soldiers swore much more devoutly. Michelle stood with the nuns as they spoke to the abbé, and the sunshine fell softly on the little girl's hair and made it glow, so that the abbé was reminded of Armelle, who had also stood there as a child, with the spring breeze puffing out her dress. Michelle said that she would say very long prayers indeed that night, for having allowed France to win the war.

Madame Bisberot had been converted, too, for she said that she was prepared to start in praying to St. George Bernard Shaw right away, but the centrally heated lady of easy virtue said that she would stick to the French saints and address her devotions to St. Guy de Maupassant and she thought that her gentleman friend would approve her choice. The abbé was rather sorry that Bessier hadn't waited behind to tell him whether he had been converted, too, but the abbé knew that Bessier couldn't really be glad about France's forthcoming victory, because Bessier thought that France was fighting an imperialist war.

But the abbé forgot all about Bessier when Rachel asked him to lunch with her in a restaurant, because France was going to win the war. Rachel was still wearing the dark blue velvet dress which the abbé had said that he liked, but she was wearing another hat which he didn't like. However, the abbé forgot all about Rachel's hat, too, when she suggested that they should begin their lunch with hardboiled eggs in mayonnaise. After that the abbé had a sauerkraut with sausages without sauerkraut, because the abbé liked sausages and didn't like sauerkraut.

LVIII

ARTHUR didn't seem to be much better at praying than Francis had been. All through the feasts of Saints Antoninus, Gordian and Epimachus, Saints Nereus, Achilleus, Domitilla and Pancras, Saints Boniface, Jean Baptiste de la Salle, Ubaldus, John Nepomucen and Pascal Baylon he and Alphonse prayed, but still the German army poured on, trampling under their feet the fair land of France.

LIX

THE abbé Gaston never liked it when the Colonel began bringing cigar smoke down his nostrils, because it generally meant that the Colonel was going to say something rude about religion. The abbé couldn't bring his own cigar smoke down his nostrils without spluttering and choking and the inability to do so made him feel at a disadvantage when attempting to answer the Colonel's gibes. On Monday the tenth of June 1940, therefore, when the Colonel brought two thick clouds of smoke out of his nose after dinner in mess, the abbé knew that he was in for something unpleasant.

"Well, one thing's certain and that is that the Pope must be feeling very pleased about this," the Colonel said.

The abbé felt as immediately miserable as he had foreseen. Looking round the table, he saw that the younger officers were already grinning in anticipation of his public defeat. Only the Major, who came to mass on Sundays, gave him an encouraging smile. The abbé rather liked the Major, not only because he was pious, but also because he was the only officer who was as distressed as himself at the military disaster which was overtaking France. But liking the Major didn't help the abbé to answer the Colonel, because to answer the Colonel the abbé had to know the right words, and only the wrong ones kept coming to the front of his mind. In desperation he drew deeply at his cigar, swallowed a vast quantity of smoke, and coughed and choked as usual when he tried to exhale it through his nostrils.

"His Holiness must be feeling sadder than anybody else in the world," the abbé said when he had finished spluttering.

"Nonsense," the Colonel said, snorting two magnificent clouds of smoke down his nostrils. "The Austrians are Catholics, aren't they? The Bavarians are Catholics and the Italians are Catholics. The French are bad Catholics and the British are Protestants. Of course, the Pope must want the other side to win. It's 1914 all over again."

"Perhaps it's Christianity that the Pope wants to win the war," the abbé Gaston said gently.

"Why doesn't he say so then?" the Colonel asked angrily. "Why doesn't he excommunicate Hitler and Mussolini?"

The abbé didn't know why the Pope hadn't condemned the German air raids and excommunicated Hitler and Mussolini, but he supposed that there was something about it in theology somewhere, which only a very holy bishop like the Pope could understand. Perhaps it was that the Church was like a boat, into which every man swimming in the sea had a right to clamber. Perhaps it was that the Church was like a lamp, held up above a storm for all men to see. But the abbé felt that he could not say any of these things to the Colonel, who was such a dab at bringing cigar smoke down his nostrils.

"I am afraid that there are many things which will not be explained till the last day," the abbé Gaston said, almost as much to himself as to the Colonel.

"Perhaps that will be explained on the last day also," the Colonel said as the sirens suddenly began to shriek. The abbé knew that the Colonel was afraid of air raids because the Colonel was never able to bring cigar smoke down his nostrils while the bombs were falling. The abbé didn't like air raids either, but he didn't think that he was as afraid of them as the Colonel was. Indeed the abbé rather liked what he thought of as the in-between part of air raids. He didn't like the wailing of the sirens and he didn't like the noise the bombs made when they fell, but he could be quite brave when he was listening to the hum of the airplanes overhead. The hum of the airplanes overhead reminded the abbé of the noise the rotary brush had made in the barber's shop when he was a boy. They didn't have rotary brushes in barber's shops any longer; instead they had airplanes that dropped bombs, because of progress.

The sirens wailed into silence in diminishing shrieks, like a giant carpet cleaner ceasing to function. As the benevolent burr of the airplanes drew nearer, the abbé puffed vigorously at his cigar, although he didn't attempt to bring any smoke down his nostrils. In the past week the abbé had used the General's cigars a lot to steady his nerves, because there had been quite a lot of air raids. In the courtyard of the hospital the dead were piled so high that the orderlies had to use a ladder to stack the corpses, and the abbé was always taking brief burial services, praying over as many as thirty bodies at a time that God would be kinder to them than men had been. But it was especially when the incendiary bombs fell that the abbé found it hard to believe that the world was love and not a chemistry. Being burned to death must be very like being tortured to death, the abbé thought, and he sometimes wondered whether in 1936 the driver of that underground train had really extinguished the little blue lamp accurately at Louis Blanc after all.

The telephone rang as the first bomb fell. A junior officer crossed the room slowly to answer it. The abbé knew that the young man walked slowly in order not to seem afraid. That was one of the reasons why nobody ever suggested going down to the cellar when the siren sounded; the other was that there wasn't any cellar.

"For you, sir," the young officer said to the Colonel when he had spoken into the telephone.

More bombs fell as the Colonel crossed the room. The bombs came down with a whistle and exploded with a bang. Soon the noise was so great that the Colonel had to bawl into the telephone in order to make himself heard at the other end. The abbé tried the rector's tip of being frightened to the greater glory of God, but he wasn't very successful. The bombs ceased falling almost as soon as the Colonel had finished speaking into the telephone, and the nice part of the air raid began again. Then the all clear sounded and the abbé felt afraid once more, because the all clear sounded even more disagreeable than the alert. As there were no longer any bombs falling the Colonel was able to bring cigar smoke down his nostrils as he walked back to the table.

"It's the General," the Colonel said. "He says we're scuppered. He says the Germans are at Noyon. He says we've to beat it at once."

The abbé Gaston tried not to see the smirk of relief which played briefly round the other officers' lips. The smirk came from the corners of their mouths and vanished into their moustaches. The abbé could feel the smirk running quickly along beneath his own beard. He could even feel it expanding across his soul. The abbé chased the smirk away because he was ashamed to be a soldier who was afraid of facing danger. When he glanced at the other officers again they were all trying to look miserable. Only the Major wasn't trying to look miserable because the Major was looking miserable.

"Are we never going to stand and fight?" the Major asked. "We've run from Sedan. We've run from Arras. We've run from Beauvais. Are we going to run from here as well?"

"It's a strategic retreat, the General says," the Colonel said. "Of course we're going to stand and fight, but at a place and time of our own choosing and not of Hitler's. Perhaps in front of Paris. Perhaps on the Loire. Perhaps at the Pyrenees."

"It's a disgrace," the Major said. "It's not as though our troops were tired. They haven't seen the enemy. They haven't even heard a shot fired."

"Trouble with you, Benestier, is that you are too big for your boots," the Colonel said. "Orders are orders and we've got to obey them. Who do you think you are? Gamelin?"

"I hope that I am right when I think that I am an ordinary decent Frenchman," the Major said.

"What you think is no concern of mine," the Colonel said. "I happen to think you're my second in command. So you can run along and give orders for the men to fall in with their bicycles in the courtyard in ten minutes' time. And don't stand there nodding your head like a Chinese mandarin. Do what I say and look slippy about it. Skids on!" The Colonel waved one hand angrily at the Major and with the other he began filling the pockets of his tunic with fruit. "Silly bastard," he said when the Major had left the room. "Come on, you chaps. Fill up. It's no use leaving anything for Hitler." The Colonel laughed harshly and inverted a bottle over his mouth, sucking down gulps of champagne and gobbing all over his chin on to his uniform as he sucked.

"I think that what the Major says is right," the abbé Gaston said, realizing that he ought to have spoken before now in defense of his friend. But they were all too busy cramming their pockets with fruit to pay any attention to what the abbé said.

The candlelight shone softly on the senior officers' medal ribbons and made them look beautiful. The concatenated little rectangles of red and blue and green and yellow silk were like rows of miniature colored railway carriages. But the abbé thought that it was unlikely that the senior officers would win anymore medals unless progress also meant that decorations were to be awarded for looting.

A subaltern stuck an orange in each of the breast pockets of his tunic and said that he was Cleopatra. When they had finished pilfering what was on the table the officers began ransacking the larder. The Colonel tried to eat a whole Camembert cheese at once but stuck in the middle and threw the unconsumed portion with a splash against the wall and shoved another whole cheese in his pocket instead. The junior officers ran out of the mess and came back with their own and the senior officers' packs. The officers undid their packs and threw out the iron rations and the socks and the shirts and began to cram in butter and bottles of wine and chocolate and hunks of raw meat. They crammed in chickens and carrots and tins of sardines. One officer rammed half a pound of butter down into his field boots and said that the butter gave his feet a delicious sensual feeling, like making love to a pretty girl among flowers. When the officers had packed all they could they flung the rest of the food on the floor and started kicking it about. A young captain sat on some eggs and said that he was trying to hatch them and then wiped the seat of his breeches on the curtains. When the officers had broken all the crystal and the china they began to throw Camembert cheeses at the splash the Colonel's Camembert cheese had already made on the wall. The abbé Gaston couldn't stand the spectacle any longer and went downstairs and out into the courtyard.

Outside the sky was calm and dark blue with stars in it. In the sacristy of Saint Clovis they had a vestment just like the sky which was used on Palm Sundays and other holy occasions when the rector sang a penitential mass himself. When the abbé puffed at the sky the stars seemed to go out and the sky turned red, but when the abbé looked closely he saw that it wasn't his cigar which had made the sky turn red, but a fire burning on the horizon, in the direction of Noyon.

The men had already fallen in in the courtyard and they stood patiently beneath the sky, poor perplexed soldiers with packs on their backs. Watching them, the abbé thought that they looked like saints stamped on a stained glass window, and he prayed a little for them, that they might endure. Some of the soldiers had bicycles and some of them hadn't. The glitter of the stars fell on the handlebars of the bicycles and on the steel helmets of the soldiers and made them look brittle.

The Major came walking out of the stained glass window and told the abbé that he had better put his cigar out. The Major said that at night the glowing cone of a lighted cigar could be spotted by hostile aircraft from as far away as fifteen miles. The abbé Gaston felt less brave when he was no longer smoking his cigar.

The Colonel and the other officers came running noisily out of the house. "Fall in!" shouted the Colonel, but as the soldiers had already fallen in he shouted at them to number off instead. The soldiers numbered off raggedly, in alternating spurts of enthusiasm and boredom.

"The even numbers will ride the bicycles and odd numbers will follow on foot," the Colonel ordered. "I myself shall take command of those on bicycles and Major Benestier will command those following on foot." Some of the bicycles clattered to the ground when the odd numbers who had bicycles handed them over to the even numbers who hadn't bicycles. A noncommissioned officer hurled filthy words at the silent faces of the soldiers beneath the sky. When the non-commissioned officer had finished swearing at the soldiers he went up and whispered to the Major.

"What's that dungheap whispering about?" the Colonel asked angrily.

"He says, sir, that some of the even numbers can't ride bicycles," the Major said. "He says that only those who were able to ride bicycles were allowed to fall in with bicycles."

"This is no time for insubordination," the Colonel shouted. "If the even numbers can't ride bicycles then they'll have to learn." As he spoke, the siren began to wail again, slitting the silence of the night with tin screechings. "Follow me, those with bicycles," the Colonel commanded, jumping on the bicycle which the non-commissioned officer wheeled up to him. "Come on, you men. The enemy will be here any moment."

The even numbers who could ride bicycles rode out of the courtyard after the Colonel and the even numbers who couldn't ride bicycles fell off them or ran for a little pushing the bicycles. The hum of rapidly approaching airplanes could be heard as the Major ordered the even numbers who couldn't ride bicycles to fall in again and hand the bicycles over to odd numbers who could ride them. Some of the bicycles clattered to the ground again as they were handed over. The hum of the approaching airplanes grew louder. The stars shone on brightly in the sky.

The Major ordered the soldiers who could ride bicycles to fall in under the command of the senior officer who could ride a bicycle and the soldiers who hadn't bicycles to fall in under the command of the senior officer who hadn't a bicycle. When the two groups had been formed the Major ordered them to retreat in the direction of Paris and to report to the commander of the first brigade which they encountered and which appeared prepared to resist the enemy. The soldiers with bicycles mounted them and rode quickly through the doorway, and those on foot followed scarcely less rapidly. The abbé Gaston found himself standing alone in the courtyard with the Major. Side by side they stood and listened to the airplanes tearing their way invisibly through the muslin of the stars.

"I forgot about you and your limp, Monsieur l'abbé," the Major said. "I ought to have given you a bicycle, too."

"The last time I rode a bicycle was in 1908 when I went to meet the Apostolic Delegate," the abbé Gaston said. "I had a puncture and the Apostolic Delegate had to come and meet me instead."

"In the meantime perhaps we'd better take cover," the Major said.

They went back into the mess upstairs because the doors of the downstairs rooms were locked. The Major said that on second thoughts they would have been safer lying flat out on their bellies in the courtyard, but the abbé said that he felt braver lying under the table. Indeed under the table was the only place they could lie because of the broken glass and the slush of butter and cheese covering the rest of the carpet. The bombs began to fall again, whistling down upon the town.

"Sometimes it's not easy not to be frightened," the Major said.

"Perhaps good soldiers only pretend not to be frightened," the abbé said.

"Even so there don't seem to be many good soldiers left in France," the Major said.

The noise which the bombs made when they exploded made it difficult for them to talk much. The noise was greater than it had been before because anti-aircraft guns fired back with a bang and a crack. The abbé tried to make himself feel braver by imagining that all the bangs and the cracks he heard were anti-aircraft guns flying back. The raid finished suddenly and the abbé and the Major lay on for a little underneath the table listening to the silence. When they went out into the courtyard again the stars were beautiful above their heads but there were fires burning on the edge of the town.

"Looks as though the hospital has been hit again," the Major said.

"In that case I'd better go and see if anybody needs me," the abbé said.

"You at least are a brave man," the Major said.

"I'm only brave because I cannot ride a bicycle or run away," the abbé said.

"I'm only brave because I'm not brave enough to be a coward," the Major said. As the Major said this flames sprang up on the edge of the town, floating over the sky like scarlet sails. "In any case I'm not brave enough to go back and face my friends and tell them that I ran away. I'm going north to try to find a unit that means to stand and fight. Who knows? We stopped them in 1914. We may stop them again. They say that our seventy-fives are beginning to get the measure of the German tanks. And there are rumors that Russia has declared war on Germany. The fortunes of war are fickle, Monsieur l'abbé. Even yet it may be we who end up in Berlin."

The abbé remembered the sermon he had preached on the Fourth Sunday in Lent. If what the Major said was true then perhaps it was Stalin who was going to make things come all right before the First Sunday in Advent. Looking at the flames on the edge of the town, the abbé said a little prayer for Stalin, that Stalin might believe in the Lord Jesus. The flames on the edge of the town no longer looked like scarlet sails, the abbé thought. On the Place du Maréchal Haig the abbé had seen young women wearing scarves like the flames, and the scarves had sometimes leaped up against the sky, too, when the wind had blown in them and spread them out.

"I'd like to come with you," the abbé said, looking out towards Noyon where there were more flames, and trying to believe that it wouldn't really hurt, being squashed flat under the treads of a tank.

"Your place is at the hospital," the Major said and shook hands with the abbé and walked away into the night.

It was always the same, the abbé thought sadly as he watched the Major go. The people he admired and liked had always gone swiftly out of his life. The nun who had liked his sermon in 1911 in Tunis had sailed the next day for China. The unassuming Scots bishop *in partibus* who had explained to him about haggis in 1913 had become an Apostolic Visitor to the Uniate Copts. The penitent who had tried to push through the grille of the confessional the teaspoon she had stolen from Rumpelmayer's had married a Moslem. The Lord certainly seemed to protect his priests from the danger of permanence in human affections.

The abbé was frightened standing alone in the torn apart world. From the distance came the rumble of guns. The abbé stuck his unlighted cigar in his mouth to give himself courage. The end of the cigar was damp and soggy and shreds of bitter tobacco came loose on the abbé's tongue.

Flames were coming out of the windows of the west wing of the hospital when the abbé Gaston arrived in the courtyard. Close up, the flames no longer looked like sails or young women's scarves blowing in the wind. Close up, the flames were red and yellow and there were blue streaks and green streaks in them, too, and the flames made a roaring noise as they swept out of the windows. The courtyard was full of ambulances and orderlies were carrying the wounded on stretchers out of the wards. A doctor shouted to the abbé that they were evacuating, but the abbé went on up the stairs into the ward on the east wing where the seriously wounded lay.

The red haired nurse who came to holy communion every Sunday confirmed what the doctor had shouted at the abbé. She said that as there weren't enough ambulances to go round they weren't evacuating the soldiers who had been wounded in the stomach, as they were certain to die anyway. The red haired nurse said that she would have liked to have stayed with the soldiers who were wounded in the stomach until they died, but that the Colonel had given them all orders to leave the hospital immediately, as the Germans were expected any minute. As the siren sounded again all the lights in the hospital went out and the nurse ran from the ward.

The abbé went from bed to bed, feeling in the darkness for those which were still occupied and helped a little by the light of the flames. Most of the soldiers were too ill to speak and the abbé could give them only conditional absolution and trust in the Lord for the rest. The soldiers who were wounded in the stomach cried. out for their mothers and for their wives, and some of them cried out for God as well, because now that they knew that they were going to die the soldiers who were wounded in the stomach were no longer afraid to acknowledge the meaning of the world. The abbé had brought the holy oils with him and he anointed their limbs and traced the last mercies upon their bodies. A boy of nineteen lived longer than the rest and he told the abbé that he was in love with a girl with fair hair and whose name was Denise. The abbé sat beside the boy and held his hand until he died and then he knelt in the increasing light of the flames and prayed that the Lord might receive all those poor bewildered souls into everlasting dwellings.

The Germans still hadn't arrived in the town when the abbé Gaston left the hospital. There was no air raid taking place and the flames seemed to have died down a little and in the middle of the dark blue sky the stars still shone brightly. The abbé licked out at the cool night with his tongue and drew a deep breath down into his lungs. As he walked with his head held up to the sky the abbé decided that he, like the Major, would go north to Noyon.

In the center of the town the street were full of soldiers. Some of the soldiers walked on the pavements but most of them marched in tight formation in the middle of the road with the splash of the stars on their steel helmets and on their rifles and on the buckles of their equipment. The abbé asked a soldier who was walking on the pavement where the soldiers who were marching in the middle of the road were going. The soldier said that the soldiers who were walking on the pavement were soldiers who were retreating but that the soldiers who were marching in the middle of the road were poor dopes who were going to have seven kinds of hell knocked out of them by the Germans. The abbé Gaston told the soldier that it was very wrong of him to talk that way about gallant men who were perhaps going to have the honor of dying for France. The soldier said that it wasn't for France that the soldiers who were marching in the middle of the road were going to die, but for the two hundred families and for the rich and that there was no honor about that as far as he was concerned and that he himself was retreating so fast that the high command soon wouldn't be able to see him for dust.

"Take hold of yourselves, men," an officer who cantered up on horseback shouted to the soldiers who were walking on the pavement. "General Huntziger has ordered us to die rather than yield the soil of France. The enemy can't go on advancing forever if we stand up to him. We mustn't let our first defeat become a rout. We must act like soldiers instead of like cowards. There are buses waiting by the side of the forest to take north again all those of you who have become separated from their units. Follow me, all those of you who've still got some guts left." The officer said these things several times over and then clopped away on his horse again.

The abbé knew his way to the side of the forest because he had carried the Blessed Sacrament in procession there, on the feast of Corpus Christi. The soldiers seemed to know the way, too, but the abbé couldn't tell if it was the same soldiers who were walking there, because he was always among different soldiers as they all walked much faster than he did. Even so the soldiers seemed to be in a great hurry to get to the buses. As he limped along after them the abbé Gaston thanked the Lord in his heart for having made French soldiers brave again. He hoped that when he reached the edge of the forest there would still be room in a bus for him to be brave, too.

When the abbé arrived at the edge of the forest he found two columns of buses drawn up: one pointing in one direction and the other in the opposite. But the abbé knew at once which were the buses that were going to the front because all the soldiers were scrambling into them and no soldiers at all were getting into the other column of buses. Some of the soldiers seemed to be using rather strong language for men who were about to risk their lives for France in a righteous war, but the abbé was sure that the Lord would forgive the soldiers, because they were going to be so brave.

The abbé lined up behind a group of men waiting to board the last bus but three in the column. The bus was a Paris bus painted over a dull yellowish green. To his surprise the abbé managed to secure his favorite little second class seat against the partition with nobody facing him and only one soldier sitting beside him. There was no light in the bus so the abbé couldn't take out his breviary and say his office. Instead he began to murmur the *Benedicite* and the beauty of the words as he said them helped him not to hear the bad language that was still so inexplicably going on all round about him.

"*Benedicite sol et luna Domino: benedicite stellae coeli Domino. Benedicite omnis imber et ros Domino: benedicite omnes spiritus Dei Domino.*" The abbé Gaston enjoyed calling upon the sun and the moon and the stars of heaven and the dew and all the spirits of the Lord to bless the Lord and he hoped that the Lord would let him get as far as the bit about the whales and all that moved in the waters before another airplane came along and dropped a bomb on them. "*Benedicite glacies et nives Domino.*" The engine of the motor bus joined with the ice and snow in praising the Lord and magnifying Him forever.

The bus gave a jerk and began to move forward through the darkness. It was difficult to see the darkness moving backwards because the darkness was the same everywhere, stuck glossily against the windows of the bus, so that the abbé felt and heard the motion of the bus rather than saw it. But when he looked very hard through the window the abbé thought that he could see the trunks of trees moving. And once he even saw the officer on horseback cantering along beside them and the officer on horseback seemed to be angry about something, for he was shaking his fist at the bus as he rode along beside it. But the bus soon gathered speed and the officer was left behind and the shiny darkness was jammed tight up against the windows again and the abbé said the remainder of the psalm out at the hidden fields. *"Benedictus es, Domine, in firmamento coeli: et laudabilis, et gloriosus, et superexaltatus in saecula."* When the abbé had finished saying these words the inside of the bus became ugly again, filled with harsh sounds and the smell of coarse tobacco and feet. The abbé turned to the soldier sitting next him.

"How long do you think that it will take us to get to Noyon?" the abbé asked.

"Noyon?" The soldier had a stupid, brutish look and small glazed eyes and at first he seemed puzzled by the abbé Gaston's question. "Noyon?" he repeated, and then he smiled as a scrutiny of the abbé's cassock seemed to help him to understand the significance of the abbé's question. "We're going much further than Noyon. In fact I shouldn't be surprised if we ended up in Berlin." The soldier winked one of his ugly little eyes as he said this, and it was the sort of mean little wink that the abbé had always disliked when he had seen it, but this time the abbé knew that it couldn't really be a mean little wink, because of what the soldier had just said. "Eh, Jules?" The soldier turned round and tugged at the shoulder strap of the soldier sitting behind him. "The chaplain here thinks that we're only going as far as Noyon. I've told him that we're much more likely to end up in Berlin. That's right, isn't it?"

The other soldier agreed. He agreed so much that he turned right round and knelt up on his seat to explain to the abbé. The other soldier had little green eyes and stubbly prickles of red beard sticking out from his chin like wires.

"That's right, Monsieur l'abbé," the other soldier said. "It's our seventy-fives that have done it, I expect. Anyway the Boches are running like hell. That's why they've put us into buses; so that we'll overtake them quicker, although I don't expect that we shall, because the Boches are bound to have buses, too."

The abbé Gaston was so moved that he forgave the other soldier for giving the first soldier the same sort of wink as the first soldier had given himself. In a crude age it was perhaps natural that the inarticulate should express their joy crudely.

"I always knew that God would uphold France," the abbé said when he was able to speak. "This is indeed the most wonderful news." The abbé's lips ran away from his tongue and he tried to smile at the soldiers so that they should not see the tears in his eyes.

"Of course we may have to do a bit of fighting yet," the first soldier said.

"But I expect that it will be mainly a token resistance," the second soldier said.

"Fight? I'll fight the whole German army provided France wins the war," the abbé Gaston said and thought how pleased the nuns and Rachel and Madame Bisberot would be when they learned that his sermon had come right after all.

The two soldiers seemed to understand that the abbé wanted to be alone with his thoughts, because he saw them both wink at each other simultaneously. Left to himself, the abbé began another psalm at once, praising the Lord in the firmament of His power. As he went on with his psalm the abbé could hear the soldiers laughing and joking among themselves, and he suspected that they were laughing a little at himself, for having been so foolish as to imagine that Frenchmen were still being beaten by Germans. But the abbé was too happy to care about that. *"Laudate eum in cymbalis benesonantibus, laudate eum in cymbalis jubilationis: omnis Spiritus laudet Dominum,"* the abbé praised before he fell asleep.

Dawn was beginning to break when the abbé Gaston awoke and looked out of the window to see that the bus was running through the streets of a big town. The abbé supposed that the town must be Lille although he was quite prepared to discover that it was Strasbourg. The rising sun made pretty patterns on the blinds drawn behind the closed shop windows and the abbé could see another bus with another abbé Gaston inside it sailing through brief blue and green and gold seas. At last the bus stopped between cliffs of houses that were familiar. The driver came round and stuck his head in at the door.

"Place du Maréchal Haig; all change," the driver shouted.

"Down with war!" the soldiers shouted back, rising to push their way out of the bus.

The abbé Gaston didn't require to wait for the soldiers' mockery before he wept.

There weren't many people in the church of Saint Clovis when the abbé Gaston said mass there on the morning of the fourteenth of June. There weren't many people in the streets either when he came out afterwards and stood on the top of the steps. Instead of people in the streets there was smoke in the streets. The smoke covered the whole of the city in a thick cloud and swirled round the deserted square in oily rings. There was no traffic in the square at all so that it seemed that history had at last come to a stop. The pink and pale green wash-hand basins and baths still stood in the window of the de luxe plumber's but the abbé couldn't see them very clearly because of the smoke. There was a light burning in the windows of the bank in front of which a thin line of depositors waited to withdraw their money. Everywhere there was the hum of airplanes but there were no airplanes to be seen in the sky and there was no sky to be seen because of the smoke. A group of soldiers came scattering down the causeway crying "Down with war!" The abbé Gaston lighted a cigar and puffed at it fiercely, because of strategy and tactics. The abbé didn't think that the point of his cigar could be seen from the air because of the smoke.

The abbé had prayed for the Major at mass, and he thought of him as he went down to remonstrate with the soldiers. The abbé waved his cigar at the soldiers and told them that it was a disgrace for French soldiers to run away from German soldiers. He told the soldiers that it was their duty to defend their city from the enemy. The abbé told the soldiers that God forgave soldiers very serious sins indeed when they defended cities from the enemy. But the soldiers laughed at the abbé and said that they had heard all these lies before. The soldiers said that Paul Reynaud was a dungheap and that Gamelin was a dungheap and that the British were dungheaps, too. The soldiers ran away into the smoke crying "Down with war!" The light in the window of the bank went out but the lonely queue of depositors waited on.

Madame Bisberot and Rachel came up to the abbé while he was still puffing away at his cigar in the gloom, and Madame Boulon and the centrally heated lady of easy virtue came across the square to him, too. Madame Bisberot said that all her prayers to St. Bernard Shaw didn't seem to have done much good and the centrally heated lady of easy virtue said that St. Guy de Maupassant had been a bit of a flop also. Madame Boulon said that the late Monsieur Boulon would have had a thing or two to say about all this if only he had been living, as it had been a habit of the late Monsieur Boulon's to speak his mind quite frankly. Rachel didn't say anything at all and the abbé saw that both her eyes were sad when she tossed back her hair. The abbé wondered if Rachel was worried because she was a Jewess and he patted her cheek until she smiled at him through the thick swirls of smoke.

"We tried to get on a train but the gates of the station were shut," Madame Bisberot explained.

"There's no use running away from Germans," the abbé said. "But civilians are only in the way when it comes to fighting. If I were you I'd go back home and wait till it's all over. In fact as senior officer commanding the Place du Maréchal Haig I order you all to do so."

The abbé stood puffing at his cigar as he watched them cross back over the square. Then he went and stood at the top of the steps of the church again, where he was joined by the Chanoine Litry and his curates when they came out of the church. Only the abbés Moune and Ronsard were with the rector as the two younger curates had been called up to the fighting.

"As I've said before, every one with any sense in his head seems to have beetled off," the abbé Moune said. "We might as well beetle off, too. It's silly to risk being killed unnecessarily."

"Monsieur l'abbé Moune, this is your parish and here you will remain," the rector said.

"Priests less than anybody ought to run away," the abbé Gaston said.

"You're a fine one to talk," the abbé Moune said. "I thought you were stationed in the Oise. Where's your regiment, if it comes to the bit?"

The abbé Gaston didn't know where his regiment was. He supposed that, if the Colonel had anything to do with it, his regiment must be practicing defense in depth somewhere near Bayonne. But a nun came out of the church before he could explain this to the abbé Moune. Beneath her big white coif the abbé recognized the anxious face of Sister Scholastica.

"I've been looking for you everywhere," Sister Scholastica said to the abbé Gaston. "We heard last night that you were back. Sister Marie Therese is most worried. She says that she does not know whether to evacuate the children or not. Even Sister Marie Joseph doesn't know."

"Botany has failed again, has it?" The abbé Gaston smiled as he said this, not because he was amused by his own joke, but because he wanted Sister Scholastica to smile, too. But Sister Scholastica did not smile.

"Please, Monsieur l'abbé Gaston," the nun pleaded. "We are all very distressed and we thought that a priest with your military experience might be able to help us." The abbé Gaston's confidence returned. He drew at his cigar and to his own surprise brought two clouds of smoke down his nostrils without choking. He pridefully watched the grey smoke sailing away into the black smoke and wished that the Colonel had been there to see him.

"Tell them to stay where they are," the abbé Gaston said. "Tell them that even French children do not run away from German soldiers."

At that moment there was a glitter at the end of the street. At first the glitter was only a faint glitter and it vanished for a little before it became stronger and when it came back again there was the sound of the tramp of feet as well. The glitter was the brightness made by the sun striving to shine through the smoke on steel helmets and the tramp was the trudge of soldiers. The soldiers did not shout as they came. The boots of the soldiers made a crunching noise as they came. Sometimes there was a bright yellow light on the helmets of the soldiers as they came but mostly there was just a glitter. The glitter stretched and became several glitters and sometimes there was a glitter and a bright yellow light at the same time, but always there was only one trudge of feet because the boots of the soldiers made one noise together.

"There wouldn't seem to be any doubt," the abbé Moune said.

"We can at least protect the church," the abbé Gaston said, marveling at his own presence of mind. "Monsieur le Curé, perhaps you would be good enough to go and stand at the southern door. Monsieur l'abbé Ronsard can stand at the north. Monsieur l'abbé Moune and I will remain here and guard the front door. Sister Scholastica, you will go into the church and protect the sanctuary." The abbé Gaston was proud of the calm with which he issued these orders and he wondered if the Major would have approved of them.

But the German soldiers didn't attempt to attack the church. The German soldiers marched past the church, and there was light on their steel helmets as they passed the church, and their boots made one noise all together. For more than an hour the German soldiers marched past the church and still there was the glitter of the sun on other steel helmets in the distance. As their faces came past in lines out of the smoke the abbé Gaston was surprised to see that the German soldiers didn't look any wickeder than the French soldiers, but the abbé hardened his heart against them, because they were German soldiers invading France.

LX

THE Ursuline nun had been writing to the Cardinal again. She said that her invention of the lid to protect cities from bombs hadn't been quite right in the first place, although that did not mean that it had been wrong. What was required, the nun said, was not a steel lid that slid out from under the earth on one side of the city and arched up over the city and clamped down on the other side of the city, but a steel lid that slid out from under the earth on both sides of the city and met in the middle, as there was less digging to be done that way. The nun said that she had written to the Air Ministry about her invention but that the Air Ministry had not bothered to reply. The Cardinal thought that this time perhaps he ought to send the invention on to the Pope. It was beginning to look as though Arthur might soon be grateful for a lid.

The Cardinal was still examining the nun's invention when the Chanoine Paquin ushered in the German military chaplains. The Cardinal stood up when the German military chaplains came in, but he did not invite them to sit down. The German chaplains said that they desired faculties to hear confessions in the archdiocese of Paris, and one of the chaplains said with a smile that he thought that his colleagues and himself would soon have a lot of forgiving of sins to do if all that he had heard about Paris was true. The Cardinal did not smile at the German military chaplains. The Cardinal wanted to ask the German military chaplains if they required faculties to forgive sins with bombs as well as sins with the contents of bottles and petticoats, but he realized that such a question would be unfair, as the theologians hadn't had time to think out the rules.

The German chaplains gravely inclined their heads when the Cardinal gave them their faculties. They clicked their heels because they were soldiers and they knelt and kissed the Cardinal's ring because they were also priests and the Cardinal was their pontiff. The Cardinal wondered whether Arthur would invite the German military chaplains to sit down, when they got to London.

LXI

ON Septuagesima Sunday 1941 the Place du Maréchal Haig was no longer called the Place du Maréchal Haig; instead it was called the Place du Maréchal Pétain. And inside the church of Saint Clovis there had been changes, too. The British and French flags were no longer festooned over the high altar, because Albion was again perfidious and France had ceased to have anything to festoon flags about. Over the Chanoine Litry's confessional there was a notice which said MAN SPRICHT DEUTSCH, because German was one of the five languages in which the rector knew about sin. The notice which said ENGLISH SPOKEN had gone, as the British had to sin at home these days, because of the U boats.

The abbé Gaston had said his mass at seven o'clock and was kneeling at the back of the church and making his thanksgiving. When he had finished making his thanksgiving, the abbé began to meditate on the gospel for the day. "*Acceperunt autem et ipsi singulos denarios*" the Lord had said in the parable of the workers in the vineyard, "and they received." The abbé thought that he had never really understood this parable of the Lord's, and he tried to understand it now. In spite of what priests more clever than himself had said, it was difficult to accept that those who had been wicked for a long time and just for a short time should receive the same reward as those who had been just for a long time. The abbé wondered if it had something to do with purgatory or with eternity being like a bath sponge or the underground railway in London. The abbé could think of no other explanation.

The German military chaplain seemed to understand the parable all right, because he was explaining it from the pulpit to the German soldiers who sat stretching away in long level rows in front of the abbé, like chocolates in a box. The abbé knew enough German to understand that the German military chaplain was explaining the parable, but he didn't know enough German to understand the German military chaplain's explanation. The German soldiers seemed to understand the chaplain's explanation, however, because they were listening attentively. The abbé Gaston hoped that it wasn't because of this parable that the German soldiers thought that they could go on being cruel to their enemies right up to the last moment.

The German military chaplain finished his sermon and the other German priest at the altar rose to continue the mass. The German priest at the altar was wearing the same violet vestments as the abbé Gaston had worn at the previous mass, and the hurt in the abbé's soul at the distress of France was healed a little by this hint of the universality of the Church.

In front of the abbé the poetess knelt side by side with a German Colonel. The abbé wondered whether it was because of the universality of the Church that the poetess always came to mass with the German Colonel or because she liked the German Colonel. At any rate, it wasn't about the universality of the Church that the poetess talked when she spoke about the Germans. The poetess said that the Germans were saving civilization from the barbarians and the abbé Moune had said much the same thing in a special course of Advent sermons. The rector, however, had said on the First Sunday after Epiphany that it was really Marshal Pétain who was saving civilization. The abbé Gaston still thought that only God could save civilization.

> *"Heilig, heilig, heilig! Heilig ist der Herr!*
> *Heilig, heilig, heilig! Heilig ist nur er!*
> *Er, der nie begonnen, er, der immer war,*
> *Ewig ist und waltet, sein wird immerdar."*

The sound of the strong voices rang through the church. Up at the altar the German priest made the holy signs and swung deeply into the great prayer. The kneeling German soldiers watched him attentively as they sang. Was it because French soldiers prayed less devoutly than German soldiers that the Lord had let them be routed? Was it because of their good behavior in church that the Lord had allowed the Germans to roll on in their tanks? The abbé Gaston did not know. At the altar the little bell tinkled tinnily and the abbé bowed his head as the Host rose like a white moon. Under his breath the abbé Gaston prayed the Latin words with the priest. The chalice rose in a silver silence and the abbé Gaston bowed his head again. When he looked up the German soldiers were still squarely on their knees and not standing up and scratching their ears like French soldiers. *"Hochgelobt sei, der da kommt im Namen des Herren,"* the German soldiers sang.

But in the sacristy afterwards the abbé bowed coldly to the German priest who had just said mass, and he bowed even more coldly to the abbé Moune who was talking affably with the other German priest who had preached the sermon. The abbé went quickly out into the street. In the de luxe plumber's window there were now heliotrope as well as pink and pale green washhand stands and baths.

The butcher, the baker and the wine merchant did not greet the abbé as he passed in front of their shops because the abbé no longer had enough money to buy much food and drink from them. The butcher, the baker and the wine merchant had told the abbé that they had to sell their wares at as dear a price as possible, in order to beat the Germans. They had, however, been willing to make certain concessions. The butcher had said that he would give the abbé a chicken if the abbé would give him a pair of new shoes and the baker had said that he would give the abbé as many chocolate eclairs as he could eat at a single sitting if the abbé would give him a new double-breasted overcoat. These offers had not been of much use to the abbé, who had only prayers to barter.

The abbé did not look into Madame Bisberot's window as he passed in case the fashions and hair might have changed again and he might be tempted to ask Madame Bisberot for another advance on royalties on the submannequin. The abbé also didn't want to have to smile at Madame Bisberot if he caught sight of her through the window because he disapproved of Madame Bisberot now that she was so busy making dresses for the wives of German officers. He was also afraid of having to smile at Rachel because he was frightened of the consequences of being seen smiling to a Jewess. The abbé knew that it was cowardly of him to be afraid of seeing Rachel, and he tried to justify his prudence by arguing that the less contact Rachel had with other people the less she was likely to have with Germans.

The centrally heated lady of easy virtue did not smile at the abbé when she met him on the doorstep, perhaps because she was still annoyed that St. Guy de Maupassant had been so inadequate. But the abbé thought that there were perhaps other reasons for her discontent: the wrinkles were beginning to run like tracks across the centrally heated lady of easy virtue's face and even her gentleman friend had been unable to find coal for her flat. The centrally heated lady of easy virtue had become the frozen lady of difficult vice.

On his way upstairs the abbé met a German officer standing outside the door of a flat on the fourth floor. He bowed coldly to the officer when the officer saluted him but he did not smile at the officer when the officer smiled at him. The abbé went on up the stairs thinking miserably of the catastrophe which had come upon France.

But as soon as he was in his little room the abbé forgot about the German officer. St. Elizabeth of Hungary was sitting on the bed washing her hind leg in the position that always made her look as though she were playing the 'cello. The abbé sat down on the bed and stroked the cat, which arched its back and began to purr. A pigeon came and strutted on the ledge of the window against the pale blue silk sheet of the morning sky, but the cat paid no attention and went on rubbing its head against the back of the abbé's hand. Still stroking the cat, the abbé began his daily prayer for the repose of the souls of the faithful departed. This prayer now took the abbé twenty-two minutes because the alive people he knew kept on changing so quickly into dead people.

The bell rang before the abbé had got very far down his list of names. The abbé rose and went to the door where he discovered that his caller was the German officer whom he had passed on the staircase. The sun shone on the German officer's leather leggings as he stalked into the room, and the sun shone on the buttons of his, too, and sent out a spray of silver light from each of them. The abbé was not surprised to see that the German officer looked very young as most people looked young to the abbé these days, even His Holiness Pope Pius the Twelfth. The abbé did not know whether the German officer was twenty-five or thirty-five because the abbé was getting too old accurately to read the gradations of youth.

"Perhaps if you were to close the door we might be able to talk in greater privacy," the officer said.

The abbé Gaston shut the door, although he felt that he ought to have left it open, to show that he had no desire to talk in privacy with an enemy of France. And when he came back into the middle of the room again the abbé did not know whether he had shut the door from charity or from cowardice, so thin was the line dividing turning the other cheek from the desire to avoid battle.

"If you will be so good as to sit down," the abbé Gaston said.

The German officer sat down in the chair in which Bessier usually sat when he came to see the abbé. The abbé wondered if Bessier's disapproval of the war as a reactionary imperialist plutodemocratic war would make Bessier approve of the German officer sitting there. "Monsieur l'abbé, I want to talk to you about Jews," the officer said.

The abbé was so startled that he scarcely noticed the German officer's good French. More than ever life was becoming like a bad detective novel, the abbé realized miserably, and he himself was becoming less and less able to deal with its complexities.

"I am afraid that you and I are not likely to agree about Jews," the abbé said slowly. The abbé did his best to look brave and defiant as he said this but he felt frightened inside. The moment seemed unimportant with the ordinary sky outside the window stamped on it, but the abbé knew that it wasn't the sky stamped on the moment that was important, but what the German officer was going to say next.

"I am not obliged to agree with you, but you are obliged to agree with me," the German officer said. "The Führer has ruled that the Jews are the enemies of our civilization."

Although he had read in the newspapers that Germans talked in this absurd way, the abbé had never really believed it. He knew now that it was as true as the sun making all those lovely glows and shines on the officer's leggings and buttons. The German officer's jargon was as pompous as Bessier's when Bessier talked about communism. The abbé realized with despair that the new idols were even more foolish than the old idols, whose silence had perhaps made it possible to believe in their wisdom.

"It is men as a whole who are the enemies of their civilization," the abbé said. "You may remember what Socrates said." But the abbé himself no longer remembered what Socrates said because he was so afraid of what the German officer was going to ask him next.

"I came here to talk about Jews, not about philosophy," the German officer said. "Monsieur l'abbé, are you hiding any Jews from the German military authority?"

"Of course not," the abbé said. Behind what he hoped was his outward calm the abbé thought rapidly. There was no reason to believe that anyone had been talking about Rachel. From the fact that he himself had seen the German officer standing outside the door of a flat on the fourth floor it was obvious that the officer was asking everybody in the house the same questions. And priests were especially suspect, the abbé knew, because so many of the clergy had sheltered Jews. There was no reason to imagine that the German officer knew anything specific unless either Madame Boulon or the centrally heated lady of easy virtue had been talking either to the other tenants or to the German officer. And the centrally heated lady of easy virtue must have been out when the German officer called because he himself had met her going out to do her shopping. In any case these were risks which he was required to take, as was also the Lord's possible disapproval of his having told a lie. "I am concealing no Jews from the German military authority," he said.

"I have another question to ask you, Monsieur l'abbé," the German officer said. "Do you know of anyone else who is hiding or helping Jews to hide from the German military authority?"

"I know of nobody who is doing so," the abbé Gaston said.

"Monsieur l'abbé, are you quite sure that you are telling me the truth?" the German officer asked. "Remember that we have means of verifying the accuracy of your statement."

It was impossible for the abbé to tell what the German officer was thinking. The German officer's stare was cold and non-committal. There was a bulge at the back of the German officer's head and there was a bulge at the front of his head. Contemplating those bulges, the abbé was afraid and he began to wonder if the abbé Moune had been talking. The abbé Moune liked the Germans and disliked the Jews. Walking one day with the rector on the square after lunch, the abbé Moune had said that the Germans had brought order to Europe and that the Jews had brought disorder. The abbé Moune had said that the Jews had crucified Christ and that therefore it was wrong for Jews to own big chains of department stores and newspapers. The abbé Moune had also said that it was right only for Christians to own big chains of department stores and newspapers, because Christians had been redeemed. The abbé remembered that he had told the abbé Moune that it was to make men meek and merciful and not prosperous that the Lord Jesus had died on the cross and that sometimes the Jews were better at these things than the Christians. Remembering these things, the abbé Gaston wondered more than ever if the abbé Moune had been talking, but he knew that this, too, was a risk which he would require to take. The officer sat on in the abbé's chair with only the Lord to love the big bulges on his head.

"I repeat what I have said," the abbé Gaston said. "I am concealing no Jews from the German military authorities. And I know of nobody who is doing so."

The German officer rose and walked towards the door. The sun shone on his leggings and the sun shone on his buttons. His big broad breeches scooped the air. "I thank you, Monsieur l'abbé," he said. "That is all that I require to know." He opened the door for himself and went out. He closed the door behind him with a click. The abbé sat listening to his footsteps diminishing away down the staircase.

The abbé prayed a quick prayer of thanksgiving but he thought even more quickly. The German officer would probably come back again to question the centrally heated lady of easy virtue. He might interrogate Madame Bisberot. He might call on the rector. Although it seemed that none of these persons had spoken so far, all of them must be warned at once. And Madame Boulon must be warned, too, if she hadn't told the German officer about Rachel on his way out.

There was no answer when the abbé rang the bell outside the centrally heated lady of easy virtue's flat, so he concluded that she must still be out doing her shopping. But Madame Boulon was behind her curtains, and she scowled at the abbé as he opened her door. The abbé was nervous, not only because of the scowl, but also because Madame Boulon's political sympathies were uncertain these days. One day Madame Boulon would say that the Germans were polite and correct and the next day she would say that if the late Monsieur Boulon had been alive he would never have kow-towed to the Germans, not the late Monsieur Boulon.

"About that German officer," the abbé began timidly.

But in spite of the scowl it was one of the days when the late Monsieur Boulon would not have kow-towed to the Germans. Madame Boulon said so quite forcibly. She said that the late Monsieur Boulon would have risen from his grave in the Cimetière de Pantin if his wife had betrayed a defenseless Jewish girl to a German officer, however much the German officer had threatened her. She said this so loudly that the centrally heated lady of easy virtue, coming back from doing her shopping, heard her, and stopped to ascertain the cause of the commotion. In spite of her annoyance at the inefficiency of St. Guy de Maupassant, the centrally heated lady of easy virtue promised that she, too, would not tell the German officer about Rachel, however often he called. The abbé Gaston thanked them both warmly and crossed the square to Madame Bisberot's, comforted by the perverse nobility of the perverse.

Madame Bisberot was as reassuring. She said that the German officer had called but that she had told him nothing. There was nothing to worry about, she said. Rachel, she said, was so un-Jewish looking that she was able to parade in gowns in front of German officers and their wives without their suspecting her race. And in the sacristy the rector was reassuring, too. He said that the German officer had already called at the presbytery and that he had told the German officer nothing. The abbé Moune, the rector said, had not been there when the German officer had called: The abbé Gaston went into high mass with a thankful heart.

LXII

ALTHOUGH his head was wobbling about more than ever on the eve of Pentecost, 1941, the Cardinal did all the public praying himself, that the Holy Ghost might come and lighten with celestial fire, and that God might flood the world with the brightness of His heavenly radiance. He breathed upon the waters of the font and poured the oil of catechumens into the waters and blessed the waters. He lay on his face in front of the altar and prayed that the Lord would have mercy and that Christ would have mercy and that the Lord would have mercy. And the people prayed with the Cardinal, that Christ might graciously hear them and that all holy monks and hermits and all holy virgins and widows might pray for them. Then they lighted the candles upon the altar and in a trembling voice the Cardinal sang the first mass of the Holy Ghost, that the rent might be mended in Christ's garment, which was the Church.

LXIII

IN 1943 there was still no traffic in the Place du Maréchal Pétain apart from German staff cars which tore round the square occasionally, with hard faces sitting in the back beneath high caps. Sitting in his room one December evening, the abbé Gaston was glad of the silence, because he hoped that it would help him to meditate more effectively.

The abbé had recently read in a pious book that in winter certain holy men and women had been able to increase the temperature of their bodies to that of an August day by reflecting upon the attributes of God. The holier you were the hotter you became, the author had said and had cited the example of a Franciscan friar who, in 1724 and in Compostella, had boiled an egg in the cold water of his bath while reflecting upon the Indivisibility of the Trinity. Although the abbé was now much too poor to have an egg to boil, he greatly desired to feel in his body the heat of an August day, because it was a bitterly cold night and the abbé had no coal to burn in his grate. In the old days the abbé had been able to rely on a little warmth coming through the floor from the flat of the centrally heated lady of easy virtue underneath, but for three years now even the youngest and the most beautiful ladies of easy virtue in Paris had no longer been centrally heated, and the abbé didn't suppose that any of them were much good at meditating on the Trinity.

The abbé Gaston soon didn't think that he was much good at meditating on the Trinity either. He began by thinking of a clover leaf, which was how they had taught him in the seminary. But even when he had thought for quite a long time about the three leaves growing on one stem the abbé didn't feel any warmer and he muffed his frozen hands in the broad sleeves of his cassock until his meditation should begin to work properly. St. Elizabeth of Hungary must have felt cold, too, for she came and rubbed herself against the abbé, meowing as she did so. The abbé knew that the cat was meowing because she wanted food, but he had no food to give her. Nor had he any food to give himself. The abbé made do on one meal a day now and sometimes he was so famished that he felt like eating St. Elizabeth of Hungary. He felt like eating her now until he looked into the cat's big yellow eyes and saw that she was as unhappy as he was. If only St. Elizabeth of Hungary had been like a clover leaf, the abbé reflected, with three St. Elizabeths of Hungary growing out of one stem, then perhaps he could have lopped off one without the other two feeling anything and have had St. Elizabeth of Hungary a la mayonnaise. The abbé was not surprised when this meditation failed to produce any warmth in his body.

The abbé Gaston placed the cat on the floor and tried again. But by now he was so cold that he could think only of how cold he was. He was so cold that he thought that nobody else in the whole of Paris could be as cold as he was. Intellectually, of course, the abbé knew that everybody in Paris was just as cold as he was, but he did not know it emotionally. Feeling the cold, the abbé supposed, was like feeling the presence of God. God was in all the rooms of all the houses in Paris, but when the abbé thought about God it seemed to him that God could be only in his own room. The supernatural thought slid in almost without his noticing it, but it did not make him feel any warmer, perhaps because the thought was pantheistic. At the seminary the abbé had often got bad marks because of pantheism. It was the immanent and the transcendent Presences of God that the abbé got muddled up.

But the abbé felt warm all at once when the bell rang with a sharp ring. Although it was more than two years now since the German officer had called to ask about Rachel the abbé was still frightened every time the bell rang. He was frightened in case either Madame Boulon or the centrally heated lady of easy virtue or Madame Bisberot or the rector or all of them might have changed their minds and told the German officer about Rachel, or that the German officer might have found out about Rachel for himself. And the abbé was especially frightened that the abbé Moune, who frequently met Germans, might meet the German officer and tell him about Rachel without even being asked to do so. The abbé knew that the German officer was still in Paris because he had seen him only a few days ago in the street.

However, it was not the German officer whom the abbé found standing on the landing when he nervously opened the door. Instead it was Bessier, accompanied by another man. Both men advanced quickly into the room while the abbé shut the door, and they were both red in the face and out of breath. Bessier wore his usual shabby suit, and the seat of his shiny trousers winked first on one side and then on the other as he walked in front of the abbé into the middle of the room. Bessier's companion was a raw-faced young man of about twenty-five who was dressed in a baggy suit which seemed a little too large for him. Bessier went back to the door and listened with his ear against the wood. Then he came back into the middle of the room again, his shoulder rounding up ever so slightly when he moved his artificial leg.

"Jean, I know that we can count on you," Bessier said.

The abbé nodded, and he tried to smile as he nodded, because he was sure that he had nodded unenthusiastically. Although the abbé liked people to think that they could count on him, he didn't always like it so much when they actually did count on him. Looking at Bessier's flustered face, the abbé was sure that Bessier was going to ask him to do something unpleasant. Continuing to cover his fears by an appearance of benevolence, the abbé tried also to smile at the strange young man, who stretched his lips out over his teeth and quickly closed them again.

"We want you to help the Resistance," Bessier said.

The abbé had heard quite a lot about the Resistance Movement, and he was not altogether surprised to learn that Bessier belonged to it, because since the twenty-first of June, 1941, the reactionary imperialist plutodemocratic war had become for Bessier a progressive and righteous war. The abbé knew that the Resistance Movement tried to counteract the bad detective novel things which the Germans did to the world by doing other detective novel things to the Germans. And the abbé didn't know whether he approved of all the things that the Resistance Movement did. The abbé couldn't help thinking that war had degenerated a lot since he himself had fought in one.

"I think I understand," he said dismally, although he knew that he did not understand at all, and he hoped not to have to understand very much, because he was frightened enough about Rachel as it was and did not wish to have to be frightened about blowing up a gas works as well.

"You can't possibly understand until you've let me explain," Bessier said. "My friend here is a British airman. His plane was shot down in the north a few days ago, but he himself got clear in his parachute."

"But of course I understand," the abbé said, smiling quite genuinely now, because he had also heard of the Resistance Movement aiding Allied airmen to escape and it was an activity of which he approved. "You want me to shelter your friend for a few days before you pass him on?" The abbé spoke quite eagerly now that he was certain that Bessier was not going to ask him to blow up a gas works.

"It's not quite as easy as all that," Bessier said. "I've been doing the passing on already. Unfortunately we were followed."

"But you managed to shake them off, I hope?" the abbé said, fearful once more.

"There was only one person to shake off," Bessier said. "And we shook him off by killing him. And not very far from here either. An officer, too, worse luck."

The abbé was deeply miserable. He was both shocked and frightened, but chiefly he was frightened. He did not approve of killing even enemies in cold blood, and he did not want to have to shelter an airman who had helped to do such a thing, but especially he was afraid of the danger to himself.

"There's nothing to get the jitters about," Bessier said, looking sternly into the abbé's terrified face. "Nobody saw us do it. And nobody saw us come in here."

"I'm glad of that," the abbé said simply and tried to control his shaking limbs.

"But they're bound to find out any moment now," Bessier said. "And then the whole district will be in an uproar."

Quaking with fear, the abbé tried to listen out through the black curtains on the window. But however hard he listened he could hear no uproar. He could hear only the silence of the coldness of the night. Even so he was still frightened. For the abbé knew that the strength of the Germans was that they did not make noisy inefficient uproars like the French made. The strength of the Germans was that they made quiet efficient uproars. The abbé was still trembling when he had finished listening.

Then the British airman spoke for the first time.

"Help me," the airman said in English and pointed with his forefinger at his own chest.

This time the airman smiled with his eyes as well as with his mouth, and the abbé began to think that he liked him better. When he smiled with his eyes the airman did not look as though he could have dropped bombs on women and children or murdered a man in cold blood. Instead the airman looked benign, banal and stupid. But the abbé knew that the crime of the cold men in the chancelleries was that they had taught benign, banal and stupid men all over the world that cruelty was their duty and that out of the screams of widows would come Augustine's City of God. Thinking of this, the abbé wondered why archbishops did not condemn air raids as angrily as they condemned birth control. But although he disliked both killing in cold blood and air raids the abbé knew that he did not dislike the airman, because he understood that the airman had been caught up in the wrong meaning of the world, because of the politicians.

"Of course I'll help you," the abbé said. He did not really wish to help the airman, because it was dangerous, but it was to do dangerous things that he had become a priest, and the Lord upheld his priests when they did dangerous things, as He had promised in the gospel.

"The first thing you've got to do is to keep this officer here tonight," Bessier said. "And tomorrow I want you to put him on the train for Lyons. Jean, please listen to what I am saying. This may be a matter of life or death for all of us."

"Of course, I'm listening, Philippe," the abbé said, but he knew that he hadn't been listening properly and that it was because he knew as well as Bessier that it was a matter of life or death for them all that he hadn't been listening properly.

"And on second thoughts I don't only want you to put him on the train," Bessier said. "I want you to travel with him as far as Lyons. He doesn't speak much French and he's less likely to arouse suspicion travelling in the company of a priest."

"That's a little more difficult," the abbé said, glad to have an excuse to offer and ashamed of being glad. "I've got duties here you know."

"Don't talk nonsense," Bessier said. "All you've got to do is to tell your superiors that you've got private business away from Paris." The abbé thought that it was extraordinary how enthusiastic about the war Bessier had become now that the war had changed into a progressive war. "There's no need to state the real reason for your journey. The less people that know about that the better."

"I can always try," the abbé said.

"In the meantime I'll leave you some money for food," Bessier said. "And I'll come back and tell you about the tickets and things tomorrow."

Listening to Bessier, the abbé wished that men would suffer pain and discomfort for the big cause of the world as readily as for the small cause of country. But the abbé knew that he himself was to blame, too. He also had shown the lesser courage when, in his field boots and his forage cap and smoking his cigar, he had stopped soldiers in the street and asked them to fight for France. He had never stopped men in the street and urged them to serve the Lord. He had preached, safely in churches where his exhortations were expected. Patriotism was only a relative loyalty. The real loyalty was to all men and women on soil beneath the sun. It was this that men must understand.

"Of course I'll do what you want," the abbé said.

It was quiet in the abbé's room after Bessier had gone. It was quiet in the room and it was quiet in the street and it was quiet over the roofs of Paris without any light on them. The abbé did not know what to say to the airman and the airman did not seem to know what to say to the abbé.

"I'm afraid it's too late to go out and buy food tonight," the abbé Gaston said.

"No compree," the airman said. *"Oui, oui, couleur rouge, no compree."*

"It is too late to search for food tonight," the abbé said in uncertain English. "The shops are no longer open. The shops are shut."

"Oui, oui, couleur rouge," the airman said.

"That is very good French," the abbé said.

"Mademoiselle, voulez-vous coucher avec moi," the airman said.

"That is not such good French," the abbé said.

"No offense, padre," the airman said.

Down in the street there was the noise of soldiers' boots marching on the square. The abbé and the airman both looked frightened as they listened. The noise of the boots drew nearer and it seemed as though the soldiers were marching on gravel because of the nails on the soles of their boots. But the soldiers did not stop. The soldiers marched round the church and out of the square until it was no longer possible to hear the sound of their boots. It was quiet in the street and in the room again.

"A near 'air cut, I think you say," the abbé said in English.

"Oui, oui, couleur rouge," the airman said.

"I expect that you 'ave a lot of near 'air cuts in the hair," the abbé said, still in English.

The airman did not answer. Instead he nodded. And as he nodded his eyes grew brighter and began to look like miniature targets, with rings of different shades of blue around the iris.

"I'm dreaming of a white Christmas," the airman began to hum.

"Is that a hymn?" the abbé asked.

"No bloody fear," the airman said. "Sorry, padre. No offense meant."

"Are you a Christian?" the abbé asked.

"Church of England," the airman said.

"I have never been in an airplane," the abbé said. "Sometimes I wonder what it must feel like. Are you never frightened?"

"Everybody gets in a flap occasionally," the airman said. "Sleigh bells ringing," he hummed.

"I think that I should get in a large flapper if other men were to fire guns at me while I was flying in the air in an airplane," the abbé Gaston said.

"One gets used to everything," the airman said. "No use binding."

"I think that you must be very brave," the abbé said. "But even when you are frightened it must be a consolation to know that you are fighting in a righteous war."

"If you ask me there's no such thing as a righteous war," the airman said. "There's only war. And war's war whichever way you look at it."

"At least you do not do the terrible things that the Germans do," the abbé said.

"What's sauce for the goose is sauce for the gander," the airman said. "I'm dreaming of a white Christmas," he hummed.

The abbé thought about all the cruel things that were happening in the world and tried to feel them within himself. But however hard the abbé thought about the pain that there was in the world he still could not feel the hurt in himself but only a sadness that he could not feel the hurt.

"The light seems to have gone from the world," the abbé said.

"The light seems to have gone from Paris, too," the airman said. "Say, what about a dekko at the Folies Bergère?"

"Quite out of the question," the abbé said. "It's full of German officers for one thing."

"It's not the German officers I want to see," the airman said. "For all the things I used to know," he hummed.

"Bed is the best place for you," the abbé said.

"*Oui, oui, couleur rouge,*" the airman said.

"I expect that the bed will be rather narrow for both of us," the abbé said.

"*Oui, oui, couleur rouge,*" the airman said.

The abbé knelt and said his prayers while the airman was undressing. He prayed for all the unhappy people that there were in the world and that somehow God's kingdom might come. The airman was already in bed and asleep when the abbé had finished praying.

The abbé Gaston was feeling more frightened than ever when he and the airman left for the Gare de Lyon the next evening. And his fright increased when the airman began to sing as soon as they stood on the landing outside the abbé's door.

"Sleigh bells ringing," the airman sang.

"Please," the abbé begged, "There is a lady underneath."

"Lead me to her," the airman almost shouted.

"Please," the abbé begged again. "We are not yet out of danger."

"*Oui, oui, couleur rouge,*" the airman said.

The one minute light wasn't working anymore because of the war so they had to go down the six long flights of stairs in the dark. On the way down the abbé memorized again what Bessier had told him when he had called at the flat that morning to give the abbé his final instructions. On his arrival at the Gare de Lyon the abbé was to say to the booking clerk: "The pink rabbit has a blue tail," and the booking clerk would give him his tickets and his reservations. In the train he was not to speak to the airman and the airman was not to speak to him, and if anybody tried to speak to the airman both he and the airman were to pretend that the airman was dumb. When they got to Lyons the abbé would find waiting on the platform a man with a red tie, a blue pullover and brown shoes to whom he was to say: "Norwegians build fine bridges." And, when the man had replied, "Yes, but the Swedes make better fountain pens", the abbé was to hand over the airman to him and the man with the red tie, the blue pullover and the brown shoes would arrange for the next stage in the airman's journey to the Spanish frontier.

Although the rector hadn't shown any curiosity about the abbé's journey, Madame Boulon had not been so discreet when the abbé had asked her to look after St. Elizabeth of Hungary for him. She had asked so many questions that the abbé was not surprised to find her standing on the wrong side of her curtains when he came down the stairs with the airman.

"I shall need money for the cat's food," Madame Boulon said. She did not look at the abbé as she spoke, but at the airman who was standing behind the abbé. The abbé gave Madame Boulon some of the money which Bessier had given him because he had no money of his own to give. The abbé thought that it was quite fitting that the Resistance should contribute to the support of St. Elizabeth of Hungary since the cat, too, was enduring discomfort for France.

"You've got a friend with you, I see," Madame Boulon said when she had taken the money.

"Yes," the abbé said, feeling both stupid and guilty.

"The late Monsieur Boulon always used to like travelling with a friend," Madame Boulon said. "He said it made the journey seem shorter." Even in the darkness the abbé could see her looking hard at the airman as she spoke, peering at him out of her rheumy eyes. "The Russians are doing well," she went on. "They always seem to do better in winter than in summer."

"It's because of the snow, I expect," the abbé said.

Madame Boulon said that in her opinion it wasn't because of the snow, but because Stalin had transferred all his munitions factories behind the Urinal Mountains. But the abbé was too frightened to be amused by Madame Boulon's mispronunciation or to give her the chance of repeating it. He pushed the airman through the front door and followed him quickly.

Outside the cold trees looked like etchings of themselves. Their leafless branches were spread like black veins across the sky. The dark bulk of the church sailed slowly beneath the watery stars. And although it was not yet curfew the square was empty except for the titanic tart who stood lugubriously beneath her now unlighted lamp. As the abbé and the airman walked along the pavement the abbé Moune approached noiselessly towards them out of the darkness.

"Good evening," the abbé Moune said. "The rector told me that you were going away for a little."

"Yes, but not for long," the abbé Gaston said. He was frightened to walk on at once in case he aroused the abbé Moune's suspicions.

"So I see, as you've got no luggage," the abbé Moune said.

"Yes, I've got no luggage," the abbé Gaston said.

"But you've got a friend," the abbé Moune said.

"Yes, I've got a friend," the abbé Gaston said.

"It is always better to travel with a friend than with luggage," the abbé Moune said. "Good night, Monsieur l'abbé Gaston. I hope that you have a pleasant journey."

"Good night, Monsieur l'abbé Moune," the abbé Gaston said.

The abbé Gaston was disturbed by his meeting with the abbé Moune and he was still more disturbed by the abbé Moune's tone. He waited with the airman in the shadows at the corner of the square until the abbé Moune's footsteps had died away on the pavement and even then he waited on a little, to make sure that the abbé Moune was not going to come creeping back again. While they were waiting a German staff car swerved into the square and its veiled headlights threw a wavering pool of light on the cobbles. The car was quickly gone, but almost as quickly it was back again, throwing the same thin light in front of it, and vanishing this time in another direction. The abbé was both intrigued and frightened and he stared hard into the darkness to see if he could see the abbé Moune lurking in the shadows, but all the shadows in the square were abbé Mounes, skulking in their cassocks. The silence was so deep that it was as frightening as the darkness and out of the silence came a rustling sound like a woman walking rapidly in a silk dress, but it was only dead leaves being blown along the pavement. As the abbé was recovering from his emotion the staff car came swinging round into the square again but this time it stopped beneath the trees and all its lights went out. The abbé decided that it would be imprudent to wait any longer and led his companion down into the underground.

Although there weren't many people waiting on the platform the train was crowded when it came in. Because all the buses on the streets had been stopped half the red first class compartment had been partitioned off and turned into a second class compartment in order to accommodate the extra passengers. The abbé knew which was the red first class compartment because of the German officers sitting in it, but even in the red first class compartment the abbé and the airman had to stand, as there were not enough seats to go round. *"Oui, oui, couleur rouge,"* the airman murmured, for once appropriately. "Please," the abbé Gaston whispered, sure that he saw a German officer looking at them.

The train drew out of the lighted cone of tiles into the dark cone of tunnel and the ticket inspector began to work his way along between the seats. The ticket inspector had some difficulty in climbing over the suitcases and parcels with which the civilian passengers had encumbered the passage. The ticket inspector didn't ask the German officers to show their tickets because the German officers travelled first class for nothing.

The ticket inspector smiled at the abbé as he punched the airman's ticket and the abbé's and he asked the abbé if the rules of religion hadn't changed yet. The ticket inspector said that the rules of politics seemed to be changing faster than ever and that even the rules of the underground railway had changed since the war. But the abbé didn't listen much to the ticket inspector because he saw that the airman was ogling a girl with a pair of lips like bicycle tires. The train rolled on between reams of **DUBO, DUBON DUBONNET** and the airman started to wink at the girl with lips like bicycle tires. The abbé was glad when the train reached the Gare de Lyon.

It was dark in the railway station and there were long queues of people waiting in front of the booking offices. Most of the people were shabbily dressed and had thin unhappy faces and an ugliness in their eyes because of the hard things that life had done to them. "Awful bunch of old crows," the airman said, referring to the women in the queue. The abbé deemed it wise not to answer although he knew that the women in the queue were mean and miserable only because others had been mean and miserable to them and because they had been cheated of the shining thing and had no glow in their hearts.

When at last they reached the guichet the abbé Gaston made the airman stand behind him while he whispered through the horseshoe of aperture at the bottom of the glass window.

"The blue rabbit has a pink tail," the abbé said.

"Pink rabbit blue tail," the booking clerk corrected without smiling. "All right; you'd better come round to the back."

The abbé Gaston and the airman went round to the back, although it was really the side, because the employees' door opened at right angles to the guichet. The booking clerk made them come into the office where they stood blinking at him in the strong light. The booking clerk had a lean unhappy face like the people waiting outside in the queue and he wore over his eyes a shade which was black on top and green underneath.

"Everything's there," the booking clerk said, handing the abbé a bunch of papers. "Tickets and permits. The young man's got an identity card, of course?"

"He came to us with one," the abbé said. The abbé had seen the forged identity card with which the airman had been provided in the north. It described the airman as an accountant.

"Photograph on it of course?" the booking clerk asked.

"Of course," the abbé said.

"Well, you'll just have to risk that," the booking clerk said.

"Risk what?" the abbé asked, wishing that his stomach wouldn't seem to turn to liquid every time he received a new fright.

"Listen," the booking clerk said. "They're watching all the trains. I'm pretty sure they suspect something."

"In that case we'd better not travel," the abbé said.

"You've got to travel," the booking clerk said. "It's too late to cancel things now. They're waiting for this young man at Lyons."

"But if we're going to be caught," the abbé Gaston said.

"You won't be caught if you do what I tell you," the booking clerk said. "Listen. There's only one thing to do: go into the lavatory and change clothes."

"But that's impossible," the abbé said.

"Listen," the booking clerk said. "They're looking for this young man and they're much less likely to suspect anything if he travels as a priest."

"But the identity cards," the abbé said.

"You'll have to swap over of course," the booking clerk said. "In any case they don't always look at them."

"But if they do look at them?" the abbé said.

"You'll have to risk that," the booking clerk said.

"But the photographs," the abbé Gaston said.

"I've already told you that you'll have to risk that," the booking clerk said.

"But I've got a beard," the abbé said.

"You'll have to risk that, too," the booking clerk said, opening the door for them to go out. "Don't say I didn't warn you."

The abbé decided to take the booking clerk's advice as it was obvious that the booking clerk was much more experienced in these matters than himself. The airman laughed loudly when the abbé explained to him what they had to do, but the abbé reprimanded him sharply, and together they went down into the tiled lavatory which was empty except for a huge despondent negro. When the negro had left, the abbé and the airman went together into one of the small wooden compartments, where they changed clothes. The tiled lavatory was still empty when they came out again and the cisterns gurgled as they flushed the dismal porcelain stalls. The airman's suit was too big for the abbé and the abbé felt that it might fall off him at any moment so he undid his waistcoat and tightened his braces up as far as they would go. The abbé's cassock was a little too short for the airman and the flat clerical hat wobbled precariously on top of his big head, but it was the airman's expression which chiefly perturbed the abbé. Although in the course of his life the abbé had seen a good many unspiritual looking priests he did not think that he had ever seen any quite as unspiritual looking as the airman. There was about the airman an appearance of rippling worldliness beneath which the presence of the apostolic mark could not even be suspected.

"Here is your breviary," the abbé said, handing the airman his little black book with the gilt edges. "For safety's sake you'd better pretend to be reading it most of the time."

"*Oui, oui, couleur rouge,*" the airman said.

"Please stop saying that," the abbé said, a little angrily, he was afraid. "To begin with, it's nonsense and in any case you don't say it well enough."

"What do I say instead?" the airman asked. "Abide with Me"?

"Once and for all you say nothing," the abbé said.

"But when do I start converting people?" the airman asked.

The abbé did not answer the airman and they went back up the steps into the station. It was the first time for many years that the abbé Gaston had worn lay clothes and he felt that people must be staring in astonishment through his waistcoat at the priest underneath. But nobody appeared to be paying any attention to him and this made the abbé sad a little, that the appearances of his priesthood could vanish so quickly from the world and not be missed. Nobody appeared to be paying any attention to the airman either, although the airman was walking with a jaunty unclerical stride.

"I'm dreaming of a white Christmas," the airman began to hum, elongating his mouth and showing all his teeth.

"Please," the abbé Gaston whispered.

"Singing about Christmas is singing about religion, isn't it?" the airman asked.

"You must not speak at all," the abbé Gaston said. "Especially must you not speak English. You must remember that the Germans are on the lookout for you and that we are in danger all the time."

"O.K. by me," the airman said. "Keep your wool on."

They had to go down steps again to reach the platform, and before they reached the bottom of the steps the abbé could hear the steam hissing from the engines. Ordinarily it excited the abbé to travel and he liked listening to the noise engines made when they were standing in stations but tonight he was too frightened to be excited. Even when he thought of the rails running in lines of silver through the long darkness of France the abbé was still frightened.

At the entrance to the platform ticket inspectors and German military policemen were waiting. The ticket inspectors stood on one side of the iron gate and the German military policemen stood on the other side of the iron gate. One of the ticket inspectors wore a red hat and the other wore a black hat. The German military policemen all wore the same kind of hat except that some of the hats had more braid on them than others, and the abbé supposed that this must be because they belonged to officers. As there was a small crowd of people in front of them the abbé stood back a little on the steps and watched what was happening. He saw that the ticket inspectors were examining the passengers' tickets and noting things down on paper and that the German military policemen were examining the passengers' faces and noting nothing down on paper. Occasionally the German military policemen asked a passenger to produce his identity card but for the most part they just looked into the passengers' faces.

When the people in front of them had passed through the iron gate the abbé advanced first towards the ticket inspectors and the military policemen, and the airman in his cassock came behind him. The abbé tried to assume a worldly expression by thinking as hard as he could about sauerkraut with sausages without sauerkraut and he hoped that the airman behind him was trying to think a little about religion. It was the inspector with the red hat who first took the abbé's ticket and scrutinized it, and funnily enough he seemed to be thinking about food, too. "Of course I don't like it in tins," he said to the inspector with the black hat as he handed him the abbé's ticket for him to look at also. But the inspector with the black hat did not bother to look at the abbé's ticket at all. "I agree; it tastes much nicer fresh," the inspector with the black hat said as he handed the abbé back his ticket. And the hard faced young German military policemen scarcely seemed to lower their gaze on the abbé. *"Ja, ja, so ist es, Karl,"* one of the German military policemen said to another across the abbé's beard. The abbé stood waiting on the platform without daring to look round. "Easy as taking candy off a kid," the airman said as he sidled up beside the abbé.

"Please," the abbé said.

"Sorry; isn't that a religious thing to say?" the airman said.

"French priests do not talk English," the abbé said. The third class railway carriage smelt of garlic, onions and raw carrots and the compartment in which their seats had been reserved smelt of stale biscuits as well. The compartment was lighted by a dim pale blue lamp which drooped from the roof like a technicolor tear, and of the eight seats in the compartment four were already occupied. In the corner by the window a middle-aged woman with rocky cheeks sat balancing a shrouded bird cage on her lap and opposite her a dismal little man was picking his teeth with a nail file. Next to the middle-aged woman sat another man trying to lean his head against a pillow without disordering the hair net with which he had covered his scanty hair. Opposite him a small boy sat swinging his legs. The airman sat next to the small boy and the abbé sat in the corner next to the corridor. The man with the pillow behind his head bowed so deeply to the airman in his cassock that he had to rearrange his hair net.

The abbé Gaston wanted to tell the airman that he must bow back to the laity when they saluted him, but he knew that he couldn't talk to the airman with all those other people in the carriage. To the abbé's delight the airman opened the breviary and began to look as though he were reading it. The airman did not open the breviary at the proper place and he did not move his lips as he read, but the abbé did not suppose that anyone would notice these things. The small boy peeped over the airman's arm to see what the airman was reading, but his interest soon vanished and he started swinging his legs again. The other three people in the compartment stared at one another in sullen silence, trying, perhaps, not to see their own mediocrity in their neighbors'. Two German military policemen tramped down the corridor and a few minutes later they came tramping back again, but they did not enter the compartment.

It was a little later that the priest came into the compartment. The priest had a big fluffy white beard which looked as though it were made of cotton wool. He slid a small leather satchel on to the luggage rack and sat down in the corner opposite the abbé Gaston. The man with the hair net leaned forward and bowed deeply and untied his hair net all over again, but the priest with the fluffy white beard paid no attention. The priest glanced at the airman with brief professional interest but he neither smiled or bowed. He rose again, removed his flat clerical hat and placed it on top of the leather satchel. When he sat down again he covered his head with a dark blue beret which he pulled from the pocket of his cassock.

The priest spread his legs wide out on either side of him and began to read a newspaper. The priest did not seem to find the world very shocking as he read because he read without apparent emotion, his little eyes moving coldly backwards and forwards along the print. He read quickly, too, because soon the top of his newspaper was curling over and tickling the abbé Gaston's unwontedly trousered knee. The priest with the fluffy white beard saw quite clearly that the top of his newspaper was curling over on to the abbé Gaston's knee, but he read on without altering his position and still keeping his legs well spread out.

The abbé Gaston glanced at the airman to see how he was taking the appearance of the priest. The airman was still pretending to read his breviary although he was still reading it in the wrong place, and the abbé hoped that the priest wouldn't notice this. He also hoped that when the priest had finished reading his newspaper he wouldn't attempt to engage the airman in conversation. The abbé felt that he must make some plan with the airman about this contingency. He looked at the priest to make sure that he was still reading his newspaper and then turned round to sign to the airman to follow him out into the corridor. But the airman was no longer pretending to read his breviary. Instead he was staring up at the doorway and showing all his teeth in a broad smile.

In the doorway stood a young woman of the type that had been such a hurdle to anchorites and stockbrokers. Even to the abbé Gaston's uninstructed eye it was immediately obvious that the girl had all the measurements of misdemeanor. Her hair was soft and golden, fluffier even than the priest's beard, and it didn't look as though it would make the tiniest of whispers if it fell off her head into a holy water stoup. Her eyelashes stood up in little crescents of black spikes and her painted lips were shaped like two miniature admirals' hats held one upside down beneath the other. Her legs gleamed like glass and her unbuttoned overcoat showed a white silk blouse coming high up under her neck. She came into the compartment with slow undulation as though trying to walk on an invisible tightrope. Her smell filled the compartment and subdued all the other smells, and her smell was of honey and chocolate and fresh flowers. Next the abbé the airman made a noise like air escaping from a tire and his eyes span round and round like marbles. Remembering the airman's selection of French sentences, the abbé Gaston was terrified.

The priest with the fluffy white beard looked briefly up as the girl entered. However he did not pull in his newspaper or alter the position of his legs, and although the abbé Gaston pulled in his legs the girl had still to step over the priest's legs in order to get to her seat. As she did so her long thighs came up against her dress and rounded it, and the airman in his cassock made a sizzling sound. The man with his head against the pillow disarranged his hair net for a third time. The abbé Gaston rose with alacrity:

"Allow me, Mademoiselle," the abbé said, taking her suitcase from the girl.

"You are very kind, Monsieur," the girl said. "I am afraid that you will find it rather heavy." She made the statement slowly and gravely, almost as though she were defining a philosophy, and she stood with the fingers of her left hand on her left hip and the fingers of her right hand behind her right ear, and leaned back a little, as if a wind were blowing from behind her and she wanted not to lose her balance.

The suitcase was big and heavy, but although the abbé had a great deal of difficulty in getting it on to the luggage rack he glared at the airman when the airman seemed to be on the point of rising to help him. As he heaved the abbé tried not to see the airman staring at the girl and he eventually succeeded in lifting the suit case on to the luggage rack. But the suitcase was too big to fit easily into the space between the man with the hair net's suitcase and the priest's satchel. The priest's satchel was jerked and his flat clerical hat was sent tumbling down on top of his newspaper.

The priest did not smile when his hat fell on top of his newspaper. Without a word he rose and put his hat back on the rack and then sat down and opened his newspaper again with a loud flap. It was obvious that he was angry and the abbé Gaston was sorry that he was angry, because the abbé thought that the meaning of the world was darkened when priests got angry because their hats were knocked down on top of their newspapers. The priest still sat with his legs wide out beneath his cassock and he neither moved nor looked up when the abbé went back into his corner.

The girl had to sit with her knees close together because of the way the priest with the fluffy white beard sat with his legs spread out. The girl sat with her back upright against the wooden partition and her knees were white where they pressed against the silk of her stockings. Although the airman kept staring at her the girl sat looking straight in front of her, with her big eyes expressionless in her still face. Carriages on the next platform began to move slowly backwards and for a moment the abbé thought that the train was leaving the station. But it was only the carriages of another train backing into the opposite platform and the world jerked silently to a standstill again when the abbé looked out at it through the other window. Up at the head of the train the invisible engine began to hiss more loudly, as though it, too, were gazing at a blonde.

Out of the corner of his eye the abbé Gaston saw the airman beginning to smile again. The abbé nudged the airman with his elbow and the airman stopped smiling and began to read his breviary, although he still kept looking up at the girl. But the girl paid no attention and sat with an expression of chilly continence on her face, as though to imply that her soul had got into the wrong sort of envelope. The German military policemen came back along the corridor and this time they looked into the compartment, but they moved quickly on again. Doors banged all along the train and the guard blew his whistle. The abbé knew that the train was really leaving now because the people still standing on the platform began to move backwards as well as the carriages drawn up alongside the next platform.

The man with the hair net was the first to close his eyes. His eyes fluttered for a little and then his mouth opened and his eyes stayed closed for good and the abbé knew that he was asleep. The priest with the fluffy white beard closed his eyes shortly afterwards and his newspaper slid down his cassock and fell on the floor. The boy sitting next to the airman fell asleep with his head hanging forward and the man and woman in the far corner soon fell asleep, too. The girl sat tightly in her dark blue skirt with her steep silk legs close to each other. The airman watched the girl and the abbé Gaston watched the airman watching the girl.

The train ran on through the night. The train ran on through the night but it was impossible to see the night because of the black curtains on the windows. And sometimes it seemed that it was the night that was being pulled past the train and sometimes it seemed that the train was moving forwards instead of backwards. The abbé Gaston tried to say his prayers to the rumbling of the train and soon the train was saying his prayers for him. *"Ave Maria,"* said the abbé Gaston, and *"gratia plena"* said the train. The abbé's eyes were just about to close when he saw that the priest's were open again. And the priest's eyes were no longer small. The priest's eyes were wide with astonishment and they were fixed on the airman.

The abbé Gaston turned his head cautiously. The airman was neither asleep nor was he pretending to read his breviary. Leaning forward across the compartment, the airman was staring at the girl and as he stared his right eyelid kept going slowly up and down, like a tiny blind. Fortunately the girl did not appear to have noticed the airman's signals, for she still sat gazing straight in front of her, with the same expression of aggressive virtue in her eyes. But it was enough for the abbé that the priest with the fluffy white beard had noticed what the airman was doing, and the abbé thought quickly and for once was speedily inspired. Beginning himself to wink energetically with his left eye at the airman, he slid his foot along the floor until it touched the airman's. The abbé felt rather than saw the priest's glance shift from the airman to himself and then return to the airman and then come back to himself again. The airman appeared to understand what the pressure of the abbé's foot against his own had meant for he immediately switched his winking right eye directly on to the abbé. They went on winking at each other like this until the priest shrugged his shoulders and closed his eyes again.

"Please do not be stupid," the abbé whispered when he thought that the priest was soundly asleep again.

"Sorry, padre, but I could do with a basinful of that," the airman whispered back.

"We are still in danger," the abbé said.

"Oui, oui, couleur rouge," the airman said.

"You must keep out of the basin till we get to Lyons," the abbé said.

" 'I'm dreaming of a white Christmas'," the airman said.

The abbé Gaston gave it up. He managed to keep awake until the airman closed his eyes and then the wheels of the train began to be dreaming of a white Christmas, too.

The train had stopped when the abbé Gaston awoke. It was still night. The abbé could feel the darkness outside the drawn curtains and the pale blue lamp burned on with no chinks of light coming in to disperse its meagre glow. Outside there was a hissing of steam, and the hissing didn't seem to come only from the engine but from underneath the carriage as well.

The girl was still awake. She was sitting as she had been sitting when the abbé had fallen asleep, with the lamp casting a brightness on the lining of her opened overcoat. But the abbé saw that the girl was no longer looking straight in front of her. The girl was looking at the airman, who was also awake and who was winking at her again. Down went the airman's eyelid and up it came again, so deliberately that it seemed to the abbé that it ought to have made a click. The girl sat watching the airman with a puzzled expression on her face. The airman leaned slightly forward.

"*Oui, oui, couleur rouge,*" the airman whispered.

The abbé Gaston's dismay turned to terror when he realized that he was not the only person watching the girl's face. A German military policeman was standing in the doorway with another military policeman behind. him. Hoping that neither of the military policemen had been able to observe the advances of the airman, whose back was turned a little towards them, the abbé himself started winking again, but this time he winked at the girl and as he winked he once more slid his foot along the floor of the compartment and kicked the airman sharply on the shin. He did not look at the airman as the airman turned to expostulate but went on winking across the compartment at the girl, raising and lowering his right eyelid as he had seen the airman do. Slowly the girl's gaze shifted from the airman's face to his own and still the abbé winked on. And when his right eyelid was sore with winking the abbé began winking with his left eyelid. The girl's face quivered and broke into a smile. The abbé screwed up his right eye and jerked his head in the direction of the corridor, in a manner which he hoped was both predatory and imperative. The girl hesitated. Then she rose and walked wigglingly towards the door. Somewhat to the abbé's surprise the German military policemen stood aside to let her pass and they also stood aside to let the abbé pass when he followed her.

The girl was standing half-way down the corridor with her back to the nothingness of the black curtain. She wore her overcoat loosely about her shoulders, with the sleeves hanging empty down her sides. The abbé Gaston remembered with a smile that the abbé Moune had once said in a sermon that girls who walked about in their overcoats with the sleeves hanging out empty were a deceitful bait in a lewd age. The girl smiled at the abbé's smile, but when the abbé drew level with her, her face was grave.

"It does one good to stretch one's legs," the girl said.

"I agree with you, Mademoiselle," the abbé said.

"One's limbs get stiff sitting in the same position all the time," the girl said.

"I am entirely of the same opinion," the abbé said.

"It does one good to stretch one's legs," the girl said.

Was such the compendium of baseness, the abbé Gaston wondered. The lower slopes of Avernus must be slippery indeed if these were its beginnings. The abbé looked closely at the girl. Even in the dim light he could see that her face was very young beneath the plaster and the pigment. Was it possible that the label on the bottle did not always indicate the contents?

"Exercise is certainly a good thing," the abbé said and then remembered the German military policemen. He realized that the train must have stopped at the frontier between occupied and unoccupied France. The abbé had never understood why the Germans still controlled the old frontier now that the whole of France was occupied and he did not attempt to do so now. The important thing was that the German military policemen must now be examining the airman's papers and that they would soon be examining his own. The abbé prayed that the airman would have the sense not to speak and that the German military policemen would not look too closely at his identity card on which the airman was photographed in civilian clothes and described as an accountant. There was also the matter of his own identity card. Before the abbé could recover from his new fright two German military policemen came out of the compartment in which he had left the airman and went into the next. From their unperturbed expressions it did not look as though they had discovered any irregularity.

"They are not terrible," the girl said.

The abbé wanted to say that he thought that they were very terrible indeed, but he decided that the girl would not understand. Underneath her woad she was probably only nineteen or twenty. At the time of Munich she had been a child. She could know nothing even of recent history. All her grown up life she had been used to the presence of German soldiers in France. And the very young no longer seemed able to be surprised that the world was cruel and bitter and that the sun shone down upon sadness. Probably she wasn't even surprised that a priest had winked at her in a railway compartment, and about this, too, the abbé decided that it would be prudent not to speak.

"Let's hope that they won't be terrible with us anyway," the abbé said.

The girl smiled, but even when she smiled her eyes had no light in them, and no wonder at the mystery of things. And when her lips had finished smiling they went back into their static switchbacks again. The paint on the girl's lips glistened damply in the damp light and the regularity of their curves made them look austere, although the abbé knew that they must be very wicked, because all the best theologians said so.

The abbé was still looking at the girl's lips when the German military policemen came out of the other compartment. They examined the girl's papers when she presented them but they waved aside the abbé's when he nervously held them out.

"I told you they were not terrible," the girl said.

"Perhaps we'd better be getting back now," the abbé suggested. He was anxious to reassure himself about the airman.

The girl nodded.

"Perhaps I shall sleep now," she said. "It does one good to stretch one's legs."

The train rolled on again, but even when one listened very hard it was impossible to tell whether it was the train that was rolling past the night or the night that was rolling past the train. The priest with the fluffy white beard slept; the man with the hair net slept; the man and woman in the far corners slept; and the small boy slept. Even the girl slept and when her eyes were closed her face looked as though it were made of soap and would melt if left for long in water. Only the airman and the abbé Gaston remained awake.

"Where have you been?" the airman asked.

"I have been talking to the basin," the abbé whispered back.

"You're a fast worker, padre," the airman said.

"It was like taking a kid from candy," said the abbé Gaston, who prided himself on his rapid acquisition of foreign tongues.

When he returned to Paris a few mornings later the abbé Gaston was feeling proud of himself, and he rather thought that the Major would feel proud of him, too. It was true that he had muddled up the password and that he had said "Swedes build fine fountain pens" instead of "Norwegians build fine bridges," but the main thing was that he had handed over the airman to the right man. The abbé was sure that the Major would think highly of him for that.

Even the sky above the church in the square seemed to think highly of the abbé, for it was as blue as the sea. And from behind Madame Boulon's curtains came the smell of a cooking so pleasant that the abbé was sure that it was rabbit. Perhaps the butcher had rabbits again. Perhaps he even had rabbits or bits of rabbits that were cheap. The abbé felt that he could do with a bit of rabbit that was cheap. He knocked at Madame Boulon's door, intending to ask her where she had found her rabbit.

But Madame Boulon did not seem pleased to see the abbé. And especially she did not seem pleased for him to see the rabbit cooking, for she kept standing in front of the pot on the range, with the steam rising in clouds behind her head.

"I did not expect you back so soon," she said. "Really, Monsieur l'abbé, I don't know how to tell you. First of all, the cat..."

"What about the cat?" the abbé asked anxiously.

"Lost, Monsieur l'abbé, lost." Madame Boulon screwed her face into contortions of sorrow. "One moment she was there and the next she was gone. What could I do about it, Monsieur l'abbé?"

"Perhaps she'll come back again," the abbé said unhappily. "Cats are wonderful at finding their way home, you know."

"Monsieur l'abbé, I shall be frank with you," Madame Boulon said. "I do not think that your cat will ever come home again. Butchers kill cats in time of war, Monsieur l'abbé. They kill them and sell them as rabbit. I know, because the late Monsieur Boulon told me. He said that that was what butchers did in Paris in 1870."

The abbé Gaston nodded sadly. He knew that Madame Boulon had killed the cat and was even then stewing it, but he also knew that he was not going to say anything about it. And it wasn't because of Christian charity that he was not going to say anything about it; it was because he was afraid of Madame Boulon.

"And that's not all," Madame Boulon went on. "The Gostepa's been here. There's an officer in your room this very minute. I had to give him your key because he asked for it. He seemed surprised to learn you'd been away."

Once again Madame Boulon's mispronunciation did not make the abbé Gaston smile. He forgot all about St. Elizabeth of Hungary having been turned from cat into rabbit. He turned and went unhappily upstairs and he did not even hear the wireless when Madame Boulon turned it on full blast behind him. The abbé hoped that the Major was going to go on being proud of him.

LXIV

MADAME Boulon turned down the wireless a little as soon as she realized that it was the statesman who was speaking. She never really understood what the statesman was saying and it was also dangerous to listen to the statesman; but it might also be dangerous not to have listened to the statesman, if the other bandits won the war.

The statesman spoke from North Africa, and he had learnt a lot of new words from the British Broadcasting Corporation, passing through London. The statesman said that the occupation of France by German troops was an unwarrantable infringement of the national sovereignty of France. He said that he knew that he had been criticized for not saying this sooner, but that his conscience was clear, as in politics it was no use telling people the truth before their minds were ready to receive it. The statesman said that the people of France must take heart as in North Africa he and his colleagues were drawing up a blueprint for the future. Above all they must not be scared by the communist bogey. The statesman said that it was very important indeed that the people of France should not be scared by the communist bogey.

LXV

THE abbé Gaston climbed the stairs with a thumping heart. The abbé's heart always thumped when he was frightened and he felt sure that if ever he became a martyr the executioner would be bound to hear this sign of his terror.

When he reached the sixth floor he found the door of his room half-open and inside his room he could see a German officer rummaging through his papers. When the officer turned his head a little the abbé was surprised to recognize the German officer who had visited him before. The officer looked a little older perhaps but the abbé knew him at once, because of the bulges at the front and the back of his head.

"I hope that I do not interrupt," the abbé tried to say ironically as he entered the room.

The German officer turned round with a start but quickly recovered his composure.

"You write interesting sermons, but I do not think that you will convert the world," the officer said. The sun did not seem to shine on his leggings as brightly as it had shone before and the abbé wondered if this was because the officer's leggings were getting old. "Monsieur l'abbé, I am sorry to have to inform you that this is more than just a routine perquisition."

One of the pigeons from the church alighted on the window ledge. The abbé watched the pigeon but he was too afraid to see the pigeon properly.

"In fact I have every reason to suspect you of a grave offense against the occupying military authority," the officer went on. "Monsieur l'abbé, a little more than a week ago an officer of the German army was killed in this district. Apparently he had been murdered in the street." The abbé was relieved that the officer did not look him in the face as he said this, and then he realized that the officer was looking at his hands, and the hands betrayed guilt, too, the abbé had read. "But perhaps you do not know that. I understand that you have been away from Paris."

Theoretically the abbé Gaston had always imagined that he would be able to stand before the Lord on the last day without a tremor, because his heart had been as clean as he could make it. He knew now that this would not be so as he was unable to stand even before his fellow men without his knees shaking. The abbé thought miserably back to 1936. Had that driver on the underground train put the little blue light out at Château-Landon or had he waited till Louis Blanc? Although he knew that superstition was a sin, the abbé would have given a lot to know.

"Perhaps if we were both to sit down," the abbé said, closing the door.

"We can discuss this matter just as well standing up as sitting down," the German officer said. But he sat down all the same. As he sat down his breeches bulged out in semi-circles of hoop on either side of them and the abbé was sure that there must be wire inside them. "Monsieur l'abbé, why have you been away from Paris?"

The abbé's fright increased. Had Madame Boulon been talking? Had she said anything about the young man who had accompanied him on his journey? Madame Boulon had killed St. Elizabeth of Hungary. There was no more health in Madame Boulon. The pigeon looked peaceful as it began to walk up and down the window ledge, but the abbé was still frightened.

"I went away with a friend," the abbé said.

"A Jewish friend?" the officer asked.

The abbé was so relieved that he almost smiled. The General had once told him that the Germans always made the mistake of barking up the wrong tree. The Germans would never have been any good at war at all if their enemies hadn't made the greater mistake of barking up no tree at all, the General had said.

"Of course not," the abbé said.

"In that case you will be able to produce to me this Jewish girl whom you are concealing," the officer said. "There is no need to look surprised, Monsieur l'abbé I think now that you lied to me two years ago. I think that you lied because I do not believe that it is only since my last visit that you have been concealing an Austrian Jewess. Come, Monsieur l'abbé. Things will be better for you if you are reasonable."

The abbé Gaston was silent. The pigeon walked up and down on the window ledge, slowly, as though it were thinking of gentle things. The shadow of the pigeon walked up and down with the pigeon. And sometimes the shadow of the pigeon was a long shadow and sometimes it was a short shadow, and sometimes, too, it was a straight shadow and sometimes it was an oblique shadow, because that depended upon the sun.

"You do not need to be afraid, Monsieur l'abbé," the German officer went on. "At least you do not need to be very afraid. We have no reason to suspect that this Jewish girl was responsible for killing the German officer. But because a German officer has been killed we are forced to be more strict about Jews. We do not like it when German officers are killed. Jewesses do not like German soldiers. And still less do Austrian Jewesses like German soldiers."

The abbé was so frightened again that it was difficult for him to think consecutively. Either the abbé Moune or Madame Boulon or the centrally heated lady of easy virtue must have been talking, the abbé realized. And in 1936 that driver on the underground must have put out the little blue light at Château-Landon. Soon, if he didn't speak, the threats would come. And if he didn't speak then the bad detective novel things would happen to himself instead of only to other people.

"I admit that I lied to you," the abbé managed to say at length, and once he had said one sentence it was easier for him to say others. "But if I lied it was because I wished to be merciful. And now, Herr Hauptmann, I am going to ask you to be merciful." The abbé felt a little braver when he had said this.

"The Führer has said that there is no mercy in war," the officer said. "War is a stark thing." The young man pushed out the stock phrases as though he had invented them himself and the abbé was reminded a little of Bessier, when Bessier spoke about communism. And the abbé thought again how imprudent it had been of the Lord to have made people grow upwards instead of downwards, so that when the feet and the hands were strong the mind might have been strong, too. "You have ribbons in your lapel, Monsieur l'abbé. You must understand that as well as I do."

"War is an affair among men." But as soon as he had said this the abbé knew that it was not true, as women and children were also killed in modern wars, because of progress. Then the abbé remembered Otto Braunschwig and was suddenly hopeful. "And even in war I was merciful," he cried, sure now that he had found a way to persuade the German officer. He told the German officer about Otto Braunschwig and about the battle and about the shells bursting in fire over the canal at night. And as he told the officer about these things the abbé was certain that the Lord was going to work a miracle and change the bad detective novel into a good detective novel, in which the German officer would turn out to be Otto Braunschwig's son or at least his nephew. "You see, I have a right to speak," the abbé said when he had finished his story. "I never asked a favor for sparing Otto Braunschwig's life. But I ask one now. I ask you to spare this girl because I spared Otto Braunschwig."

But the Lord worked no miracle. The Lord remained silent in heaven. The officer rose and paced the room. The sun shone on the officer's leggings and buttons as he paced the room.

"Pity is a weak emotion," the officer said at length. "It is because of pity that France has lost the war. And in the long run it is our terror which will prove the greater mercy. Men do not know how to be either happy or good. Men must be governed into happiness and virtue. Only when Germany has conquered the whole world will all men be happy and good. That is why the Führer's voice must be listened to."

"It is God's voice that must be listened to, and God's voice is a whisper and not a shout," the abbé Gaston said. And as the abbé said this he knew that what he said was true. Even priests had to listen hard to hear God's voice, although they had the mark upon them. Even priests had to scrub their souls and scour their souls and flatten themselves out before they knew what it was that God would have them do. Even priests who touched the Thing touched it through a veil.

"Shout or whisper, it would be as well if God's voice were to tell you to tell me where that Jewess is," the German officer said. The officer came and stood over the abbé and all the buttons of his tunic shone in a row of little silver moons as he looked down upon the abbé, and the bulges at the front and the back of his head looked bigger than ever. "Monsieur l'abbé, I am not joking. Either you will tell me here and now where this Jewish girl is or I shall have to ask you to accompany us to our headquarters. We have means of making people speak, you know."

The abbé Gaston thought of many things. He thought of how easy it would be to speak. He thought of his mother and of the Major and of St. Peter being crucified upside down. He thought of the safe men in their councils and he thought of the saints who had endured great pain that the light might go on shining into the world. He thought of all those things and from his shaken heart a prayer leapt up to the Lord, that the Lord would give him strength.

"I shall not speak," the abbé heard himself say in a small voice. "Even though you do terrible things to me I shall not speak. I shall not speak because it would be wrong to speak," he said.

To the abbé's surprise the officer laughed. The officer was still laughing when he walked away from the abbé and sat down in his chair again. And his laugh had softened to a smile when he next spoke to the abbé and there was no longer any threat in his voice.

"I am glad that you spoke like that," the officer said. "I am glad because it proves to me that you are a brave man. And if you are brave the Austrian Jewess whom you are protecting is probably brave, too, and would not commit the cowardly crime of murdering a German officer in the street." The officer seemed pleased with his logic, for he still went on smiling. "You see, we have to be so careful. The most stupid muddles occur when we are not careful. For example, only last month a consignment of Balaclava helmets was due to be sent to a division of our soldiers fighting in Russia. Our soldiers who were fighting in Russia were very cold and they had great need of Balaclava helmets. But when the parcels arrived at the front they were found not to contain Balaclava helmets at all, but women's brassieres and knickers instead. Our soldiers on the Eastern front were not pleased and the officer who was responsible got into serious trouble." The German officer laughed again and seemed very amused that the soldiers on the Eastern front had received women's brassieres and knickers instead of Balaclava helmets.

The abbé Gaston laughed, too, only it wasn't about the women's brassieres and knickers that he was laughing. The abbé was laughing because he was sure now that the Lord was going to let him die the easy way, sliding straight from a warm bed into paradise. Probably it wasn't only the German officer who had been testing him. Probably the Lord had been testing him as well, as He had once tested Abraham over Isaac. The abbé laughed on at the thought that the Lord was going to let him go on being a comfortable Christian.

"And about Austrian Jewesses we have to be even more careful," the German officer said when he had finished laughing. "And although your own courageous conduct helps me to believe that your friend is herself courageous I must still ask you to allow me to see her and judge for myself."

The abbé began to feel frightened again, although he did not feel quite as frightened as before. He looked at the pigeon still walking up and down against the square of blue sky and he tried to see the Lord's smile upon himself in the square of blue sky.

"I promise you that no harm shall come to her if she is as you have given me reason to believe that she is," the officer went on. "I need scarcely tell you that I am failing to do my duty in exercising this clemency. This girl is both an Austrian and a Jewess and is therefore doubly subject to our jurisdiction. However, as you were once merciful to a German soldier, Monsieur l'abbé, I also shall be merciful to this girl. But to protect myself I must at least see the girl to whom I am expected to be merciful."

"I am afraid that is impossible," the abbé said. He hoped that the Lord might still be testing him, but he didn't think it likely that the Lord would test him in the same way twice. And he tried to believe that torture was painful only at the first impact.

"I see that you still do not trust me," the German officer said, rising abruptly from his chair. "Fortunately there is no need for you to trust me. I can go and see this girl for myself, but I think that it would frighten her less if you were to accompany me. You see, my informant not only told me that you were concealing an Austrian Jewess; he also told me where she was hiding. Well, Monsieur l'abbé? Do I go alone? Or do you come with me?"

The abbé Gaston stood up at once, and in his heart he praised a great praise to the Lord. Of course the abbé Moune or the rector or Madame Boulon or the centrally heated lady of easy virtue or whoever the officer's informant had been had also told him where Rachel was working. And it wasn't at all extraordinary that the German officer should have come to see him first. It was only natural that he should attempt to assess the character of the protégée through testing the character of her protector. The Germans had always been very clever at that sort of thing. And there was no reason to believe that a German officer could not be merciful. The Germans also had the holy words read to them out of the holy book.

In Madame Bisberot's window the hair on the wax mannequins' heads now fell so far down their shoulders that it made them look like small girls at a party. But the wax mannequins also looked much stupider than small girls at a party. Their expressions were no longer menacingly idiotic but had become arrogantly imbecilic again and progressively imbecilic as well, with a touch of paleolithic imbecility round the eyes. But the abbé Gaston didn't notice the wax mannequins very much. As they were about to move into the doorway the abbé was struck by a suspicion which made him accelerate his step and lead the German officer along to the corner of the square, where they stopped.

"Please," the abbé said. "You are sure that you have been telling me the truth?"

"Why should I do otherwise?" the German officer asked. "The fact that you once lied to me does not entitle me to lie to you."

But the abbé Gaston was too concerned to blush. "You're sure that you really know where this girl works?" the abbé asked.

"I did not say that I knew where the girl *worked,*" the German officer said. "I said that I knew where she was *hiding.* That is not quite the same thing. But if I must prove my truthfulness to you I shall tell you that she is both working and hiding inside that dressmaker's establishment into which you so nearly led me." The officer smiled triumphantly at the abbé as he said this.

But it was the gladness in the officer's smile that made the abbé realize that he was lying then as before. The German officer had laid a trap for him and he had fallen into it. The German officer had only heard vague rumors about Rachel and nobody had told him where she was working. And because he had almost led the German officer straight into Madame Bisberot's the German officer had guessed that that was where Rachel was working. The German officer had tricked him once, but what was worse the German officer might trick him again. The German officer might not be merciful to Rachel after all.

"Please," the abbé Gaston pleaded. "Please, Herr Hauptmann. I shall do anything you want if only you'll be merciful to that girl."

The officer was still smiling as he answered and this time the abbé thought that there was mockery as well as triumph and gladness in the officer's smile.

"I have already promised you that," the officer said. "But first I must see the girl."

"There is no need for you to see the girl," the abbé persisted. "I tell you that she is harmless. And if you leave her alone I'll do anything you want. I'll pay you money. Listen, Herr Hauptmann, I've got a government bond. It's worth nearly ninety thousand francs. I'll sell it and I'll give you the money if only you'll let this girl alone."

"Monsieur l'abbé, it is a grave offense to attempt to bribe an officer of the German army into neglecting his duty," the officer said sternly. "Whatever you say I am going to see this girl for myself whether you come with me or not. But if you are wise I think that you will come with me." When he had said this the officer began to walk slowly back along the pavement.

The abbé Gaston followed wretchedly. He was ashamed of the stupid way in which he had betrayed Rachel and he was frightened of what might happen to her. And whether he accompanied the officer or not Rachel would be bound to think that he had denounced her deliberately. At the door of the shop the abbé made a last attempt to dissuade the officer from his purpose.

"You may be glad of my help one day," the abbé said. "The Allies are going to invade soon. And they have said that they will punish all war criminals and members of the Gestapo. It may help you if I am able to say that you were merciful to a Jewess."

"The Allies have been going to invade for two years now and even if they do not invade I may still be merciful to your Jewess," the German officer said, but the abbé knew from the officer's smile that he had no intention of being merciful to Rachel.

"I tell you I'll do anything you want," the abbé Gaston pleaded. "Whether the Allies come or not I'll do anything you want."

But the German officer only smiled and opened the door of the shop.

Madame Bisberot began to explain about the wax mannequins as soon as she came to greet them. She said that it was because of American cinema actresses that the wax mannequins were wearing their hair longer, as fashions in hair were international even in time of war. She did not say anything about fashions in imbecility and she did not say anything about royalties, but the abbé was much too worried about Rachel to remark either omission.

"I've come to see Rachel," the abbé explained unhappily.

"Mademoiselle Rachel is preparing for the dress parade," Madame Bisberot said and pointed upstairs, from where a noise like the throbbing of a motor car engine came. "She will not be able to see you just now, but perhaps you and your friend would like to see the parade." The abbé would have preferred to nurse his sorrow downstairs, but the German officer said that he would like very much to see the dress parade. And as they went upstairs the noise of a motor car engine throbbing separated out into the noises of people talking. Mounting miserably behind the officer, the abbé did not suppose that the people were talking about spiritual matters, or even about sensible matters. Listening to the racket, the abbé concluded that this, too, was one of the causes of modern wars, that men and women no longer talked about sensible matters. But the abbé was in too great a despond to be able to think for long about the causes of modern wars.

The room in which the abbé and the German officer found themselves was crowded with women sitting on chairs, waving their arms in the air and talking at the top of their voices, almost certainly not about spiritual matters. Even when two women were sitting together both of them went on talking at once, so the abbé concluded that they must be cleverer than they looked, to be able to talk so loudly and listen at the same time. And most of the women were so ugly that St. Anthony could have seen them in their baths without interrupting a prayer. Hermits could have swabbed them down without trepidation. In spite of his anxiety about Rachel, the abbé Gaston began to wonder if the moral theologians had always used the right telescope.

Some of the women were accompanied by men, and there were German officers there, too, but none of the men seemed to be talking much. There was not much room left for the abbé Gaston and the officer, but Madame Bisberot brought them chairs and they managed to squeeze in at the back. The mannequin parade began almost immediately.

From another room girls began to come out wearing silk dresses. The silk dresses were green and pink and yellow and black and red and most of the girls who walked in them looked as though they were made of silk, too, so that the abbé was forced to revise his thoughts about the moral theologians. Each girl walked slowly round the room in her dress, revolving upon herself as she walked, and wibbling and wobbling a little. The abbé didn't think that he liked the wibbling and wobbling, although he knew that it was very historical and that quite a lot of it had gone on in the Bible. But when Rachel came in she walked demurely with her eyes cast down and the abbé could not see whether she was feeling happy or sad. She did not seem to notice that the abbé was there, and the abbé was glad of this, because he would have found it difficult to smile back at her when he felt so guilty and frightened in his heart. "There's a pretty girl," the German officer beside him said.

The same girls began to come in again wearing different dresses, but this time the abbé didn't look at them very much, because the German officer's remark had encouraged him to hope again. But so that he shouldn't feel too optimistic the abbé deliberately thought a sad thought, and the sad thought that he thought was the regret that men and women should not pay the same attention to the appearance of their souls as they did to that of their bodies. The abbé had often preached on the ugliness in the sight of God of a soul in the state of mortal sin but none of the mortal sinners in the congregation had ever blinked an eyelid. Perhaps what was wanted was a spiritual mannequin parade, with St. Benedict and St. Dominic and St. Francis and St. John Chrysostom walking past holding up their holy faces.

The abbé was still thinking about a spiritual mannequin parade when Rachel came out of the little room again. She was wearing a black dress which made a noise like water as she walked and her eyes were still lowered so that it almost looked as though she were asleep. Once again she did not see the abbé watching her and she smiled at nobody as she passed and her face was calm and long and grave.

"She's the loveliest thing I've ever seen," the German officer seated beside the abbé said.

The abbé's optimism came surging back again and turned into the certainty that the German officer would be merciful to Rachel after all. Even when he found out that the girl whom he admired so much was the Jewess for whom he was looking, the German officer would still want to be merciful to her, because men were rarely unkind to girls whom they admired physically, at least at the beginning of their acquaintanceship. This much at least the abbé's penitents had taught him, if he himself had taught them nothing. So sure of this did the abbé become that his vision began to blur when the girls came out for the third time, wearing different frocks again, for the abbé had always found worldliness rather wearying. The abbé blinked and tried to keep awake. The abbé blinked and fell asleep.

The abbé dreamed that he had been made a bishop and that the Pope was telling him that as he was now such an important priest it wasn't sinful for him to live in a palace. And the palace in which the abbé now lived was a very grand palace indeed for it had a bathroom and a soft armchair to sit in. And the Pope said that this wasn't worldly at all, so long as the abbé remembered that a bishop was only a presbyter empowered to ordain other presbyters and sat humbly in his soft armchair and his bath to God's honor and glory. And the Pope said that it was quite all right for the abbé to have a really smart cassock now that he was a bishop and three changes of underclothes as well, although these were not a matter of liturgy and the Sacred Congregation of Rites hadn't laid anything down about combinations. And the Pope also said that he was very sorry that he hadn't thought of making the abbé Gaston a bishop before, because in his opinion, and strictly between the abbé and himself, the present lot weren't such great shakes by any means.

The abbé Gaston awoke to music, but it wasn't Gregorian music in a cathedral. It was the sort of music the abbé had often heard coming from the centrally heated lady of easy virtue's wireless set and it sounded like brakes being applied suddenly to a heavy lorry or like a man dying in agony in a dungeon. But this time the wails and the moans and the groans came from a gramophone and to this dismal din the pretty girls in the lovely dresses were revolving slowly round the room in the arms of the men who had been watching the mannequin parade. Some of the ugly women were revolving, too, but it was only with the pretty girls that the German officers were revolving. And all the pretty girls and the ugly women and the German officers and the other men seemed suddenly to have become very unhappy and they circled round the room in determined gloom and with their mouths tight shut, as though thinking of their dead grandmothers and trying to chew nails. The abbé Gaston realized that he was witnessing a modern dance.

The abbé himself had danced as a small boy with little girls in satin frocks and loose brown hair. And as a bigger boy he had seen his parents dance polkas and waltzes and sometimes to this very day the abbé would catch himself humming The Blue Danube under his breath in the confessional, while waiting for penitents. And in all those dances the small boys and the little girls and the grown-up men and women had laughed as they danced, as David had laughed when he had danced before the Lord. The abbé could not make up his mind whether the dancers he saw now were sad because the music was sad or whether the music was sad because the dancers were sad. Watching the misery of revelry, the abbé was puzzled.

Observing the abbé's perplexity, Madame Bisberot explained to him that the dance he was looking at was called a tango, and that it had been invented in South America, where even the moon was passionate. She said, however, that she had heard that an even more wonderful dance called the boogie-woogie or the jeepie-weepie had been invented in North America and that was why the Americans were fighting the war so bravely, because they wanted all nations to dance the boogie-woogie or the jeepie-weepie together. As Madame Bisberot said this Rachel passed in the arms of the German officer, and the abbé tried to smile at her, but Rachel did not seem to see the abbé and passed on sadly with her long face held gravely in the shining casements of her hair.

The dancing went on and on and the abbé Gaston tried to go to sleep again and dream that he was a bishop and allowed to do all sorts of special holy things. But he could not go to sleep because of the music, which still seemed to be about the moon being passionate in South America. The abbé hoped that the boogiewoogie or the jeepie-weepie would sound more cheerful and that it would be possible to dance it before the Lord, as the Americans were fighting for righteousness.

The abbé noticed that Rachel and the German officer danced all the sad gloomy dances together and he wondered if this meant that they, like the moon in South America, were passionate. It would, he realized, make things so much simpler if they were to fall in love with each other because then the German officer wouldn't want to send Rachel to a concentration camp, at least not immediately. The abbé sometimes thought that he understood about the quick beginning part about falling in love, because young women were sometimes so lovely to look at, but he didn't think that he understood much about the going on part, because the women who were so lovely to look at were rarely so lovely to listen to. The abbé thought that the going on part must be much more difficult than living in a monastery. He was still thinking this when the German officer came up to him.

"And now, Monsieur l'abbé, perhaps you'll be good enough to introduce me to your little Jewess," the German officer said.

The German officer's words were still ringing in the abbé's ears as he knelt at the back of the church to thank the Lord for having worked a miracle after all. "You'd have saved us both a lot of trouble if you'd told me that she was so beautiful," the German officer had said.

The abbé also thanked the Lord for having made the abbé Moune, the rector, Madame Boulon and the centrally heated lady of easy virtue more steadfast than he had imagined them to be.

Up at the high altar the abbé Ronsard was saying a funeral mass and the coffin lay on the catafalque beneath a black velvet pall. The abbé Gaston prayed for the departed soul, too, although he found it hard to be sorry for the dead these days, as there were so many unpleasant things that could no longer happen to them.

LXVI

IN the summer of 1944 the Cardinal began to sleep badly. Tonight as usual, he tried counting other Cardinals entering the Sistine Chapel, but this exercise was no longer very soporific, because the Cardinal now knew more dead Cardinals than he knew live Cardinals and the dead Cardinals could no longer enter the Sistine Chapel. Only last year poor Arthur had died, but Bernard, although only an archbishop as yet, seemed much better at praying than Arthur had been, to judge by the way that the Germans were beginning to scurry out of France. The Cardinal thought that he would rather like to meet Bernard.

The Chanoine Paquin glided in through the darkness. But it wasn't a very dark darkness because there was moonlight in it and the Cardinal could see the Chanoine Paquin's pyjamas trousers peeping out from under his cassock. The Cardinal lay quite still as the Chanoine Paquin began to pour embrocation on his chest. Sometimes he went to sleep quite easily when the Chanoine Paquin rubbed his chest with embrocation and the stiller he lay the sooner he fell asleep.

"I'm growing old," the Cardinal murmured as he felt the blob of liquid fall on the middle of his chest. At first it was a small cold blob but it became a warm big splash as the chaplain began to rub. "It is sad to grow old when one has loved life so much as I have done," the Cardinal said and knew at once that he said a sinful thing, because priests had no right to love the world so much that they were afraid to die. "An English lord once said something about power but my memory's so bad now I don't remember what it was although I don't think that it was anything good," the Cardinal said and hoped that this would do for repentance.

The chaplain did not say anything but rubbed on in circular motions as though the Cardinal's chest were a plate which he was trying to dry. And as the chaplain rubbed the Cardinal thought of the little

Benedictine cemetery with the old worn crosses engraved with the names of long dead priests and of the grass very green under the trees. They had buried the Cardinal's confessor there only that morning and the Cardinal had said the last prayers at the graveside and his mitre had tickled the back of his head quite a lot. It had been very quiet in the little Benedictine cemetery.

The Cardinal began to feel sleepy as the chaplain rubbed. He felt so sleepy that he wanted to tell the chaplain to stop rubbing, but he didn't do so in case he would wake himself up. Instead he lay in silence and thought about Bernard and how very good at praying Bernard must be, with all those victories mounting up.

LXVII

PARIS was now liberated, although in the city the sound of firing could still be heard coming from the suburbs. Even so the Church of God had still to go on with her humdrum shuttle service to supernatural glory, because God kept pumping new souls into the world and sucking old souls out of the world.

Among the old souls recently sucked out of the world had been that of the poetess and in the presbytery of Saint Clovis they were planning the ceremonies for her funeral, which was to be as slap up as circumstances permitted. The abbé Moune, who had just taken down a portrait of Marshal Pétain and was nailing up in its place a picture of General de Gaulle, said that the poetess had been lucky to have died when she did otherwise she might have been prosecuted for collaboration. The abbé Ronsard, who had administered the last sacraments to the poetess, said that the poetess had died a very French death indeed, and that almost her last words had been "Long live General de Gaulle," although the abbé Ronsard was glad to say that she had managed to squeeze in something about Jesus having mercy on her soul as well. The rector said gently that they must not be too hard on the poetess as perhaps most people had been a little wrong about the Germans, although he for one had never despaired of an Allied victory. The abbé Ronsard asked whether they would have a black or a white pall for the poetess' funeral, and pointed out that white was usual for the unmarried. The rector said with a smile that he thought that a pale grey pall would perhaps be more suitable.

The abbé Gaston, who had been invited to take part in the discussion, listened in amazement. All through the war the abbé Moune had kept saying that only the presence of German soldiers on French soil was preserving the country from anarchy. In more than one sermon the rector had preached that Christians ought to be grateful to Marshal Pétain because he had given religion back to France. Neither the rector nor the abbé Moune had ever approved his concealment of Rachel, although the abbé Gaston was now prepared to believe that neither of them had reported the fact to the Germans. And even the abbé Ronsard had bleated from the pulpit that it was easier to serve the Lord in agricultural countries than in industrial countries. Lately, of course, these pronouncements had diminished, although only three months ago the abbé Moune had agreed with a German chaplain in the sacristy that the Allies would never dare to invade France.

But the abbé Gaston did not doubt that the new found patriotism of his colleagues was sincere. They were not wicked men, the abbé Gaston knew, otherwise they would not have given up the world for God to put His mark upon them at their ordination. They were only weak men and it was of weak men that God had made the Church. And that was the wonder of the Church, that the Holy Ghost should be able to hold it together, when God had made it of such weak men. And the Lord always had His arms about the Church, that the Church might not fall apart, when weak men stood at its altars.

The poetess wasn't the only parishioner who had died, because God kept sucking ordinary souls out of the world as well, as even arrivals in eternity had to be staggered. The butcher who hadn't been to mass since the Third Sunday in Lent, 1901, had died, too, and the clergy were not very sure that he had repented properly. "Between the stirrup and the ground, mercy sought and mercy found," the abbé Gaston remembered having read in an English poem and that was the best he could hope for the butcher. And as the rector agreed that such a last minute change of heart had indeed been possible it was decided to give the butcher Christian burial, on condition that there would be no ostentation, because of the bad effect it might have on other butchers. The rector was to officiate the next day at eleven o'clock at the funeral of the poetess, and the abbé Gaston was to bury the butcher at noon.

When these arrangements had been made the abbé Gaston left and went out into the street. It was not very late in the evening yet and the sky was still blue above the church. From the distance came the noise of guns firing, but people seemed to be getting used to liberation and nobody was paying much attention, and the people in the square were still mostly mean little persons, hurrying past with averted eyes. In the de luxe plumber's window the wash-hand basins and baths were no longer pink, pale green and heliotrope but were red, white and blue instead and had been arranged in the pattern of the French flag. The abbé stopped to admire them and was joined by Madame Boulon and the centrally heated lady of easy virtue, who both found the display patriotic.

The centrally heated lady of easy virtue told the abbé that she was very pleased by the Allied victory which she had never been afraid to foretell. The centrally heated lady of easy virtue said that she and her gentleman friend had been in the Resistance all along but that of course they had been unable to tell anybody, because it had all been so secret. And Madame Boulon said that she had been in the Resistance as well and that it had been very secret, too. And the centrally heated lady of easy virtue and Madame Boulon thought it very wonderful that they should both have been risking their lives for all that long time without either of them knowing that the other had been risking her life, too, because it had all been so secret. They asked the abbé Gaston if he had been in the Resistance also and appeared rather shocked when he said that he hadn't. It was everybody's duty to have been in the Resistance, they said. Concealing a Jewess was all very well, they said, but it wasn't as brave as having been in the Resistance.

The church was still open, and the abbé went in to say a few prayers. But there was so much hammering going on in the church that the abbé found it difficult to pray at all. Behind the high altar workmen were nailing up the French, the American and the British flags. And the Hammer and Sickle was being nailed up as well, as the rector had said that they mustn't forget that the Russians had been fighting for righteousness, too, even if Stalin hadn't got certain points of Christian doctrine quite right yet. There was nailing going on outside the rector's confessional, too, for the MAN SPRICHT DEUTSCH notice was coming down and the ENGLISH SPOKEN notice was going up again. The rector had said that he expected to have quite a lot of confessions in English to listen to, as one couldn't expect even American crusaders to go on being crusaders all the time.

Although the abbé was no longer sure that the Lord wanted France to be freer than any other country, he thanked the Lord for making her people happy again. And he thanked the Lord for having made Rachel safe once more, and he prayed that the Lord might have made the German officer safe, too, since the German officer had been kind to Rachel. And above all he thanked the Lord for having made Frenchmen united and he prayed that great blessings might flow from this. The abbé's prayers and his thanksgiving slid into silence as the hammering ceased and the workmen left the church. The evening sun shone through the stained glass window and made pools of blue and gold and crimson on the sanctuary, and the abbé thought that the different colors looked very beautiful.

The abbé was disappointed that there were not many other people in the church. The abbé thought that the church ought to have been filled with people, thanking God for having freed Paris. But that was the way of the world, the abbé knew. People came to church when they were sad and went to the Boeuf-sur-le-Toit when they were happy. The abbé's heart went out to a young man and a young girl who came in and knelt down on the other side of the aisle, a little in front of him. It always touched the abbé to see young people praying.

The abbé watched the young man and the young girl as he prayed for them and with them. The young man was wearing a shabby civilian suit and the young woman was wearing a light summer coat. Both the young man and the young woman seemed very devout for they buried their faces deeply in their hands. The girl's hair was fair where it showed beneath her hat and some of her hair came down on her shoulders and it was very soft and shining. It wasn't until the young man and the young woman raised their faces from their hands that the abbé recognized Rachel, and then he recognized the German officer as well, because of the bulges at the front and at the back of his head.

The abbé was disturbed by the sight of the German officer. German officers had no longer any right to be in Paris, even in civilian clothes. It was the civilian clothes which made the abbé realize that Rachel and the German officer had not come into the church to pray and that their devotion was a simulation. They must have followed him into the church because they wished to speak to him and were afraid to do so in the streets. His fear increasing, the abbé was on the point of rising and going across and asking them what they required of him when the sacristan came out of the sacristy to change the curtains on the tabernacle door.

The sacristan wore a sleeveless surplice over his unbuttoned cassock and he had a big bleary face and a sticking out moustache. The sacristan did not genuflect as he approached the altar. He changed the tabernacle curtains from red to white, because today had been the feast of St. Zephyrinus and tomorrow would be the feast of St. Joseph Calasanctius and God's time was marked that way. St. Zephyrinus had been a martyr in the reign of Heliogabalus but St. Joseph Calasanctius had only lived a holy life. The sacristan did not look as though he were very interested in St. Zephyrinus and St. Joseph Calasanctius and he left the sanctuary without genuflecting. The abbé Gaston looked round guardedly. There was no one else in the church except the German officer and Rachel and himself.

Rachel looked round, too, and she smiled at the abbé with her lips but, as the abbé had expected, her eyes were grave and troubled. The abbé made a motion with his head and they came and knelt down beside him. Rachel knelt next to the abbé and the German officer knelt on the far side of Rachel. Beneath her open coat the abbé saw that Rachel was wearing the dark blue velvet dress which he liked so much. They all knelt for a few minutes in silence in case the sacristan should come out of the sacristy again.

"We are in trouble and we want you to help us," Rachel whispered. She did not turn her face as she spoke but went on staring straight in front of her.

"This secrecy is absurd," the abbé Gaston whispered back. "What's more it's dangerous. We'd much better talk openly in the porch." The abbé was a little angry as he said this because now he thought that he knew what they were going to ask him to do for them.

"But Karl is known in the district," Rachel whispered again. "People may recognize him."

"We shall have to risk that," the abbé said and rose and walked away down the church towards the door. He was still angry as he limped down the aisle. He was still angry because he knew more than ever what they were going to ask him to do for them. But the abbé thought that he had had enough of doing hard things to please the Lord. Behind him he felt the safety of the church and the quiet prayers that had been said in it down the centuries and the quiet prayers that would still be said in it. Tomorrow they would be saying white masses out of the holy book and then black masses out of the holy book, and it was to do this that he had been ordained, to say masses out of the holy book. The abbé waited impatiently for Rachel and the German officer to join him in the porch.

"I was afraid that you might be angry," Rachel said as she came up to him. When he looked closely into her face he saw that she was not looking as beautiful as she usually looked. There were little prickles of sweat on her nose again and he noticed for the first time that her teeth were irregular. The abbé realized that she was lonely and unhappy and frightened beneath the paint and powder on her face.

"Angry, of course not," the abbé said, beginning to be ashamed of his irritation and of his fear. "Surprised a little perhaps, but angry, no."

"We are in trouble," the German officer said. "I have not been able to escape. I have tried to escape, but it was too late, because the city had already fallen."

"But surely there is no need for you to escape," the abbé Gaston said. "Surely you can give yourself up. The French soldiers are honorable soldiers. They will imprison you until the end of the war and then you will be free. Like that you will be neither wounded or killed." The abbé thought that this was a very sound argument.

"You see, we are in love," Rachel said. She was very quiet as she said this. The sun shone in at the door of the church in a slanting beam and more gold fell on the gold of her hair and made it glow a great deal. The sun itself was blue when the abbé looked at it, but beneath the blue sun there was the rim of another gold sun. And when the abbé turned away from the sun it was all a gold sun again, and it went on shining on Rachel's hair.

In spite of his understanding about the beginning part of love the abbé had always been perplexed by the emotion, because of its many manifestations. There was the kind of love that made people stand close up against each other in underground trains with their lips stuck together like hosepipes, and the contemplation of this kind of love had helped the abbé to approve the Lord's decision that there would be neither marrying nor giving in marriage in heaven. Then there was the kind of love that made people look seasick when they held hands in public places and there was also the kind of love which he had to reprimand so frequently in the confessional. All in all the abbé considered it best not to think too much about love, and he tried not to think about it now as he stood looking at Rachel with the sun shining on her.

"Love's like sardines," the abbé said quickly. "It'll keep if you put it in a tin. And that's what you've both got to do: put your emotions in a tin until the war's over." He tried to smile as he spoke, but he knew that it was not a very successful smile, because of the hard thoughts behind it. "Our friend here gives himself up and is made a prisoner; and you wait for him until the war is over."

"Monsieur l'abbé, I do not think that you understand," the German officer said. "They are no longer taking prisoner officers who have been policemen. I have not been a bad or a cruel policeman but they will be unlikely to believe that. And Rachel cannot stay behind either. She has been seen too much in my company to make it safe for her to remain in Paris. Already Madame Bisberot has been saying unkind things. Soon she will also be doing unkind things."

"All that is true," Rachel said. The sun had gone from her hair now because the golden bar had moved along a little. The golden bar was shining on the abbé himself now and it made him blink as he stood in it.

The abbé knew that what the German officer had said was true. The liberation of Paris had made people behave badly as well as nobly and cowardly as well as brave deeds had been done.

"I hate to have to remind you of your promise, Monsieur l'abbé," the German officer said quietly. "But you promised that if I were kind to Rachel you also would be kind to me. I know that it is not altogether fair to remind you of this, because I was kind to Rachel for her own sake rather than for yours. But if I do remind you, Monsieur l'abbé, I ask you to believe that I do so more for Rachel's sake than for my own."

The abbé was acutely miserable, and acutely frightened, too. He knew they wanted him to help them to escape and that if he were caught doing so he would be tried and shot as a traitor.

"I think that I said that when the Allies came I would give evidence for you that you had been kind and merciful to a Jewess," he said. "And that I am still willing to do," the abbé said. "I am willing to go with you now to the police station and testify in your favor."

But the German officer shook his head slowly.

"That was only one of the things that you said you would do," he said. "You also said that you would do anything I wanted. Well, what I want you to do is not to give evidence in my favor. What I want you to do is to help Rachel and myself to escape." The German officer said this gently and there was gentleness, too, in his eyes as he looked at the abbé. "I realize that I am asking rather an unfair thing and we shall both understand if you refuse. We should find it easier if you helped us but if you do not help us we shall do our best to help ourselves."

"We shall understand if you do not wish to help us," Rachel said.

"We shall not think unkindly of you," the German officer said. "And I shall not hold you to your promise." In spite of the bulge at the front and at the back of his head the German officer's civilian hat was too big for him and it fell down over his ears as he spoke: The German officer had to pull his hat up on to his head again.

The abbé Gaston did not smile when the German officer's hat fell down over his ears. The abbé was remembering his promise to the German officer and he knew that he had meant what he said when he had promised it. The German officer had been merciful to Rachel and, whether or not it was because he had fallen in love with her that he had been merciful to her, it was the abbé's duty to be merciful to the German officer. And the abbé knew that the Lord had poured rivers in all countries and that the Lord wanted all men to be happy where they slept, because all men were in the Lord's glance and none more than others. And in the soundlessness of the abbé Gaston's heart the Lord said that this was the lie, that men should live tightly within themselves and within their countries.

"Of course I shall help you," the abbé said. The words were out now and he could not take them back, but even so he tried to take them back. "But I still wonder if you would not be able to help yourselves more easily without me," he said. "This war is not like any other war. It is a fluid war." The abbé smiled gratefully in his beard as the technical term came to help him. "You have only to go to the gates of Paris. There is still fighting in the woods. At night it will be easy to slip through to the German lines. It will be easy because there are no lines to speak of, neither on one side nor on the other. I should be willing to come with you, of course, but I am afraid that I should only be in the way. And there would be no point in my crossing to the German lines, too, because I should have to cross back again."

"We have already thought of that," Rachel said. Her teeth chattered as she spoke and she pulled her coat about her, although the sun was still streaming into the porch.

"The men of the Resistance are watching all the gates," the German officer said. "They are watching even the southern and the western gates. But in a week's time they will be less vigilant. We shall have further to travel, of course, but it will not be so dangerous. In the meantime we must hide."

"And even I can no longer hide in Madame Bisberot's," Rachel said.

The abbé Gaston thought quickly, still trying to find an easy solution. His own room was too small, and besides Madame Boulon would almost certainly recognize the German officer. The presbytery was no good either. All the doors which had been open to the enemy yesterday were closed to him today and in the whole of Paris the abbé could think only of the convent. The nuns would almost certainly not refuse to shelter even an enemy in distress. He would be exposing the nuns to a risk, of course, but he would be exposing himself as well, and he thought that the nuns would be willing to run the risk when he had explained to them about the German officer having saved Rachel. And it wouldn't take long to accompany the German officer and Rachel to the convent in the underground.

"I think I know a place," the abbé said and was silent again as the sacristan came out to lock up the church. The sun was no longer blue or gold as they moved down the steps of the church, but was beginning to turn red and its glow fell softly all over the roofs of Paris and warmed them. The sun began to look big as well as red because it was coming down to the edge of the sky.

"Once again you are kind," Rachel said. "I think that you are very kind indeed."

"Neither of us shall ever forget your kindness," the German officer said.

"Perhaps it would be safer if you were both to be silent a little," the abbé Gaston said. "You both speak French with an accent and it is better that this should not be remarked."

None of them spoke anymore when the abbé had said this and they all three walked in silence towards the entrance to the underground. As they walked the abbé felt ashamed of having spoken sharply to Rachel and the German officer. He knew that he had done so because he was afraid, and was even hating them a little for having made him afraid. He was irritated and frightened at the thought of having to make a journey in the underground in the company of the German officer. And his fear obsessed him so much that he forgot that the underground had not been running for the past few days, so that his displeasure escaped him again when they arrived at the entrance to the underground and found the iron gates at the foot of the steps shut and padlocked.

"Just our luck!" the abbé exclaimed bitterly. "That would happen, of course."

"It is no doubt because the electricity has been sabotaged," the German officer said.

"Or it is perhaps because they are afraid that the tunnels have been mined," Rachel said.

Ashamed again of his anger, the abbé began to think that it was not because of sabotage or the danger of mines that the underground was not running, but because the Lord wished to punish him for having spoken crossly to Rachel and the German officer, who were also His servants.

"We shall have to walk," the abbé said sadly, but this time he managed to keep the irritation out of his voice. The convent was a long way off and he had not walked so far since he had been wounded in the first war. He would probably be so tired when he reached the convent that he would have to ask the nuns to allow him to stay the night. It was fortunate that the funeral of the butcher who hadn't been to mass since the Third Sunday in Lent, 1901, was not until twelve o'clock next day.

"Is it far?" the German officer asked.

"It is very far," the abbé Gaston said.

"I do not care how far it is as long as I am with you," Rachel said, thrusting her arm through the German officer's and smiling up at him.

The abbé thought that this was a stupid thing to say, and this was another thing which the abbé did not understand about love, that people in love should say such foolish things to each other. He thought it still more stupid to say such things when there were so many other people standing with them looking at the closed gates of the underground and likely to be suspicious of anyone talking in a foreign accent. Two or three people, the abbé saw, looked closely at Rachel after she had spoken, and one scruffy little man in a green suit in particular, but the abbé did not want to speak crossly again.

"*Liebchen,*" the German officer murmured.

Although the German officer said the German word softly the abbé Gaston heard it and he saw at once that the scruffy little man in the green suit had heard it, too. The abbé led the way quickly up the steps.

"It is imprudent to use German words in public," the abbé said gently when they reached the top of the steps.

"I beg your pardon," the German officer said. "It was foolish of me. I am afraid that I was carried away."

"I shall let go your arm so that you will be carried away no more," Rachel said.

The windows in the houses on the right side of the street were all shining with gold and silver and pale green as well as they started to walk up the pavement, because the sun had come down low on the sky now and was big and red on the horizon at the end of the street. They did not speak as they walked because of what the abbé Gaston had said. At first Rachel and the German officer walked too fast for the abbé with his limp and they had to keep falling back again until they remembered to match their pace to his. There were not many people in the street because already the people had begun to get used to being free again and the ordinary things had to go on being done in houses and most of them meanly. There was no traffic in the middle of the street. Occasionally little groups of men with armbands marched quickly up the causeway with a swaggering air and before they reached the end of the. street they couldn't be seen anymore as the sun was shining on them so strongly. There was not much noise in the street, although here and there was the drool of a wireless playing dance music and once a screech as well as the tin ghost of a wax soprano howled about love.

It was not until they reached the top of the street that the abbé Gaston heard the footsteps behind them. It was because they were deliberate footsteps that they attracted the abbé's attention. However, the abbé did not look round at once but waited until they were crossing into the next street, when he pretended that he was looking back to see if there was any traffic coming. The abbé saw that the scruffy little man in the green suit was walking about fifty yards back on the pavement.

There were two streets branching off at the top of the street and the abbé took the one to the right that ran up a hill into the blaze of the sky. When they were a little way up the street the abbé heard the footsteps crossing, too, and then on the pavement behind them, but he did not look round. The sky was green and purple as well as red now, but they could see only a strip of it hung like a banner at the end of the street between the high cliffs of the houses. The abbé waited until they had reached the end of this street also before he drew the attention of his companions to the footsteps sounding on the flagstones behind them.

"I think that we are being followed," the abbé said. Although he wanted to add that it was because of their imprudent conversation at the entrance to the underground, he did not do so. "I think that we had better try to dodge about a little," he said.

So at the top of the street they turned down another street running in the opposite direction. There were beginning to be stars on the strip of the sky at the end of this street as they were walking away from the sun now. They walked down the street with their faces held up to the coolness of the new stars and the abbé tried not to think of the footsteps which might turn down the street after them, but only of the stars in the sky. But the abbé listened all the same for the footsteps. And when he heard them again he looked round quickly and saw that it was the same little man who was following them, although he couldn't distinguish the color of the little man's suit any longer because of the darkness coming down.

"I am sure now that we are being followed," the abbé said and was surprised that he did not feel more frightened. He was even a little exhilarated as he made Rachel and the German officer turn sharply to the right again on reaching the end of the street.

At the top of this next street there was a café of the type that sold both coal and drinks, and light was coming from the windows, in front of which the proprietor was standing in his shirt sleeves, preparing to pull down the iron shutters. "It's the hell of a life," the proprietor was shouting at the shutters in the heavy accent of the Auvergne. "If it's not the Germans it's the Americans." The abbé Gaston made a decision immediately. He pushed Rachel and the German officer into the entrance to the café and followed quickly himself before the proprietor had finished pulling down the shutters.

There were a few men in workmen's clothes standing along the counter, mooning into their drinks. The abbé Gaston and Rachel and the German officer went and stood beside them. The abbé did not look round while the proprietor was finishing pulling down the shutters. The shutters came down with a clang because they were made of iron and they seemed to come down quickly. When the abbé turned round he saw that a shutter had come down in front of the door as well. He was glad of this and hoped that this shutter, too, had been pulled down before the little man had turned the corner.

The proprietor came back into the café and stood behind the counter with the shiny back of his waistcoat reflected in the mirror behind the bottles. The proprietor's face was shiny, too, and it looked as though it had been polished. The proprietor's wife sat perched on a stool in front of the cash desk staring at a candle burning in a saucer. There was no electric light in the cafe. There were only candles burning in saucers and bottles.

"So we are wetting the liberation?" the proprietor asked, standing in front of the abbé Gaston with an inquiring look.

"That's it," the abbé said. He knew that, as a priest, he had no right to be in a café and he hoped that the proprietor would ascribe his misdemeanor to the exceptional times. He slid his boot gently against the German officer's shoe as an indication that the German officer should not talk.

"Quite like a church, isn't it?" the proprietor said, nodding his head at the candles. "Ought to make you feel at home. Well, what's your tipple? As a matter of fact there's no choice. There's only red rotgut and white rotgut. Those blasted Germans have drunk everything else."

The abbé ordered three glasses of red rotgut. It cost fifteen francs a glass and the abbé thought this very dear and he grudged the money, as he was saving up to buy Michelle a New Year present.

"It's the hell of a life," the proprietor said. "If it's not the Germans it's the Americans and if it's not the Americans it's the Germans."

"All the same we are free," a man along the counter said.

"As long as they don't bomb us," the proprietor said. "One can't even light a candle at night without having to pull down the bloody shutters."

"A candle or electric light, it's the same thing," the man along the counter said.

"They don't give you any electric light and still you've got to pull down your shutters," the proprietor said.

"A candle is the same as electric light," the man along the counter said.

"That's because of astronomy," a second man along the counter said. "The moon is a candle if it comes to the bit."

"All the same we resisted the enemy," the first man along the counter said.

"A German once asked me the way to the Folies Bergère and I showed him the way to the Panthéon," the second man along the counter said.

The wine was sour and the abbé Gaston did not enjoy drinking it. He drank it quickly and then he had to stare at his empty glass for a long time. He did not wish to talk to the proprietor and he could not talk to

Rachel or the German officer because of their accents. And he did not want to go out into the street again immediately in case the little man in the green suit might be hanging about. He looked at Rachel standing beside him and saw that her eyes were sad and tired.

He looked along past her at the German officer and the German officer was looking tired, too.

"Quite like a church, isn't it?" the proprietor said, nodding his head at the candles again. "Ought to make you feel at home that."

The abbé Gaston made his beard grin in the middle. But it wasn't a very good grin and the abbé could see that the proprietor was watching closely out of his darting little beady eyes. He raised his glass and drank the thin rim of wine that remained at the bottom.

"Well, good night and thanks," he said.

"Good night and thanks, Monsieur l'abbé," the proprietor said, but he came with the abbé and his companions to the door. "You'll have to go out quickly because of the light," he said. "Even a candle the Germans can see a long way off."

"It's because of astronomy," the second man along the counter said. "The moon's a candle, I tell you."

"The moon can't be a candle because it's got seaweed on it," the proprietor said as he bent to slide up the shutter.

The shutter slid up with a clang and the abbé and Rachel and the German officer stepped through quickly. And as soon as they were standing on the pavement the proprietor slid the shutter down again with a louder clang than before. The sky was all covered with stars now, above their heads and at both ends of the street. The sky was drawn right down behind the houses at the ends of the street, but the sky moved back behind other houses as they walked towards it and the stars were still as far away as ever when the abbé Gaston looked up at them.

"I rather think that we have shaken him off," the abbé said. There was no one at all in the street, and the next street when they came to it was empty, too.

"There does not seem to be much joy," the German officer said.

"The people have suffered too much for that," the abbé Gaston said.

"If Germany had conquered, Germany would have brought happiness to the world," the German officer said. "There would have been dancing and laughter, but behind the dancing and the laughter there would have been discipline."

"You cannot force happiness upon people," the abbé Gaston said. He was disappointed that the German officer should still talk like that when the Germans had done so many wrong things.

"I think that wars do not bring happiness," Rachel said. "It is true that there is a great misery in the world, but when men fight to cure it they make only a greater misery."

"Peace does not bring happiness either," the German officer said. "The counting houses are fields of battle, too."

Happiness is obedience, the abbé Gaston wanted to say, but he did not say it, in case it would sound like preaching. He limped along in silence with his eyes fixed on the sky and always there was a coolness on his cheeks, because of the coolness in the sky.

"I used to think that we could cure it all, but now I am not so sure," Rachel said. "I used to think that all we had to do was to distribute equally among people the goods that there were in the world so that a man should not have six oranges when his neighbor had none."

"There will always have to be inequalities but what inequalities I confess that I do not know," the German officer said. "There must be authority and it is not quickly that men learn to govern."

"It is from the people that I think that order will come, and then happiness will go back to them, but how that will happen I also do not know," Rachel said. She, too, walked with her face held up to the sky, and her face seemed very small and pale with only the faint light of the stars upon it. "In all countries the people are foolish and often they are also wicked as well."

"That is why authority must come down to the people from those who are more intelligent than they are," the German officer said.

"We wish for the same thing perhaps, but we wish for it to come about differently," Rachel said.

"And our way has failed," the German officer said. "Your way may succeed, but our way has failed."

"Your way has failed because it was the wrong way," the abbé Gaston said. "It is not by machine guns and thumbscrews that the truth shall be made known. You have brought a misery to the world which this century will not see healed." The abbé said this severely, but he tried not to sound angry, because anger was not his privilege.

"I may have threatened but I never tortured," the German officer said. "And even when I threatened I threatened that good might come."

"It is evil to do evil that good may come," the abbé Gaston said.

"Perhaps our way will be the right way after all," Rachel said. "It may take a thousand years but perhaps in the long run our way will be the right way."

"The trouble is that the world has been offered two wrong ways," the abbé Gaston said.

"Tell us a little about the right way," the German officer said.

"Yes, tell us, please," Rachel said.

They walked on in silence through the silent streets, and the abbé Gaston tried to tell them about the right way and about how simple it was. "Men have only got to humble themselves," he began, but as soon as he had said these words they began to bore him as he knew they must be boring his listeners. They had heard it all before, of course. Every Sunday from thousands of pulpits and in reedy voices the true things were said and every Monday the false things were done again. To the clap of his own boots on the pavement the abbé tried to discover why simple things had become obscure. There was science, of course, and its cold story about the world, and there were the cruelties with no Hand held out, and it was difficult because of the foolish words to find the right words. Every morning as he stood at the altar the abbé knew that he had the right words and the grand words, because God had placed them in the holy book, but these were words that were meant to be used to God alone and whispered only, because they were very holy words. "It is perhaps by acts that it is easier to explain," the abbé said when he had thought about these things for a little longer.

"*Your* acts are all right anyway, Monsieur l'abbé," the German officer said.

"You were kind to Rachel," the abbé said. "It is only natural that I should be kind to you. And even if you had not been kind to me I hope that I should still have been kind to you. Even although you are the enemy of France it is still my duty to be kind to you.

"Lately I have found it hard to understand about these things," the German officer said.

Sometimes there was the sound of gunfire in the distance and flashes of light on the horizon. Sometimes, too, there was the sound of rifle fire and of machine guns as well, and occasionally searchlights striped the sky and made some of the stars go out. But mostly there were silence and darkness and they walked alone in a round of roofs. When they met other people in the street they walked without talking. The other people seemed to be in a hurry, too, and the abbé Gaston was never very afraid of them. Even when there was nobody in the street they generally walked without talking, and the abbé thought that this was best. Rachel walked again with her arm through the German officer's arm and the abbé thought that they seemed very close to each other. Their bodies threw no shadows as they walked because there were no lamps lighted in the streets and there was no moon in the sky but only stars.

The Place de l'Etoile was deserted when they reached it. Most of the avenues running out of it seemed empty, too, when the abbé Gaston looked down them. The abbé calculated that it would still take them an hour to reach the convent, and he chose the Avenue Kléber instead of the Avenue Foch, as he thought that it looked less suspicious to walk through streets than through woods. There was no sound of firing now, but as they turned into the long canal of street the abbé heard a buzzing noise. At first he thought that it was the drone of a German airplane coming to bomb the city. But the noise came down on the ground behind them and quickly grew. It was only when the car screeched to a standstill beside them that the abbé remembered the scruffy little man in the green suit.

The scruffy little man in the green suit sat in front of the car beside the driver. The German officer and Rachel and the abbé Gaston were made to sit behind. Two men armed with rifles stood leaning against the back of the front seat and facing them, and another man with a rifle stood on each running board. All the men with rifles wore civilian clothes with armlets round their sleeves. The men standing up inside the car kept their rifles tucked up under their arms and pointing at their prisoners. When the car turned a corner the muzzles of their rifles slipped down and pointed at the floor of the car, but the men always brought their rifles quickly back into position again. The men hanging on to the sides of the car did not point their rifles at the abbé and Rachel and the German officer as they had to keep on holding on to the car and carrying their rifles at the same time. The scruffy little man in the green suit never looked round, not even when the car jolted badly. "It is foolish to talk with a German accent in the street these days and it is still more foolish to talk

German," the scruffy little man had said when he had arrested them. And that was all that the scruffy little man had said, except to tell them to get into the car quickly.

The car had turned round as soon as they had got into it, and it was now running along beside the river. The abbé could see the river when he looked out of the side of the car past the man standing on the running board. The river was shining and black and there were blue and silver gleams on its surface and sometimes there were gold gleams mingling with the silver gleams. Then the wall came high up and the abbé couldn't see the river for a little and then the wall went down again and the road came nearer the river again and the abbé saw the river again and the river was a strip of moving mirror with glows and gleams and glisters upon its gloss. The abbé Gaston threw his thoughts at the beauty of the river and tried not to be afraid, and he threw his thoughts at the cathedral, too, when he saw it, riding up upon the river and obliterating it.

The car swerved away from the river and ran among ugly houses. There were red and blue advertisements for drinks and soaps painted on the ends of the houses and they were illuminated briefly in the glare of the headlights. And even to the advertisements the abbé Gaston clung a little because they were familiar and seemed to promise that life would go on being familiar, too. The abbé knew that they had been captured by members of the Resistance and as the advertisements flashed by he caught out at them in hope, because they had framed his thoughts before when he had been unhappy.

The car left the houses behind and began to run along between trees. The abbé could not see the trees at the side of the car very well because there the trees were only another darkness flung upon the darkness of the night. But he could see the trees in front of the car lighted up by the lamps and their leaves pale green at the top of high arches. The abbé thought that it was imprudent of his captors to be driving a lighted car through the night with the German airplanes so near. However, he was too frightened to think about this for long and his fright was the whole of him, and it was with fright that he thought about his fright.

The lights from the lamps hit the leaves of the trees when the trees were far away and made the leaves turn silver on the top branches. But even about the beauty of this the abbé could not think, and always his terror came back to him. He knew that it was foolish of him to be afraid because being shot meant only dying and dying meant wearing reality right side up and seeing the glory. The abbé knew these things, but he did not feel them. As he sat there with the man in front of him pointing his rifle at him the abbé felt that death was a going out forever and he did not want to go out forever, and least of all painfully. To console his despair he clutched at the customary consolations, recalling a sermon he had preached to the nuns only a few weeks ago. Reality was reality not because one felt it or did not feel it, but because it existed. China was real and yet one didn't feel China unless one went there. Revelation was like mathematics, and even Einstein couldn't feel mathematics. God and His City waited whether one believed in them or not and the saints were there in spite of those who had never heard of them. These reflections made the abbé feel a little less miserable, but not for long.

The car left the road and ran on to a track. The driver drove more slowly now and the car lurched from side to side. The abbé bumped up and down on his seat and the men with rifles in front of them had difficulty in standing upright. The trees were close up all about them and the abbé could hear the tools rattling in the boot of the car. The car came to a standstill and the driver switched out his lamps. The trees vanished into more night. The abbé still could not see the trees when they made him get out of the car although he could smell the freshness of the leaves. In front of him the abbé could see pink lines of light coming from a doorway.

The men with the rifles stood all round them and the scruffy little man ordered them to march towards the doorway. Rachel and the German officer were made to walk in front and the abbé was made to walk behind. The scruffy little man kicked at the door when he came to it and the door was opened immediately. The room into which they were marched was filled with more men in armlets.

The room was a small room with cheap wallpaper peeling from the walls. There was no carpet on the floor and the only furniture was a table and a few chairs and benches running round the walls. A burly young man with curly black hair sat at the table which was littered with papers. There were also on the table three bottles with candles burning in them and this was the only light in the room. Two young men stood beside the man who was sitting at the table and the other men were sitting on benches round the walls. There were rifles stacked in a corner and all the men had cartridge belts strapped round their waists. Most of the men wore dark blue sweaters but some of them wore dark blue flannel shirts instead. Black curtains were drawn across the windows and there was a black curtain on the back of the door, too. But the curtain on the back of the door was not big enough and the abbé supposed that this was the reason why he had seen the pink lines of light.

The scruffy little man in the green suit made the abbé and Rachel and the German officer stand in front of the table. The four men with rifles stood beside them. The young man with the curly black hair gazed coldly at the abbé and Rachel and the German officer. One of his legs was crossed over the other and his big boot swung backwards and forwards beneath the table. "What's it this time?" the young man with the curly black hair asked. "More collaborators?"

"Germans trying to escape, I think," the scruffy little man in the green suit said.

"We'll interrogate them separately," the man with the curly black hair said. "Like that they'll probably all tell different lies." His boot went on swinging all the time that he was speaking, and it still went on swinging when he had finished speaking, backwards and forwards.

"The French priest speaks French with a French accent so perhaps he is really a priest after all," the scruffy little man in the green suit said.

"We'll soon find that out," the man with the curly black hair said. He sat in silence for a moment, swinging his boot and sucking in air through his teeth. "You realize that this is summary justice," he said, switching his cold face full on the prisoners. "Your interrogation will be your trial. We have no time to waste on formalities these days." His boot swung on beneath the table and his nose looked colder than the rest of his face, perhaps because it was so thin. "We shall begin with the girl," he said to the men standing beside him. "Have the other two taken upstairs and put in separate rooms."

The abbé Gaston had not time to study the expression on Rachel's face because he and the German officer were marched away immediately. He caught a glimpse of her hair hanging softly about her cheeks and of the candlelight making it seem softer still, and of her summer coat half-open, too, he caught a glimpse, and of her dark blue velvet dress beneath.

Two of the men who had driven with him in the car accompanied the abbé and the German officer. They were marched along a dark corridor and up an uncarpeted stair. The German officer was put in one room and the abbé Gaston was put in another.

The room in which the abbé found himself was in darkness and there were no curtains on the window. The abbé could see the stars again, shining far above the trees, and he walked towards the window so that he could see them better. But the guard who had accompanied the abbé reached the window before him and stood with his back against it.

"No nonsense," the guard said. "If you're going to die you're going to die our way."

"Surely you know that a priest would never try to commit suicide," the abbé said.

"I've heard that tale before," the guard said.

The phrase rang on in the abbé's mind. Everybody in the world had heard tales before and none of them were clean tales, and this, too, was part of the tragedy, that men no longer believed clean things.

As his eyes grew accustomed to the darkness the abbé saw that there was no furniture in the room. The guard walked up and down from the window to the door with his rifle slung over his shoulder. The abbé's bad leg was tired after so much walking and he stood and leaned against the wall. He wondered what Rachel was saying downstairs and if she were trying to shield the German officer and himself. He wondered whether they would interrogate the German officer or himself next and what the German officer would say when they questioned him.

The abbé Gaston had never liked lying, even of the supposedly sinless sort. He decided that the only thing for him to do was to tell the truth. The truth could be harmful only to himself; it could not be harmful either to the German officer or to Rachel, who were both German subjects attempting to escape from an enemy country. The abbé did not think that the men of the Resistance could punish either the German officer or Rachel for having made this attempt, which was quite in accordance with the laws of warfare. It was true that Rachel had been an Austrian refugee, but Austria was now part of Germany and the abbé hoped that the tribunal would not inquire too closely into the ethics of her flight. His own case alone was doubtful. Indeed it was so doubtful as to be almost certain, unless of course, he were to tell the tribunal that he had also helped a British officer to escape. The abbé did not think that he would tell the tribunal about the British officer. It would sound like bragging and he did not suppose that the tribunal would be likely to believe him. Words of grandeur occurred to the abbé as he made this decision. The words were from the eighteenth psalm and they formed the offertory for the Third Sunday in Lent: "*Justitiæ Domini rectæ, lætificantes corda, et judicia ejus dulciora super mel et favum: nam et servus tuus custodit ea.*" And that, the abbé suddenly knew, was why one must never despair: because the justices of the Lord were right, rejoicing the hearts. And one day all would be made clear, because the judgments of the Lord were sweeter than honey and the honeycomb, and His servant kept them. The abbé whispered the lovely words to himself, to give himself heart.

"Talking to yourself, eh?" the guard asked, coming close to the abbé in the darkness.

"I talk to myself for two reasons," the abbé said, less frightened now because of what the words had done to him. "I talk to myself because I like to talk to somebody intelligent and because I like to hear somebody intelligent talk." The joke was an old one which one of his professors at the seminary had told the abbé, and it often amused him still.

"Funny, aren't you?" the guard grumbled.

They came for the abbé shortly after that. The abbé blinked his eyes when he entered the lighted room again. The man with the curly black hair was still sitting at the table and his boot was still swinging. The two men who had been standing beside him were now seated on upturned boxes on his right and his left, and one of them was breaking off the stalactite of candlegrease which had flowed down the edge of one of the candles and hardened. Rachel and the German officer were seated among the men on the benches round the wall, with armed guards separating them. The abbé wondered what they had said when they were questioned, but he tried not to worry too much, because the justices of the Lord were right, rejoicing the heart, and His judgments were sweeter than honey and the honeycomb. He smiled at them and they smiled unhappily back.

"Look at me and not at your friends," the man with the curly black hair said. "What is your name?"

"My name is the abbé Jean Gaston," the abbé said.

"And you are a priest?" the man with the curly black hair asked.

"I am a priest," the abbé said.

"A French priest, eh?"

"That also is correct," the abbé said.

"Then what are you doing in the company of two Germans?" the man with the curly black hair asked.

"I was helping them to escape," the abbé said.

"Please say that again so that there may be no mistake."

"I was helping them to escape," the abbé said.

"You were aware of what you were doing?"

"I was aware of what I was doing," the abbé said.

"You were aware that you were aiding the enemies of France to escape from the people of France?"

"That is not quite correct," the abbé said. "I was aware that I was aiding one enemy of France to escape from the people of France. The girl is not and has never been an enemy of France. The girl is an Austrian refugee."

The man with the curly black hair exchanged glances with the men sitting on either side of him. His face was cold as he went on with his questioning, and his nose still looked colder than his face, and his big boot still kept on swinging, backwards and forwards.

"And why should you aid even one enemy of France to escape from the people of France?" the man with the curly black hair asked.

"A little because of theology, perhaps," the abbé said. Once again the man with the curly black hair exchanged glances with the men seated on either side of him, and this time he smiled a little.

"Perhaps you do not know that you are talking to communists," he said.

"Whoever I am talking to it is still my duty to tell the truth," the abbé said.

"And so it was because of theology that you were helping these people to escape?"

"A little, I hope," the abbé said. "The girl is an Austrian refugee. She is a Jewess whom I helped when she first came to France in 1938."

"You have told us most of that before," the man with the curly black hair said. "I would prefer it if you were to tell me a little about the man."

"The man is a German officer," the abbé said. "That is all that I know about him."

"At least you must know his name."

"I know that he is called Karl," the abbé said. "And I only know that because I have heard the girl call him by that name."

"Am I to understand that you're asking this tribunal to believe that you have risked your life and your reputation for one whose name you do not know?"

"I'm afraid that I am," the abbé said.

"I suggest that you know perfectly well that this man's name is Karl Rummel."

"I know nothing of the sort," the abbé said.

"I suggest also that you know that he is a member of the Geheimstaatspolizei, commonly known as the Gestapo," the man with the curly black hair said. "I suggest that you have not only been aiding him to escape. I suggest that you yourself were also attempting to escape and that you were doing so because of the crimes which you have committed against the French community. I suggest that you are both a collaborator and an informer, Monsieur l'abbé."

"That is not true," the abbé said angrily. "I admit that I had an idea that this man belonged to the German police administration but I did not know that he was a member of the Gestapo. And I am not a collaborator or an informer. I served France in the first war and I served her in this. And even when I was no longer a soldier I helped the Allies of France in the same way as I have helped this man who is technically her enemy." It was the abbé's resentment which led him into telling the beginning of the story of the British officer in spite of his determination not to mention it, and it was his resentment which made him check it, because for the moment he was more angry than afraid and he did not wish to appear to be trying to curry favor with the tribunal.

"A lot of people helped both sides but they were prudent enough to do so in a different order," the man with the curly black hair said. "Perhaps you will tell us how you came to make the acquaintance of this officer."

"I made his acquaintance in 1941," the abbé said. "He came to inquire if I was concealing or helping to conceal any Jewish persons. I lied and said that I was not."

"For theology's sake?" The man with the curly black hair winked at the men sitting on either side of him at the table, first at one and then at the other. Then he turned back to the abbé again and his big boot went on swinging under the table and his nose looked very cold down the middle. "But perhaps you would tell us why you wished to befriend this girl."

"That is simple," the abbé said. "I befriended her when she first came to Paris in 1938. I found her work. And I went on befriending her after the Germans came."

"That is not telling us *why* you befriended her."

"I befriended her because the Germans had done cruel things to her in Vienna," the abbé said. "And I went on befriending her because I knew that if the Germans found her in Paris they would do still more cruel things to her. It is cruelty that is the sin."

"If that is so why should you attempt to protect a member of an army which has done cruel things to France?"

"That I shall try to tell you," the abbé said. "In 1943 this officer came back again. He told me that he knew now that I had been lying to him and he tricked me into showing him where the girl was working. And I promised him that if he would leave her alone I should help him to the best of my ability if ever the need arose. He saw the girl, liked her and no harm came to her."

"Because you had promised to help him to escape if ever the Allies came to Paris?"

"I did not promise him exactly that," the abbé said. "And I do not think that it was because of my promise that this officer spared the girl. I think that it was because he fell in love with her."

"In that case it would seem that you were no longer bound by your promise."

"That was not the way I looked at it," the abbé said.

"Monsieur l'abbé, I do not think that you are telling this tribunal the truth."

"I know that I am telling you the truth and that is all that matters," the abbé said.

"This man is an officer of the Gestapo," the man with the curly black hair said, and as he spoke his boot began to swing more violently and the white line down the middle of his nose seemed to grow broader. "We know that because we have lists and photographs. We are not sure about the girl, although the evidence suggests that she is an agent of the Gestapo. But we are quite sure about you, Monsieur l'abbé. You are a French priest and you have been caught helping an officer of the Gestapo to escape."

"I have already told you that I did not know that he was an officer of the Gestapo," the abbé said. "And I know that he himself has never done a cruel thing."

"How do you know that?"

"Because he himself told me so," the abbé said.

There was laughter at this, but the man with the curly black hair did not laugh.

"And it was because he told you that he had never done a cruel thing that you yourself were attempting to escape with him?" the man with the curly black hair asked.

"That is not true," the abbé said. "I was not attempting to escape with him."

"Monsieur l'abbé, I suggest that you knew that he was a member of the Gestapo."

"That is not true," the abbé said. "But even if I had known that he was a member of the Gestapo it is possible that I might still have helped him to escape."

"Why?"

"For one thing, because of my promise to help him if he helped the girl," the abbé said.

"And for the other thing?"

"The other thing is a little more difficult and I do not know if I should have had the grace to do it for the other thing alone," the abbé said. "The other thing is what God has said clearly and men have blurred. The other thing is that we do worse to ourselves when we do to others the evil that they themselves have done to us."

"Very nice theology, I'm sure," the man with the curly black hair said. "But there is no need to worry on that score. Neither their deaths nor your own will hurt very much. But there is one other thing I want to know and I want to know it very badly." The man with the curly black hair suddenly stopped swinging his boot and he leaned his whole cold face across the table at the abbé and his eyes were hard and threatening and without pity. "Do you know of the whereabouts of any other Gestapo officers or the names of those who have been helping them?"

"Of course not," the abbé said.

"That is what we shall have to find out and it may hurt a little," the man with the curly black hair said and turned to the guards. "Take him upstairs again." They did not have to give him many blows with the belts with the buckles before the abbé Gaston was sure that in 1936 the driver in the underground must have put the little blue lamp out at Château-Landon after all.

The sun was shining on the leaves of the trees outside the window when the abbé Gaston awoke the next morning. The leaves were pale green in the sunshine and thin and frail and almost transparent against the sky, but the abbé was too frightened and sore to notice their beauty. His chief pain was in the head, where the buckle of the belt had struck him several times, and when he touched his right eyelid with his hand he could feel that it was puffed and swollen. There were pains in his body as well, for the belt had struck him all over, and the men had kicked him with their heavy boots. When he stretched on the floor the abbé found that he could still move his legs although they were sore, too. He did not know whether he had been unconscious or asleep. He thought that he must have been unconscious first and asleep afterwards as he seemed to remember lying on the floor while it was still dark. The man who had guarded him before was guarding him now, sitting with his back against the wall, and with his knees drawn up and his rifle between them.

"It won't be much longer now," the guard said when he saw that the abbé was awake.

The abbé licked his lips, which were dry and crusted. He tried to speak and quickly stopped. The effort was too great for him and he did not think that he had anything to say.

"We had to do it," the guard said. "We had to make sure that you weren't hiding any others. We've got to be certain that we've kicked all those swine out of France."

The abbé did not answer. It was obvious that the man was ashamed of having hurt him so much, but the abbé did not know how to make him less ashamed, so he said nothing. Beneath his cracked lips he offered his pain to the Lord, that the Lord might hallow it and fit it in.

The door opened and another guard entered.

"We're starting with the officer, but he wants to see the priest first," the other guard said to the guard who was guarding the abbé.

The abbé understood and managed to rise painfully to his feet before his guard told him that he might go. Both guards came with him. The first few steps hurt the abbé but soon the stiffness in his legs wore off although the pain in his head and his body remained. One guard walked on either side of him. Their young ears were clamped in tight against their heads like little pink wheels. The abbé thought of how old his own ears must look, with all the hairs growing out of them.

The German officer was sitting on the floor in a little bare room like the one the abbé had just left. A guard with a rifle was standing by the window. The German officer stood up as the abbé entered.

"They are going to shoot me now but I do not think that I am afraid," the German officer said.

"It is not weak to be afraid," the abbé Gaston said.

"But it is weak to show it," the German officer said. "Before I die I should like to thank you for all that you have tried to do for us."

"Please," the abbé Gaston said.

"It is useless to attempt to apologize for the wrong that we have done to you because the wrong is too great," the German officer said. "Both Rachel and I think that you are a very good man."

"These things are nothing," the abbé Gaston said.

"I have said good-bye to Rachel," the German officer said. "In a few minutes they will be shooting her also. They are not going to shoot us all together. They are going to shoot us one after another."

"There are different ways of doing these things but I do not understand very much about any of them," the abbé Gaston said.

"I loved Rachel," the German officer said. "I loved her at night and I loved her in the morning. That is how you know you love a girl: when you love her in the morning."

"About these things also I do not understand," the abbé Gaston said.

"I loved her in all her dresses, but I think that I loved her best in her red dress," the German officer said. The bulges at the front and at the back of his head were as big as ever and the abbé tried not to think of what the rifle bullets would do to them. "I have said good-bye to Rachel," the German officer said. "And now I think I should like to say good-bye to God."

"These are not altogether the right words to use," the abbé Gaston said.

"No nonsense, mind," one of the guards said. "We'll have a man posted under the window just in case."

The three guards went out of the room. The abbé took from the pocket of his cassock the thin little silk stole which he always carried with him. The stole was white on one side and violet on the other. The white side was for giving holy communion and the violet side was for hearing confessions. The abbé put the stole over his shoulders with the violet side upwards. He knew that there would be no opportunity of using the white side.

The sun was coming in at the window when the abbé had finished hearing the German officer's confession. The sun was lifted above the trees in a big blue and gold ball and it sent quick little shining lights all over the floor. The pattern of the lights on the floor looked like water moving.

"It is not easy to die on such a morning," the German officer said.

"It will be quickly over," the abbé Gaston said.

"There must be some hurt all the same," the German officer said.

"Perhaps a quick little hurt but it will be a very quick little hurt," the abbé said.

"It is not the hurt of which I am afraid," the German officer said. "It is of leaving Rachel. I love Rachel. I wanted to love her for a long time. I wanted to love her when she was old and to think of how much I had loved her when she was young. She had a new green dress. I never saw her in her new green dress.".

"These things are hard, but behind them there is a gentleness," the abbé Gaston said. "That is the real mystery, that all hard things turn into a gentleness."

"I love Rachel, and I do not think that it is just her body that I love, although her body is very beautiful."

"It is of loving God that you must think now," the abbé Gaston said. "The time is short. You must think a lot of loving God. You must pray a great prayer in your heart so that you may love God."

"It is difficult to love God when one is stood up to be shot by cold men," the German officer said.

"It is not the cold men you must think of," the abbé Gaston said. "It is the small voice at the bottom of your heart that you must listen to."

"My shoelace is undone," the German officer said. "I must not die untidily with my shoelace undone."

"I shall tie your shoelace for you if you will only listen to the small voice at the bottom of your heart," the abbé Gaston said.

"I shall tie my shoelace myself and try to listen to the small voice at the bottom of my heart at the same time," the German officer said.

"That is the lie that men have told the world: that there is no gentleness and no voice at the bottom of the heart," the abbé Gaston said.

"I have found it easier to tie my shoelace than to listen to the small voice at the bottom of my heart," the German officer said.

"I am not good at explaining these things but I know that what I say is true," the abbé Gaston said.

"I hear them coming," the German officer said. "If you see Rachel before she dies you will tell her that I died thinking of her and that I was sorry that I never saw her in her new green dress."

"If I see her I shall tell her these things," the abbé Gaston said. "And now kneel down while I give you my blessing." And as he made the sign of the cross and murmured the holy words, the abbé tried to tip out over the young man all the yearning and the sorrow which he felt for him and for the rest of the world, because the yearning and the sorrow which the abbé felt was a great spread out pity, as he knew the Lord's must be also. "And try to think of God and not of green dresses," he said, when he had finished blessing the young man.

"And you will come with me?" the German officer asked. "Perhaps I shall find it easier not to think of green dresses if you will come with me."

The three guards came in again. Their big boots walked through the shimmering dapples of light on the floor. There were other men standing outside in the passage and they carried rifles, too.

"If you are ready we are," one of the guards said.

The German officer bit at his lips. His eyes shone so brightly that for a moment the abbé Gaston thought that he was going to weep. But the German officer caught at the tears in time and he squared his shoulders and threw back his head.

"I am ready," he said.

"If you don't mind I should like to come, too," the abbé Gaston said;

"We are shooting you separately and we are shooting you last of all," the guard said.

"You are shooting me last of all but I should still like to come, too," the abbé Gaston said.

They marched out into the corridor. The abbé Gaston and the German officer went first and the three guards came behind. But in front of the abbé Gaston and the German officer were the men with rifles already standing in the corridor and they all went downstairs in that order. There was nobody in the big room in which they had been tried the night before. The men who had been sitting on the benches stood drawn up in a single line outside in the sunlight and the man with the curly black hair was giving them instructions.

The sun shone into the abbé's eyes and made him blink and it hurt him when he blinked with his right eye because it was so swollen. The sun shone on the men who were waiting outside and the sun shone on the men who marched with them across the grass. The sun made their bodies throw oblique shadows, which walked with them. The sun shone on the leaves of the trees and the sky was blue with no clouds in it, and the abbé knew again that the Lord's justices were right, rejoicing the heart, and that His judgments were sweeter than honey and the honeycomb, and that behind what men had done to the world the Lord's meaning lay. The abbé wanted to say something of this to the German officer, but he hadn't the words and there wasn't time, as they had soon reached the beginning of the trees.

Their guards split away on either side of them when they reached the trees. The man with the curly black hair came across the grass and helped the guards to bind the German officer against one of the trees. His lips were thin and tightly closed but there was a shame about his eyes and, as he watched him, the abbé knew that the stink which had come upon the world had come upon it because men had been afraid to listen to the voice at the bottom of their hearts. "Say 'Lord Jesus, into Thy Hands I commend my spirit,' and these things will pass quickly," the abbé said to the German officer when they had finished binding him to the tree.

"Blindfolded?" the man with the curly black hair asked the German officer.

"Not blindfolded," the German officer said.

The man with the curly black hair stood away from the tree and he made the abbé Gaston come with him and stand among the guards.

The German officer stood with the sun shining on the tree behind him and with the leaves making moving shadows on his face. The bulge in front of his head was big and plain and the abbé could see part of the bulge on the back of his head as well, because he was looking at the German officer sideways. The abbé tried to pray, but his lips and his heart were dry as he knew that this same sharp lonely thing must happen to him also and the sun go on shining on the trees after it had happened. The man with the curly black hair gave a command and the men in the firing squad raised their rifles to their shoulders. He gave another command and they fired. The German officer's head fell forwards on to his chest and his knees slumped beneath him. For a little there was no blood on the German officer's face and then there was blood on his face, but it was not very much blood. The man with the curly black hair walked quickly back to the tree and fired a shot with his revolver into the back of the German officer's head.

"Just to make sure," the man with the curly black hair said as he came back and stood beside the abbé Gaston.

The abbé Gaston would have liked to have gone and said one last prayer over the German officer's body, that the Lord might gather his soul and lift it up. But the guards marched him back to the little house immediately. They said that Rachel, too, had asked to see him before she died, and the abbé hoped that she also might be reaching out to the Lord.

But as soon as he saw Rachel he knew that she was not reaching out to the Lord, and his sadness deepened, both for her and for himself. She was sitting on a small stool in a bare room. The room was cold as there was no sun shining into it. She still wore her summer overcoat open over her blue velvet dress, which was shiny and pressed down where it fell over her knees. Her hair hung in untidy streaks about her head. Her eyes were big and somber and her lips were trembling. She did not speak until the guards had left them alone together.

"I heard the shots," Rachel said.

"It was very quick," the abbé Gaston said. "He told me to tell you that he died thinking of you."

"As I shall die thinking of him," she said.

"He said that he was sorry that he had not seen you in your new green dress," the abbé Gaston said.

"We used to joke a lot about my new green dress," she said. "I do not feel like joking now. I am very frightened. Tell me: was Karl frightened?"

"He was very brave and he died a good death," the abbé Gaston said.

"A good death?" she asked. "I am afraid that I do not understand."

"Karl died with his thoughts fixed on God," the abbé Gaston said.

"Even that I do not understand," she said.

"It is important that you should understand," the abbé Gaston said. "The mercy of God is a long and a strong rope and it's never too late to catch hold of it."

"That I think I understand a little," she said.

"These things are written in men's hearts as well as in books," the abbé Gaston said.

"Even so I am still afraid to die," she said.

"You must not be afraid to die," the abbé Gaston said, but the words when he said them sounded unconvincing. Instead of talking he stroked her cheek. "My *poor* Rachel," he said.

"I do not think that I am looking very beautiful today," she said.

"Of course you are beautiful," the abbé Gaston said.

"But my eyelashes are not sticking up properly," she said.

"I'm old fashioned and I like them better the way they are," the abbé Gaston said.

"Please kiss me," she said.

The abbé Gaston put his arms around her and kissed her on both cheeks. Her body was warm and sweet and soft smelling in his arms and for the first time since his mother had died the abbé Gaston felt the touch of a woman's hair on his face. And when she began to weep he felt her tears also, and his own tears mingled with them. When they had finished kissing each other they were both still weeping.

"You have been very brave and kind to me and I love you a lot and if there is a heaven I hope that you will pull me up into it," Rachel said.

"We must not be silly like this," the abbé Gaston said. "We must not forget that we have both got to be brave."

They dried their eyes and looked away from each other for a little. The abbé Gaston was ashamed of himself for not having been able to convert Rachel and he asked the Lord to forgive the weakness of his words. When he looked at Rachel again she was no longer weeping.

"You went with Karl and saw them fire?" she asked.

"I think it was easier for him that way," the abbé Gaston said.

"I heard first a lot of shots and then another shot," she said.

"It is not necessary to think about that," the abbé Gaston said.

"The second shot was in case he was not killed the first time?" she asked.

"There is no need to think about that," the abbé Gaston said.

"Is it because they stand a long way off that they may not kill the first time?" she asked. She watched him sadly when he did not answer. "Please tell me the truth," she said.

"It is usual for them to stand a long way off," the abbé Gaston said.

"You must ask them to shoot me from close up," she said. "Promise me that you will ask them to shoot me from close up. I shall be brave if only you will ask them to shoot me from close up." She came back into his arms and wept again and her long hair was like silk against his cheek, and even where her hair touched his beard he could still feel the softness of it. "Promise me that you will ask this for me and that you will come with me."

"It will be quickly over and you will not be hurt," the abbé Gaston said.

"But promise me that you will ask," she said.

"I promise you that I shall ask," he said. "And I shall come with you, too," he said.

She dried her eyes again and stood listening to the silence.

"They will come quickly now but I am no longer afraid because I know that you will ask them to shoot me from close up," she said. Then she smiled at him and her face was beautiful and the beauty was still there when she was sad again. "Always I talk of myself and it is of you that I should talk when it is because of me that you, too, are going to die," she said.

"Sooner or later we all must die," the abbé Gaston said. "I am old now and I have seen many lovely things but chiefly I think I have seen ugly things and that is why I shall try not to be afraid when they come to do the thing to me."

They were silent as the footsteps sounded on the wooden flooring of the corridor. The footsteps came quickly and they stopped outside the door. The guard who had been guarding Rachel came into the room.

"We are ready now," the guard said. "Mademoiselle wishes me to come with her," the abbé Gaston said.

"You will not forget to ask also the other thing?" Rachel said.

"I shall not forget to ask the other thing," the abbé Gaston said.

They marched down the stairs and out into the green and blue and gold morning. The sun still shone on the trees and some of the leaves were pale yellow in its light. The same men still stood waiting to fire and the man with the curly black hair left them and came across the grass with the guards to help to bind Rachel to the tree. There was no sign of the German officer's body anywhere.

The sun shone down on Rachel's blue dress when they bound her to the tree and made all the flattened velvet bits show. The sun shone down on her hair and made it bright and gold and glowing, and she looked very young as she stood there with the men binding ropes round her body. At first she kept her eyes shut but after a little she opened them and she began to weep when she saw what they were doing to her. The tears streamed down her cheeks and moisture came out of her nostrils, too.

"I am afraid that I am not very brave," she said. "I do not wish them to do this thing to me. But if they must do it I wish them to do it from close up. I wish to know one minute something and the next minute nothing. I do not wish to know first an agony and then nothing."

"Mademoiselle wishes to be shot from a close range," the abbé Gaston said.

"Your request is unusual, Mademoiselle, but we shall do as you wish," the roan with the curly black hair said. "But first we shall bandage your eyes and then the men will come close up. It is not pretty to look at men pointing rifles at you from close up."

"You must not mind if I still go on crying when you have bandaged my eyes," Rachel said. "I shall go on crying because I am not brave, but I should be less brave if you did not shoot me from close up."

She said the words jerkily, between sobs. As they bandaged her eyes, the abbé Gaston was stricken for her because of all the hard things that the world had done to her and because of the hard thing that the world would still do to her, standing there with the sun shining on her hair. The abbé did not look as the men came closer with their rifles, advancing slowly across the grass and their shadows creeping with them. There was nothing that he could say to comfort her, and very little that he could pray, but a hope went out from him that for unbelievers, too, there might be a mercy, and a gentleness when the last of the hard things had been done to them. *"In manus Tuas . . ."* the abbé began to say for her as the man with the curly black hair made him stand away from her, but he stopped half way, miserable because of her loneliness and of his own loneliness and of the loneliness of all men.

When the man with the curly black hair gave the command some of the firing squad pointed their rifles at her breast and some pointed them at her face. The abbé did not look and then he looked and even when he looked he could not see, because of his tears. The girl stood and the rifles pointed and the girl's dress was blue and her hair was gold where the sun shone upon it. The man with the curly black hair gave the second command. The men fired. And where the girl's face had been there was a big red hole, and in her breast there was another red hole and blood was running down her dress. "*Justitiæ Domini rectæ, lætificantes corda, et judicia ejus super mel et favum: nam et servus tuus custodit ea,*" the abbé murmured in an attempt to make things come right again. But things would not come right again, and they didn't come right again when he was marched away from her, because of the terrible thing which he had seen.

They told the abbé that they would shoot him in five minutes' time and they left him alone in a room with a guard. And the abbé Gaston thought of the failure that his life had been. He had been a priest for more than forty years. Morning after morning he had stood in the holy place and said the holy words. He had preached many sermons. For more than forty years he had had the words and the ointments and the balms, but even a little of the soreness of the world he had been unable to heal, and the same wounds still ran in the same places. He had inspired nobody and his ministrations had left the lukewarm unmoved. If his wisdom and his skill had been greater Armelle might still have been alive. If his words had been persuasive Rachel might not have died in despair and unbelief. He had been unable to refute Bessier's Marxist errors. And the abbé knew that all priests were not as clumsy as he had been. Priests with whom he had been at the seminary had converted atheists and communists and notorious sinners. And he, with the Lord's arm about him day after day for forty years, had not converted a single unbeliever, except in North Africa, and that was a very long time ago. The abbé Gaston could hope only that he had done some unconscious good.

The abbé began to pray to the Lord for mercy, because he had been an unworthy priest. But although he knew that up to the very last minute there was time for acquiring merit he could not pray very well, because of his fear. In his fright and in his sorrow he wanted to lie flat down on the floor as he had done in the sanctuary on the day on which he had been ordained, but he felt that he could not do that with the guard watching, and he was still too stiff and sore to kneel. So he told the Lord how sorry he was standing up, and how frightened he was, too, and he covered his face with his hands, but no tears ran against his fingers, because his fright was greater than his sorrow, and the misery was hard within him and would not be melted. But in his soul he lay flat out on the floor and in his soul he tried to be more sorry than frightened, because he was God's priest and the Lord had put the mark upon him. When the abbé uncovered his face he saw that there were two men standing beside him instead of only one. At first the abbé did not look at the second man because he thought that the second man was another guard come to fetch him and he was afraid to know that his death was so near.

"So it *is* you after all?" the second man said in a familiar voice. The abbé looked round with a start and saw that the second man was Bessier.

"Philippe!" the abbé exclaimed and half held out his hands, but quickly drew them back again when he saw that Bessier did not extend his hands to meet them. The abbé could feel the muscles of his face slipping away from him until his jaws seemed to touch his chest and the muscles of his face would not come together again for him to make sensible sounds with his lips, and his mind ran away from him, too, so that he could not have made sensible sounds anyway. And there was a mist of tears in front of his eyes and for a little he could no longer see Bessier properly. And when he could see Bessier again he still could not speak, because of the turmoil in his heart.

Bessier's face was expressionless and it was impossible to tell what he was thinking. He told the guard to leave the abbé and himself alone together. He walked to the window and back again. He was wearing a blue jersey and baggy breeches with leather leggings. Although he walked almost without a limp his artificial leg made his shoulder go up and down a little. He did not speak until he had finished walking up and down the room. And when he did speak his voice was hard. "Well, Jean, this is a pretty kettle of fish," he said.

The abbé tried to speak. At first no sounds would come out of his mouth. It was gulping sounds that came first and it was a little time before he was able to say words.

"I was thinking of you a minute ago and now you are here," the abbé said. Gulps still came out of his mouth between each word.

"Thinking of me explains nothing," Bessier said.

"Anyway I am glad to be able to say good-bye to you before they shoot me," the abbé said. There were still gulps in his voice as he said this. The abbé found it difficult to be brave with Bessier standing there watching him, because he had known Bessier for so long and the lines had come upon their faces together.

"Nobody shoots anybody here unless I give the order," Bessier said.

"But they have shot the others," the abbé Gaston said. The hope rose swiftly within him that the bad detective novel was at last going to turn into a good detective novel and that he was going to be set free. And the hope made his voice gulp as fear had made his voice gulp, and he was more ashamed of the gulps than he had been before when he remembered how Rachel and the German officer had died tied up against the tree. "As they have shot the others they must surely shoot me, too," he said and the gulps in his voice were bigger than ever.

"They had no business to shoot the others," Bessier said, beginning to walk up and down the room again. Almost it was as though he were still trying out his artificial leg and the abbé was reminded of when Bessier had first walked before him on it, in the hospital ward, twenty-five years ago. "If I had been here they would not have shot the others without a fair trial And the trial which they had was not a fair trial. We are fighting this war to make France clean and we shall never make France clean if we do the sort of things the Germans did. Even communists have their Holy Ghost, but perhaps you do not understand that." Bessier smiled briefly as he said this, but he was soon grave again. "You are the only one they had a right to shoot. They had a right to shoot you because you are a Frenchman and you were caught committing a treasonable act." He stopped walking up and down and came and laid his hand gently on the abbé Gaston's shoulder. "Tell me, you silly old man: why did you do this thing?"

The sudden and unexpected kindness touched the abbé. Once again it was some time before he could speak.

"Perhaps a little for the same reason as I helped the British airman," the abbé said at length.

"I was hoping that you wouldn't remind me of that," Bessier said. He walked away from the abbé again and stood by the window.

"I am not reminding you of anything," the abbé said. "I am trying to explain, perhaps to myself as well as to you." The abbé was a little glad of Bessier's displeasure as it made it easier for him to justify himself, and took the gulp away from his voice. He told Bessier about Rachel and about how the German officer had tricked him into showing him where she worked. He told Bessier about his promise to help the German officer in case of need if the German officer refrained from imprisoning or deporting Rachel. And as he spoke the abbé saw from Bessier's expression that the men downstairs had not told him what he himself had told them about Rachel being a Jewess and the German officer having protected her. He saw, too, that Bessier understood this explanation: "You see, I could scarcely have done otherwise when he had helped Rachel," he said, and was ashamed of the eagerness in his voice.

"I am beginning to understand," Bessier said. "But surely you must have suspected that he belonged to the Gestapo?"

"I did not know whether he belonged to the Gestapo or not, but I did not think that he had been guilty of meanness or cruelty," the abbé said. "And in any case it is my duty as a priest to try to love men at a distance no less than near men. And bad men no less than good men," he added when he had thought about this for a little longer.

"Let's leave theology out of it, please," Bessier said. "The point is that although you helped an enemy of France you had what you considered a perfectly sound reason for doing so."

"That's it," the abbé said and again tried to curb the eagerness in his voice. "He was charitable and I had to be charitable, too."

"And I think that it was a sound reason, too," Bessier went on, as though the abbé hadn't spoken, and he walked up and down the room again as he thought his thoughts out aloud. "And you risked your life to help a British airman. And you sheltered me when I was in trouble." But Bessier was no longer thinking aloud when he came and stood close to the abbé again. Bessier spoke directly to the abbé and he looked severe as he spoke, with his face tired and white and the hardness in his eyes. "I think that I love you, Jean," he said, but there was no gentleness in the words both on account of the tone in which he said them and of the hardness in his eyes. "But however much I love you I should still order you to be shot if I thought that you had been a traitor," he said.

"I think that I understand that, Philippe, although treachery is hard to define," the abbé Gaston said. This time there was no eagerness in the abbé's voice because of the stern way in which Bessier was looking at him.

"I am going to let you go," Bessier said. "I am going to let you go because I am persuaded that you acted from right motives. And perhaps it may also be a little of a punishment to let you go. Perhaps you will feel a little guilty that the others have died and you haven't."

"That will perhaps be so," the abbé said and he tried to speak a little sadly as he wanted Bessier to go on believing that it would be a little of a punishment for him, to be allowed to go free when the others had died.

"There is only one condition," Bessier said. "You must not talk. And that you must not do both for our sake and for your own. The story will do neither of us any good."

"I think perhaps that I ought to tell my rector," the abbé said.

"You will tell nobody and we shall tell nobody," Bessier said. "That is the bargain."

"If you insist," the abbé said.

"I do insist," Bessier said.

They were silent as they walked down the stairs together. The room below was still empty. They walked out into the sunlight among the trees. Their bodies threw oblique shadows on the grass which crept back under their feet and disappeared. The man with the black curly hair and the men with the rifles were nowhere to be seen.

"Will they have missed you at the church?" Bessier asked.

"I don't think so," the abbé said. "I have a funeral at twelve."

Bessier looked at his watch.

"You'll still be in time if you walk quickly," Bessier said.

"I shall walk as quickly as my bruises allow," the abbé said.

Bessier nodded dully. He did not seem to think that the abbé's bruises were important or to be concerned about them. He walked along with his shoulder moving up and down ever so slightly.

"I sometimes think that we are both of us out a little for the same thing," Bessier said when they reached the edge of the road. "And perhaps we are going to have our reward sooner than we imagine. Men of all parties and beliefs have helped to free France."

"And this time I think that we have learned our lesson," the abbé Gaston said as he looked up into the blue sky and saw the sun shining in it. And in his optimism he forgot about his fright and the terrible things that he had seen and he thought only of the happiness of France, with her green fields free once more. "These things must not happen again."

"These things happen because there are rich men and there are poor men," Bessier said. "It is wrong that this should be so. It is only when there are no more poor men that there will be no more wars." There was sadness in his face as he shook hands with the abbé. "You'd better think up a good lie to tell about that eye of yours," he said, and smiled a little.

The abbé Gaston did not think that Bessier wished to be thanked for having saved his life. He did not attempt to do so. The sun shone on his wise old cassock as he moved off down the road and made all the worn bits shine. In the distance there was the rumble of gunfire. but the abbé did not hear the guns. Already his liberty was beginning to be a punishment to him.

LXVIII

IN September 1945 the Bishop of Saracen called to see the Cardinal and interrupted the Cardinal's new method of saying the Angelus, which was to move slowly along the mantelpiece in his study, touching with the points of his fingers a different part of the cold marble at each petition. The Bishop of Saracen was wearing a military uniform and he told the Cardinal that he had come to France as a chaplain to the forces. Although he had grey hair on his temples now, the Cardinal thought that the Bishop looked as young as when he had first seen him, at the Eucharistic Congress in Chicago in 1926. They talked the holy shop of prelates and of how good they both thought Bernard was at praying. And they rejoiced that the rent had been mended in Christ's garment, which was the Church.

LXIX

IN November 1945 the abbé Gaston's catechism class had been put back till four o'clock in the afternoon, and even at that hour he was late for it, because the rector had kept him talking in the presbytery.

The rector talked a lot to the abbé Gaston these days. The abbé Moune had lately been made rector of the church of St. Rémy and there was nobody else for the rector to confide in. The other priests were all new, except the abbé Ronsard. But the rector said that he could not talk much to the abbé Ronsard. Indeed it was chiefly about the abbé Ronsard that the rector had been complaining today. Once again the abbé Ronsard had been putting sugar instead of salt on babies' tongues at baptism, and this time the rector had been more than ordinarily angry, as sugar cost three hundred francs a pound on the black market. When the abbé Gaston had pointed out that sugar didn't invalidate the sacrament the Chanoine Litry had said sharply that salt certainly invalidated his coffee. The rector had also grumbled about the abbé Moune, who was now the Chanoine Moune and whose sermons were attracting a large part of the congregation away from Saint Clovis. Sometimes the abbé Gaston wondered if the rector would have taken him into his confidence so much if he had known about the German officer. But the abbé remembered his promise to Bessier and stifled his conscience and said nothing.

The children were waiting in the church when the abbé Gaston arrived. The little girls sat on the epistle side of the altar and the little boys sat on the gospel side of the altar. They stopped fidgeting and giggling as the abbé entered and the abbé thought that this must be because of his beard, which was beginning to turn quite white and to look as though it were made of cotton wool. The abbé Gaston looked at the little girls and the little boys, and he loved all of them, all the way down the church, even the naughty ones. And when they were unable to tell him about the marks which distinguished the Church of God the abbé loved them still and he told them about the signs which the Lord had put out, for all men to see. The Church of God was a ship on the ocean and a lamp held up in the darkness and a lake in a desert and a blazing fire on a winter's night, the abbé Gaston said. The Church of God was all these things, the abbé Gaston said. And he blessed the children with a big wave of his hand and smiled at them as they left the church.

The abbé still went on thinking about the Church after the children had gone, for the American soldiers began to come into the church for the evening mass which was their special privilege. The American soldiers behaved very devoutly in church, although they didn't always behave as devoutly on the boulevard. Watching them as they knelt and prayed, the abbé Gaston thought that they looked indeed like crusaders, and he wondered if the tilt of the Church was shifting from east to west, and if from the west grand new things would come and a great light. The American chaplain did not seem to share the abbé's hopes. When he had read the gospel he told the American soldiers that they were a dirty lot of lying, thieving, drunken, lecherous buccaneers. The abbé Gaston listened in astonishment for a little and then went out into the street.

The Place du Maréchal Pétain was now called the Place du Maréchal Stalin, but there was still no traffic on it, apart from jeeps and military lorries, and there weren't many of these. The abbé Gaston limped across the square, without looking to right or left. The abbé was thinking about money problems.

Three thousand francs did not go very far these days, especially when twelve hundred of them had to be set aside for rent. It was fortunate that his rent hadn't been increased since everything else was about eight times dearer than it had been in 1938, and even then the abbé had found it difficult to make both ends meet. Although the rector was paying the abbé three times what he had been paying him before the war there was still a big hole to be filled in. And mostly the abbé couldn't fill in the hole, and the hole remained, in the middle of the abbé's stomach.

The shops were brightly lighted round the square and looked as though they had lots of things to sell. The abbé thought that he would try the butcher first, because he was hungry and wanted some meat. The butcher was a new butcher with a face like Pope Benedict the Fifteenth, although the abbé didn't think that the resemblance went much further. The abbé Gaston showed his meat coupon to the butcher and the butcher said that he was very sorry but he had no meat to sell against it. The abbé said that he didn't understand as he could see for himself that there was meat hanging up at the back of the shop. The butcher said that the meat which Monsieur l'abbé thought he saw was such a very special kind of meat that it wasn't meat at all. The abbé said that he didn't want to be difficult and that he would make do with a very small chop and that he would be willing to pay as much as thirty francs for it. The butcher laughed as Pope Benedict the Fifteenth had never laughed and said that the smallest chop which he could sell Monsieur l'abbé would cost a hundred francs, and that wasn't a black market price, but a parallel market price. There was all the difference in the world between a black market price and a parallel market price, the butcher said. The abbé Gaston decided that he would have to sup on bread and cheese. The greengrocer looked at the abbé Gaston's ration coupons with interest and admired their design. He said that he was sorry that he had no cheese to sell against them. He said that Monsieur l'abbé must not think that the smell he smelt in the shop was really the smell of cheese, because it was the smell of a special brand of Gruyere with so many holes in it that it wasn't cheese at all and that it was really the holes that Monsieur l'abbé smelt. The greengrocer said that as a special favor he would let the abbé have a piece of the holes for seventy-five francs. The abbé Gaston decided that he would have to sup on bread without cheese.

The baker was a little more obliging. He honored the abbé's bread ticket and gave him half a pound of bread. The abbé had to pay fifteen francs for this. The baker said that he was sorry that he had no chocolate eclairs, as he knew how fond of them Monsieur l'abbé was. He said that, strictly in confidence, he knew that the hairdresser had quite a number of chocolate eclairs and that the hairdresser was quite willing to let them go in exchange for a new spare tire. The sooner the new spare tire, the sooner the chocolate eclairs, the baker said.

The abbé Gaston liked good wine and he never felt sinful about it, because of the miracle which the Lord Jesus had performed in Cana of Galilee. But he did not look in as he passed the wine merchant's window with his roll of bread under his arm as he knew that even the sourest rotgut cost a hundred francs a bottle these days. Looking in at lighted windows, however, made the abbé feel warm and less hungry, so he looked in at Madame Bisberot's window, knowing that he would be unlikely to want to buy anything there.

He saw with surprise that the wax mannequins' hair and faces had changed yet again. Their hair no longer fell down the back of their shoulders but was piled up on top of their heads and twisted into little knots like his own mother's had been, when he was very young. Their expressions were now a startling compound of arrogant, progressive, paleolithic and neolithic imbecility, relieved by the faint surprise of pterodactyls disturbed in their sleep. The abbé decided that with prices what they were it was time that he had another advance on royalties.

When Madame Bisberot came to greet him in the front shop the abbé was a little afraid that she would want to talk about Rachel. And about Rachel the abbé could not talk, not only because of Bessier, but because of the very terrible thing which had happened to her. But apparently Madame Bisberot didn't want to talk about Rachel, probably because she would have had to talk about the German officer as well, and that was dangerous these days, with everybody in France having been in the Resistance all along. Madame Bisberot merely smiled and waited for the abbé to speak first.

"I see that fashions in hair styles and expressions have changed again," the abbé said gently, feeling both ashamed and hungry as he spoke, but chiefly feeling hungry.

Madame Bisberot's smile vanished immediately. Her eyes shrunk back into their sockets as though pulled by invisible strings. When she spoke she spoke fluently and purposefully.

Hair styles and expressions were not the only women's fashions that had changed, Madame Bisberot said. Fashions in women's bodies had changed as well and they had changed because women's bodies themselves had changed. Although she did not wish to go into details, she thought that the change was due to the war and to the number of big guns which had been fired. In the first world war the big guns had changed the weather and the month of September had never been the same since. In this war, she said, the big guns had changed the shape of women's bodies as well and they were no more likely to recover from this war than the month of September from the first. Madame Bisberot said that as a result of this she had been forced to change the bodies of her wax mannequins as well as the heads, and that this had been most inconvenient, as she still had a very poor bank overdraft.

The abbé Gaston didn't know whether Madame Bisberot was lying or not about the shape of women's bodies having changed, although he was pretty sure that she had got the cause wrong. He went sadly back into the street and tried not to think of how hungry he was or of how long he would have to make his loaf of bread last. Then the happy thought came to him that perhaps it wasn't now that Madame Bisberot had lied, but rather when he had first spoken to her about his invention. Perhaps his invention had never really been any good at all. Perhaps it was because of pity that she had given him the two thousand francs in 1932 and helped Rachel in 1938. Worldly people, he knew, told that sort of lie to poor priests sometimes, when they wanted to help the poor priests without the poor priests knowing it. This thought cheered the abbé and made him feel a little less hungry and cold.

The covered wagon for forgetful crusaders was already waiting at the corner of the square, and two American military policemen in white helmets and white belts were waiting beside it. On the terraces of the cafes the forgetful crusaders sat with their feet on the tables, pouring rye on top of Benedictine and not looking as though they were thinking about the new tilt of the Church. The crusaders, the abbé felt, didn't always behave as well as the enemy soldiers who had been fighting against righteousness, but this, too, he supposed, was part of the mystery.

And beneath the trees the pretty women walked. Their high heels made a clacking little noise on the pavement and their faces were dim in the darkness. There was no moon in the sky but only stars. And the brittle light of the stars fell upon the fur coats and the silk stockings of the pretty women as they walked and made them shine a little in the darkness. And the gentleness of the night and the gentleness of the stars fell softly upon the pretty women and made them seem mysterious as they walked and beautiful sometimes, too. And the abbé Gaston said a little prayer for the pretty women as they walked, that the Lord Jesus might be kind to them.

It was cold in the street and the abbé's breath came up out of him and made a big cloud in front of him, like steam from a kettle. But the cloud that the abbé's breath made was not too dense for him to see the little black kitten crouching against the wall, almost at the exact place where the abbé had found Rachel lying seven years previously. The kitten was very small. It stood up and arched its back and meowed when the abbé stooped to pick it up. The kitten's meow was sometimes a hoarse little meow but more often it was a silent pink little meow which made a tiny blot of mist on the night beside the big blot of mist made by the abbé's breath. The abbé wondered whether the kitten had strayed or whether people had put it out to starve, forgetting that mercy was upon animals also.

It was cold in the abbé's room, too, and he warmed his hands on the kitten, and the kitten warmed his body on the abbé's hands. The abbé had no milk to give the kitten so he broke his loaf in two and pulled out some soft crumbs of bread and gave them to the kitten. The kitten seemed to like the bread for it began to purr. The abbé decided to call the kitten St. John of the Cross, whose feast it was that day, and hoped that his botany was better than Sister Marie Joseph's.

The kitten began to suck the abbé's fingers and to lick them and to press its paws up and down in the palm of the abbé's hand. And the kitten seemed to laugh at the abbé, and the abbé laughed back at the kitten, and he rubbed his cheek against the kitten's soft fur, glad that the Lord had made all things joyfully.

LXX

THE statesman was not allowed to speak very much these days, and when he was allowed to do so he took good care to be progressive, because the statesman knew in which direction the hurricane was howling. The statesman said that the true blueprint for the future was a just and lasting peace. The statesman said that the nineteenth century had been the century of the dirty tyke but that the twentieth century was going to be the century of the common man. The statesman said that Frenchmen who had died resisting the unwarrantable infringements of reactionary fascism and Nazi-dominated totalitarianism upon their national sovereignty had inscribed their names forever in the golden scrolls of history. The new big words insulted the dead as effectively as had the old.

LXXI

IN December 1946 the abbé Gaston felt that he was now old enough and respectable enough looking to be able to talk to pretty girls on the steps of the church after mass on Sundays without incurring the rector's disapproval.

Michelle was now sixteen and her fair hair was soft and wavy and it hung about her head like a little bright cloud, glowing with gold. Today she was wearing a new green hat and coat and the abbé thought that she looked very lovely as she stood with the nuns in the frail winter sunshine. And the abbé was moved to reflect upon eternity as he saw her standing there so young and so like her mother and Paris still the same with its grey roofs friendly in the watery brightness of the sun and the pigeons strutting on the pavement and only himself so much older, with all those strings of Advents and Lents behind him. Wondering once more whether eternity was like the London underground or a bath sponge, he suddenly realized that he hadn't been listening to what the nuns and Michelle were saying. Michelle was learning to be a seamstress, he heard one of the nuns say, and then the nun broke off, perhaps because she had seen he hadn't been listening.

"There's a rumor that a Cardinal is head of the black market in Rome," Sister Scholastica said.

"I hope that's not an article of faith," the abbé Gaston said.

"Perhaps it's only an impious belief," Sister Marie Joseph said.

The nuns and the abbé laughed, glad to have something to laugh at in liberated France. Michelle did not laugh much, perhaps because she was too young to understand the joke.

The abbé Gaston was quickly sad again as he went back into the church. He had still to say the twelve o'clock mass and he was tired and cold with so much fasting. It seemed likely, too, that he would have to go on fasting for the rest of the day as all that he was going to have for lunch was a piece of dry bread. The government decree that prices should come down five per cent had resulted in an increase of fifteen. Sometimes the abbé thought that he did not understand the arithmetic of freethinkers.

And the abbé was also worried because his right eye was bothering him and he was beginning to see double with it. As subdeacon at the high mass he had sung *"Lætamini gentes cum plebe ejus"* twice instead of once and he was sure that the rector had noticed. The trouble was that it had been a very special high mass with a Monsignore who had come all the way from Clermont-Ferrand to preach the sermon. The negro had arrived to lay his silver-knobbed walking stick and his yellow chamois leather gloves on the altar of St. Peter of Alcantara during the gospel so as not to miss anything, and the rector himself had climbed up into the pulpit to pray "Send us priests, holy priests", so that the Monsignore from Clermont-Ferrand could save his breath for the sermon. Then the very young deacon with the red hair had kept moving much too quickly for the abbé with his limp, charging about the sanctuary as though it were a football field. The abbé had been late at least twice, and once he had bumped into the young deacon and the young deacon hadn't seemed to like it much.

So the abbé wasn't surprised to find the rector waiting for him in the sacristy, looking angry as well as old. The abbé didn't notice it much when the rector looked only old because the abbé looked old himself and always saw other people's old faces against the morning's memory of his own reflection in the mirror and so was often able to believe that they looked young. But when the rector looked angry as well as old all the lines on his face deepened and he made the abbé Gaston feel young as well as frightened. The abbé waited timidly to hear the criticism which he felt he had deserved.

"We're almost out of candles and incense again," the rector said.

Although he knew that the recurring shortage of candles and incense was a serious matter, the abbé was so relieved that it wasn't about himself that the rector was angry that he almost laughed.

"It's no joking matter," the rector reproved. He went on to tell the abbé Gaston what the abbé already knew: that even at high mass on Sundays the prevailing shortage of wax forced them to light only two candles on the altar and that the amount of incense they burned in the thurible required an act of faith either to see it or to smell it. In every church in Paris it was the same, the rector said, but the knowledge didn't make their own shortage any easier to bear.

"All the same, they seem to have plenty at St. Rémy's," the abbé Gaston said.

"Don't talk to me about those gangsters," the rector said. "They've made a corner in candles and incense, I know. It makes my blood boil every time I think of it."

"Black market, you mean?" the abbé Gaston asked.

"The blackest of the black," the rector said. "That church is nothing more than a hot bed of sanctity."

The abbé Gaston did his best not to smile.

"Gangsters or not, we've got to put our pride in our pocket," the rector went on. "Beggars can't be choosers. Either we've got to buy candles and incense from the Chanoine Moune or we've got to find out where he gets his supplies from. Personally I'm inclined to think it's the Jesuits, although I shouldn't put it past those rascally Benedictines."

The abbé Gaston began to feel unhappy again; he thought he knew what was coming.

"As you know, the Chanoine Moune and I are no longer on good terms," the rector went on. "Especially since I criticized his views on finance at the chapter meeting. I was wondering if you wouldn't like to go along and call on him this afternoon."

"I should scarcely say that I was on good terms with him either, Monsieur le Curé," the abbé Gaston said.

"Oh, you're on good terms with everybody," the Chanoine Litry said. "Everybody likes you. Why, only last week somebody told me they thought you were a saint. Probably the Chanoine Moune thinks you're a saint, too. Now if I were to give you the money there would be no reason why you shouldn't take a little walk along to Saint Rémy this afternoon and try to do a little business with the blackguard, would there?"

"I suppose not," the abbé Gaston said reluctantly.

"He'll probably try to do you in the eye, of course, but he's got us up against the wall and I don't care what I pay," the rector said. "You can start by offering him two thousand five hundred francs for two dozen tall altar candles and three pounds of incense." The rector took out two thousand franc notes and a five hundred franc note from his pocket book and handed them to the abbé Gaston. "If he asks for three thousand tell him it's all right by me and that I'll pay him the other five hundred tomorrow. Only be sure and bring the stuff back with you. We've got to take precautions against his raising the price to four thousand before delivery." The abbé Gaston did not know how he was going to carry two dozen tall altar candles and three pounds of incense through the streets with his limp and with his right eye bothering him into the bargain. But he decided that it would be imprudent to risk offending the rector by appearing to make difficulties.

"I'll do my best, Monsieur le Curé," he said.

"And take care that the candles don't have false bottoms and that the incense isn't mixed with tapioca," the rector said as he left the sacristy.

The abbé Gaston had still half an hour to wait before he said mass and he tried to fill in the time by praying for the repose of the souls of the faithful and of the unfaithful departed. This now took him twenty-seven minutes, as the abbé's way of praying for the dead was to say a little puff of prayer with a face floating in the middle of it and he found it hard to remember the faces quickly, as there were so many of them. Trying to race against time, he soon gave it up as a bad job and started to pray instead for those who were that day being killed on fields of battle, and for those who were being wounded, too, as this was the only ointment he could bring to them.

The English priest came in while the abbé was still praying for the French soldiers who were being killed and tortured in Indo-China. The rector had told the abbé about the English priest, who was to say his mass privately at the altar of St. Peter of Alcantara. The English priest was carrying a big bag with him and the abbé supposed that he must be leaving for England as soon as he had said mass.

The English priest and the abbé Gaston bowed to each other and smiled at each other, saluting and greeting their common burden and privilege. And as he watched the English priest begin to vest the abbé thought again of the universality of the Church, and his heart was gay once more within him, because of the strong cords which the Lord had let down. The Church of God was holy with the holiness of trees, the abbé thought, which shaded men in all lands.

The abbé Gaston was still merry when he went in to say his own mass, wearing the old crumpled flapping faded purple chasuble which the sacristan always laid out for unimportant priests in Advent and Lent. The chasuble didn't fit properly round the neck and the abbé had always to keep pulling it back into position, but he didn't worry about that today, because he had seen that the mercy of the Lord was to all heads and hands and feet. Nor did he worry when he sometimes saw the same words twice in the holy book and sometimes said them twice, too, because he knew that the Lord's arms were about him, when he stood in that place.

When he returned from saying his mass the abbé Gaston was surprised to find the English priest still in the sacristy. The English priest was back in his overcoat again and he was walking up and down as though he had something on his mind. He was still doing so when the abbé Gaston had finished making his thanksgiving. The abbé Gaston wondered if the English priest were lonely and wanted to make friends.

"It is nice to see our English brothers again in France," the abbé said in his careful English, which he had not spoken since he had helped the British airman to escape.

"It's very difficult for us to come to France these days," the English priest said. "Currency restrictions, you know."

The abbé Gaston understood a little of the terrible terminology of the times. He nodded sympathetically. "The Government only allows us seventy-five pounds,", the English priest said.

"But that is a lot of money," the abbé Gaston said. The abbé knew that the English apostles and especially the American apostles lived much more comfortably than the French apostles, but seventy-five pounds still seemed to him a large sum to spend on a holiday. He tried to do a quick sum in his head, but the English priest had done it before him.

"Thirty-six thousand francs," the English priest said. "It's enough for a nun to see life on, but it's no good for a secular priest."

The abbé did not tell the English priest that he himself was lucky if, with his own three thousand francs added to what the rector gave him, he had thirty-six thousand francs to spend in a year.

"I've got something here that may interest you," the English priest said as he opened his bag. The bag was long and deep and was filled with tall candles lying neatly piled on top of one another. And on top of the candles there were tins laid out, which, the abbé guessed, contained incense.

"Really!" the abbé exclaimed.

"An invisible export," the English priest explained. "At least as far as my bishop's concerned I hope that it's invisible." He watched the abbé Gaston closely. "Well, what's your offer?"

"Do you mean to say that you wish to sell those very beautiful candles?" the abbé Gaston asked.

"Candles and incense," the English priest said. "Hard currency, of course. You can have the lot for twenty dollars."

The abbé Gaston shook his head sadly. He would have liked to have been able to buy the lovely candles and the tins of incense. The transaction would have saved him an awkward interview with the Chanoine Moune and a difficult walk back carrying his purchase.

"I am sorry but I have only French francs," he said. "French priests do not have American dollars to spend."

"What about your Cardinal?" the English priest asked. "Hasn't the old boy got any real money tucked away in his mitre?"

"Our Cardinal is a very holy man and I am sure that he has only the ghosts of his own holy thoughts tucked away in his mitre," the abbé Gaston said quietly.

"Pity," the English priest said. "In that case I suppose I'll have to be apostolic and let them go for French francs. On a dollar basis, of course. They're not utility candles, you know, and the incense isn't austerity either."

"I should love to buy them, of course, but I am afraid that I shall have to do a little sum first to see if I can afford them," the abbé Gaston said.

"The sum's easy," the English priest said. "The rate of exchange is a hundred and nineteen point twenty. Say a hundred and twenty to make up for my honesty in not charging you the black market rate. Twenty dollars at a hundred and twenty make two thousand four hundred. Two thousand four hundred francs and the goods are yours."

The abbé Gaston was surprised that the sum asked by the English priest should so nearly equate the amount entrusted to himself by the rector, and almost he was tempted to see the Lord's doing in the matter. But it wasn't so easy to see the Lord's doing in the English priest's expression, as he stood with his hand held out. At first the English priest didn't seem to want to give the abbé any change when the abbé handed him the two thousand five hundred francs, but the abbé insisted, surprised a little at his own firmness. However, the English priest helped the abbé to lift the tall candles and the tins of incense out of the travelling bag and to lay them out on top of the vestment chest, and the abbé was grateful to him for this.

It wasn't until the English priest had left the sacristy that the abbé began to wonder whether the English priest had stolen the candles and the incense from his own sacristy or whether he had purchased them for invisible export. But he speedily decided that it was not his responsibility to know as he himself had purchased the goods honestly with the money which the rector had given him. Probably, too, it was only on the surface that the English priest was grasping and commercial. Probably deep down inside him the English priest was very holy and loved the Lord a lot. That was the great wonder the Lord worked on priests when He put His mark upon them, making even those with the appearance of scallywags holy underneath. The abbé Gaston put the hundred francs change in his purse to give to rector when he should see him next and resolved to think no more about the English priest.

Out on the square the Sunday afternoon traffic was beginning, and it was almost all French traffic again, because most of the crusaders had now gone home. There was still no petrol allowed for pleasure, but the pleasure cars were there all the same, rolling round the square on their big tires. The shape of the cars had altered since 1938, but the shape of the people behind the windscreens was still the same, and their faces were hard and hating, and the hair of the women was hard, too, and it didn't look like their crowning glory at all. And the men and the women looked all the same, as though they, like the cars, had come out of a tin womb, and they all drove in the same selfish manner. The abbé was very careful when he crossed the street, especially as his right eye wasn't working properly.

Even on the pavement men and women walked with hatred in their eyes, scowling at one another. The abbé Gaston could not make up his mind whether it was because of the atom bomb or because of the black market or because of the unkindness and the fright that had come upon the world that they loathed one another. And as he passed them he tried to smile out at them from beneath his beard, to make the world seem less lonely for them and for himself, too, but always their eyes were hard with no answer in them.

The abbé didn't smile at the greengrocer and at the baker as he passed them standing outside their shops as he didn't wish to get into conversation with them. He had no money to spend that day and wouldn't have much until the end of the month, when the rector paid him. But he smiled at the butcher, because the butcher smiled at him first and the abbé didn't want to appear rude even although he had no money to buy meat.

"Good morning, Monsieur l'abbé, and what can I do for you today?" the butcher asked, coming right out in front of the abbé and stopping him in the street. The abbé didn't think that the new butcher was anymore pious than the old butcher had been, but he tried not to judge what went on in the new butcher's heart.

"Nothing, I'm sorry," the abbé Gaston said.

"That's a pity," the butcher said. "I have a most succulent steak. And very cheap, too. Only a hundred francs."

"I'm afraid that I shan't have a hundred francs for quite a little time yet," the abbé Gaston said.

"I could let you have it on credit," the butcher said. "It's the juiciest steak you ever saw."

"I can't afford to run up bills," the abbé Gaston said and suddenly remembered the hundred francs change which the English priest had given him. And within the abbé the processes described by Jean-Jacques Rousseau began to work, rhyming convenience with conviction. The rector had authorized him to spend two thousand five hundred francs on the purchase of candles and incense. If he had spent only two thousand four hundred francs the saving was due to his own ingenuity. The hundred francs didn't really belong to the rector at all. The hundred francs were his own to spend as he liked. And even if they weren't his own he could always pay them back to the rector at the end of the month. The arguments raced through the abbé's mind. The abbé Gaston was very hungry and he wanted that steak. The abbé Gaston was very hungry and he bought that steak.

Madame Boulon and the centrally heated lady of easy virtue were talking together at the door when the abbé Gaston arrived back home. Madame Boulon was saying that it was a disgrace that she couldn't buy a motor car in France when Germans could buy motor cars in Germany. The centrally heated lady of easy virtue said that there were no motor cars in Germany for Germans to buy and that she had been told this by her gentleman friend who was now occupying Germany, and that was why he didn't come to see her quite so often, the dirty cad. Madame Boulon said that that didn't matter and that it was unjust that she shouldn't be allowed to buy a motor car in France when Germans were allowed to buy motor cars in Germany. The abbé Gaston raised his hat politely and left them arguing.

St. John of the Cross was a big furry black cat now and he was waiting up against the inside of the abbé's door when the abbé opened it. He gave his silent pink isosceles triangle meow and rubbed his back against the abbé's legs. St. John of the Cross was a reactionary fascist warmongering cat who didn't believe much in blue-prints for the future, and the abbé had had a lot of difficulty in keeping him away from the pigeons.

The cat smelled the steak at once and ran in front of the abbé with his tail stuck up like a mast in the air. Then he came back and rubbed his body against the abbé's legs again and jumped up and reached out at the parcel of steak with his paws, so that the abbé had to chase him away to the window where he sat looking at the pigeons, strutting there. The abbé laid the steak down near the stove, lit the gas ring and began to melt the fat in the frying pan. Then he went across to the window and shut it, in case St. John of the Cross might be tempted to attack the pigeons.

Down on the square the little girls were passing two by two, with the nun tied on to the end of the procession. The little girls and the nuns looked dumpy and squat, seen from so far up above. The little girls were new little girls, of course, and the abbé wondered what had happened to all the other little girls whom the old nun had taught. Then the flattened out little procession turned a corner and the abbé saw that the nun tied on to the end was no longer an old nun but a young nun instead. The old nun must have slipped away into eternity, the abbé thought, and whether eternity was like the London underground or a bath sponge he still didn't know. The Church Militant was a tapestry in time, the abbé thought, with the old faces pulled away past time until they were absorbed into stillness, the abbé thought. Perhaps eternity was chiefly a stillness, the abbé Gaston thought.

And when the abbé turned back from the window he discovered that St. John of the Cross was chiefly a stillness, too, and that there was no longer any steak lying near the stove. The cat sat staring at the abbé out of his big round black and yellow target eyes which seemed to understand all about metaphysics. Then he began to wash himself, carefully licking his paws and passing them slowly over his face. The abbé Gaston extinguished the gas and sat down and tried to decide whether he had really intended to pay the rector back those hundred francs at the end of the month.

LXXII

IN 1947 when the Cardinal made the Chanoine Paquin a bishop he invited the Bishop of Saracen and Shorty to be the co-consecrators, because Shorty had become a bishop, too, although it had been a narrow shave, as the slippery joker from the Vatican had caught him reading *Forever Amber*, from spiritual motives.

So they lighted the candles on the altar and the Cardinal sat on his throne and they brought the holy vestments to him. And they prayed that the Lord might have mercy and that Christ might have mercy and that the Lord might have mercy. They asked all the holy angels and archangels to pray for them. They asked all the holy orders of blessed spirits to pray for them. They asked all the holy patriarchs and prophets to pray for them. They asked all the holy apostles and evangelists to pray for them. They asked all the holy disciples of the Lord to pray for them. They asked all the holy innocents to pray for them. They asked St. Cosmas and St. Damian to pray for them. They asked all the holy bishops and confessors to pray for them. They asked all the holy doctors to pray for them. They asked all the holy priests and levites to pray for them. They asked all the holy monks and hermits to pray for them. They asked St. Cecily to pray for them. They asked St. Anastasia to pray for them. They asked all the holy virgins and widows to pray for them. They asked all the holy men and women and saints of God to make intercession for them. They asked the Lord to deliver them from anger, hatred and ill-will, from plague, famine and war, by His baptism and holy fasting, by His holy resurrection and admirable ascension. They asked the Lord to have mercy and Christ to have mercy and the Lord to have mercy. And the Cardinal and the Bishop of Saracen and Shorty all laid their hands upon the Chanoine Paquin, that he might receive the Holy Ghost.

And the Cardinal prayed that the new bishop's deeds might shine with the splendor of gold and the gleam of jewels, and he bound the new bishop's head with a white cloth, and they all prayed that the Holy Ghost, who was the forefinger of God, might come. And the Cardinal anointed the new bishop's head with oil and made the sign of the cross upon him and gave peace to him. And he prayed that the new bishop's feet might be beautiful and announce peace and that he might not confuse darkness with light and that his union with God might be as the perfume of the oil which flowed down from Aaron's beard upon his garments. And the Cardinal kissed the new bishop, that peace might be with him.

LXXIII

THE abbé Gaston was glad that he had been able to get to confession before he was taken into hospital, because he wouldn't have liked to have had to confess to the rector about the hundred francs change and the steak. The abbé had confessed his sin to a Dominican friar, and the friar had given the abbé such a blowing up that the confessional had seemed to rock. Even when the abbé said that he had already made restitution the friar had gone on pitching into the abbé. The friar had told the abbé that what he had done was worse than if he had been married to six wives at once, since wives were a greater temptation than steaks, if St. Anthony were to be believed. The friar had told the abbé that it was conduct such as his that was responsible for wars, plagues, pestilences, famines, two-piece bathing suits and the atom bomb. The abbé Gaston was dangling over hell fire by a thread, the friar had said. But in spite of all that the friar had said the abbé had been happy when he had come out of the confessional, because such was the effect of sanctifying grace. And in spite of the fact that he was lying in bed in total blackness with a bandage round his eyes, the abbé Gaston was still feeling happy now, because of the great sin which had been lifted from his soul.

Ever since he was a small boy the abbé Gaston had liked lying in bed when he was ill. When he had been wounded in the first war he had liked lying in bed afterwards. Even now when there was a chance of his losing the sight of his right eye the abbé still liked lying in bed. The part before the operation had not been pleasant, of course. He had been afraid of what would happen when they took his right eye out of his head and tried to stick the retina back into its proper position. But now that the doctors had told him that his right eye was almost certain to get better again the abbé was no longer afraid.

The doctors had asked the abbé if he had ever received a severe blow on the eye, but the abbé hadn't told the doctors about the blows which the men of the Resistance had given him with their buckled belts. Quite apart from his promise to Bessier, the abbé hadn't wished the doctors to think him a traitor. The doctors had said that there was a chance of his losing the sight of both eyes if he didn't have his right eye attended to properly. And there was still a chance of his losing the sight of his left eye if his right eye failed to heal, they said. The abbé tried not to think about this as he still wanted to go on being a priest at the altar.

The abbé Gaston thought on in the warmth of his bed and was happy in spite of the things he had to be frightened about. He had still to be frightened about if he was going to see clearly with his right eye and he had still to be frightened about how he was going to be able to eat enough with prices going up and up all the time. In 1914 the abbé Gaston had been able to buy a whole meal with wine for a franc and although the cheapest meal now cost a hundred francs the faithful still went on putting single francs into the collection plate. The abbé had also the communists to be frightened about, in spite of what the statesman had said.

Deep in the darkness the abbé heard the door open. He thought that he could feel the slice of light let into the room but almost immediately the darkness was dense again and he supposed that he hadn't felt anything at all. The footsteps that came into the room were heavy and he could hear the sound of legs against cloth. The abbé knew that his visitor was the rector even before the rector began to speak. The abbé loved the rector these days almost as though he had striped fur and could meow and purr at the same time. For it was the rector who had offered to pay all the abbé's expenses at the hospital so that he could have a room to himself and be properly treated in the darkness. And today as always when he called the abbé thanked the rector for his kindness.

"It is nothing," the Chanoine Litry said. "You have done a great deal for the parish. It is only right and natural that we should help you when you are ill and in trouble."

The abbé liked to hear the rector praise him, although he knew that it was vain of him.

"I shall try to work hard when I get well again," the abbé said. And as always he wanted to be able to be fair to the rector and to tell him what had caused the hurt to his right eye.

"You really ought to go away for a period of convalescence, but I don't think that we can afford that," the rector said. "The faithful aren't too generous these days. The Voluntary Contribution is a disgrace. Out of fifteen thousand families in the parish only three thousand practice their religion. In 1946 out of those three thousand only three hundred and thirty families subscribed to the Voluntary Contribution although we preached special sermons about it and handed out envelopes to everybody. And the sum they gave was ridiculously inadequate. And it's the same all over the archdiocese. Although prices have gone up fifteen times since 1938 the Voluntary Contribution has increased only four times. People willingly pay thirty five francs for an iced cake, but they won't put thirty five francs in the collection plate or anything like it."

With the tip of the cool sheet drawn up under his beard the abbé Gaston was silent. He had heard the figures before, on the last Sunday of the previous year, when the rector had delivered his customary financial harangue to the congregation. In view of such dismal statistics it did not look as though the rector would ever be able to pay him more than he was paying him now. "I sometimes think that it is our duty to take you to live with us in the presbytery, but I feel that it is a little late in the day to attempt to obtain permission," the rector went on. "And the authorities are getting very strict about these matters." The rector did not refer to the previous occasion on which he had made this offer or to the reasons which had led him to abandon it. "Besides, you are used to your liberty and you can take it from me that most of these young priests are very difficult to live with. But there is no doubt that you must take greater care of yourself in future and that I must help you to do so. I am thinking of paying you a round sum of seven thousand francs a month in future. Where it's going to come from I don't know, but I think I can promise to make it come from somewhere."

The abbé Gaston was happy in the big black darkness when the rector had gone. On seven thousand francs a month he could live like a Benedictine monk, even if prices still kept increasing. And there was also his own two hundred and fifty francs a month. He could have meat once a week on that and St. John of the Cross could have fish twice a week. The cat deserved some compensation for having been left so long with the centrally heated lady of easy virtue. The abbé had been afraid to leave the cat with Madame Boulon in case St. John of the Cross might turn into stewed St. Elizabeth of Hungary.

The door opened again and there were footsteps again and there was the quick sound of a woman's dress with the footsteps. The noise was a little like the sound of tissue paper being distantly crumpled and so the abbé guessed that it must be a silk dress, with a young woman walking inside it. And there was another noise as well, but it was chiefly the quick noise that the abbé heard, and it was a watery noise as well, the abbé thought. Then the quick noise quickly stopped and soft arms were flung round his neck and a warm cheek was laid against his beard and smooth hair fell across his mouth and the smooth hair, too, was like silk in the darkness.

"Michelle, you must be gentle with Monsieur l'abbé," an elder woman's voice said. "You must remember that he's been very ill."

Lying in the darkness the abbé Gaston could feel the peace of the nun. He knew from her voice that she was Sister Jeanne Françoise. He could feel the cool linen of her coif and her hands folded in her lap. And he could feel Michelle sitting beside him in her new frock and her soft hair falling down her shoulders. And he could feel the kind loving things which they were both thinking about him.

"We have a new nun at the convent," Sister Jeanne Françoise said.

The abbé Gaston nodded in the darkness and made a sound which he hoped didn't sound too uninterested. Words were things which he had to build with his breath and he was tired after his conversation with the rector. Even about the holy things of God it was an effort for him to talk. And they were always having new nuns at the convent: thin nuns, fat nuns, blotchy nuns, pasty nuns, cross-eyed nuns, snub-nosed nuns. They all cemented the Church Militant, he knew, but he was uninterested all the same.

"She is a very pretty nun," Sister Jeanne Françoise said. "She has the loveliest ankles in all Paris."

"She must have looked lovely at dances," Michelle said.

"The men were all mad about her," Sister Jeanne Françoise said. "She and I used to be worldly together and eat Neapolitan ices during Lent. Gisele, her name was. And now she's plain Sister Catherine of Siena."

" 'Neither delighted He in any man's legs,' " the abbé Gaston wanted to preach at them, but it was too much effort. And why shouldn't the loveliness of women praise the Lord, the abbé thought. Why shouldn't a pretty ankle sing his psalm? The strains of old waltzes came back to the abbé and he saw his mother dancing again on his father's arm, with the bunch of her dress and petticoats held away from her and reflected like a huge carnation on the polished floor. The abbé Gaston hadn't been supposed to see the ball, but he had crept half-way down the stairs in his flannel nightdress and peered at it through the banisters.

The music cradled him as he lay there in the darkness, and old images passed before his mind. He saw again the glow from the candelabra on the women's colored dresses and his mother's ankles, which had been pretty, too, and the square lamps of the horse cabs waiting in the street. Even when there had been no dances there had always been horse cabs, and in his bed he had used to listen to the sound of the horses' hooves. His blinds had never been drawn at night and the lamps of the cabs had thrown wavering pools of light on the ceiling and the wavering pools of light had travelled like lanterns all round the ceiling until they had disappeared with the sound of the horses' hooves. Priests and nuns were rather like those wavering pools of light, the abbé thought: they came in and they went out the same way, and always there were new wavering pools of light to take their place, for the Church of God was a gentle moving on. The abbé wanted to tell Sister Jeanne Françoise what he had thought, but the thought slid away from him before he could get it on to his lips, and he was sleepy again and worldly and warm beneath his blankets.

The door opened again and there were more footsteps and more voices in the room. It was Bessier and his son, the abbé realized, and he spoke to them a little and asked them how they were. And he told them that he himself was quite well and that the doctors had practically promised that his right eye would get better again.

The abbé Gaston always felt awkward when two different kinds of his friends met in his presence, and he felt that he had to keep on talking now in case Sister Jeanne Françoise and Bessier might start saying rude things to each other about Stalin and the Pope. From his bed he made a vague mumble of introduction. He said that Bessier was an old friend of his by whose side he had fought in the first world war, but he did not say that Bessier was a communist. Of the new important things he did not talk at all, because even of a little struggle he was afraid, although he tried to persuade himself that he would be brave about the big struggle when it came. Of the fact that there would be no big struggle at all if people were brave about little struggles he tried not to think.

But Bessier apparently did not want to say anything rude about religion. The abbé could feel this as soon as he himself stopped speaking. Bessier and his son were thinking warm loving thoughts about him, too, and he could feel the friendliness of them all lapping round his bed. The abbé Gaston gathered his darkness about him and decided that he would only listen.

"I'm very worried indeed about your eye," the abbé heard Bessier say, and he knew why Bessier was worried about his eye and he was glad that Bessier was worried about his eye. And he lay in a great cozy indolence because Bessier was worried about his eye.

Soon they all began to talk together in a friendly manner and the abbé lay in silence. Perhaps he had been wrong about Bessier and Sister Jeanne Francoise. Perhaps there was no great difference between them. Perhaps they searched the same goal along different roads and perhaps that was what everybody else in the world was doing. Perhaps there would be no struggle after all, but only a big peace instead.

Soon there was young laughter as well as voices, so the abbé knew that Michelle and Bessier's son were talking together. The laughter was the kind of laughter that had used to come upstairs from his mother's dances. There was the sound of water in the laughter and there was the sound of bells as well. When there had been laughter in his mother's drawing-room there had been music, too, and the women's dresses had looked like the petals of flowers held upside down. The women's dresses had been blue and gold and green and red and they were there again in color before his eyes as he thought about them, spread out and with a shine upon them.

The laughter and the music grew dimmer and even the laughter had gone entirely when the abbé woke. But he could still see the women's dresses, blue and gold and green and red and with a shine upon them, and he lay on thinking about them until he fell asleep again.

LXXIV

THE new Bishop tried not to look down at the silver buckles on his shoes as he sat in the parlor of the convent, with the nuns all round about him, like big pale blue life buoys floating on invisible water. For the new Bishop knew that silver buckles were vanity if he looked upon them as honoring himself instead of as honoring God, who made bishops. The new Bishop knew that Bishops wore fine raiment only because the thing that God had pressed down into them was holy. The new Bishop knew that bishops were dust and that to dust they would return.

The nuns brought tea to the new Bishop, and cake and cream buns as well, and they sat round in a circle to watch him drink and eat. The nuns talked to the new Bishop as they sat with him, and it was of holy things that they mostly talked, because they were nuns.

It was Sister Catharine of Siena who did most of the talking. She said that she was a new nun and that she had once met the Bishop before, many years ago when she had been in the world, seeing only the glimmer and not the glow. She said that it was she who had taught the bishop how to eat cream buns without making a mess of his fingers and that she was glad to see that the new Bishop had remembered her lesson. And the nuns all laughed with their eyes as well as with their mouths, because they were good and holy nuns.

The new Bishop blushed and asked Sister Catherine of Siena if her name had been Gisele when she had been in the world and had seen only the glimmer and not the glow. And the nun said that her name had indeed been Gisele but that now it was Sister Catharine of Siena because she had seen the glow. The new Bishop said that he had never forgotten the lesson which Sister Catherine of Siena had taught him and that it was probably because he had known how to eat a cream bun without making a mess of his fingers that the Pope had made him a bishop. And the nuns all laughed at this joke, too.

The new Bishop tried not to look down at the silver buckles on his shoes, because he knew that it was not in order that they might eat cream buns with nuns that the Pope made bishops, but that they might hand on the glow.

LXXV

THE Feast of St. Peter and St. Paul was generally one of the sweaty feasts of the Church, and in 1947 it was no exception to the rule. The abbé Gaston felt sorry for the new Bishop up at the altar, in all his heavy red vestments. For the Cardinal was getting too old to do all the ordaining himself and his fingers creaked at the joints, even when the Holy Spirit came out of them.

In 1947 as in 1914 and as in 1466, in Greek and in Latin, the litanies of supplication were roared, that the Lord might have mercy and Christ hearken, and that all the holy apostles and evangelists and all the holy disciples of the Lord might pray for them; that Saints Fabian and Sebastian might pray for them; that Saint Gregory and Saint Ambrose might pray for them; that Saint Augustine might pray for them; that all holy priests and levites, monks and hermits might pray for them; that the Lord would spare them and pardon them and rule and preserve His holy Church; that it might please the Lord to grant peace and concord to Christian rulers and to lift up their minds to heavenly desires; that it might please the Lord to bless, hallow and consecrate these chosen ones; that Christ might hearken and that the Lord might have mercy. Lying upon their faces, they prayed that the Lord might accomplish all these things.

The new Bishop had asked the abbé Gaston to preach a short sermon to the young men. The abbé's right eye was working properly again now and he hoped that his voice was working properly as well, as he had such solemn things to say to the young men.

The abbé Gaston told the young men that they had been stretched out on the floor of the church like a lovely white carpet before the Lord, and that this was a symbol of priests' lives, because priests flattened themselves out before the Lord. He said that it was only when they all lay down together that they became a carpet but that when they separated they were doormat and that men would clean their feet upon them. The abbé said that it was the strips of doormat that made the carpet, as God was honored by their service of others, as that was the rule.

The abbé told the young men that they were doing a great and a glorious and a shining thing, but that the world would see it as a dull thing, as that, too, was part of the mystery. When they were old priests nobody would ever remember that they had been young priests. When they died their shadow would be swallowed up in the shade of other forgotten priests, and the Church of God would move on again in other young priests. For the Church of God was a river and it flowed rapidly, the abbé Gaston said. And even if they became bishops they would still be forgotten, for bishops bobbed downstream quite quickly, too, the abbé Gaston said.

But this was the great and the glorious and the shining thing, the abbé Gaston said: to stand on the right meaning of the world and to proclaim it boldly. For it was what went on on the other side of television and jet airplanes that mattered, and that was invisible, as that, too, was the rule. The world was like a garment which men wore inside out, and the priesthood was like a glimpse of the other side of that garment, the abbé Gaston said. Tremendous things were done that day to their souls and tremendous things would be done by their hands and by their mouths and it would all be made plain on the last day, the abbé Gaston said.

The Church of God was flowing on more rapidly than even the abbé Gaston's now apparently well right eye could see, for when he went back into the sacristy they told him that the Chanoine Litry had died.

LXXVI

IN 1947 the pretty girls from Madame Bisberot's still walked on the square after lunch. And although both the girls and their fashions had changed more often than the abbé Gaston could remember, they still looked the same girls, with the same foolish wisdom on their faces. In long skirts, in short skirts, in narrow skirts, or in wide skirts, they always looked the same girls as they walked up and down beneath the trees.

The abbé Gaston found the new rector talking to the new pretty girls on the square, and the new rector's new curates stood talking to the new pretty girls with him. The priests laughed a lot as they talked with the pretty girls and the wind blew in the pretty girls' frocks and made lovely colored patterns in the air.

The new rector was called the Chanoine Paiseau and to the abbé Gaston he looked far too young to be the rector of an important city church. The new rector had strong dark hair. He wore a beret instead of a shovel hat and a dyed black battledress blouse on top of his cassock with his fountain pens and his pencils clipped in a row along the pocket. The new rector had been in the Resistance Movement and he liked talking about it.

The new rector left the pretty girls as soon as the abbé Gaston came towards him, but the new curates went on talking to the pretty girls. The abbé Gaston didn't think that he liked the look of the new curates at all. They were far too noisy and boisterous and one of them was hatless and had brilliantine on his hair.

"I expect that you are surprised to find us talking to these young women," the new rector said as he joined the abbé Gaston. "Perhaps even you are shocked. But in a modern age one has got to be modern. I feel that a great opportunity is open to the Church if only priests will get on a common footing with the people. In the past we have been too standoffish. In the Resistance Movement priests weren't standoffish and that is why we were able to do so much good. The Church needs to say the old things with a new voice. But perhaps it is a little hard for you to understand that."

The abbé Gaston smiled sadly behind his beard as he remembered his own high hopes of more than thirty years ago.

"I am old, Monsieur le Curé, but I am not so old that I cannot understand that new methods have to be used in new ages," he said.

"I am glad of that," the new rector said as they walked slowly up towards the de luxe plumber's window. "It makes what I have to say to you easier. Monsieur l'abbé Gaston, I shall be frank with you. I do not altogether like your somewhat anomalous position in the parish. I prefer my priests to be regularly attached to the archdiocese and to live in the presbytery. Like that I can keep my eye on them better and see that there is no inefficiency. As you know, I have had to get rid of the abbé Ronsard."

The abbé Gaston knew, but he didn't know why. He didn't know whether the abbé Ronsard had been fired for singing *"Ite, missa est"* instead of *"Benedicamus Domino"* on the second Sunday in Advent or for having appeared in black vestments at a wedding. Whatever the reason, the abbé Ronsard had been sent to make his mistakes at Issy-les-Moulineaux and the abbé Gaston was very sorry, because the abbé Ronsard had been the only priest left at St. Clovis who had known him when his beard was as strong and dark as the new rector's hair.

"There is also the question of finance," the new rector continued. "I have been given to understand that you have certain private means."

"Private means in France have a habit of becoming so private that it is difficult even for their recipients to be aware of them," the abbé Gaston said.

The new rector did not smile. He walked on jauntily with his head thrown back and his beret bulged out at an angle. The new rector looked like a military chaplain all the time.

"I understand that the late Chanoine Litry was in the habit of making you a small monthly payment for your services," the new rector said.

"For the last few months the late Chanoine Litry was giving me seven thousand francs a month," the abbé Gaston said.

The new rector whistled, rather vulgarly, the abbé Gaston thought.

"In that case the late Chanoine Litry must have been a greater financial wizard than I am," the new rector said. "The parish cannot possibly support such a charge. Collections keep getting smaller and smaller and the Voluntary Contribution looks as though it were going to disappear altogether. As it is we've had to raid the cleaning fund to have the organ repaired. Times are hard, I know, Monsieur l'abbé Gaston, but I am afraid that you'll have to open your mouth a little less widely. Four thousand francs a month is my limit and I am sorry to say that it is a case of take it or leave it."

The abbé Gaston tried to smile bravely but behind the gap in his beard he could feel the sadness of his own face. A few months ago seven thousand francs a month had seemed a large enough sum. Since then, however, prices had increased thirty per cent and it looked as though they were going up still higher. The abbé Gaston did not know how he was going to be able to live on an income of four thousand francs a month. His own private income of two hundred and fifty francs a month could do little more than buy one decent meal. The abbé Gaston wasn't greedy and he would gladly have served the Lord for nothing, but even to serve the Lord for nothing he had to be strong enough to walk to his work. St. John the Baptist, he knew, had lived on locusts and wild honey, and he had got off rather lightly, the abbé Gaston thought.

"Of course it's a case of take," the abbé Gaston said quietly.

"I am glad that you have seen things so reasonably," the new rector said. "And, if I must go on being frank, even the payment of four thousand francs a month is a business arrangement. In other words, it is strictly a payment for services rendered. This parish cannot afford extravagances. This parish is a microcosm of the Church of God and the Church of God is rather like the Resistance Movement: indeed it is a Resistance Movement against the world, the flesh and the devil."

The abbé Gaston did not think this a very clever phrase. In fact he thought it more likely to retard the cause of religion than to advance it. He had always distrusted the use of military metaphor and simile when applied to the Church. If Christians had indeed been soldiers they would have all been shot for treachery long ago.

"And in the Resistance Movement we didn't tolerate slackers," the new rector said.

"In the first world war we didn't tolerate slackers either and the first war lasted longer than the Resistance Movement," the abbé Gaston said a little resentfully.

"I know, I know," the new rector said. But it was clear that the new rector had no desire to talk of the first world war or of the abbé Gaston's experiences in it. The abbé Gaston tried to resent this and failed. For the new rector the world and the priestly life were almost only beginning, and for himself they were slowly ending. The abbé Gaston stayed for a little longer listening to the new rector hinting how much more eventful his own short life had been than the abbé Gaston's long life. Then he crossed slowly to the underground and left the new rector to talk to the pretty girls with his glossy new curates.

The abbé Gaston was going to call on Bessier to try to persuade him to agree to the marriage of his son with Michelle. The abbé's mission was an intimation as well as a request, as Bessier's son had been afraid to tell his father. There was also the question of Bessier's son being baptized. Bessier's son said that he could no longer accept the doctrines of communism after the unapostolic deeds of its adherents. The abbé was afraid that it was going to be a stormy interview.

It was while he was waiting for the policeman to stop the traffic that the abbé Gaston first saw the little dark bar in front of his right eye. He blinked and it was gone, and he knew that what he had seen must have been an illusion, as the doctors had told him that his eye was healed for always. The policeman stood in the middle of the road and he saw only one policeman and not two policemen. The policeman was a new policeman and the traffic was new traffic but it surged on just as speedily as the old traffic, with the drivers still resisting supernatural grace behind their windscreens. The abbé stood for a long time waiting for the policeman to stop the traffic and while he was waiting he saw the little dark bar again twice, but he knew that he must have been mistaken, as the doctors had told him that his eye was healed for always. And when he saw two policemen instead of one policeman he still knew that he must have been mistaken, because of what the doctors had told him.

The traffic went on and on. Lorries, buses, taxicabs and private cars pushed past in jerks and thrusts and spurts. There was no petrol for private use but still the shining expensive private cars rolled on with the shining expensive private faces seated inside them. In 1947 it was as in 1927 and Frenchmen didn't seem to have learned anything from the years which had passed in between. On the high seats of the green buses the drivers drove ferociously, for theirs was now the power if not the glory. The traffic went on and on and the policeman made no sign of stopping it. Finally, the policeman moved away from the middle of the road and came and stood beside the abbé on the pavement.

"Please, Monsieur l'agent, aren't you going to stop the traffic?" the abbé Gaston asked.

"The crossing's been changed," the policeman answered surlily.

"Where's it been changed to?" the abbé Gaston asked.

"It's been changed, I tell you," the policeman said. The abbé gave it up. He could not see where the crossing had been changed to as the traffic seemed to be stopping nowhere on the square. He was in a hurry to get to Bessier's flat because Bessier had written to say that he could wait for him only till three o'clock. Although more little dark bars kept falling across his right eye, the abbé decided to try to cross the road in between the spurts and the jerks and the thrusts and the spurts. He waited until he saw a gap that he thought was likely to last for some time and advanced carefully on to the road. But before he had got half way across a jeep with two long-haired civilians in it charged down on him and forced him to hurry back to the pavement again. The long-haired young civilians turned round and jeered at the abbé as they passed.

"Couldn't you stop the traffic a moment for me?" the abbé Gaston asked the policeman.

"The crossing's been changed, I tell you," the policeman said.

"I was wounded in the last war and I've got a limp and also I'm not seeing very well," the abbé Gaston said.

"I haven't received any instructions to stop the traffic here," the policeman said.

"But I'm a disabled ex-soldier, I tell you," the abbé Gaston said.

"Write to your member of parliament if you've got any complaints to make," the policeman said.

The abbé felt hurt and angry as he wandered away to look for the new crossing. It took him some time to find it. His right eye kept on bothering him, so that it was still difficult for him to cross the road when the traffic stopped.

The corridors of the underground were full of workers returning to the automobile factory. Along the dark passages the surge of sub-men swept, sweating a hymn to Stalin, the father of the world. More than once the abbé was nearly knocked off his feet and more than once he bit back an expostulation, because he knew that the Lord loved the sub-men, too. The employees had been disinfecting the station again and both the corridors and the platform were covered with a damp greasy paste. The abbé had great difficulty in not falling when he placed the rubber tip of his stick on the slippery surface. He had to use his stick a lot, because of his limp and because he was seeing so badly with his right eye.

First class travel on the underground had been suppressed since the second of January, and the red first class carriages which still ran in the middle of the train were always more crowded than the green second class carriages. When the train came in the abbé got into the last green carriage so as to have the shortest possible distance to walk to the lift at Buttes Chaumont. Two men carrying lavatory seats and motor car tires barged in in front of him and the abbé nearly tripped over the feet of another man carrying a wash-hand basin. Eventually he found a little corner of seat next a glassy eyed man in a blue overcoat. The glassy eyed man was carrying a chair turned upside down on his knee and he had a brief case wedged in between his body and the wall of the carriage. The glassy eyed man moved neither the upturned chair nor the brief case in order to give the abbé more room.

The train shot off into the tunnel. Instead of DUBO, DUBON, DUNBONNET the walls of the tunnel said ESPERE, ESPERONS, ESPEREZ, in black letters upon yellow. But the little blue lamp was still the same and it was lighted and its crescent of white lettering still said PORTE ST. GERVAIS as it had done in 1936, although the abbé couldn't see the lettering very clearly because of his eye. The dark bars were falling more frequently now and the abbé was too worried by them to make any conjectures as to the station in which the driver was going to extinguish the little blue lamp; When he looked up at the blue lamp the dark bars fell across it but when he looked down at the floor of the carriage they were gone. He tried shutting his right eye and looking at the little blue lamp only with his left eye and he felt the dark bars rising up behind the closed eyelid. He opened his right eye again and looked up with both eyes at the little blue lamp and this time he saw two little blue lamps and they were both lighted and they both had crescents of white lettering upon them. He shut both his eyes again in terror.

When at last the abbé opened his eyes again he was seeing normally. The little blue lamp was out, and the train was pulling up the slope from

Jaurès to Bolivar. The compartment was almost empty. The glassy eyed man next him had gone and the two men with the lavatory seats and the motor car tires had gone, too. The abbé Gaston sat plump in the middle of the seat and stretched out his legs.

There was nothing the abbé liked better than travelling in an uncrowded underground compartment. The movement soothed his thoughts so much that he sometimes thought that if he hadn't been a priest he would have liked to have been a driver of an underground train. He began to forget about having seen two little lighted blue lamps now that he was no longer seeing even little dark bars. The train rounded into the Buttes Chaumont station in the long loop of lighted loveliness that always delighted the abbé. Each time he saw the carriages in front of him curving into the station he felt a sense of immortality as the lights and the motion were always the same and he was still alive to see them the same.

Because he had been travelling in the last carriage the abbé Gaston arrived at the lift in plenty of time. The liftman was the same liftman as in 1936. He looked a little older and much crosser. He stood with a scowl on his face until the last of the passengers had entered the lift and then he banged the doors noisily in the name of Stalin and of Molotov and of Vishinsky.

To the abbé's surprise Bessier was waiting for him at the entrance to the underground. Bessier stood at the top of the steps with his hands in his pockets and his shoulders broad against the afternoon sky. The collar of his shabby coat was turned up about his ears because of the cold. The communists in France practiced both discipline and poverty, the abbé knew, and this he admired, and he wished that Christians would be as austere. The abbé was a little afraid when he saw Bessier as he hadn't expected to have to begin talking about Bessier's son quite so soon.

"It's nice of you to come and meet me," the abbé said.

"An idea I had," Bessier said. He shook the abbé's hand limply and gravely. "I'm getting polite in my old age. In any case I have the whole afternoon in front of me."

"But what about your office?" the abbé asked. "I thought you said you had to get back."

"Since this morning I have no longer any office to get back to," Bessier said. He walked along beside the abbé with scarcely any limp although his shoulder still moved ever so slightly up and down. "In other words, I've been fired. For deviations. We, too, have our heresies, you know."

The abbé did not know what to say to that. He was sorry for Bessier's sake that he had been dismissed, and glad for Bessier's sake, too, because he knew that communism was the cruelest lie that had ever been preached to the world. In the end he managed to make an inarticulate sound of condolence.

Bessier walked on for a little in silence and beneath his coat his artificial leg jerked a little.

"All my life I have tried to fight against the dirty dogs," Bessier said as they passed beneath the mournful trees. "And now I find that those who fight against the dirty dogs are dirty dogs themselves. And yet it is not right that some should be rich and that others should be poor. It is not right that some women should wear fine silks and that others should starve." There was a preaching tone in Bessier's voice as he said this, and the abbé realized that even the communists found it hard to produce new words all the time.

"Somebody once said that the thing which requires most courage is to profess a true faith in spite of the false people who also profess it," the abbé Gaston said. He knew that this applied to Christianity and not to communism, but he hoped that Bessier would find comfort in the saying.

They were crossing the Avenue Simon Bolivar as the abbé said this. A gleaming American limousine shot round the bend and forced them to retreat on to the pavement. Behind the windscreen sat a heavy jowled man with a girl with hair like frozen syrup and an expressionless slab of face. Bessier swore after the car as it passed, using words which gave the abbé pain, "The old rich are swine," Bessier said. "And the tragedy is that the new rich will be even greater swine. Always rich men are swine and especially in France are they swine. There is need for a great cauterizing of the world, but who has clean enough fire to do it I no longer know," Bessier said.

The abbé Gaston wanted to say that only the Holy Ghost had clean enough fire to cauterize the world but he knew that such words were distrusted because they had been said so often. Often the abbé thought that the only hope of converting the world was to be silent until the old holy words had had time to sound new again. In the meantime priests preached best by not preaching.

In front of the commissariat two policemen stood with holes in their faces where they yawned. The abbé supposed that they must be new bored policemen as the bored policemen he had seen standing there in 1936 must have grown into more important bored policemen. Then suddenly the abbé saw four bored policemen and almost immediately no bored policemen. He threw out his hand and clutched Bessier's arm.

"It's my eyes," the abbé said. "I can no longer see."

"Stand still a little and perhaps your sight will come back," Bessier said. "Sight's a funny thing, you know. It goes and it comes back."

"I do not think that it will ever come back," the abbé said. "I think that I am going blind. Then I, too, shall be without a job. My new rector is not like my old rector. He will no longer employ me if I cannot see."

"The holy dirty dogs are even dirtier than the unholy dirty dogs," Bessier said.

They stood for a little and the abbé could feel the tenderness in Bessier's arm. Bessier loved him, the abbé knew, and he knew that he loved Bessier, too. In spite of all the big different things between them he and Bessier loved each other. They had a stretch back over the dead years together and that was why they loved each other. Slowly the blackness in front of the abbé's eyes turned to greyness and out of the greyness emerged the outlines of the shop of the Spanish barber who had cut the abbé's hair too short in 1924.

They walked on while the abbé could still see. The abbé could see the advertisement for Byrrh painted on one end of Bessier's house but he couldn't see the advertisement for Cinzano because it was at the far end. The same dirty children still played noisily in the street.

The abbé was glad that Bessier took him into a room in which they were alone. He didn't want to have Madame Bessier being sorry with him about his eyes. He wanted only Bessier to be sorry with him about his eyes, because he had known Bessier down all those years and wasn't ashamed to be sad with him. He saw the bottle of brandy when Bessier took it off the shelf but he didn't see the liqueur glass very well when Bessier handed it to him.

"There's only one thing left and that's Lourdes," the abbé said as he took a sip at the brandy. The idea grew in his mind as the brandy warmed him and he began to calculate. It would cost money to go to Lourdes and it was certain that the new rector would not finance his journey. It was equally certain that the new rector would cease to employ him if he could no longer see properly. There was only one thing to do and that was to sell his bond. The hundred thousand franc bond would probably bring in only about seventy thousand francs but even with prices as they were such a sum would be more than enough to pay for a journey to Lourdes. Of course there would be no three thousand francs income once he had sold his bond, but it was better to lose three thousand francs a year than four thousand francs a month. There was also the possibility that he might not be cured, but he would have to risk that. The Lord liked people who took risks. And perhaps he wouldn't have to sell the whole of his bond in order to go to Lourdes. The brandy worked quickly and so did the abbé's optimism. "Yes, Lourdes is the only thing left," he said again.

"If you think that way it's always an idea," Bessier said.

"I should have expected you to mock at me rather than to encourage me," the abbé said.

"You forget that I am partly responsible for your trouble," Bessier said. "Or at least so I consider myself."

"That's nonsense," the abbé Gaston said.

"And in any case I've grown too old to mock any longer at things I do not understand," Bessier said. "And there are very many things that I do not understand."

"You are patient with me," the abbé said. "You are more patient with me than I am with you. You are in trouble, too, but it is only of my own trouble that I talk."

"These things are natural," Bessier said.

"Will you be able to find another job?" the abbé asked, although it was still chiefly about his own eyes that he was thinking. He saw a little better now and he closed his eyes to rest them.

"I shall find something but it will not be the same thing," Bessier said. "Like you I wanted to reform the world but the world will not let itself be reformed. There is a muck upon us that no man can shift. But perhaps you do not care to talk about that, you who still think that you can shift the muck."

"Perhaps it is your son who will be able to shift the muck," the abbé Gaston said gently, realizing that this was his opportunity to say what he had come to say. "I came here to talk to you about him. He wants to marry Michelle. He is afraid to tell you himself."

"She seems a nice girl," Bessier said. "I do not see why my son should be afraid to tell me that he wishes to marry her."

"It is to tell you something else that he is mostly afraid," the abbé said. "You see, he also wants to become a Christian." When he had said this the abbé opened his eyes again, to watch Bessier's face as best he could.

But Bessier's expression did not change.

"I have told you that I no longer mock at things which I no longer understand," Bessier said. "And as long as he does not become a rich Christian I do not greatly care. I do not think that such things are important."

"I think that they are very important indeed," the abbé said.

"I think that it is more important that I should be sorry for you when you are in trouble and that you should be sorry for me when I am in trouble," Bessier said. "I think that it is more important that I should help you home when you cannot see properly."

"These things are important, too," the abbé said. They sat on in silence. The abbé kept blinking first one eye and then the other, to see if he could see properly. Sometimes he could see Bessier's face and even the tired lines upon it and the greyness of it, but more often he could see only a blur. He tried to think about Bessier's unhappiness instead of about his own unhappiness and always he came back to thinking about his own unhappiness. The important things were waiting to be said to the world, but even to each other he and Bessier could not get them said.

"Perhaps some day somebody will find the right words and the whole world will be persuaded," the abbé Gaston said.

LXXVII

EVEN although he was now a bishop, the new Bishop still came in the middle of the night to rub the Cardinal's chest with embrocation. Sleepless, the Cardinal lay waiting for him in the darkness. And as he waited the Cardinal thought of the great distress which had come upon his brother bishops and priests in the east. In Poland and in Hungary, in Czecho-Slovakia and in Yugoslavia persecutions were raging and Christians were martyrs again. The Cardinal was glad that he was not a Cardinal in Warsaw or in Budapest. He did not think that he would have been much good at being a Cardinal in Warsaw or in Budapest. The Cardinal thought that it was a good thing for the other Cardinals that they had such a good prayer as Bernard on their side.

The new Bishop stole in through the darkness. The embrocation made the Cardinal feel so sleepy that he couldn't go on thinking anymore about the new strong Church which the Bishop of Saracen said God was raising up in the west.

"I'll give you my blessing," the Cardinal murmured drowsily when the new Bishop had finished.

"Just a minute and I'll put on the light," the new Bishop said.

"There's no need to do that; it works in the dark," the Cardinal said.

LXXVIII

SOME days the abbé Gaston saw better than other days, but even on his best days he never saw very clearly, so that he knew that the Lord hadn't worked even a tiny miracle on him, although he had been at Lourdes for more than a fortnight now.

Today at lunch he saw out of his left eye clearly enough to distinguish the blur of stubble on the Most Reverend Don Miguel's chin, for Don Miguel Ortiz was a Reverendísimo now, having recently been promoted a bishop by the Holy See. But it was only for a very short while that the abbé Gaston was able to see the blur of stubble on His Excellency's chin, and at no time could he see the stubble itself well enough to imagine himself striking a match on it, as he had used to do. The blur was a blue blur for a minute. Then it was a grey blur for a little longer. And then the grey blur merged into a bigger grey blur, which became the whole of the Bishop of Puerto Pobre himself, stubble, big belly and all.

That afternoon the Reverendísimo Don Miguel Ortiz was going to carry the Blessed Sacrament in procession from the Grotto and bless the sick as they lay on their stretchers. The abbé Gaston was hoping for great things from this. Every afternoon the abbé had had a different Bishop raise the Blessed Sacrament over him and it had done no good. And now the abbé could hope only that it was by a Bishop whom he knew personally that the Lord wished his eyes to be healed.

The Reverendísimo Don Miguel's breath still smelt of acetylene as he told the abbé Gaston about the great spiritual progress which had been made by the Church in Latin America. He said that this spiritual progress was so great that even His Excellency Don Esteban de los Puentesamarillos had been converted. His Excellency Don Esteban de los Puentesamarillos now visited brothels only on the greater festivals of the Christian year and this high virtue had increased not only the morale of the whole army but their military efficiency as well. At the last summer exercise the men of the third regiment had scored more bulls' eyes on the open range than for the last twenty years. That fact alone ought to convince the froward that God advanced those who obeyed His commandments, the Bishop of Puerto Pobre said.

The Bishop of Puerto Pobre did a lot of eating and drinking as well as a lot of talking, the abbé Gaston saw well enough to make out. The Reverendísimo Don Miguel no longer tipped the sardine tin into his mouth so that he could drink out the oil, perhaps because he thought the gesture unepiscopal, perhaps because the waitress didn't leave the sardine tin lying on the table long enough. But His Excellency got back on the rest of the meal what he lost on the sardines. His Excellency had also an omelette, fried sole, roast veal, salad, cheese and strawberry ice and fruit, and he poured himself out half a bottle of Pouilly and half a bottle of Châteauneuf du Pâpe.

The abbé Gaston did not eat as well as the Reverendísimo Don Miguel. The abbé was paying a pension price of six hundred francs a day, and for that he was served with six radishes, a piece of high fish and two boiled potatoes and five cherries to wind up with. Watching the Bishop of Puerto Pobre wolf his way through his elaborate meal made the abbé feel quite hungry. But the abbé knew that he could not afford to eat as well as His Excellency if he were to give the Lord a good chance of curing him. Even the thinnest slice of meat would have cost the abbé a hundred and fifty francs extra. The abbé was glad when the Reverendísimo Don Miguel asked to be excused in order that he might prepare himself for the solemn thing that he was about to do that afternoon.

As usual the English girl staying in the hotel offered to lead the abbé Gaston down to the basilica. Even with both his eyes not working properly the abbé could see that the English girl wasn't wearing many clothes. In fact all that the English girl seemed to be wearing were big bands of sticking plaster round her middle and on her top, but the abbé couldn't be sure of this, as he was seeing so badly.

It was hot in the sun, and it was when the sun was bright that the abbé saw worst of all, so that the English girl had to take his arm and lead him gently. The abbé could feel the people in the street better than he could see them, and sometimes he could see the sparkle of the river as well. And when he shut his eyes he could still feel the people in the street and the sparkle of the river, too. He was glad that the English girl was there to hold his arm even although she was wearing only sticking plaster. The abbé wouldn't have liked to have bumped into the people of the street, especially as many needed the Lord's help more badly than he did.

The English girl had told the abbé that she had come to Lourdes for sun baths and not for religion, and so she left the abbé when they reached the basilica. And the abbé said a little prayer for the English girl as she walked away from him in her sticking plaster, because he knew that even pagan kind hearts were God's. And when he had said this prayer he made his way slowly down the broad open space between the stretchers till he reached the steps of the middle church, on which he sat down. The abbé had told the Reverendísimo Don Miguel that this was where he generally sat, and the Bishop of Puerto Pobre had promised to make a very big sign of the cross with the Blessed Sacrament over him, so that the Lord might lay His hand upon the eyes of His priest, that His priest might see the excellent land again.

In front of the church, the whole length of the esplanade and in two long lines facing each other, the rich lay on their stretchers. Although the abbé Gaston couldn't see them very well he could make out the white smear of the blankets covering them. There were the sick in bath chairs, too, and those who could not walk except on crutches. And even if he had been able to see properly the abbé knew that he could not have distinguished the nature of all their maladies. Their maladies were mostly beneath blankets, in their stomachs, in their kidneys, in their lungs, but that did not matter, the abbé supposed, as the Blessed Sacrament, Whose fragment was the whole, could pierce through blankets, if God so willed. And beneath bandages round heads the Blessed Sacrament could pierce also and heal lupuses and dry up running sores and put new flesh on gaps in faces and wash away the pus, if God so willed. Suffering was a mystery, the abbé had been taught and had taught others, and so, too, was God's shortening of it. And one must not try to see behind the veil too much, because suffering was the rule.

A priest stood up in front of the stretchers and the sick began to pray that the Lord Jesus might have mercy on them and that Mary might intercede for them and that Christ might hear them. The priest was a Spanish priest and he prayed in Spanish, but the people prayed in Italian and French and English and Dutch as well, that the Lord Jesus might have mercy on them and that Mary might intercede for them and that Christ might hear them. The priest prayed first and the people prayed afterwards and when the people prayed their prayers rose in a storm from their stretchers. The priest prayed and the sick prayed and the people prayed and their prayers were a great noise beneath the sky. But heaven was silent and the summer afternoon was blue and gold and green and ordinary, because that, too, was the rule.

Behind the sick the worldly stood, the smooth men with the cold eyes and the young women with the sleek flanks and the old women with the dyed hair, who had come up from Bagnères-de-Bigorre and Bagnères-deLuchon to see what manner of man this was. The abbé Gaston tried not to listen as he heard them talking behind him on the steps. "He's got all he can ask for: a fast car, the woman he loves and money in his pocket," he heard a woman say. And the abbé knew that it was this that caused unhappiness, not to know the meaning of the world. Then the abbé heard another voice and it was the voice of an old peasant woman. "They've gone to fetch the Lord," the old peasant woman said, and the abbé's heart reached out to the old peasant woman, because she knew the meaning of the world. And almost immediately the tinkle of a bell was heard as God was carried tinnily from the basilica to the Grotto. The abbé liked listening to the sound of the little bell beside the river.

The singing began, and the strong words rose in a roar and behind the sick on the other side of the esplanade the abbé could see a white blob which he knew was the top of the canopy, as God was carried along the river bank by His badly shaven Bishop. The abbé sang for a little, too, and as loudly as he could and he was happy as he sang with the people and they all made a noise about the true things together.

But the abbé did not sing for long. Soon he began to pray. He tried to pray that others rather than himself might be healed, and that the Lord might staunch their wounds and stem the evil flowings from their sores. Yet he could not feel their misery as he could feel his own misery of not seeing properly and of not knowing how he was going to be able to live if the Lord did not heal his eyes. For the abbé had not been able to lunch on six radishes, high fish and five cherries every day since he had been at Lourdes. Occasionally he had eaten a steak and sometimes a strawberry ice as well, and all those extras would certainly swell his bill. The sale of his bond had brought him in only sixty-seven thousand francs. And this sum wouldn't last forever, not at the present cost of railway fares, steaks and strawberry ice cream. As the Bishop and his ministers drew nearer, the abbé Gaston forgot all about other people's unhappiness and thought only of his own. With his eyes open he prayed that the Lord might disperse this blackness which had come upon him and make him able to be a good enough priest again to earn four thousand francs a month.

The Bishop approached slowly along the line of stretchers, tracing a blessing over each. In his hands he held the monstrance, but he did not touch the monstrance with his hands, because the monstrance held the Holy Thing, and the Bishop was not holy enough to touch even that which held the Holy Thing. The Bishop held the monstrance through the humeral veil and he raised the monstrance above each sick person and blessed him with it, that the Lord might send out His power upon them. And always there was a silence from heaven and the summer afternoon was blue and gold and green in the silence, because that was the rule, and no man might tell God what He should do. Bound in his vestments and with his priesthood heavy upon him, the Bishop blessed the sick and the sore and the maimed, and always there was no miracle, because that was God's Will.

The abbé Gaston decided that he would keep his eyes open when the Bishop held the Blessed Sacrament over him, so that the healing might come full upon them. The thumping silence of the blessings drew nearer and the sweat ran down the abbé's face into his beard as he prayed that this time the Lord might make him whole. And when the Bishop stood over him and the abbé raised his eyes to the monstrance it seemed almost that God had heard his prayer. For the abbé saw not only the Host and the sparkle of gold behind it but the blur of the stubble on the Bishop's chin as well and the great solemn look on the Bishop's face as he did the thing for which he had been made a priest. But as soon as the Bishop had passed on the abbé began to see badly again, and the Bishop and his assistants walked away from him in a white mist. And tears as well as sweat ran down the abbé's face into his beard, because he had waited for so long upon the Lord.

The Holy Thing had gone and the procession had gone and the sick had gone when the English girl came to help the abbé Gaston back to the hotel. The abbé was seeing a little better again and he was no longer weeping. Although he still didn't think that the Lord had worked a miracle on him he wanted to find out if he was seeing better than he had been seeing yesterday, so he asked the English girl to lead him down towards the river. The abbé thought that he could tell more easily how he was seeing when he watched the ripples on the water.

Today the water looked as though it were moving sideways instead of longways and this was because of the ruffles which the breeze made upon the water. But the abbé wasn't seeing well enough to notice the ruffles and he could feel only the water in front of him and it was cool beneath his face. The English girl was wearing a soft white dress now and it blew out in the breeze towards the water, and this, too, the abbé could feel better than he could see. And the abbé felt the wave of her white dress all about him as she led him homewards through the hot streets.

LXXIX

THE statesman was silent. The statesman was silent for a long time, in secret diplomacy.

LXXX

THE abbé Gaston was no longer able to be polite to God at the altar. He had to carry the chalice and the paten down the steps with him immediately after the last gospel, because of his limp and his eyes that still wouldn't see properly. He had also had to learn all the changing bits of the mass by heart, so that when his eyes played tricks on him he could still say out the right words.

Behind him as he knelt at the foot of the altar steps on a hot summer's day in 1948 the abbé could feel the restlessness of the small congregation, although he didn't allow himself to be disturbed by it. He knew from long experience that congregations at weddings were rarely devout. He was happy enough to hear Michelle and young Bessier answering the responses and glad when he heard the centrally heated lady of easy virtue joining in as well. The abbé prayed rapidly because he knew that was the best way of concentrating on his intercession, and then went out into the sacristy to take off his vestments.

Almost immediately the wedding group was round him, and he had to postpone his thanksgiving. He showed Michelle and young Bessier where to sign in the register and he stood laughing with the nuns while they signed. The abbé was pleased that his eyes were working well enough for him to see that Michelle was looking very pretty in the white satin dress which the nuns had made for her. And young Bessier was looking handsome, too, with almost as much brilliantine as the third curate on his hair. Michelle was wearing her mother's glass necklace and brooch, which was the only wedding present that the abbé had been able to afford to give her.

Apart from the nuns there weren't many guests at the wedding. Bessier, who had been given leave from his new job in the accounts department of the iron foundry, was there with his wife, and Madame

Boulon and the centrally heated lady of easy virtue were there as well. The centrally heated lady of easy virtue dabbed at her eyes with her handkerchief and said that weddings always made her weep in streams when she thought of all the lovely things she had missed.

The abbé apologized for not being able to come to the wedding lunch. He said that the resident chaplaincy at the convent began right away and that he had promised to start evangelizing the nuns that very afternoon. The nuns all giggled at this and asked the abbé if he would like to come back with them now and begin converting them in the underground. But the abbé said that he would have to wait for the Chanoine Paiseau, who had promised to look into the sacristy to say good-bye. After that he had to go back home and get his luggage. He told the nuns that he would be able to manage all right, because a little girl from the catechism class had promised to come and carry St. John of the Cross for him.

The abbé walked to the door of the church with them all and watched them go down the steps. But the sun quickly blinded the abbé's eyes and soon he wasn't able to see even Michelle's white dress. He went back into the sacristy to make his thanksgiving and to wait for the new rector.

A young priest with curly hair came into the sacristy and began to put on black vestments for a funeral. The abbé Gaston wasn't sure whether the young priest was a new new curate he hadn't seen before or an old new curate whose face he hadn't remembered clearly. The abbé Gaston was always getting the new curates' lineless faces mixed up and calling them by the wrong names, and so he didn't know whether to smile at the young priest or to look solemn. The young priest took no notice of the abbé Gaston and tied himself tightly into his vestments. The acolytes arrived with grins on their scruffy faces. The young priest and the acolytes went out on to the sanctuary and began the funeral mass.

The contrast between the wedding and the funeral didn't shock the abbé Gaston. The abbé knew that the Church of God wasn't only a ship on the ocean and a lamp held up in the darkness and a lake in a desert and a ladder let down; the abbé knew that the Church of God was a tunnel as well, with souls always shooting through it like trains. More than thirty-five years ago he had taken up his curacy at Saint Clovis during a funeral, and he thought it quite fitting that he should be leaving Saint Clovis forever in the middle of another funeral. He thought it fitting, too, that a very young priest should be standing where he himself had so often stood, with his arms outstretched like the branches of a tree, in the holy place.

"Please, Monsieur l'abbé, I met Monsieur le Curé in the street and he told me to tell you not to wait for him as he has got an important appointment," a child's voice said behind the abbé.

It was the little girl from the catechism class. She was a chubby faced child of about eleven. In one hand she carried the abbé's straw suitcase; in the other she held a small basket from which a cat's meows were coming.

"I thought you were going to wait for me in my room," the abbé Gaston said. "That suitcase is much too heavy for you to carry."

"But I met Monsieur le Curé and I had to come and tell you what he said," the little girl said. "So I thought I might as well save you a journey and bring the suitcase and the pussy over here."

They left the sacristy at once, because of St. John of the Cross' meows. The abbé carried the suitcase and the little girl carried the basket with the cat in it. Fortunately the suitcase was light, as most of the abbé's underclothes had worn out during the war and he had not been able to replace them. Even so, with his limp and his bad sight, he had difficulty in carrying his suitcase down the steps. He held his stick and the suitcase in one hand and with the other he clung on to the railing. As the suitcase banged against the railing the abbé tried not to feel hurt that the new rector had not come to say good-bye to him. The steps of the church still looked the same, and the square of streets looked the same, too, just as they had looked thirty-five years ago, when the abbé Gaston had seen them for the first time.

They had to wait quite a long time at the new crossing before the policeman stopped the traffic for them. The same sort of people still shot past in the same sort of cars, but the abbé could not see them very well, and he was glad of this, as he was beginning to be envious of them. The abbé sometimes wondered what it must feel like to be a rich blind man and to be driven about all day in a motor car.

From the loudspeaker above the entrance to the de luxe plumber's shop came the rasp of the noon news: Monsieur Yves de Chataigneau, Mr. Bedell Smith and Mr. Frank Roberts had seen Mr. Molotov again. Mr. Ernest Bevin had said that the Allies would not be bullied out of Berlin; a Swedish diplomat had said that the Russians would not be able to make war for another three years; an Argentinian diplomat had said that the Russians were ready to make war at once; a British Field-Marshal had said that the Russians could capture the whole of Europe in thirty days but were unlikely to be such cads as to attempt to do so; the representatives of forty-six nations had squeaked that they desired a just and lasting peace and blueprints from the future; a Danish farmer had predicted that in seventy-five years' time all the inhabitants of the world would have died of starvation; six Trappist monks had been murdered by communists at Yanckiaping. The only good tidings was the announcement by a Mexican scientist that a gigantic glacier was approaching rapidly from the Arctic and would shortly cover the whole surface of the earth.

Down in the underground the ticket inspector was punching tickets instead of inspecting them. Commenting upon his new occupation, the ticket inspector pointed out to the abbé that the rules of the underground railway as well as politics were changing these days, as there was no longer any first class travel and therefore no need for inspectors. He said, however, that he had heard rumors that the rules were shortly going to change back again and that there would be first class travel again. And the ticket inspector asked if there was no change of the rules of religion changing temporarily like those of the underground, so that the faithful might have a let up. But the abbé said that that was the hard part about religion, that there was never a let up and that it was third class travel all the way.

The train rattled through the tunnel and the walls sang ESPERE, ESPERONS, ESPEREZ, but the abbé couldn't see the letters. The little girl sat next him with the cat in its basket on her knee and the abbé sat with the suitcase on his knee. Opposite them a fat old woman sat, smiling at the little girl. The cat was quiet for a little and the abbé felt awkward sitting there in silence and not talking to the little girl.

"What is your name?" he asked the little girl. "My name is Armelle," the little girl said.

"That is a very pretty name," the fat old woman opposite said.

But the abbé Gaston was no longer listening. Although he knew that there was no supernatural significance in the coincidence he was thinking of the other Armelle and of how she had used to look like a daisy when she walked across grass in her small white frock, and of her little girl's hair tied up with pale blue ribbon. And of Otto Braunschwig and of Rachel and of the Major and of the Chanoine Litry and of all those people whom the Lord had taken from him the abbé thought, too, and of whether God would raise them up young or old on the last day.

The train rattled on through the tunnel, but the abbé didn't notice the stations, because he was thinking about the Lord's mysteries and about how imperfectly he understood them. One of them, however, he thought he was beginning to understand, and that was why all the workers in the vineyard were paid a penny, whether they had borne the heat and burden of the day or not. He thought that it was because so much of the labor was its own reward just as so much of the world was its own punishment. The abbé Gaston suddenly realized that he had been very happy as a priest. And even now that he was almost blind as well as lame and would have to learn kilometers of epistles and gospels off by heart, the abbé knew that he was going to be very happy indeed as resident chaplain to the nuns. The abbé Gaston almost laughed aloud as St. John of the Cross began to meow.

"It's a cat," he explained unnecessarily to the fat old woman opposite, who was still talking to the little girl. The train rattled on through the tunnel. The abbé Gaston began to pray silently for the six Trappist monks who had been murdered at Yanckiaping. And for the rest of the world the abbé prayed, too, that the Lord Jesus might lean down, and touch it, and smooth it out.

THE END

www.ingramcontent.com/pod-product-compliance
Lightning Source LLC
Chambersburg PA
CBHW031312160426
43196CB00007B/497